# Current Trends in Business and Economics

# Current Trends in Business and Economics

Edited by
Marshall Blair

Willford Press
www.willfordpress.com

Published by Willford Press,
118-35 Queens Blvd., Suite 400,
Forest Hills, NY 11375, USA



ISBN: 978-1-68285-638-3

**Cataloging-in-Publication Data**

Current trends in business and economics / edited by Marshall Blair.
p. cm.
Includes bibliographical references and index.
ISBN 978-1-68285-638-3
1. Business. 2. Economics. 3. Economic development. 4. Managerial economics.
I. Blair, Marshall.
HF1008 .C87 2019
650--dc23

For information on all Willford Press publications
visit our website at www.willfordpress.com

Willford Press

Printed in China.

# Contents

# Preface

The world is advancing at a fast pace like never before. Therefore, the need is to keep up with the latest developments. This book was an idea that came to fruition when the specialists in the area realized the need to coordinate together and document essential themes in the subject. That's when I was requested to be the editor. Editing this book has been an honour as it brings together diverse authors researching on different streams of the field. The book collates essential materials contributed by veterans in the area which can be utilized by students and researchers alike.

Business refers to any activity, which is carried out for the purpose of earning profit. Business entities can be divided into sole proprietorship, partnership, corporation, cooperative, franchises, etc. The organizational setup of a business is based on the functional domains of manufacturing, finance, marketing, research and development, etc. The discipline of economics studies the production, distribution and consumption of goods and services. Such analyses are of significance in business and finance. Managerial economics attempts to use economic methods to optimize business decisions through cost minimization and profit maximization. This book strives to provide a fair idea about the disciplines of business and economics and to help develop a better understanding of the latest advances within these domains. It outlines the processes and applications of these fields in detail. Managers, economists, researchers, academicians and students will be assisted by this book.

Each chapter is a sole-standing publication that reflects each author's interpretation. Thus, the book displays a multi-facetted picture of our current understanding of application, resources and aspects of the field. I would like to thank the contributors of this book and my family for their endless support.

**Editor**

# 1

# Risk Preferences and Obesity: A Behavioral Economics Approach

**Sumati Srinivas**[1]

**ABSTRACT**

Risk aversion has been shown to have a negative effect on adverse health behaviors such as smoking and heavy alcohol consumption. However, the significance and sign of the effect of risk aversion on the tendency to be obese has not been established in previous research. Additionally, the knowledge of specific health risks arising from obesity has been shown to have a significant negative effect on obesity, although the interaction between health risk awareness and risk aversion has not been studied. This paper fills this gap in the literature by studying the relationship between risk preferences, health risk knowledge and the occurrence of obesity within. In this paper, data from a nationally representative survey of adults in the United States is used to determine the significance of measures for both risk aversion and health risk knowledge on the likelihood of obesity, while controlling for the usual variables shown by previous research to be predictors for obesity. Risk aversion is found to have a positive and significant effect on obesity within the general population; however, this effect loses its significance within sub-populations who exhibit awareness of the health risk from obesity, as measured by two different proxy variables.

Keywords: Behavioral economics, health risk knowledge, measures of risk preference, obesity, risk aversion.

## 1.0 INTRODUCTION

The relationship between individual risk preferences, as exhibited in economic experiments, and the propensity to indulge in risky health behaviors has not been established in the economics literature. Cutler and Glaeser (2005) show that there is little correlation between 5 different forms of risky health behaviors (smoking, heavy alcohol use, being obese, not taking recommended medication and not undergoing medical tests), and concludes that individual characteristics such as genetics and behavioral-specific factors are likely to be important drivers of such health behaviors. Due to the conceptual importance of risk preferences in models of decision-making, individual risk preferences may be

[1] Radford University, USA. E-mail: ssrinivas@radford.edu

implicated as one of the individual characteristics that drive the propensity to engage in such behaviors. But the direction in which risk aversion might influence a specific type of health behavior remains unclear.

Dave and Saffer (2008) study risk preferences within a model of alcohol demand and find that risk aversion has a significant negative effect on alcohol consumption. Similarly, Barsky et al (1997) find that their experimental measure of risk aversion is significantly and negatively associated with behaviors such as smoking and failing to hold insurance. However, Picone et al (2004) find that risk-averse individuals are less likely to take needed medical tests, possibly because they do not want to discover they are at risk for a difficult or expensive procedure.

## 1.1 OBESITY AS A HEALTH BEHAVIOR

Obesity prevention, as a health behavior, may have more in common with preventative care than thrill-seeking behaviors such as smoking or heavy alcohol consumption. However, Anderson and Mellor (2008) study obesity/overweight as a health behavior, along with smoking, heavy drinking and seat-belt non-use, and find that risk aversion (as measured by an experimental lottery-based instrument) has a significant negative effect on all these health behaviors. While these results are consistent with other studies with regards to behaviors such as smoking and drinking, there are several reasons why the relationship between obesity and risk aversion found by Anderson and Mellor (2008) is worth investigating further. Firstly, the study includes both overweight and obese respondents under a single category, though it would be of interest to study the risk preferences of the narrower group of obese respondents. Secondly, as noted in the study, the sample of respondents exhibited much smaller rates of obesity/overweight than the national average. Thirdly, also as noted in the study, the sample of respondents were highly educated, with 30% holding a graduate degree, and it is possible that this introduces a bias into the relationship between risk aversion and obesity/overweight. The last point is especially relevant in the light of Davis et al (2010), who found previous results showing a significant relationship between obesity and risky decision-making in the Iowa Gambling Task (reported in Davis et al, 2004) became insignificant once education levels were added to the model. This study addresses these issues by using a nationally representative survey of the U.S population aged between 45 and 52 years, as well as focusing on the relationship between risk aversion and obesity, instead of the larger population of overweight respondents.

## 1.2 HEALTH RISK KNOWLEDGE

Any model of behavioral determinants of obesity will also need to take into account the levels of health risk knowledge exhibited by individuals. Unlike health behaviors such as smoking and alcohol consumption, which require a deliberate action to indulge in the unhealthy behavior, the tendency to become obese may not always manifest itself as deliberate action to become obese, e.g., by over-eating. Instead, obesity may be the result of not indulging in preventative behaviors, such as paying attention to the nutritional content of food and taking part in regular exercise. For example, Kan and Tsai (2004) show that the acquisition of health risk knowledge by itself can have a significant effect on obesity.

## 1.3 EXPERIMENTAL MEASURES FOR RISK PREFERENCE

As with any study on risk preferences, the fidelity of the survey instrument used to measure risk preference is an important aspect of the design of the study. The instrument used in this study to measure risk aversion is a version of the hypothetical gamble between two prospective sources of income described in Barsky et al (1997). An important issue with using this instrument is that there is no incentive provided, and therefore the response to the gamble may not capture true risk preferences. To mitigate this concern, this study uses the respondent's self-assessment of risk preference in combination with the experimentally determined value, in order to arrive at a robust measure of risk aversion. Previous studies, such as Dohmen et al (2011) have shown that self-assessment of risk preference is usually consistent with propensity to engage in real-life risky behaviors, and therefore the use of such an assessment in combination with the experimental measure provides more confidence that the respondent's risk preference is being accurately measured.

### 1.4 RESEARCH QUESTIONS

To summarize, this paper advances the research on the relationship between obesity and risk preferences in the following ways:

- Construction of a measure of risk aversion that combines experimental results with the respondent's self-assessment of risk preferences.
- Investigation of the relationship between risk aversion measured in this fashion, and obesity in a diverse, nationally representative sample of adults aged between 45 and 52.
- Comparison of the results obtained for sub-populations who exhibit awareness of health risk.

## 2.0 DATA

The NLSY79 is an ongoing survey of a nationally representative sample of 12,686 men and women living in the United States. The respondents have been surveyed annually every year from 1979 to 19 94, and once every two years from 1994 to 2010. The NLSY79 respondents were aged 14 to 22 at the beginning of the survey, and this study uses data from the 2010 wave, when they were aged between 45 and 52. Due to attrition, the sample size of respondents who answered the relevant questions in the 2010 wave used in this study is 7,369.

### 2.1 RISK AVERSION

The NLSY79 provides a rich set of individual characteristics for each respondent, and the 2010 wave included questions on risk preference detailed below:

> **RISK 1:** Suppose that you are the only income earner in the family, and that you have to choose between two new jobs. The first job would guarantee your current total family income for life. The second job is possibly better paying, but the income is less certain. There is a 50-50 chance the second job would increase your total lifetime income by 20 percent and a 50-50 change that is would cut it by 10 percent. Which job would you take: the first job or the second job?

Respondents who chose the second job in response to question RISK1 were asked the following question:

> **RISK 2:** Suppose the chances were 50-50 that the second job would increase your total lifetime income by 20 percent, and 50-50 that it would cut it by 15 percent. Would you take the first job or the second job?

Respondents who chose the first job in response to question RISK1 were asked the following question:

> **RISK 3:** Suppose the chances were 50-50 that the second job would increase your total lifetime income by 20 percent, and 50-50 that it would cut it by five percent. Would you take the first job or the second job?

Also, all respondents were asked to self-rate their attitude towards the question below.

> **RISK 4:** Are you generally a person who is fully prepared to take risks or do you try to avoid taking risks? Rate yourself from 0 to 10, where 0 means "unwilling to take any risks" and 10 means "fully prepared to take risks."

For this study, we denote all respondents who chose the first job in response to questions RISK1 and RISK3 in addition to self-rating their risk preference between 0 and 4, as being "risk averse." As described earlier, this combination of the experimentally-determined risk preference and self-rated score should prove more accurate than risk preferences determined purely through hypothetical gambles.

### 2.2 HEALTH RISK KNOWLEDGE

Three questions from the 2010 wave of the NLSY79 are used to control for the awareness of the respondent of health risks posed by obesity.

> **HEALTH 1:** When you buy a food item for the first time, how often would you say you read the nutritional information sometimes listed on the label - would you say always, often, sometimes, rarely or never?
> **HEALTH 2:** Are you now trying to lose weight, gain weight, stay about the same, or are you not trying to do anything about your weight?
> **HEALTH 3:** How often do you do light or moderate activities for at least 10 minutes that cause only light sweating or slight to moderate increase in breathing or heart rate?

Respondents who answer that they read the nutritional information always or often in response to HEALTH 1 are coded with the value 1 for a created variable called "Read Nutritional Information". Similarly binary variables are created for respondents who answer that they are trying to lose weight in response to Health 2 (called "Trying to Lose Weight") and for respondents who answer that they never (or are unable to) exercise in response to question HEALTH 3 ( called "Never Engages in Exercise).

### 2.3 BODY MASS INDEX (BMI) & OBESITY

The Body Mass Index (BMI) was calculated for each participant based on their height and weight in 2010. Per the usual guidelines, respondents were coded as obese if their BMI is greater than or equal to 30. Where overweight is shown as a variable in the analysis, the definition of overweight used is that the BMI is greater than or equal to 25 and less than 30.

## 3.0 ANALYSIS

### 3.1 SUMMARY STATISTICS

Summary statistics for the key variables used in this study are shown in Table 1. These statistics are in line with previous research, showing a risk aversion rate of 38.6% which is slightly lower than previous estimates such as Dave and Saffer (2008), who estimated it at 42.9% for this age-group – but within reasonable limits of consistency, given that this study is using a two-pronged method to confirm risk aversion. The percentage of obese respondents, 37.4, is also consistent with previous studies on the US population.

**Table 1:** Summary statistics key variables

| Variable | Mean | Standard Deviation |
|---|---|---|
| Risk Aversion (1=Averse) | 0.386 | 0.487 |
| Overweight (1=Overweight) | 0.752 | 0.432 |
| Obese (1=Obese) | 0.374 | 0.484 |
| Read Nutrition Information (1=Yes) | 0.497 | 0.500 |
| Never Engages in Exercise (1=Never) | 0.262 | 0.439 |
| Currently Trying To Lose Weight (1=Trying) | 0.465 | 0.499 |
| BMI | 29.166 | 6.200 |

To explore the distribution of BMI further, Tables 2-4 show the percent quantiles for the distribution of BMI within the risk-averse respondents and the not risk-averse respondents for three populations: Table 2 shows the distribution for the full sample, Table 3 for the sub-sample of respondents who were coded as reading nutritional information while shopping for food, and Table 4 for the sub-sample of respondents who were coded as trying to lose weight.

**Table 2:** BMI quintiles for full sample population

| Percent | Not Risk Averse | Risk Averse |
|---|---|---|
| 1 | 18.5979 | 19.1284 |
| 5 | 20.9803 | 21.2547 |
| 10 | 22.4263 | 22.5941 |
| 25 | 24.9637 | 25.0647 |
| 50 | 27.9865 | 28.3396 |
| 75 | 32.075 | 32.7305 |
| 90 | 36.4879 | 37.7855 |
| 95 | 39.7973 | 41.5976 |

**Table 3:** BMI quantiles for sub-sample who read nutritional information

| Percent | Not Risk Averse | Risk Averse |
|---|---|---|
| 1 | 18.5595 | 19.2027 |
| 5 | 20.7988 | 21.1599 |
| 10 | 22.3125 | 22.4327 |
| 25 | 24.8865 | 24.9586 |
| 50 | 27.8913 | 28.1639 |
| 75 | 32.0946 | 32.6099 |
| 90 | 36.5765 | 37.5852 |
| 95 | 39.6211 | 41.5976 |

**Table 4:** BMI quantiles for sub-sample trying to lose weight.

| Percent | Not Risk Averse | Risk Averse |
|---|---|---|
| 1 | 21.2846 | 21.4806 |
| 5 | 23.4908 | 23.1702 |
| 10 | 24.9586 | 24.5247 |
| 25 | 27.1219 | 27.4324 |
| 50 | 30.3411 | 30.7276 |
| 75 | 34.3852 | 35.3002 |
| 90 | 39.0556 | 40.4133 |
| 95 | 42.717 | 43.754 |

Each of these tables shows that the risk-averse population has a higher BMI threshold in every quantile of the BMI distribution. For the full sample, the 90 percent quantile is a full point of BMI higher for the risk-averse population when compared with everyone else. The sub-sample of respondents who read nutritional information have a lower BMI, and the sub-sample of those trying to lose weight have a higher BMI, at every quantile when compared to the overall population. This can be explained by the higher likelihood that respondents who are trying to lose weight are motivated to do so due to being overweight or obese, compared to either the general population or respondents who regularly read nutritional information. Interestingly, the risk averse population in both sub-samples show a higher BMI threshold in every quantile, similar to the overall population. Thus, the summary statistics provide early support for the idea that risk aversion, and not risk-taking, may be associated with higher BMI.

## 3.2 ESTIMATION RESULTS

Next, the following model specification is estimated:

$$Logit[Prob(O_i = 1)] = \beta_0 + \beta_1 X_i + \beta_2 R_i + \beta_3 H_i$$ **Equation (1)**

where $O_i$ is a dichotomous variable which indicates whether the respondent is obese at the time of the survey; $X_i$ represents a set of individual characteristics such as age, gender, educational level and household income & net-worth that have been shown to influence the tendency to become obese; $R_i$ is a dichotomous variable that codes the risk aversion of the respondent as described in Section 2; $H_i$ represents the 3 different methods to capture health risk knowledge of the respondent which are described in Section 2.

Estimation results are shown as Odds Ratio Estimates in Table 5 for readability. Many of the variables shown as having significant effects on obesity in Table 5 are well-established predictors of obesity, thus giving confidence to the study methodology and survey measures used. The strongest significant negative effect observed in Table 2 is that when the respondent is trying to lose weight, followed by race and whether the respondent reads nutritional information on food labels. These are all expected results; but the interesting finding for the purpose of this study is that risk aversion has a significant, positive effect on the likelihood of being obese. In fact, the positive effect of risk aversion is large enough to offset the negative effect of the variable that captures whether the respondent reads nutritional labels.

**Table 5:** Odds ratio estimates for determinants of obesity

| Odds Ratio Estimates | | | |
|---|---|---|---|
| Effect | Point Estimate | 95% Wald Confidence Limits | |
| Race (1=Not Hispanic or Black) | **0.706*** | 0.63 | 0.791 |
| Regular Exercise (1=No Exercise) | 1.025 | 0.913 | 1.151 |
| Years of Schooling | **0.964*** | 0.94 | 0.989 |
| Household Net Worth | **0.938*** | 0.919 | 0.961 |
| Reads Nutritional Labels (1=Yes) | **0.869*** | 0.782 | 0.966 |
| Age | 1.008 | 0.986 | 1.031 |
| Married (1=Yes) | **0.943*** | 0.904 | 0.984 |
| Risk Averse (1=Yes) | **1.196*** | 1.079 | 1.325 |
| Trying to Lose Weight (1=Yes) | **0.619*** | 0.594 | 0.645 |
| Gender (1=Female) | 0.913 | 0.822 | 1.015 |

(* indicates significance at 5% Level).

Tables 6 and 7 further explore the idea of health risk information and its effect on the relationship between risk preference and obesity. Table 6 shows Equation 1 re-estimated with a sub-sample of the survey population who read nutritional information on food labels, and Table 7 shows the re-estimation with the sub-sample who are trying to lose weight.

**Table 6:** Determinants of obesity (sub-sample of respondents who read nutritional info).

| Odds Ratio Estimates | | | |
|---|---|---|---|
| Effect | Point Estimate | 95% Wald Confidence Limits | |
| Race (1=Not Hispanic or Black) | **0.731*** | 0.62 | 0.863 |
| Regular Exercise (1=No Exercise) | 1.038 | 0.868 | 1.241 |
| Years of Schooling | 0.966 | 0.932 | 1.001 |
| Household Net Worth | **0.927*** | 0.908 | 0.95 |
| Age | 1.031 | 0.998 | 1.065 |
| Married (1=Yes) | **0.887*** | 0.832 | 0.945 |
| Risk Averse (1=Yes) | 1.08 | 0.929 | 1.255 |
| Gender (1=Female) | **0.807*** | 0.692 | 0.942 |
| Trying to Lose Weight (1=Yes) | **0.555*** | 0.52 | 0.592 |

(* indicates significance at 5% Level).

Demographic and economic variables such as race, marital status and net worth continue to be significant determinants of obesity in the sub-population of respondents who reporting reading nutritional labels. In addition, gender shows a significant effect, with women being significantly less likely to be overweight and education loses significance at the 5% level, though it continues to be associated with a slightly lowered chance of obesity at the 10% level of significance.

**Table 7:** Determinants of obesity (sub-sample of respondents trying to lose weight).

| Odds Ratio Estimates | | | |
|---|---|---|---|
| Effect | Point Estimate | 95% Wald Confidence Limits | |
| Race (1=Not Hispanic or Black) | **0.581*** | 0.495 | 0.682 |
| Regular Exercise (1=No Exercise) | 0.973 | 0.821 | 1.154 |
| Years of Schooling | 0.969 | 0.937 | 1.003 |
| Household Net Worth | **0.933*** | 0.914 | 0.967 |
| Age | 1.003 | 0.972 | 1.035 |
| Married (1=Yes) | **0.928*** | 0.875 | 0.984 |
| Risk Averse (1=Yes) | 1.061 | 0.918 | 1.227 |
| Gender (1=Female) | **0.637*** | 0.547 | 0.741 |
| Reads Nutritional Labels (1=Yes) | 1.009 | 0.871 | 1.169 |

(* indicates significance at 5% Level).

The sub-population of respondents who are trying to lose weight show similar characteristics to those who read nutritional label s, with the demographic variables representing gender and race both having much stronger effects while retaining significance. Remarkably, neither of these two subsamples show significant effect of risk aversion on the likelihood of being obese though the effect of the demographic variables remains similar.

## 4.0 DISCUSSION

This study uses an experimentally-obtained of risk preference, which is further validated by a self-assessment, to show that risk aversion is significantly associated with higher levels of obesity in a representative sample of the US population. Further, when knowledge of health risk is taken into account, using proxy measures for nutritional awareness and motivation to lose weight, the significance of risk aversion with regard to obesity disappears, and demographic factors are found to have both stronger and wider-ranging effects on the likelihood a respondent being obese.

The results also show that many demographic and socioeconomic determinants of obesity, such as race, income levels, years of schooling and marital status, are significant determinants of obesity in the overall population. This is consistent with the research literature on obesity risk, and increases the confidence that the relationship shown between risk preference and obesity is indeed a new finding, which is not correlated with the well-known socioeconomic factors. Further, the fact that gender emerges as a significant determinant of obesity risk in the sub-samples of respondents who have greater health risk knowledge provides an independent verification of Kan and Tsai (2004), who similarly found gender-specific effects of the health risk knowledge on obesity.

This difference in the significance of risk aversion in the two sub-samples provides us with a valuable clue as to the nature of the mechanism that may be linking risk aversion and obesity in the full population. Since risk-averse individuals have been shown to be less likely to avail themselves of health risk information and tests, the same effect might make them averse to discovering facts (such as nutritional information) that can reveal unwelcome facts about their current diets. Such an effect would, obviously, disappear when looking at risk-averse individuals in sub-populations who have already made the decision to avail themselves of health risk information. Thus the results consistently support the hypothesis that risk-averse behavior is significantly associated with greater obesity risk.

## 5.0 CONCLUSIONS AND POLICY IMPLICATIONS

This study advances the strand of research that seeks to determine whether the classification of obesity as a risky health behavior in much of the prior research is valid, and whether obesity might be better characterized by a failure to engage in healthy, preventative behaviors. The correct characterization of the behavioral profile of people who are likely to become obese is an important policy consideration, given the economic impacts of increasing obesity in the US population. In particular, as Mullahy & Sindelar (1994) demonstrate, policy that does not take risk preferences into account may seriously underestimate the cost of health interventions, and undermine economic models of healthcare. Therefore, if a set of risk preferences were seen to be significantly associated with obesity, the set of policy tools being used for economic modeling of obesity and related health issues can be calibrated to better fit individual heterogeneity in decision-making.

The need for incorporating behavioral economics into the design of incentives for healthy behavior have been well-studied in the research literature. In particular, as Volpp et al (2009) show, there is enormous potential for improving health outcomes if incentives are designed with the biases that inform decision-making are taken into account. While behavioral patterns such as time discounting have been researched for their effect on health, this study indicates that policies that are targeted towards risk averse populations might provide enhanced health outcomes, since the findings indicate that such populations are at heightened obesity risk, even after accounting for the usual socioeconomic and demographic factors. As previous research in health policy shows, the same bias that causes poor health-related decisions can be used to make incentives more effective once the bias is understood. In this case, if risk-averse populations are at greater obesity risk, structuring incentives as penalties will be expected to generate better outcomes than structuring them as benefits. And regardless of the actual design, policies that do not take into account the risk preferences of the population will have sub-optimal outcomes compared to policies that do take this important factor into account.

Future research can look at the complete question of the propensity to seek health risk information, and how it interacts with risk preferences, given that risk preferences do not appear to be significantly associated with obesity risk in individuals with better health awareness. Longitudinal studies that measure changes in risk preference, and investigate the relationship between such changes and health behaviors will also provide insight into the design of optimal health policies. Given the importance of obesity risk to public health and related economic issues in the United States, the results shown here indicate that the structuring of incentives to specifically appeal to risk-averse individuals is an area of research that needs urgent and sustained focus from policy-makers.

## REFERENCES

Anderson, L. R., and Mellor, J.M.. (2008). Predicting health behaviors with an experimental measure of risk preference." Journal of Health Economics 27(5), 1260-1274.

Barsky, R. B., et al. (1997). Preference parameters and behavioral heterogeneity: An experimental approach in the health and retirement study. The Quarterly Journal of Economics 112(2), 537-579.

Cutler, D., and Glaeser, E. (2005). What explains differences in smoking, drinking, and other health related behaviors? American Economic Review 95(2), 238-242.

Dave, D., and Saffer, H., (2008). Alcohol demand and risk preference. Journal of Economic Psychology 29(6), 810-831.

Davis, C., et al. (2004). Decision-making deficits and overeating: A risk model for obesity. Obesity Research 12(6), 929-935.

Davis, C., et al. (2010). Immediate pleasures and future consequences. A neuropsychological study of binge eating and obesity. Appetite 54(1), 208-213.

Dohmen, T., et al. (2011). Individual risk attitudes: Measurement, determinants, and behavioral consequences. Journal of the European Economic Association, 9(3), 522-550.

Kan, K., and Tsai, W. (2004). Obesity and risk knowledge. Journal of Health Economics 23(5), 907-934.
Mullahy, J., & Sindelar, J. L. (1994). Health, income, and risk aversion: assessing some welfare costs of alcoholism and poor health (No. w4649). National Bureau of Economic Research.
Picone, G., et al. (2004). Effects of risk and time preference and expected longevity on demand for medical tests. Journal of Risk and Uncertainty 28(1), 39-53.
Volpp KG, Pauly MV, Loewenstein G, Bangsberg D. (2009). P4P4P: an agenda for research on pay- for-performance for patients. Health Affairs, 28(1), 206-214.

# 2

# Income Inequality: Do Different Inequality Measures Show Different Impacts on Economic Growth, at the State Level? An Analysis of the State of New Jersey[1]

**Bertram C. I. Okpokwasili, Ph.D.**[2]

**ABSTRACT**

This paper investigates whether the use of different inequality measures is instrumental in determining impact on economic growth at the State level. We find that different measures show different levels of significance with respect to economic health. We study New Jersey income distribution and shares from 1964 to 2014, using graphs and statistics. The dual analyses approach and the use of different inequality measures enabled conclusions to be reached, that only one view and one inequality measure would have made difficult, if not misleading. New Jersey Real GDP/Capita (RGC) was going up, whether or not the inequality measure was getting better. Inequality had little or no effect on the direction of the RGC. Economic Growth is not a good measure of the effects of inequality.

Keywords: Economic growth, gini coefficients, quintiles, real GDP/capita.

---

## 1.0 INTRODUCTION

Research papers tend to fall on either side of the argument whether inequality is helpful to economic growth. Even though the Gini coefficient is the most widely used income distribution tool, other measures such as the Atkinson Index, the 20/20 measure (ratio of 1$^{st}$ Quintile Mean Income/ 5$^{th}$ Quintile Mean Income) amongst others, have been employed at various times. The question investigated in this paper is whether the claim of impact might depend on the inequality measure used. It is relative rather than absolute inequality that matters more on people's lives and behavior. It is of relevance, therefore

[1] I am grateful for the numerous changes which both the editor of the journal of business and the peer reviwers suggested in order to make this paper better in every respect. I incorporated many of them in the final copy of this paper. To the extent that this paper has any redeeming quality, the praise should go to these reviewers and the editor. I take responsibility for any shortcomings.

[2] Associate Professor, School of Business Administration, Georgian Court University, Lakewood, NJ

that studies be made of inequality variations at the local and state levels. That is another contribution this paper makes.

The Gini coefficient, even though very widely used, has been criticized for not differentiating between different kinds of inequalities. In which case, even when two Lorenz curves intersect, indicating different inequality patterns, they may still have the same Gini Coefficients[3]. The Gini coefficient is said to be most appropriate for inequalities in the middle spectrum. It may have difficulties at the top or at the bottom[4]. In this study, we use the Gini, the 20/20 measure, the various ratios of the different segments of the population and income quintiles and percentages. The 20/20 measure could also be the ratio of the 5th Quintile over the 1st. We will show that the two versions are sensitive to inequalities at different ends of the income spectrum.

There is a general agreement that in the US, at least, and in the most recent times, income inequality has grown substantially. In fact this has become a major 2016 presidential (the US) and other campaign issue[5]. But apart from politics and its implications, scholars are very much disagreed on many aspects of the inequality arguments. And these include:

- What causes the perceived income inequality in the US?
- Is the present attention given to inequality justified- is inequality harmful to growth?
- Why are scholars disagreed as to whether inequality has impact on economic development?

At the national and international levels, data is plentiful for various forms of analyses and positions. This paper seeks to use state data to explore the last 2 of the 3 questions above. One recognizes the many limitations entailed in the measurement of data on income and wealth in the country, very magnified when dealing with the states. It is also relevant to recognize that pre-tax and post-tax measurements may give different results, as well as income with or without capital gains.

We limit ourselves to pre-tax incomes, recognizing that, at the lowest levels, government transfer payments may not be fully captured as income to the poorest families. We however use total family income as determined by the Bureau of the Census, which could include total earned and unearned income.

Section 2.0 is a short review of the literature of various positions taken by researchers on income distribution and its effects.
Section 3.0, discusses the data and methodology of this paper.
Section 4.1, covers the descriptive/graphical analysis of our data on the relationship between Economic wellbeing and the Inequalities.
Section 4.2 gives the results of the empirical analysis of the relationship between economic wellbeing and income inequalities. The related tables are in Tables 1 and 2. We use the state of New Jersey experience to determine if state figures support what has been said on the national level, and what relationship, if any, exists between inequality and economic wellbeing.
Section 5.0 concludes the findings.

## 2.0 PRIOR LITERATURE AND HYPOTHESIS DEVELOPMENT

There is recently, so much interest in income distribution that many presidential statements in the most recent times have focused on the lopsided distribution of income in the United States. The heated debate on the share of national income that goes to the top 1% of the population prompted many days of sit-ins and demonstrations on Wall Street in the months preceding the presidential election of 2012. The campers claimed they were the 99 Percenters, the bottom portion of the population whose share of income the One Percenters were taking. Writing in the Los Angeles Times of February 2015, David Lauter headlined his piece as "income inequality emerges as key issue in 2016 presidential campaign". He goes

---

[3] Fernando G De Maio, 'Income inequality measures', www.jech.com, J. Epidemical Community Health 2007
[4] Fernado Maio, opcit.
[5] See Mother Jones publication of April 2, 2015- "Bernie Sanders goes Biblical on Income Inequality" by Josh Harkinson

on to quote Gallup Polls that " Although economic growth has resumed, the stock market has soared into record territory, and the number of Americans filing new claims for unemployment benefits has fallen to its lowest level in nearly 15 years, income has remained stuck except for those at the very top."[6] Interest and debate on Income Distribution are an age old intractable, yet exciting academic and social question, with as many researchers on one side as there are on the other side. The discussion on Income Distribution was very much geared toward the economic growth of developing nations. Simon Kuznets in his seminal address to the American Economic Society asked "Does inequality in the distribution of income increase or decrease in the course of a country's economic growth. What factors determine the secular level and trends of income inequalities"[7].

Kuznets would go on to observe that inequitable distribution of income deterred economic development in a developing country, and so would be of a negative consequence. In developed countries however, inequitable distribution of income would favor economic growth. His analysis would lead to what was called the Kuznets Curve. The curve which is like an inverted U shape, would have Kuznets hypothesizing that "as economic growth / development increases, inequalities first go up and then come down" [8] Kuznets would later abandon this hypothesis, for lack of plausible data, even as many economists and researchers lined up on both sides of the hypothesis.

Similar to the Kuznets curve debate, income distribution has had supporters and detractors- those who assert that income inequality is very harmful to economic growth and development (Wilkinson and Picket, the Spirit Level, 2009), and those who maintain that inequality is necessary for robust economic growth, and is good for the country (Barro, 2000)[9], also strongly argued for by economists at the Manhattan Institite (2014)[10]

Nancy Birdsall[11] extensively explored the literature on the development and lack thereof of many Asian and Latin American countries. Whether or not inequality contributes to economic development would depend on other economic and political institutions in the country, she claims. Where institutions are weak, and politicians seem not to care for the welfare of the poor, inequality grows at the expense of the poor, and development lags behind. Where more democratic institutions thrive, like the early northern farmers in the US, where labor was not as abundant as the slavery in the south, property rights were more broad-based, and thriving smallholder class supported public financing of education, thus creating local governments that were accountable to most of the citizens. In this setting equitable distribution of income enabled broad based growth, and stronger institutions.[12] Robert Barro (2000), said Birdsall, had shown structural differences in the relationship between inequality and growth in the developed and undeveloped economies. Barro apparently showed that in higher income developed countries, inequality tended to be associated with higher growth, whereas in lower income developing countries, inequality tended to be associated with lower growth rates.

Birdsall discusses what she called "constructive" and "destructive" inequality. Constructive inequality is income inequality that reflects solely differences in individuals' responses to equal incentives or opportunities, and is consistent with efficient resource allocations. "Destructive" inequality on the other hand reflects inefficient resource allocation to the rich, which has the effect of encouraging economic discrimination and reducing the incentive to invest or take advantage of economic opportunities to contribute productively.[13]

[6] David Lauter: Income Inequality emerges as key issue in 2026 presidential campaign, LA Times, Feb. 5, 2015
[7] Simon Kuznets: Economic Growth and Income Inequality; American Economic Review, March 1955, Number 1
[8] Dan Hirschman: On the Origins of the Kuznets Curve / A (Budding) Sociologist Commonplace Book, http://asociologist.com/2013/03/21 on-the-origins-of-the-Kuznets-curve
[99] Robert Barro found that in developed economies, inequality was helpful to growth, but harmful in developing ones.
[10] Eight economists, Gerald Auten of the US Treasury Dept. and others argue the positive effect of inequality.
[11] Nancy Birdsall_ Income Distribution: Effects on Growth and Development, Center for Global Development, Working Paper Number 118, April 2007.
[12] Nancy Birdsall- Income Distribution: Effects on Growth and Development
[13] Nancy Birdsall

Rebecca Blank and David Card used regional data in the US to study the causes of income inequality in the US. In a multiple regression of unemployment as the dependent variable and mean quintile incomes of the five quintiles over the period 1967 to 1991 as independent variables, Blank and Card would seem to assert that there was little or no relationship between unemployment and income shares. They would also indicate that if unemployment had any effect on income shares, it would seem to happen more after 1979 than before.

Black and Card would go on to show that wage dispersion, measured as standard deviation of log wages, has significant relationship to income shares. They would show that higher wage dispersion had a negative effect on low income earnings of families, and a positive effect on higher income earnings[14] Black and Card would claim that "The growth in earnings and income that occurs with a rise in median wages leads to some equalization, with redistribution of income away from the top quintile, and towards the second and third quintiles. The effect of wage dispersion is more clearly redistributive and is disequalizing"[15]

A book- "The Spirit Level: Why more equal societies almost always do better" by two British epidemiologists, Richard Wilkinson and Kate Picket, in March 2009, attributed all social ills to income inequality. They assert that ills ranging from infant mortality to shortened life span were all a result of inequitable distribution of income. This book was very highly received in Britain and various other social circles. It has also been criticized very strongly for lack of statistical data collection honesty and procedural miscalculations.[16]

In "Income Inequality in New Jersey: The Growing Divide and Its Consequences", the Legal Services of New Jersey Poverty Research Institute (LSNJ) would quote Wilkinson and Picket extensively as a proof of the damage inequitable distribution of income in New Jersey is doing to New Jersey residents.[17] Some of these assertions would need to be investigated further.

The Manhattan Institute in its May 2014 E/21 Economic Policy for the 21st Century argues many aspects of inequality – what in the opinion of many of these economists may be facts and fiction[18]. Eight different economists explored various aspects of inequality. But many of these are from the viewpoint that income inequality is not as bad as it seems. And some of the quotations reflecting the observations made are indeed interesting, to say the least: Professor Bruce Meyer quotes " The level of inequality is much lower for consumption than income, and since 1980, consumption inequality has risen considerably less than income inequality". Professor Philip Amour quotes in the same publication- "A shocking result emerges: from 1987 to 2007, the incomes of the bottom and middle fifth rose (by 13 percent and 6 percent), but the income of the top 5 percent declined by 5 percent- Inequality- even between the top and everyone else- fell"[19].

Much has been written and suggested as to why income inequality has grown in the US in the last quarter of the 20th Century. Many of these point to increasing wage dispersion (Blank and Card, 1993; Picketty and Saez, Feb. 2003). Picketty and Saez suggest that whereas pre-World War II top income shares were accounted for by capital accumulation, which suffered much decline because of the shocks of war and depression, from which it never recovered fully, top income shares since 1970's have reflected higher wages for CEO's and top business management. These higher earnings have persisted because the society tolerated such incomes, in addition to decline in progressive taxation since the 1980's[20]. Such high

---

[14] Rebecca Blank and David Card: Poverty, Income Distribution and Growth: Are They Still Connected? Brookings Papers on Economic Activity, Vol.1993, No.2, page 310.

[15] Blank and Card

[16] Milos Simic- "A critical reading of the Spirit Level: why equality is better for everyone, R Wilkinson and K. Pikette, January 2012"

[17] The Inaugural Annual Report from the Legal Services of New Jersey Poverty Research Institute, July 2012, pages 8 and 10

[18] The Manhattan Institute- E/21 Economic Policies for the 21st Century- " Income Inequality in America Fact and Fiction", No. 1, May 2014

[19] The Manhattan Institute, opcit.

[20] Picketty and Saez, February 2003.

incomes have helped fuel the growth in inequality in the US compared to the rest of the developed Western World. The reduction in union power in the US has also been mentioned as responsible for the rise in income inequality. There is hope, Picketty and Saez would suggest- for more progressive taxation in the future to stem the tide of inequality.

## 3.0 RESEARCH DATA METHODOLOGY

This study uses data from 1964 through 2014 of household incomes in New Jersey, derived from the March CPS (Current Population Survey) Data of the US Bureau of the Census, stored by IPUMS (Integrated Public Use Microdata Series)[21].

The data retrieved had to be sorted by years and in ascending family income order. For each year, we would break down the data in 5 income categories (called quintiles for 1/5 of the population), designating the income segments that would constitute the basis for our study. Excel's Descriptive Statistics function would be used to calculate the mean and median of each quintile.

Mark Frank had derived state inequality measures ("A New State –Level Panel of Income Inequality Measures Over the Period 1916- 2005", 2008), This had been updated to 2012 by a later publication[22]. So it was possible to get the inequalities (the Gini, Atkin 05 etc), other than the 20/20 measures, from this panel. The 20/20 (1st Quintile Mean/5th Quintile Mean) measures were calculated from our IPUMS income figures.

GDP and Personal Income figures for New Jersey were derived from various editions of the Bureau of Labor Analysis and Bureau of Economic Analysis publications. Where necessary, we reduced all the data on GDP and Personal Income to 2009 dollar denominated figures, using consumer price indexes. GDP calculation for the state is different from GDP calculation for the national economy. The major components of National GDP calculations are Consumption, Gross Investment, Government Expenditures and Net Exports. For the state, it's mainly a summation of value add for the different businesses. State GDP is calculated as the sum of employee compensation, taxes on production and imports, subsidies and gross operating surplus.[23]

First we show graphical relationships between incomes, broken down by quintiles, and state GDP/Capita. This is done at the beginning of section 4. Then we do statistical analyses using Ordinary Least Squares Multiple Regressions, based on both the modified Solow model and the modified Cobb-Douglas Production Functions. These are properly described in the sections. We are not interested, for this study at this time, in causation, we are interested in relationships, if they exist, between economic growth and various inequality distributions. We are also interested in whether it is possible that using different inequality measures might show different levels of statistically significant relationships. Personal income (employee compensation) is the major component in state GDP calculations. It accounts for about 60% of the state GDP[24]

We measure the relationship between the state GDP/Capita, the general measure of the economic health of the state, the personal income per capita and various inequality measures, including: the 20/20 (the 1st quintile /the 5th quintile) means, the Gini and the Atkinson coefficients. We use either economic growth (change in Real GDP/Capita) or simply Real GDP/Capita, to represent economic wellbeing in this paper. We recognize, however, that economic growth is not necessarily the same as economic development, nor are we under any illusions that growth represents wellbeing for all[25].

[21] https://USA-IPUMS.org/USA

[22] Mark Frank and Sommeiller- Price Series, Annual Top Income Measures for each state 1917-2012

[23] Experimental Estimates of Gross Domestic Product by State (GDP by State) for years 1963etc., Bureau of Economic Analysis, US Department of Commerce, 1985

[24] BEA (2006) GDP by State Estimation Methodology, page 7

[25] Please see Amtya Sen "Freedom as Development"1997, or Bertram Okpokwasili "economic development vs economic growth", 2007

## 4.0 STATE-LEVEL GDP/CAPITA VS PERSONAL INCOME AND INCOME INEQUALITIES

### 4.01 DESCRIPTIVE ANALYSIS

Descriptive analysis gives an intuitive view of the relationships between different income shares and economic or social parameters. These relationships may not be adequately captured by regression or other mathematical analyses.

Fig.4a demonstrates the relative growth of the mean incomes of the 5 quintiles. The bottom quintile grew, albeit very slowly, until 2010 and went down from there. The top two quintiles have grown considerably, apparently at the expense of the bottom two quintiles. All three middle quintiles grew slowly over the period. The bottom quintile grew until 2010, and started a downward trend. The top (5th) quintile grew very quickly through 2010, went down in 2011, grew in 2012 and 2013, and slowed down in 2014.

Figure 4b demonstrates graphically how the mean incomes of the bottom 20% of New Jersey residents have varied with the top 20%. The figure would be much worse when the lowest 10% is compared to the top 10% or 5%. It looked like the gain at the bottom in the 1960's lost ground consistently thereafter to 2014. Income inequality has grown consistently since about 1980

**Fig 4a:** Mean incomes for the population quintiles in New Jersey.

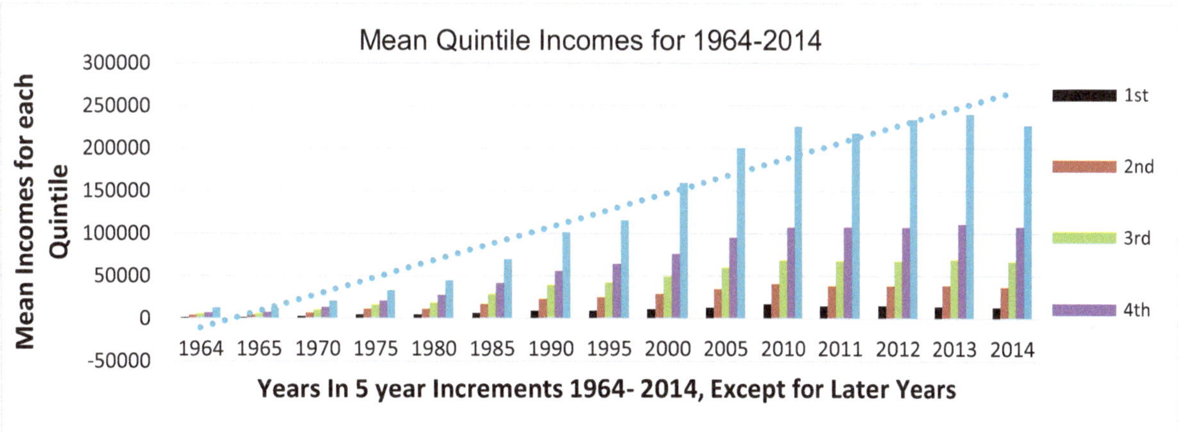


1st quintile is the bottom 20% of the population, while 5th is the top 20% of the population. We plot 5 year gaps until 2010, then yearly

Source: My calculations from March CPS Data from IPUMS 1965- 2014

**Fig 4b:** 20-20 (1st Quintile as a percentage of the 5th Quintile) Measure of new Jersey Income Distribution.

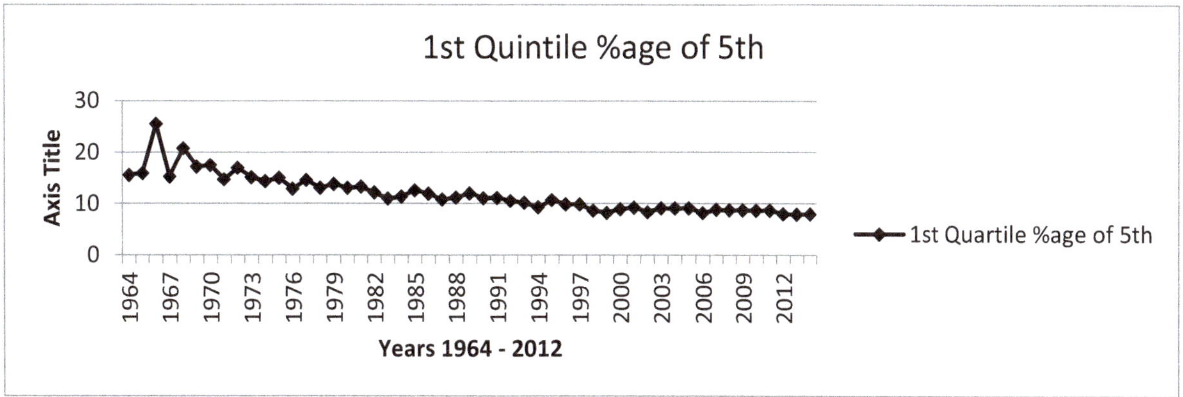


Source: My calculations using March CPS Bureau of the Census Data, from IPUMS Database.

Fig 4c gives a graphical demonstration of the movement of Real GDP/Capita versus the three measures of inequality (the 20/20 not in percent, the Gini and the Atkin05 (in %age terms) over the study period. It is very clear that the Gini and the Atkin05 were moving higher along with the Real GDP/Capita. That is the way it should be if inequality worsened throughout the period, which would be what the two measures indicated. However, the 20/20 measure was not showing what the Gini and Atkin05 were showing. The 20/20 measure showed that for the 1964 – 1982 period, income inequality was not getting any worse, in fact it was getting better most of that time (hovering around 11.6% to 13.3%). But from 1983 to 2012, with the exception of 2001, inequality had gone from 12.7% down to 6.4% [26]

**Fig 4c:** NJ Real GDP/Capita vs Various Inequality Measures

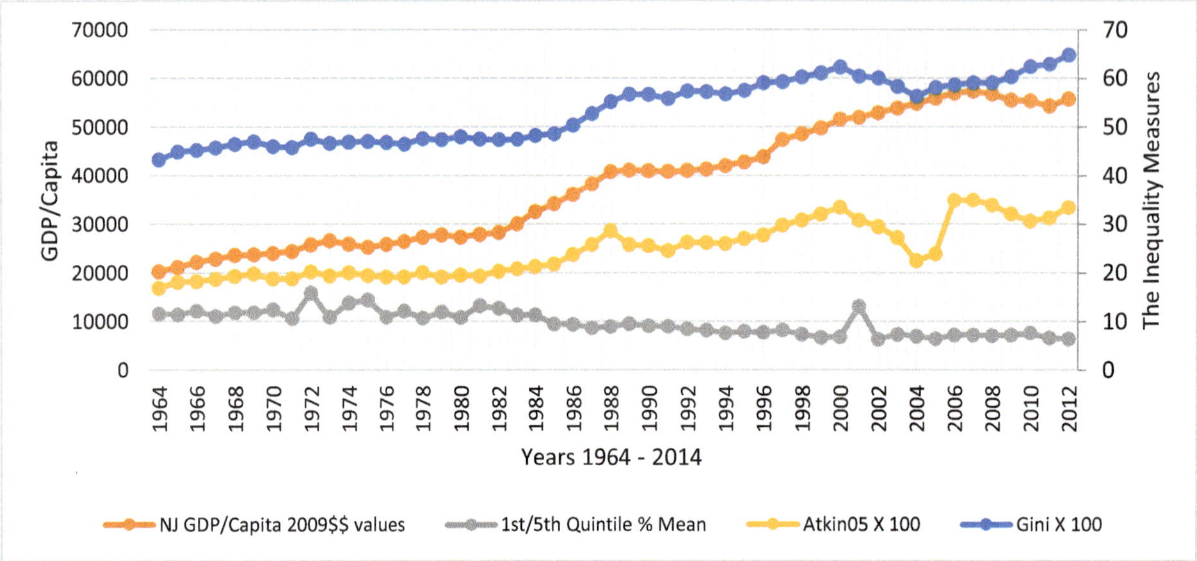


Figures 4d to 4f give graphical relationships between Real GDP/Capita (Real with 2009 dollars) and individual inequality measures. One would expect that growth in GDP/Capita would enable the 20/20 ratio (measured by the ratio of the 1st to the 5th quintiles) to go up, indicating the narrowing of the gap between the lowest earning quintile and the top earning quintile. If however this ratio continues to decrease, one would surmise that increasing GDP/Capita over the years seemed not to have a helpful impact on the lot of the bottom earners. We do the same with the Gini coefficient and the Atkin05 measure.

A look at Figure 4d, the relationship between Real GDP/Capita and the 20/20 measure of income inequality, shows what looks to us as a mixed relationship, in that between 1964 and 1980, this ratio fluctuated between 12% and 14%, but an the average tended to go up, as GDP/Capita was going up. After 1980, one observes a downward trend in the ratio for a while (between1981 and 2000) as GDP/Capita continued on an upward trend. The 20/20 ratio spikes up in the year 2001, and remains relatively flat through 2012, going down fractionally as GDP/Capita kept an upward trend.

The Gini Coefficient, in Fig 4e moves in a direct relationship with GDP/Capita from 1964 to 2008. Then there seemed to be a divergence, the Gini increasing through 2012, while the GDP/Capita, for the most part, goes in a downward direction.

The Atkins in Fig 4f, moved directly with the GDP/Capita measure except for the three years of 2003 through 2005.

The two major objectives of this paper are; one to evaluate, using state data over the years, whether increasing income inequality is helpful or unhelpful to economic growth/economic wellbeing, and

[26] Note that for the 20/20 measure lower percentages indicate worsening inequality, since we are dividing the 1st quintile by the 5th quintile.

secondly whether the use of different measures of income distribution could led us to different conclusions on this issue.

Given the figures we have just evaluated, we are able to answer the second question better than the first at this juncture. The movements of the three measures of inequality with respect to GDP/Capita are different. The 20/20 measure is definitely moving in the opposite direction as the GDP/Capita. Generally, the trend in GDP/Capita has been upward, while the trend in the 20/20 measure has been downward. So one could say, using these figures, that in New Jersey over the period in question, the bottom fifth has gotten lower proportion of the income than the top fifth, even as per capita income has increased.

**Fig. 4d:** New Jersey Real(2009) GDP/CAPITA vs 1st Quintile/5th Quintile Income Shares

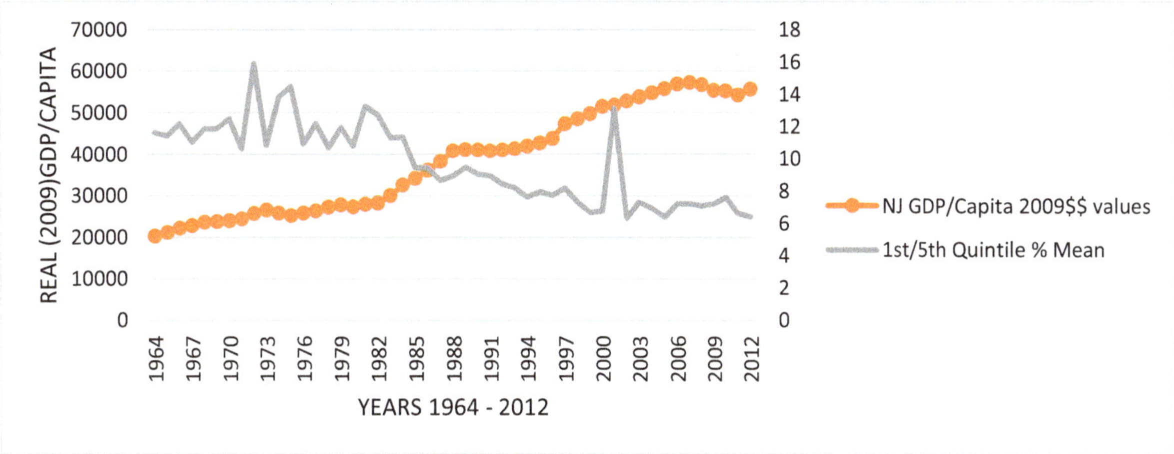


The Gini coefficient, on the other hand moved in direct relationship with the per capita GDP for most of the period in question. The Gini went up as per capita GDP increased from 1964 to 2003. One sees that as the Gini went up after 2003, the GDP/Capita went down. There were various periods where the Gini went up, while GDP/Capita went down – 1988 to 1997 for instance. The Gini would tend to show no letting off in worsening inequality over the years.

**Fig 4e:** NJ GDP/Capita vs Gini Coefficient For 1964-2012

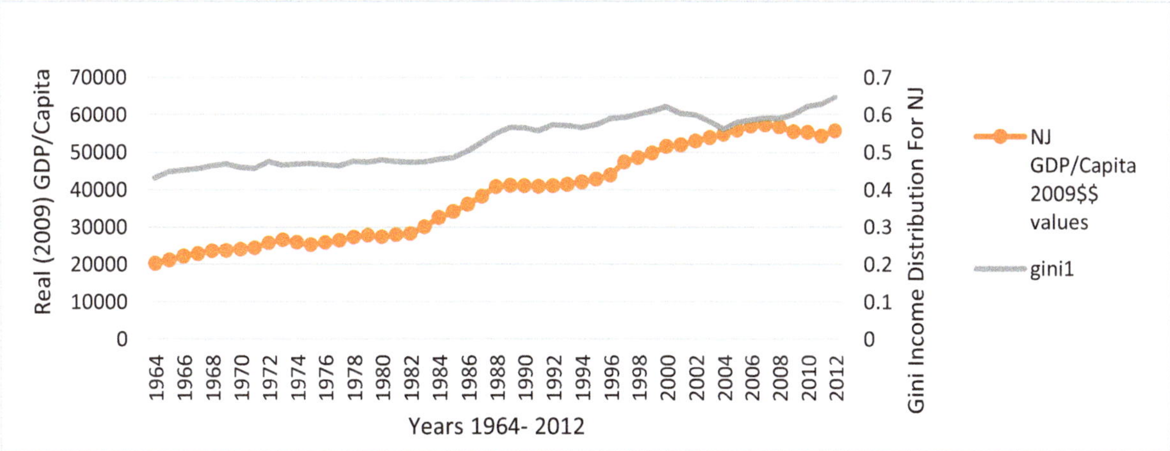


But even though we could have arrived at different conclusions using the two measures of inequality for various time frames, the long term trend for both would tend to give the same indication, namely that over the period in question income inequality increased even as the GDP/Capita increased.

The Atkin05 tended to give the same pattern as the Gini, except that from 2003, the Atkins would seem to move directly with GDP/Capita, while Gini would move in opposite direction. Between 1964 and 1985, whereas the Gini showed almost a flat (or rather unchanging) pattern of inequality, the 20/20 measure showed an irregular pattern of the relationship between the quintiles. In a number of cases showing improvement (or higher ratios), and in other cases maintaining a downward trend. After 1985, but for one spike upwards in the year 2000, it was generally downward, indicating increasing inequality. The Atkins would, except in 2003, show that it moved in the same direction as the GDP/Capita, increasing inequality as the economy grew.

**Fig 4f:** NJ Real GDP/Capita vs The Atkins Measure of Income Inequality

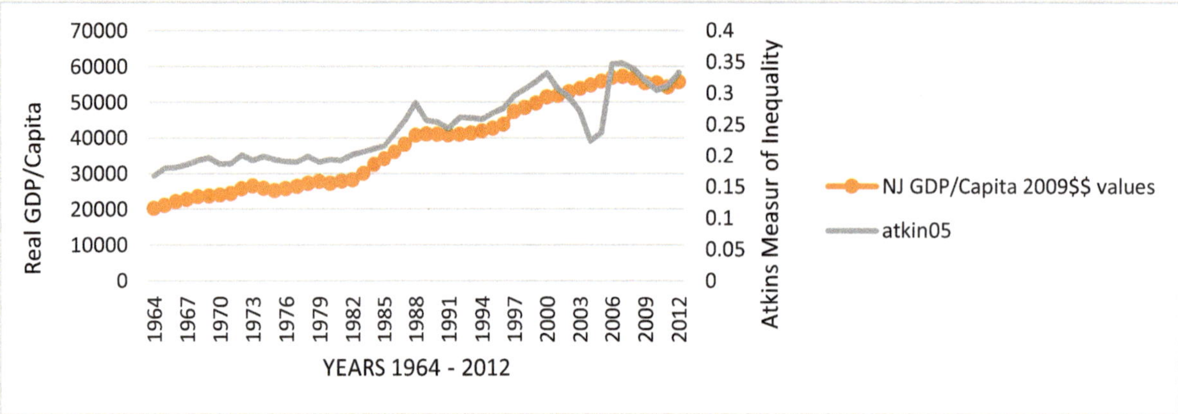


## 4.02 MAIN STATISTICAL RESULTS

This section gives the results of the various statistical analyses we did of the relationship between GDP/Capita, Personal Income and various income inequalities (the 20/20 measure, the Gini and the Atkin05 indexes). GDP/Capita measures the wellbeing of the economy, whether it is at the national level or at the State level. Even though the inequality measures we used were mainly the three mentioned above, we did explore such measures as the 5% over the 1$^{st}$ quintile, and 10% over the 1$^{st}$ quintile.

We did in some cases look at the ratio of the 5$^{th}$ quintile over the 1st quintile, rather than the reverse as we stated earlier. We had thought that both measured exactly the same thing, except one was the reverse of the other. We were surprised to see that their roles were quite different in the measurements. They exhibited different levels of significance.

Equation 4G1 is the untransformed version of the relationships we explore. These are reflected in Table-1.

$Y = \beta_0 + \beta_i X_i + \text{------------} + \varepsilon_i$ ---- G1

The Natural Log Transformation of 4G1 is reflected in equation 4G2, and the models in Table-2 give our results.

$\text{Ln}\, Y = \beta_0 + \beta_i \text{Ln} X_i + \beta j X j + \text{-------------} + \varepsilon_i$ ---------------- 4G2

Where Y = Real GDP/Capita

$X_1$ = Real Personal Income/Capita

$X_2$ = 1st Quintile Mean/5th Quintile Mean, known as 20/20 measure.

$X_3$ = The Gini Coefficient measure of inequality

$X_4$ = The Atkins measure of inequality

$X_5$ = 5$^{th}$ Quintile/1$^{st}$ Quintile

$X_6$ = Top 10%/1$^{st}$ Quintile Measure of Distribution

$X_7$ = Top 5%/1$^{st}$ Quintile Measure of Distribution

$\varepsilon_i$ = The error term

Various versions of equation 4G1 are explored, using Real ($2009) GDP/Capita as dependent variable, versus New Jersey Personal Income/Capita and various inequality measures (the 20/20 measure, the Gini coefficients, the Atkin05 measures, 10%/1$^{st}$ Quintile and 5%/1$^{st}$ Quintile) as independent variables. The statistical output is shown in Table 1. The transformed model of equation 4G1, given in equation 4G2, with various logarithmic transformations of the Real GDP/Capita and the associated independent variables, are explored also, and the statistical outputs are shown in Table2.

**Table A-1**, Models 1 through 8 reflect different measures of Inequality added to Personal Income/Capita, regressed against Real GDP/Capita for 1964 to 2012.

In all the models, the 20/20 measure shows a negative but statistically significant relationship (at the 95% level) with the economy measure of Real GDP/Capita. This is in agreement with the visual diagram shown in Fig 4e. For most of 1964 – 2012, the GDP/Person was on the rise. For most of that time, the 20/20 ratio was on the decline. Between 1964 and 1982, the 20/20 ratio had various up and down periods. The 20/20 ratio would seem, for this 64-82 period to fluctuate within a level range- between 11% and 15%. After 1982, the downward spiral had taken the ratio from 12%- 6%. This negative/indirect relationship would seem to support the theory that inequality is indeed helpful to growth in a developed setting. But this is just using the quintiles for which the top quintile contains 20% of the population. The measure with the top 5% or 1% might be different.

The Gini Coefficient, unlike the 20/20 measure, exhibited a direct relationship with Real GDP/Capita throughout the study period, except for a brief reversal between 2007 and 2010, during which period the Gini continued in an upward direction even as the economy headed downward. Once again indicating that higher inequality, measured by the Gini coefficient, would seem to be helpful to economic growth in this state setting. In certain periods when the 20/20 measure showed reduction in inequality, the Gini still indicated worsening inequality, as was the case between 1964 and 1982, and between 2007 and 2010 (Fig. 4f). The Atkins index showed a positive relationship, though statistically insignificant (at 90% and above) with Real GDP/Capita.

The 20/20 measure we used was the percentage version of the Mean of the $1^{st}$ Quintile divided by the mean of the $5^{th}$ Quintile. We used the raw decimals also in the analysis, but found no difference in the statistical significance of the model. The only difference was that the coefficient of the variable was multiplied by 100 in the non-percentage version.

In other cases, we changed the 20/20 variable to represent the $5^{th}$ Quintile divided by the $1^{st}$ Quintile. This showed substantially different statistical significance and numbers from the $1^{st}/5^{th}$ measure. There was a difference depending on which ratio was used as the 20/20 measure of inequality. This was also reflected in the graphical representations. It made some sense in that, of the two measures of 20/20 inequality, one ($1^{st}/5^{th}$) would represent a negative relationship with GDP growth. That is inequality would seem to be increasing when this measure is going down. The other ($5^{th}/1^{st}$) would show a direct relationship with increase in GDP/Capita, which means that when this ratio is increasing, inequality is increasing, the same type of measure the Gini and the Atkins05 would seem to show.

For an evaluation of our statistical analyses, we start with the:
Reference Model of Table1, the relationship between Real GDP/Capita (RGC) and Real Personal Income/Capita (RPC). We chose this as a reference, since we know that RPC would move in the same direction as RGC, since RPC is the major component of State RGC.
The equation for the reference model is approximately:
1.RGC = -622.6 + 1.118RPC + Ɛ
Since the constant term is not significant, it could, for all practical purposes be assumed to be close to zero. So our reference equation shows 1.RPC = .9009 RGC. One percentage change in the RPC changes RGC by 90%.
The adjusted coefficient of determination is 99.08%, and the beta weight is 0.9955.
What we seek in evaluating the inequality measurements on top of the RPC is their statistical significance in relation to RGC, and the possible differences in explaining the dependent variable, made by them individually and together.
Model1: Included the 20/20 ($1^{st}$ Quintile/$5^{th}$ Quintile) inequality measure with the RPC as independent variables.

The resulting equation was RGC = 4606 + 1.06 RPC - 325.8 (20/20)

The adjusted coefficient of determination ($R^2$) was 99.21%, and the betas were -0.0644 for 20/20, and 0.94 for RPC. The constant term was statistically significant, we cannot assume that it was zero. The 20/20 inequality showed a negative relationship with RGC, and showed that while it's effect is relatively very small on RGC, it has a negative effect nevertheless. A unit change in 20/20 would have the effect of changing RGC, albeit by a small amount. A 1% change in the inequality would change RGC by about 0.003%. The residuals showed Durbin – Watson statistic of 0.7437, an indication of slight autocorrelation in the independent variables. 2 would have been an ideal for no autocorrelation, and 0 would be positive autocorrelation. The Variance Inflation statistics were 3.0 for both independent variables. A figure more than ten would have been indicative of serious collinearity problems. As small as the impact of 20/20 is on RGC (Real GDP/Capita), it is nevertheless negative- an increase in the inequality increases GDP.

Model 2: Combined the Gini coefficient with RPC (Real Personal Income/Capita) as independent variables. The Gini did not show any statistical significance. The $R^2$ at 99.10%, indicating much less influence on RGC. The beta weight of the Gini was essentially the same as the 20/20, at 0.0616. The relationship with RGC is positive, indicating increase in one resulting in an increase in the other. An increase in Gini, however, is indicative of higher inequality in the state. One wonders if this might be the reason that Kuznets and others felt that increase in inequality was helpful to growth in developed economies.

Model 3: Included the Atkins05 inequality index controlling for the RPC as independent variables. The Atkin05 variable was not significant at 95% or 90% level, showed lower $R^2$ at 99.06%, and a beta-weight of 0.0074.

**Table 01:** Equation G1 untransformed GDP/Capita Dependent Variable

**Real ($2009) GDP/Capita against Real Personal Income/Capita, Various Measures of Inequality**

| Variables | | Reference Model (GDP vs PI | Module 1 with 20/20 | Module 2 with the Gini | Module 3 with the Atkins | Module4 with Atkins & 20/20 | Module 5 with 20/20, Gini | Module 6 with 20/20, Gini & Atkins |
|---|---|---|---|---|---|---|---|---|
| Intercept | $B_0$ | -622.5<br>(-1.0984) | 4606.25<br>(2.43)** | -4800.6<br>(-1.58) | -772.4<br>(-0.834) | 4550.123<br>(2.201)** | 1859.15<br>-0.482 | 1475.5<br>-0.366 |
| Real Personal Income/Capita | X1 | 1.119<br>(72.06)** | 1.06<br>(42.06)** | 1.053<br>(21.3)** | 1.1112<br>(27.6)** | 1.057<br>(25.13)** | 1.028<br>(21.44)** | 1.032<br>(20.35)** |
| 1st/5th Quintiles | X2 | | -325.8<br>(-2.87)** | | | -325.37<br>(-2.83)** | -302.72<br>(-2.58)** | -299.28<br>(-2.52)** |
| The Gini Coefficient | X3 | | | 12171.7<br>-1.4 | | | 6924.03<br>-0.819 | 8735.28<br>-0.89 |
| The Atkins | X4 | | | | 1694.26<br>-0.206 | 555.71<br>-0.072 | | -3317<br>-0.3753 |
| $5^{th}$ Q/$1^{st}$ Q | X5 | | | | | | | |
| 10%/$1^{st}$ Quintile | | | | | | | | |
| 5%/$1^{st}$ Quintile | | | | | | | | |
| $R^2$ | | 99.10% | 99.24% | 99.14% | 99.10% | 99.24% | 99.25% | 0.9925 |
| Adjusted $R^2$ | | 99.08% | 99.21% | 99.10% | 99.06% | 99.19% | 99.20% | 0.9919 |
| F statistic | | 5192.6 | 3000.9 | 2650.16 | 2543.4 | 1957.3 | 1986.46 | 1461 |
| Significance for F, p-value | | 0% | 0% | 0.00% | 0.00% | 0.00% | 0.00% | 0% |
| Degrees of Fr | | (1,47) | (2, 46) | (2, 46) | (2, 46) | -3.45 | (3, 45) | -4.44 |

**Significant at 95% confidence level. Critical T is 1.66, and the T's are in parentheses

*** Significant at 90% level. *Beta – weight values; std change in dependent variables per standard deviation change in the independent variable

**Table 01: Equation G1 untransformed GDP/Capita Dependent Variable) (cont.)**

Real ($2009) GDP/Capita against Real Personal Income/Capita, Various Measures of Inequality

| Variables | | Module 7 with 10%/1st Quintile | Module 8 with 5%/1st Quintile | Model 9 Year 64-81 with 20/20 vs RGC | Model 10 Years 64-81 with all the ineq. measures vs RGC |
|---|---|---|---|---|---|
| Intercept | B0 | -1793 (-3.12)** | -1081.62 (-2.18)** | 8021.68 (8.087)** | -67573 |
| Real Personal Income/Capita | X1 | 1.002 (31.17)** | 0.999 (32.03)** | 0.72 (23.9)** | |
| 1st/5th Quintiles | X2 | | | 28.5 (0.4383) | --76.99 (0.409) |
| The Gini Coefficient | X3 | | | | 247165.12 (4.723)** |
| The Atkins | X4 | | | | -78818.2 (-1.43) |
| 5th Q/1st Quintile | X5 | | | | |
| 10%/1st Quintile | | 377.17 (3.99)** | | | |
| 5%/1st Q | | | 266.98 (4.25)** | | |
| $R^2$ | | 99.33% | 99.36% | 97.48% | 83.17% |
| Adjusted $R^2$ | | 99.30% | 99.33% | 97.15% | 79.56% |
| F statistic | | | | 290.48 | 23.05 |
| Significance for F, p-value | | 0% | 0% | 0.00% | 0.00% |
| Degrees of Fr | | (3,45) | (3,45) | (2,15) | (3,14) |

**Significant at 95% confidence level. Critical T is 1.66, and the T's are in parentheses

*** Significant at 90% level. *Beta – weight values; std change in dependent variables per standard deviation change in the independent variable

Model 4 was a combination of RPC, 20/20 and Atkin05. The Atkin05 was not statistically significant. The RPC and 20/20 were significant at the 99% level. The $R^2$ was 99.19%, not much different from the figure in Model1, 99.21%.

Model 5 which included the Gini, the 20/20 and RPC was similar to Model 4. The Gini was not significant, and the 20/20 was. The variance inflation ratios were more than 10 each for the Gini and the RPC, indicating collinearity problems.

Model 6 combined all heretofore independent variables against the RGC. The results were more or less as in Model1, showing significance for the 20/20 and the RPC, and essentially the same level of adjusted coefficient of determination. The variance inflation factors for all but the 20/20 were above 10.

Models 7 and 8 which respectively combined the 10%/1st Quintile and 5%/1st Quintile with RPC showed more statistical significance and higher adjusted coefficient of determination than even Model1. Model 7- a combination of the ratio of the top 10% of earners to the bottom 20% (the 1st Quintile), showed statistical significance, $R^2$ of 99.30%, a beta-weight of 0.114 for the 10% and 0.892 for the RPC. It had a Durbin-Watson of 0.9559, better than any of the other Models we evaluated, and a variance inflation factor of 5.65. Model 8 included Top 5%/1st Quintile, showed an, $R^2$ of 99.33%, a beta-weight of 0.1179 for the 5%, and a Durbin-Watson of .7315, the variance inflation factors were 5.496 each, indicating no collinearity problems.

Models 9 & 10 we explored using the time period 1964-1981 to evaluate the relationships instead of the entire study period of 1964 to 2012. The 20/20 measure showed a positive but statistically insignifant relationships (which goes with what we saw on the graph fig 4e). The Gini coefficient was significant and stayed positively related to the Real GDP/Capita. The Atkin05 was insignificant and positively related.

For all the exercises of Table 1 we learn that the 20/20 inequality measure was a better indicator than its counterparts (the Gini and the Atkin05) by itself, and in combination with other independent variables, in having any impact on the overall health of the economy. Small effect in quantity, but the 20/20 measure would seem to show that as inequality increased, GDP/Capita increased.

**Table 2** explored the transformed RGC, using Logarithmic functions.

The transformed RGC (in a log-linear relationship), Ln RGC showed a much more statistical significance with the inequality coefficients and their combinations than the untransformed RGC.

We report our findings in Table 2, Models 1 thru 8. If one could equate the ln RGC as the change in RGC, we would be able to say that the Atkin05 and the Gini seemed to be more predictive than they were with the untransformed RGC. The Gini showed significance in combination with other measures. The Atkin05 did not show any significance at all. The ln (20/20) also showed significance with the Ln RGC, just the same as the ordinary $1^{st}/5^{th}$ would do with the transformed and untransformed RGC.

**Table 02:** Equation G2 transformed GDP/Capita Dependent Variable
Ln Real ($2009) GDP/Capita against Ln Real Personal Income/Capita, Various Measures of Inequality

| Variables | | Model 1 | Model 2 | Model 3 | Model 4 | Model 5 | Model 6 | Model 7 | Model 8 |
|---|---|---|---|---|---|---|---|---|---|
| Intercept | $B_0$ | 9.267 | 8.5068 | 1.681 | 1.2658 | 1.877 | 1.3165 | 0.9379 | 1.3359 |
| | | -63 | (927.6)** | (4.41)** | -3.7314 | (4.61)** | (4.456)** | (4.88)** | (4.03)** |
| Real Personal | X1 | 2.53 | | | | 0.8214 | | | 0.8251 |
| Income/Capita | | (13.66)** | | | | (18.58)** | | | (19.21)** |
| Ln X1 | Ln X1 | | | 0.8246 | 0.91659 | | 0.8257 | 0.8775 | |
| | | | | (18.64)** | (35.12)** | | (21.55)** | (35.43)** | |
| 1st/5th | X2 | -0.0072 | -0.0208 | -0.009897 | | | | | |
| Quintiles | | (-1.68)*** | (-2.179)** | (-3.002)** | | | | | |
| Ln X2 | Ln X2 | | | | -0.1353 | -0.1073 | | | |
| | | | | | (-3.91)** | (-3.08)** | | | |
| The Gini | X3 | 0.9616 | 3.6798 | | | 0.547 | | | 0.6136 |
| Coefficient | | (2.68)** | (5.456)** | | | (1.92)*** | | | (2.6)** |
| The Atkins | X4 | -0.366 | 0.96977 | | | 0.1029 | | | |
| | | (-1.134) | -1.392 | | | -0.429 | | | |
| Ln X5 | Ln X5 | | | | | | 0.1193 | 0.416336 | |
| | | | | | | | (3.545)** | (2.35)** | |
| 10%/1st Quintile | X6 | | | | | | | | |
| Ln X6 | Ln X6 | | | | | | | -0.6357 | |
| | | | | | | | | (-1.60) | |
| Ln X7 | Ln X7 | | | | | | 0.03266 | 0.3854 | 0.10657 |
| | | | | | | | -0.879 | -1.74 | (3.09)** |
| $R^2$ | | 98.64% | 92.88% | 99.20% | 99.08% | 99.21% | 0.9938 | 0.9939 | 99.20% |
| Adjusted $R^2$ | | 98.52% | 92.41% | 99.13% | 99.04% | 99.14% | 0.9932 | 0.9932 | 99.15% |
| F statistic | | 799 | 195.78 | 1364 | 2489 | | 1765.685 | 1776.7 | 1869.45 |
| Significance for F, p-value | | 0.00% | 0.00% | 0.00% | 0.00% | 0 | 6.00E-48 | 0 | 0.00% |
| Degrees of Fr | | (4, 44) | (3, 45) | (4, 44) | (2, 46) | (5, 44) | (2, 48) | (4, 44) | (3, 45) |

* Beta-weight values; std change in dependent variable per standard deviation change in the independent.
** Significant at 95% confidence level. Critical t is 1.66, and t's are in parenthesis.
*** Significant at 90% level.

Both the Gini and 20/20 measures were significant in a log-linear analysis. The Gini would seem not to have a linear relationship with Real GDP/Capita. It has a curve-linear relationship. The 20/20 measure has a linear relationship. The Atkin05 was not significant either way.

## 5.0 CONCLUSIONS AND POLICY IMPLICATIONS

There has been growing income inequality in the US in recent times. Whether one looks at the widening gaps in figures 4a and 4b, studies the Gini coefficient or the 20/20 ratio, inequality increased steadily throughout the last quarter of the 20th century and beyond.

In the state of New Jersey, the Gini fluctuated between 0.40 and 0.65. The 20/20 ratio went down from about 0.40 to 0.33. It is our determination that the inequality measures that were evaluated in this study showed relevance at different inequality manifestations and impacts.

Whereas the 20/20 measure has a relationship with the Real GDP/Capita whether one explores a direct or a log-linear relationship (see Table2), the Gini shows significance in a log-linear relationship only. The most glaring difference is that in many cases, the use of the Gini would tend to indicate that inequality is helpful to economic wellbeing- supporting the Kuznets Curve. The use of the 20/20 measure showed a mixed relationship. Before 1982 the 20/20 measure, in fig. 4e, varied from a beginning of about 11% to about 14% fluctuating along the way, while income growth was in the upward trend, indicating economic growth with decreasing inequality. A statistical analysis done for the 1964-1981 time frame (Model 9 of Table 1) showed a positive, but no statistical significant relationship between 20/20 and GDP/Capita. In which case, during half of the period studied, inequality would seem to reduce growth. After 1982, growth continued even as inequality increased. The statistical analysis showed a significant negative relationship, indicating growth in the economy as inequality worsens, the same indication from the Gini. The 20/20, however would seem to indicate, at least graphically, that at some period in time (between 1964 and 1981 in this case) the GDP would be helped with reduction in inequality.

In the measurement of any effect inequality might have had on state GDP, the 20/20 measure seemed to be the one that showed the most relevance than either the Gini or the Atkin05. The 20/20 measure (the 1st/5th ratio) was significant in both the linear model ($Y = \beta_o + \beta_i X_i + \varepsilon_i$) and the log-linear model ($Ln\, Y + = \beta_o + \beta_i X_i + \varepsilon_i$). Though very small, as to the impact, the 20/20 (X2 in the tables) would change GDP/Capita. A Percent change in the 20/20 ratio would increase Real GDP/Capita by about 0.003% as calculated in section 4A-2.

We are in a position to argue that the effect of inequality on Real GDP/Capita is so small that economic growth is not a good phenomenon to judge the full effect of income inequality on the society. Other societal ills have to be studied to evaluate the impact of income inequality. It may be creating disfunctional members of the society as suggested by Richard Wilkinson and co. Policy makers should direct their attention accordingly. We will do that in another study.

**Some Limitations of the Study**: Our studies open the door to further research. The first is that state data at this time is limited, though improving in quality and quantity. Secondly, our study did not separate long term and short term unemployment. Thirdly, we did not massage various transfer payments in and out of the income figures we used. Fourthly, earnings from capital accumulation were not considered, and finally, the top 1% and top 5% needed to be explored further, instead of just the top 20%. They might show a much more serious impact than we were able to account for.

### References

Auten, G., (2014), Historical perspectives on income inequality and economic mobility, Income Inequality in America:Fact or Fiction, Economic Policies for the 21st Century at the Manhattan Institute, E21, IssueB #1, pp 14 - 18

Awuku-Budu, C., Ledia G., Christopher A. L., and Carol A. R., (2013) A first look at experimental personal consumption expenditures by state, BEA Briefing, www.bea.gov/about/pdf/0613_experimental_pcs-by-state_statistics.pdf, (retrieved 08/06/15)

Barro, R., J. (2000). Inequality and growth in a panel of countries. Journal of Economic Growth 5(1): pp 5-32.

Benoit, K., (2011), Linear regression models with logarithmic transformations, Methodology Institute, London School of Economics., http://www.kenbenoit.net/courses/ME104/logmodels2.pdf

Birdsall, N., (2007), Income distribution: effects on growth and development, center for global development, Working paper, Number 18, www.cgdev.org

Bishop, J. A. , Subhabrata Chakraborti and Paul D. Thistle, (1991), Relative deprivation and economic welfare: A statistical investigation with gini-based welfare indices, The Scandinavian Journal of Economics, Vol.93, No 3 , http:// www.jstor.org/stable/3440184, retrieved 10/05/2013

Blank, R. M., David C., Frank L. and James M., (1993), Poverty, income distribution and growth: are they still connected?, Brookings Papers on Economic Activity, Vol. 1993, No.2. pp.285-339

Bureau of Economic Analysis, (1963-1997) Gross domestic product (GDP) by state (millions of current dollars), http://bea.gov/regional/pdf/gsp/gdpstate.pdf

Bureau of Economic Analysis GDP by State Estimation Methodology, BEA GDP by State (2014), http://www.bea.gov/newsreleases/regional/gdp_state/gsp_newsrelease.htm

Bureau of Economic Analysis (2014), SA1-3 Personal income summary state or DC, New Jersey, 1929-2013.

Chang, R., (1994), Income inequality and economic growth: evidence and recent theories, Economic Review, Federal Reserve Bank of Atlanta, July – August 1994, pp 1-10

Deaton, A., (2001), Health, inequality, and economic development, National Bureau of Economic Research, Working Paper 8318, htttp://www.nber.org/papers/w8318

De Maio, Fernando G. (2007), Income inequality measures, Dept. of Sociology and Anthropology, J Epidemiol Community Health 2007;**61**:849-852 .

Frank, Mark W.(2008), A new state level panel of income inequality measures over the period 1916 – 2005 SHSU Economics & Int'L Business Working Paper no SHSU_Eco_WP08-02., Vol.31, pp 241-263, http://www.shsu.edu/eco_mwf/Inequality measures_final.pdf

Frank and Sommeiller (2014) Price Series- Annual top income share measures for each state, 1917-2012, www.shsu.edu/eco.msf/inequality.html

Harkinson, J., (2015), Bernie Sanders goes biblical on income inequality, http://www.motherjones.com/politics/2015/04/bernie-sanders-inequality-president-interview, Mother Jones Publications, (retrieved 08/06/15)

Herb, J., and Raimy S., (2013), Health and safety baseline topic report, Environmental Analysis and Communications Group, Edward J. Bloustein School of Planning and Public Policy, Rutgers University, revised August 2013.

IPUMS – Integrated Public Use Microdata, Minnesota Population Center, University of Minnesota , https:\\cps.ipums.org

Kuznets, S., (1955), Economic growth and income inequality, The American Economic Review, Vol.XLV, number one, pp 1-28.

Kuznets Curve from Wikipedia, http://en.wikipedia.org/wiki/Kuznets_curve, retrieved Feb.27, 2015

Lauter, D., (2015), Income inequality emerges as key issue in 2016 presidential campaign, Los Angeles Times,www.latimes.com/nation/la-na-campaign-income-20150205-story-htmlpage=1, Feb. 5, 2015

LSNJ – The Legal Services of New Jersey (2012 and 2014), Income inequality in New Jersey: a growing divide and its consequences, Annual Report from the Legal Services of New Jersey Poverty Research Institute, July 2012 and December 2014.

Odedokun, M.O. and Jeffery I. Round, (2004), Detrminants of Income Inequality and its Effects on Economic Growth: Evidence from African Countries, African Development Bank .

Okpokwasili, B. (2005). Economic growth vs. economic development, a case of Nigeria. In Proceedings of the Association of Global Business, Vol. 17, #55, Nov. 17-19, 2005.

Panek, S. D., Jacob R H., and Frank T. B. (2003), Comprehensive revision of gross domestic product by metropolitan areas- Advanced Statistics for 2003 and Revised Statistics for 2001-2002

Persson, T., and Guido T., (1994). Is inequality harmful for growth. American Economic Review 84(3): pp 600-621.

Piketty, T., and Emmanuel S., (2003), Income inequality in the United States 1913-1998, The Quarterly Journal of Economics, Vol.CXV111, Issue 1 February 2003. pp 1-39

Sen, A. (2001). Development as Freedom, Oxford University Press.

Simic, M., (2012) A critical reading of the spirit level: why equality is better for everyone. What is the scientific content of the book?, http://www.environnement.ens.fr/IMG/file/stages/A critical reading of the spirit level

Taylor, T., The Kuznets curve and inequality over the last 100 Years, Conversable Economist, http://conversableeconomist.blogspot.com/211/09/kuznets_curve_and-inequality-over-last.html. Retrieved 02/27/2015

The Manhattan Institute, (2014), E21 Economic Policies for the 21st Century, Income inequality in America-Fact and Fiction,Issue B #1

US Department of Commerce, (2012) Household Income Inequality Within US Counties: 2006-2010, United States Census Bureau.

Weil, David N. (2014) A review of Angus Deaton's the great escape: health, wealth and the origins of inequality, Brown University and NBER, *Journal of Economic Literature*, 53(1): 102-14. DOI: 10.1257/jel.53.1.102

Wilkinson, R and Paul, P.,(2014), What does inequality do to our bodies and minds, a psychologist and an epidemiologist discuss. IDEAS.TED.Com, retrieved 01-09-2016.

# 3

# Foreign Aid and Economic Growth: A Panel Cointegration for Selected Turkic Republics

**Hasret Balcioglu**[1]

**ABSTRACT**

This paper considers the relationship between external aid and economic growth in Azerbaijan, Georgia, Kazakhstan, Kyrgyzstan, Turkmenistan and Uzbekistan from 1992 to 2014. These countries have benefited positively from continuous aid inflows from Turkey. In this study, the model is a panel system with the variables real GNP per capita for country and Turkish aid. From the analysis, it could be understood that all the panel unit root tests show that each variable is integrated of the first order I (1) and there is strong evidence for panel cointegration between real GNP per capita and foreign aid for the selected countries. The country-specific elasticity of real income with respect to foreign aid for most of the countries is close to one. Therefore, it can be recommended that foreign capital flows can have more positive effect on real income with the supplements of domestic savings and complements of domestic resources. Thus, it is advisable for the countries to develop their capacities to optimize the benefits from international resources with supportive integration in international markets.

Keywords: Economic Growth, Foreign Capital Flows, Panel System, Turkey, Turkic Republics.

---

## 1.0 INTRODUCTION

It is known that Turkic Republics have underdeveloped economies based on export of raw materials in exchange for assistance from Russia. With the collapse of the Soviet Union in 1991, it had been almost impossible for them to export their products (Gouliev, 1997; Vand derleeuw, 1997). These countries also struggle with low income level, high level of unemployment and low utilization level of industrial capacity. Therefore, after 1991, Turkic Republics have started a slow transition process which is called "from plan to market economy" through economic reforms and privatization (Melo et al., 1997; Aslund, 2001) but the inadequacy of the domestic economy to increase domestic revenue sources to finance the deficit by itself also makes inflows of foreign capital an important source to relieve the challenge. In

[1] Department of Business Administration, Cyprus International University, North Cyprus, Mersin 10 Turkey, E-mail: hbenar@ciu.edu.tr

consequence, the presence of these resource's gaps in one way or another shows that the domestic economy does nor have the capacity of generating enough finance to close these gaps and make the country's reliance on foreign capital inflow mandatory.

It is known that foreign aid is important as a source of income for the developing countries. It has come out as a dominant strategy for improving economic life conditions in the third world over the last half century. United Nations, World Bank and International Monetary Fund have gained the role of donor international institutes for the recipient countries (Hjertholm and White, 2003). This source of income can be divided into two main categories: Military and economic assistance. Foreign aid is given to developing countries, countries of strategic importance to the donor country and countries recovering from the war.

There are different views in the literature dealing with the impact of foreign aid on economic growth. For instance, Griffin and Enos (1970); Boone (1994); Easterly (1999); Knack (2000); Brautigam and Knack (2004) and Temitope (2013) indicate a negative relation between foreign aid and economic growth. These authors encourage the idea that foreign aid is completely consumed and it substitutes rather than compliments national resources.

There are some other studies (Singh, 1985; Lensink and Morrisey, 2000; Pallage and Robe, 2001) that make the explanation of the negative correlation between foreign aid and economic growth as the outcome of factors such as intervention of government, business cycles, economic policies and sustainability of foreign aid through the recipient countries. Some of the papers like Mosley, *et al.* (1987); Boone (1996); and Jensen and Paldam (2003) point out that foreign aid does not have any effect on economic growth.

Obstfeld (1999) indicates that lump-sum foreign policy does not have any effect on the steady-state capital stock or output level but it will increase the dynamic adjustment of steady state that begins below it. Some other studies, like Papanek (1973); Dowling and Hiemenz (1982); Gupta and Islam (1983); Hansen and Tarp (2000); Burnside and Dollar (2000); Gomanee, *et al.* (2003); Tavares (2003); Dalgaard *et al.* (2004); and Karras (2006); Fasanya and Onakoya (2012), show that there is positive correlation between foreign aid and economic growth.

The aim of this paper is to find out the relationship between the Turkish foreign aid and the economic growth in Azerbaijan, Georgia, Kazakhstan, Kyrgyzstan, Turkmenistan and Uzbekistan for the period 1992-2014. The period is selected with the consideration that Soviet Union has collapsed in 1991 and Turkey started to help those countries in the context of economy starting in the year of 1992. The selected countries are the Turkic Republics which benefit mostly from the aid of Turkey.

The study is most probably the first attempt to investigate the effect of foreign aid on the economic growth in this region using panel cointegration methodology. Panel cointegration test has significant more power that the standard cointegrations test for small samples (Hatemi-J and Irandoust, 2004).

This paper is structured in this way: Section two deals with the methodology with theoretical background. Section three explains research analysis and results while section four presents conclusions and recommendations.

## 2.0 METHODOLOGY WITH THEORETICAL BACKGROUND

In this study, the model is a panel system which is defined as follows:

$$LnY_{it}=\alpha_i+\beta_i lnA_{it}+\varepsilon_{it}, \text{ for } i=1,\ldots, N \text{ and } t=1,\ldots,T, \quad (1)$$

where $lnY_{it}$ shows the log of real GNP per capita for country i at time t, $lnA_{it}$ is the log of the Turkish aid to country i at time t, and $\varepsilon$ is the stochastic error term.

GNP per capita stands for a series of annual data and it is calculated by using population series in each country. Real US dollar is the currency used. Consumer price index of each country is used in order to deflate GNP and aid series. Data for consumer price index and GNP series were collected from International Financial Statistics and data for aid series were obtained from Turkish Coordination and Cooperation Agency (TIKA). The countries considered in this study are Azerbaijan, Georgia, Kazakhstan, Kyrgyzstan, Turkmenistan and Uzbekistan and the sample data for each country is used for the period of 1992-2014.

For making the necessary analysis, a panel version of Dickey-Fuller (1979) unit-root test is considered. It is known that Augmented Dickey-Fuller test statistics is one of the well-known test statistics for unit roots. The simplest form of the test is:

$$\Delta x_t=\gamma x_{t-1}+e_t \quad (2)$$

Shiller and Perron (1985) shows that the power of Dickey-Fuller unit-root test should be improved with the panel versions of the test which is recommended by Im, Pesaran and Shin (2003) since the test is not strong in small sample sizes. A panel version of the test is as follows:

$$\begin{pmatrix} \Delta x_{1t} \\ \Delta x_{2t} \\ \cdots \\ \Delta x_{Nt} \end{pmatrix} = \begin{pmatrix} \gamma_1 x_{1t-1} \\ \gamma_2 x_{2t-1} \\ \cdots \\ \gamma_N x_{Nt-1} \end{pmatrix} + \begin{pmatrix} e_{1t} \\ e_{2t} \\ \cdots \\ e_{Nt} \end{pmatrix} \quad (3)$$

where N shows the number of cross-sections. The null hypothesis of one panel unit root is $\gamma_1=\gamma_2=...=\gamma_N=0$. The error terms are supposed to be white noise. Levin and Lin (1993) shows the panel unit root test:

$$\Delta x_{it}=\gamma_i x_{it-1}+e_{it}\text{, for } i=1,...,N \text{ and } t=1,...,T \quad (4)$$

According to Levin and Lin (1993), the panel estimator can be defined:

$$\sqrt{NT}(\check{y}-1)=\frac{(1/\sqrt{N})\sum_i(1/T)\sum_t(x_{it-1})\,e_{it}}{(1/N)\sum_i(1/T^2)\sum_t(x^2_{it-1})}, \text{ for } i=1,...,N \text{ and } t=1,...,T. \quad (5)$$

where $\sum_i=\sum_{i=1}^{N}$ and $\sum_t=\sum_{t=1}^{T}$

In order to test the null hypothesis of panel unit root, the following equation could be used:

$$t_y=\frac{(\check{y}-1)\sqrt{(\sum_i\sum_t x_{i\,t-1})}}{\sqrt{[(1/NT)\sum_i\sum_t e^2_{it}]}} \quad (6)$$

It is clearly understood from the Monte Carlo experiments done by Levin, Lin and Chu (2002) that the power of the panel unit root test is significantly higher than the individual unit root tests.
A diverse coefficient of unit root test could be used by the Im-Pesaran-Shin (IPS) by Im et al. (2003) test and this encourages a mean of the individual Dickey-Fuller tests. The test with better size properties is written below:

$t=(1/N)\sum_i t_i$ where $t_i$ is the individual t-statistics for testing $H_0:\gamma_i=0;\forall i$, i=1,...,N (7)

The alternative hypothesis, $H_1$, in the IPS test is $\gamma_i<0$ for $i=N_1+1, ..., N$ where

$$\lim_{N\to\infty} N_1/N = c, \quad 0<c\leq 1$$

Heterogeneity could be observed within the panel.

With the usage of panel data, running panel unit root tests is significant to prevent spurious regression. In order to test for panel cointegration, Pedroni (1995, 1996, 1999) suggests the following test statistics:

a. Panel t-statistic (Parametric)

$$Z^{*}_{tN,T} = \left( \check{s}^{*2}_{N,T} \sum_i \sum_t \acute{L}^{-2}_{11} \dot{e}^{*2}_{i,t-1} \right)^{-1/2} \sum_i \sum_t \acute{L}^{-2}_{11i} \dot{e}^{*}_{i,t-1} \Delta \dot{e}^{*}_{i,t} \tag{8}$$

b. Panel t-statistic (Non-Parametric)

$$Z_{tN,T} = \left( \overline{\sigma}^{2}_{N,T} \sum_i \sum_t \acute{L}^{-2}_{11} \dot{e}^{2}_{i,t-1} \right)^{-1/2} \sum_i \sum_t \acute{L}^{-2}_{11} (\dot{e}_{i,t-1} \Delta \dot{e}_{i,t} - \lambda_i) \tag{9}$$

c. Group t-statistic (Parametric)

$$N^{-1/2} \overline{Z}^{*}_{tN,T} = N^{-1/2} \sum_i \left( \sum_t \check{s}^{*2}_i \dot{e}^{*2}_{i,t-1} \right)^{-1/2} \sum_t (\dot{e}_{i,t-1} \Delta \dot{e}^{*}_{i,t}) \tag{10}$$

d. Group t-statistic (Non-Parametric)

$$N^{-1/2} \overline{Z}^{*}_{tN,T} = N^{-1/2} \sum_i \left( \overline{\sigma}^{2}_i \sum_t \acute{L}^{-2}_{11} \dot{e}^{2}_{i,t-1} \right)^{-1/2} \sum_t (\dot{e}_{i,t-1} \Delta \overline{\dot{e}}^{*}_{i,t} - \overline{\lambda}_i) \tag{11}$$

where

$$\overline{\lambda}_i = (1/T) \sum_s \left( 1 - s/(k_i+1) \right) \sum_t \overline{\mu}_{i,t} \overline{\mu}_{i,t-s}, \text{ where } s=1,\ldots,k_i \text{ and } t=s+1,\ldots,T \tag{12}$$

$$\check{s}^{2}_i = (1/T) \sum_t \overline{\mu}^{2}_{i,t}, \quad \overline{\sigma}^{2}_i = \check{s}^{2}_i + 2 \overline{\lambda}_i \tag{13}$$

$$\overline{\sigma}^{2}_{NT} = (1/T) \sum_t \acute{L}^{2}_{11i} \overline{\sigma^{2}_i}, \quad \check{s}^{*2}_i = (1/T) \sum_t \mu^{*2}_{i,t} \tag{14}$$

$$\acute{L}^{2}_{11i} = (1/T) \sum \acute{\eta}^{2}_{i,t} + (2/T) \sum_t \left( 1 - s/(k_i+1) \right) \sum \acute{\eta}_{i,t} \acute{\eta}_{i,t-s} \tag{15}$$

The estimated error terms are obtained by the regressions written below:

$$\dot{e}_{i,t} = \breve{y}_i \, \dot{e}_{i,t-1} + \overline{\mu_{i,t}}, \qquad (16)$$

$$\dot{e}_{i,t} = \breve{y}_i \, \dot{e}_{i,t-1} + \sum_{k=1}^{K_i} \breve{y}_{i,k} \Delta \dot{e}^{*}_{i,t-k} + \mu^{*}_{i,t} \qquad (17)$$

$$\Delta \ln Y_{it} = b \Delta \ln A_{it} + \acute{\eta}_{i,t} \qquad (18)$$

where Δ is the first difference operator and the result of the equation is the standard normal distribution.

Pedroni (1995, 1996a, 1996b, 1997a, 1997b, 1998) recommends a few adjustments for both panel unit root tests and panel cointegration tests. The adjusted values are written in the manuscript to find the opportunity to compare the results with the standard normal distribution.

## 3.0 RESEARCH ANALYSIS AND RESULTS

All the panel unit root tests show that each variable is integrated of the first order I (1). After finding that all of the variables are non-stationary, it should be continued looking for cointegration which is the long-run steady state. Table 1 exhibits the estimated results for three Panel Unit Root Tests.

**Table 1:** Three Panel Unit Roots Estimated Results

| | $H_0$: I(1), H: I(0) | | | | $H_0$: I(2), H: I(1) | | |
|---|---|---|---|---|---|---|---|
| | $LL_1$ | $LL_2$ | IPS | | $LL_1$ | $LL_2$ | IPS |
| $\ln Y_{it}$ | -0,88 | -0,92 | -1,01 | $\ln Y_{it}$ | -6,78 | -7,02 | -9,13 |
| $\ln A_{it}$ | 0,21 | 0,48 | 0,14 | $\ln A_{it}$ | -8,86 | -9,12 | -11,89 |

**Notes:**

a. The first test augments the regression until the removal of autocorrelation. Potential autocorrelation is considered in the second test.
b. IPS test shows that the null hypothesis can be rejected at 1% significance level.
c. Each test is one sided-to the left side of the distribution.

It can be seen that there is strong evidence for panel cointegration between real GNP per capita and foreign aid for the selected countries. Table 2 indicates the results obtained from the Pedroni's test.

**Table 2:** Pedroni Panel Cointegration Test for Real Aid and Real GNP per Capita

| Test a | Test b | Test c | Test d |
|---|---|---|---|
| -2.38 | -2.13 | -2.02 | -1.72 |

**Source:** by Author

Tabulated data (in Table 2) show that the variables cointegrate in the panel view and three of the tests reject the null hypothesis (no cointegration) at the 1% significance level and one of them rejects the null hypothesis at the 5% significance level.

The tests are one sided therefore the 1% critical value is -1.96, the 5% value is -1.64 and the 10% critical value is equal to -1,28. The adjusted values are comparable with one sided standard normal distribution, N (0.1). Test results suggest that there is significant long-run equilibrium in the panel. The next step is to estimate the parameters considered. In Equation (1), there is the estimation of panel system with the usage of the dummy least squares method. This helps us to find the country-specific elasticities. The estimated elasticities have been shown in Table 3.

From the table 3, it could be understood that the elasticity written in column 2 is the elasticity of GNP per capita per country with respect to aid coming from Turkey except the last row. The elasticities (individually and pooled) are estimated by letting the effects individually through dummy variables to consider the scale effect.

**Table 3:** The Foreign Aid Elasticities in the Long-run Period

| Country | Elasticity | Standard Error | t-statistics |
|---|---|---|---|
| Azerbaijan | 1.268 | 0.089 | 13.54 |
| Georgia | 1.135 | 0.075 | 12.47 |
| Kazakhstan | 0.865 | 0.054 | 9.84 |
| Kyrgyzstan | 0.954 | 0.098 | 7.75 |
| Turkmenistan | 1.021 | 0.120 | 11.25 |
| Uzbekistan | 0.562 | 0.066 | 8.82 |
| Pooled Data | 0.941 | 0.042 | 21.73 |

**Source:** by Author

Each elasticities obtained is positive and statistically significant at any level of significance. From these elasticities, it can be realized that (keeping other factors constant), the foreign aid from Turkey is positively affecting the real per capita GNP of the Azerbaijan, Georgia, Kazakhstan, Kyrgyzstan, Turkmenistan and Uzbekistan. The last row in the table is important because it shows the foreign aid pooled elasticity. The elasticity is significant at all conventional significance levels and it also indicates that 10% increase in foreign aid results in 9% increase in GNP per capita in the group.

## 4.0 CONCLUSIONS

The study indicates the long-run relationship between foreign aid and real economic growth for the period 1992-2014. It concludes that the Turkish foreign aid has a significant positive impact on economic growth for Azerbaijan, Georgia, Kazakhstan, Kyrgyzstan, Turkmenistan and Uzbekistan. The country-specific elasticity of real income with respect to foreign aid for most of the countries is close to one so it can be recommended that foreign capital flows can have more positive effect on real income with the supplements of domestic savings and complements of domestic resources. So, it is advisable for the considered countries to develop their capacities to optimize the benefits from international resources with supportive integration in international markets.

## REFERENCES


Aslund, A. (2001). Transforming Post Communist Political Economies: Possible Future Directions for Economies in Transition, www.nap.edu.readingroom/books/transform/ch18htm

Boone, P. (1994). The impact of foreign aid on savings and growth, Center for Economic Performance, working paper 1265, London.

Boone, P. (1996). Politics and the effectiveness of foreign aid. European Economic Review, 40: 289–329.

Brautigam, D.A. and Knack S. (2004). Foreign aid, institutions, and governance in Sub-Saharan Africa. Economic Development and Cultural Change, 13:255-285.

Burnside, C. and Dollar D. (2000). Aid, policies, and growth. American Economic Review, 90:847–868.

Dalgaard, C. J., Hansen, H. and Tarp F. (2004). On the empirics of foreign aid and growth. Economic Journal, 114: 191–216.

Dickey, D. A.; Fuller, W. A. (1979). Distribution of the Estimators for Autoregressive Time Series with a Unit Root. Journal of the American Statistical Association, 74 (366): 427–431.

Dowling, M. and Hiemenz U. (1982). Aid, Savings and Growth in the Asian Region. Economic Office Report Series 3, Asian Development Bank: Manila.

Easterly, W. (1999). The ghost of financing gap: testing the growth model used in international financial institutions. Journal of Development Economics, 60: 423-438.

Fasanya, I. O. and Onakoya A. B. O. (2012). Does Foreign Aid Accelerate Economic Growth? An Empirical Analysis for Nigeria. International Journal of Economics and Financial Issues, 2: 423-431.

Gomanee, K, Girma, S., Morrissey O. (2003). Searching for Aid Threshold Effects: Aid, Growth and the Welfare of the Poor. CREDIT Research Paper02/05, Centre for Research in Economic Development and International Trade, University of Nottingham, Nottingham.

Gouliev, R. (1997). Petrol and Policy. Ar Publication Office, Istanbul.
Griffin, K.B., and Enos J. L. (1970). Foreign Assistance: Objectives and Consequences. Economic Development and Cultural Change, 18:313-327.
Gupta, K. L. and Islam M. A (1983). *Foreign* Capital, Savings and Growth—An International Cross-Section Study. Reidel Publishing Company: Dordrecht.
Hansen, H. and Tarp F. (2000). Aid effectiveness disputed. Journal of International Development, 12: 375–398.
Hatemi-J, A., and Irandoust M. (2004). Is pricing to market behaviour a long-run phenomenon? A non-stationary panel analysis. Emprica, 3:55-67.
Hjertholm, P. and White H. (2000). Survey of Foreign Aid: History, Trends, and Allocation. Discussion Papers, University of Copenhagen Institute of Economics.
Jensen, P. S., Paldam M. (2003). Can the New Aid-Growth Models Be Replicated?, *Working Paper No.2003–17*, Institute for Economics: Aarhus.
Karras, G. (2006). Foreign aid and long-run economic growth: empirical evidence for a panel of developing countries. Journal of International Development, 18, 7: 15–28.
Knack, S. (2000). Aid Dependence and the Quality of overnice: A Cross-Country Empirical Analysis, World Bank Policy Research Paper.
Lensink, R. and Morrissey O. (2000). Aid stability as a measure of uncertainty and the positive impact of aid on growth. Journal of Development Studies, 36: 31-49.
Melo, M. D., Denizer, C. and Tenev S. (1997). The Role of Initial Conditions and Policies in Transition Economies, *Wb, IFC, WP*
Mosley, P. Hudson, J. and Horrell S. (1987). Aid, the public sector and the market in less developed countries. Economic Journal, 97, 387: 616–641.
Obstfeld M. (1999). Foreign resource inflows, saving, and growth In The Economics of Saving and Growth: Theory, Evidence, and Implications for Policy, Schmidt-Hebbel K, Serven L (eds). Cambridge University Press: Cambridge, 107–146.
Pallage, S. and Robe M. A. (2001). Foreign aid and the business cycles. Review of International Economics, 9: 641-672.
Papanek, G. F. (1972). The effect of aid and other resource transfers on savings and growth in less developed countries. Economic Journal, 82: 935–950.
Pedroni, P. (1995). Panel Cointegration; Asymptotic and Finite Sample Properties of Pooled Time Series Tests, with an Application to the PPP Hypothesis. Indiana University Working Papers in Economics, 95-013.
Pedroni, P. (1996a). Fully ModiÆed OLS for Heterogeneous Cointegrated Panels and the Case of Purchasing Power Parity. Indiana University Working Papers in Economics, 96-020.
Pedroni, P. (1996b). Endogenous Growth, Human Capital, and Cointegration for Multi-Country Panels. Working Paper, Indiana University.
Pedroni, P. (1997a). Panel Cointegration; Asymptotic and Finite Sample Properties of Pooled Time Series Tests, with an Application to the PPP Hypothesis: New Results. Working Paper, Indiana University, April.
Pedroni, P. (1997b). On the Role of Cross Sectional Dependency in Dynamic Panel Unit Root and Panel Cointegration Exchange Rate Studies.Working Paper, Indiana University.
Pedroni, P. (1998). Testing for Convergence to Common Steady States in Nonsta- tionary Heterogeneous Panels, Working Paper, Indiana University.
Singh, R.D. (1985). State intervention, foreign economic aid, savings and growth in LDCs: some recent evidence. Kyklos, 38: 216-232.
Tavares J. (2003). Does foreign aid corrupt? Economics Letters, 79: 99–106.
Temitope, L. (2013). Foreign aid and economic growth in South Africa: an empirical analysis using bounds tests. Journal of Economics and Financial Sciences, 6(1):55-66.
Van der Leeuw (1997). Oil in Azerbaijan-Black Gold and Vile Poison, Caucasus and Unholy Alliance (Edited by Antero Leitzinger), 307-314.

# 4

# Evaluating Nigeria Cashless Policy Implementation

**Kket E Ewa[1], Egu U. Inah[2]**

**ABSTRACT**

The Central Bank of Nigeria introduced cashless policy initiative to accomplish two main macro-socio-economic policy objectives of increased convenience and greater financial inclusion in Nigeria. This study evaluates Nigeria cashless policy implementation using a four point Likert scale questionnaire administered to six hundred respondents. The results of the study show that the twin policy objectives investigated were partially achieved. Also the study reveals that social infrastructures in power and telecommunications need improvement and expansion and the need to create more awareness to encourage the unbanked to embrace banking culture. This study recommends vigorous investments on cyber security, strengthening of internet protocol and controls in the banks and enactment of relevant legislative laws to curb cybercrimes.

Keywords: Bankable, cashless policy, cybercrime, macroeconomic, transparency.

---

## 1.0 INTRODUCTION

Monetary policy is the regulation of interest rates and the money supply by the apex banks of nations geared towards controlling inflation and currency stabilisation. In Nigeria, the Central Bank of Nigeria (CBN) undertakes monetary policy so as to promote and maintain monetary stability as well as safeguard the international value of the nation's currency and manage the country's external reserves. According to Ajayi and Ojo (2006), in other to encourage economic development, a nation should encourage a payment system that is secure, convenient and affordable. Likewise, Humphrey (2004) opined that developed countries to a large extent are migrating from paper payment instruments to electronic ones. In this macroeconomic management, the payment system plays an important role being the channel through which financial resources are channelled from one segment or sector of the economy to another. It represents the crucial foundation of the modern market environment and plays three very

[1] Department of Accountancy, Cross River University of Technology, Ogoja, Cross River State, Nigeria. E-mail: uketewa@yahoo.com

[2] Department of Accounting, University of Calabar, Calabar, Cross River State, Nigeria.

important roles in the economy of any nation. These roles according to the CBN include financial stability role, monetary policy role and overall economic role (CBN, 2015).

The Nigerian Central Bank (CBN) conscious of the above and the drive for Nigeria to be the 20th developed economy by the year 2020, introduced electronic-based payment system initiatives for payment of goods, services and transfers. The scheme which began in Lagos in 2012 stipulates a cash handling charge on daily cash withdrawals or cash deposits that exceed five hundred thousand (N=500,000) naira for individuals and three million (N=3 million) naira for corporate bodies with the aim of reducing and not necessarily eliminating the amount of physical cash transactions in the economy and encouraging more electronic-based transactions in Nigeria. According to the CBN, the new policy was introduced for a number of key reasons including;

(a) To drive development and modernization of the country's payment system in line with the Nation's vision 2020 goal of being amongst the top 20 economies by the year 2020. This they envisage that 'an efficient and modern payment system is positively correlated with economic development' and is a key enabler for economic growth (CBN, 2015).
(b) To reduce the cost of banking services which include cost of credit and thus drive financial inclusion by providing more and efficient transaction options and greater reach.
(c) To improve the effectiveness of monetary policy in managing inflation as well as driving economic growth. The former CBN governor reiterated that 'the major focus of payments system reform is to increase the diversity and liquidity of payment instrument' (EFLnA, 2013).
(d) To curtail some of the negative ills associated with the high usage of physical cash in the economy which includes; high cost of cash handling associated with volume cash handling, high risk of using cash as a result of robberies and other related cash crimes, ineffectiveness of monetary policy in managing inflation and encouraging economic growth in an informal economy, corruption, leakages and money laundering.

Yaqub, Bello, Adenuga and Ogundeji (2013) highlighted various benefits expected to be derived by various stakeholders from the increased utilization of e-payment as enumerated by the CBN to include: to the customers; increased convenience, more services, reduced risk of cash-related crimes, cheaper access to banking services, access to credit and financial inclusion. To the corporations; faster access to capital, reduce revenue leakages and reduced cash handling costs. To government; increased tax collection, greater financial inclusion and increased economic development. In their study, Yaqub et al., (2013) reviewed the prospects and challenges of the cashless policy in Nigeria by only reviewing reports published by the CBN on: direct cost of cash to financial system in Nigeria, payment channels in Nigeria as at 2011, e-payment market share in Nigeria, value of electronic card-based transactions in Nigeria as at 2011 and the trend of currencies in Nigeria and in circulation as at 2011.

In spite of the perceived benefits enumerated in the policy document prior to the introduction of the policy, there are noticeable complaints from the banking public over long queues at ATM centres, fraudulent electronic withdrawals of customers' funds and non-functionality of ATM machines. This paper seeks to empirically ascertain whether the CBN achieved the two main macro-socio-economic policy objectives of; (i) increased convenience, providing more efficient transaction options and greater reach, reduced risk of cash-related crimes, cheaper access to banking services, access to credit and financial inclusion by the general public and (ii) greater financial inclusion among the citizenry and increased economic development. The following research questions are addressed in the study: (i) whether with the introduction of cashless payment system many market traders are using the other mediums of payment methods as against cash, (ii) whether bankable public are satisfied with the overall performance of the banks, (iii) whether the bankable public are satisfied with the adequacy and functionality of the ATMs and the POS in service and (iv) whether the public infrastructures in use are efficient and effective in driving the cashless policy. The study proceeds as follows, section 2 deals with the theoretical/conceptual framework. Brief review of literature is in section 3 while section 4 states the methodology followed in carrying out the study. Data analysis is dealt with in section 5 while section 6 discusses the results of the data analysed. Recommendation for policy makers and conclusions are presented in section 7.

## 2.0 THEORETICAL/CONCEPTUAL FRAMEWORK

The theory of payment system efficiency and the Central bank mandate underpin this study. The theory advocate for the strengthening of the central bank mandate of currency management, regulation and control of the volume of physical cash in circulation to ensure price stability, check inflation and manage interest rate in the economy.

The proponents of this theory Claudia and Grauwe (2001) and Marco and Bandiera (2004) opined that the central banks as regulators of monetary policy management are gradually losing their monopolistic position in the provision of liquidity and management of interest rate in the economy. Therefore, the gaps which the cash based system creates reinforces the need for a paradigm shift in monetary policy and payment system management in the Nigerian economy.

Cashless policy is an economic system where by business transactions are done not purely or predominantly in exchange for physical cash neither is it an economic system where goods and services are exchanged for goods and services (the barter system). This is an economic setting in which goods and services are bought and paid for through electronic medium. It is defined as "one in which there are assumed to be no transactions frictions that can be reduced through the use of money balances, and that accordingly provide a reason for holding such balances even when they earn rate of return" (Woodford, 2003).

The commercial banks act as intermediaries between the surplus and deficit savings units within an economy by mobilizing and facilitating efficient allocation of national savings, thereby increasing the quantum of investments and hence national output. In a developing economy such as Nigeria, financial sector development is routinely accompanied by structural and institutional changes. The Nigerian banking sector has generally been recognized to play a crucial role in the economic development of Nigeria in her quest to be the twentieth developed economy by the year 2020.

The monetary Policy management is the responsibility of the apex bank. It is the regulation of the money supply and interest rates by the apex Bank in order to control inflation and stabilize currency. This responsibility is vested on the Central Bank of Nigeria (CBN) who regulates monetary policy in order to maintain Nigerian's external reserve, safeguard the international value of the naira against other currencies, promote and maintain monetary stability. The Bank also acts as a banker and financial adviser to the Federal Government and as lender of last resort to the banks.

### 2.1 THE PAYMENT POLICY

In any country's financial system, the payment system plays a very crucial role in the economy, being the channel through which financial resources flow from one segment of the economy to the other. It represents the major foundation of the modern market economy as it has important role in monetary policy, financial stability and overall economic activity of the nation.

Given the important role that a well-functioning payment system has on monetary policy, financial stability and overall economic activity, the CBN bank formulated a set of national payment systems policy objectives as a broad guideline and framework for all payment systems initiatives. The national payments system objectives clearly spelt out include:

- **Promotion of efficiency and effectiveness by being** transparent, flexible and reliable, ensuring integration, interoperability of the sub-systems and speeding up exchange and settlement of funds and securities
- **Safety by** protecting systematic risks through containing credit, legal, liquidity and operational risks, complying with international standards and recommendations (E.g. the ten core principles for Systematic Important Payment Systems) and complying with national standards and recommendations (E.g. cheque and electronic banking standards)

- Migration to cash-less modes of payment, such as electronic debit/credit instruments, credit/debit cards, ATM-sharing and electronic Fund transfer at point of sales and real time gross settlement system(RTGS)
- **Transparency in the payment system** as one of the factors militating against widespread usage of the formal payment systems is the concern of market participants about transparency.

The goal thus of the national payment systems (NPS) is to ensure that the system is available without interruption, meet as far as possible all users' needs, and operate at minimum risk and reasonable cost. The significant points of the policy were the decision to peg customer's daily withdrawal or deposits to a maximum of =N=150,000 per individual customer and =N=1 million naira for corporate clients. This was reviewed to =N=500,000 for individuals and =N=3,000,000 for corporate in 2012 and again reviewed downwards to =N=60,000 for individuals in 2015. At the commencement of the policy, the CBN Governor Sanusi Lamido Sanusi, said the limit did not stop customers from withdrawing or depositing beyond the limit set by the apex bank, but such a customer should be ready to pay a penal fee of about 100 naira per 1,000 in bank charges to enjoy his desire. However, the recent downward review did not give room for the discretionary withdrawal with a penal fee.

The policy has other financial services ranging from customer accounts information and updates and transactions alerts which have been in existence but not widely subscribed to by account holders to payment of bills, person to person transaction and remittances in different forms. In achieving the goal of the payment system and the broad objectives enumerated, the apex bank in collaboration with the Bankers committee launched various initiatives to modernize the payment system ranging from the automation of the cheque clearing system and making it veritable platform for development of electronic payment channels, the use of POS, ATMs and mobile banking.

The policy has thus emphasised the use of; POS, ATMs and Internet banking.

The application of these products in the financial architecture of Nigeria requires enormous investments in power, telecommunication, financial infrastructures and security. The functionality and adequacy of these infrastructures is critical to the success of this policy.

According to Emecheta (2012), the implementation of the new procedures and rules based on MICR technology revolutionized the cheque clearing system thus, a centralized Automated Clearing process was established whereby with MICR Reader Sorters, necessary information on cheques are captured, built into clearing files and electronically transmitted to the clearing house, from where the net settlement position of participating banks are automatically computed and also electronically transmitted to the apex bank for final settlement. This initiative reduced clearing cycle from 5days to 3days for local instrument and from 9days to 6 days in respect of up-country instrument.

## 3.0 LITERATURE REVIEW

Cashless banking is that banking system with the sole aim at reducing but not eliminating physical cash transactions in the day to day business transactions in the economy for electronic based transactions. In other words, cashless policy is the optimal combination of electronic banking (e-banking) system and cash-based system. Electronic banking system entails the application of the following; mobile payment system, Point on sale (POS) system, credit/debit card system and internet banking system.

According to Emecheta (2012), the cashless economy policy of the Central Bank of Nigeria (CBN) was designed towards providing mobile payment services, breaking down the traditional barriers hindering financial inclusion of millions of Nigerians, bringing down transaction costs, and to secure convenient financial services to both the urban, semi urban and rural areas across the country. Regrettably, it has, however, become an albatross to some elites, the poor, uneducated and traders (Emecheta 2012). Adewoye (2013) in his study of the impact of mobile banking on service delivery in the Nigerian Commercial Banking system found that the introduction of e-banking services has improved banking efficiency in rendering services to customers in the form of transactional conveniences, savings of time, quick transaction alert and savings on service cost. He observed lack of awareness of the e-banking by the public, lack of collaboration among the banks, lack of skill manpower to drive the product and inadequate and poorly maintained public network systems like power and telecommunications to be mitigating full benefit of the service and so recommended improvement on these constraints. James (2012) investigated the acceptability of e-banking services in Nigeria and found that e-banking was significantly influenced by the age, educational background, income, perceived risk and perceived benefits, perceived ease of use, perceived risk and perceived enjoyments by the respondents customers. In their study on bankers' perceptions of electronic banking in Nigeria, Morufu and Taibat (2012) observed that bankers in Nigeria perceived electronic banking as a tool for minimising inconveniences, reducing transaction costs and customers queuing time and thus saving customers' waiting time in the banking hall.

Ajayi (2014) on his study 'Effect of cashless monetary policy on Nigerian banking industry: Issues, prospects and challenges' observed that the cashless policy has improved the performance of bankers in carrying out their duties, maximised the banks' profitability by the extended customers' base among others. However, the study observed that 'social infrastructures in Nigeria, technological infrastructures, security and limited numbers of electronic channels for cashless transactions' continue to be major challenges and problems facing the cashless policy adoption in Nigeria. The challenges enumerated above were collaborated by Yaqub et al. (2013) who further added legal, Regulatory and Socio-Cultural issues as challenges confronting the policy in Nigeria. Their study only reviewed CBN reports without carrying out independent survey of citizenry who use the facilities to establish if the benefits intended by the CBN have been achieved. Similarly, Ajayi (2014) failed to relate the banks' performances with their financial statements to establish any upward trend in their financials. Olajide (2012) in his study 'Cashless banking in Nigeria and its implications,' concluded that among other factors 'the existence of severe poverty and poor state of infrastructure must be duly considered before embarking on this project. In their study on 'benefits and challenges of Nigeria's cash-less policy, Osazevbara and Yomere (2015) citing Princewell and Anuforo stated that the CBN in 2011 estimated that 99% of over 215 million customer transactions in Nigerian banks were through ATM and over-the-counter valued at about =N=2.1 trillion. Also, that this transaction level has a significant cost to the Nigerian economy and estimated that cash distribution cost accounts for about 60% of the overheads in the banking industry. Similarly, cash management operations in the period require about 80% of the industry's infrastructure base and staff strength, (CBN, 2012). They thus concluded that electronic banking in Nigeria has positively impacted on the development of payment system in particular and the banking system in general. They also stated that the system will increase the customer base of banks as more un-banked Nigerians will be banked (Osazevbara and Yomere 2015). However, the authors have not shown in 2015 actual positive impact in the years 2012 to 2014 as postulated in their study which used 2011 pre-operational period. Secondly, the study has not shown also the growth in customer base since the introduction of the system as postulated.

Emecheta (2012) opined that Nigeria occupies the unenviable position of being number one country in Africa with largest number of people with no access to financial services. Citing a data compiled by Microfinance Information Exchange (MIX), he stated that Nigeria and the Democratic Republic of Congo (DRC) were found to have 'the largest gaps between populations living in poverty and those with no access to financial services – 80 million in Nigeria and 48 million in the DRC'.

In spite of the low bankable population, managing the few that have access to the banks is said to cost banks a huge amount of money with cash management taken a large chunk of the expenses. Similarly, the cost of printing new bank notes as a result of frequent handling is said to cost the apex Bank significant amount annually. According to Emecheta (2012), to address the above and many other issues facing the banks and the nation's economy, the apex bank introduced the cashless economy policy.

## 4.0 DATA AND METHODOLOGY

A structured questionnaire to address the research questions enumerated was administered to bank customers in urban, semi-urban and rural communities in Cross River State, Nigeria. The structured questionnaire was complemented with qualitative interviewing to address any ambiguity in the questionnaire and uneducated customers (respondents) that may be enlisted in the study. Since Nigeria is largely a cash-based economy with about 66% of cash residing outside the banking sector (Yaqub et al. 2013) but with the informal sector (petty traders, small retail & supermarket shops, educational and hospital institutions, artisans and the monthly low paid employees), to ascertain if the policy is a myth or reality, one hundred and twenty candidates each were recruited from petty traders & retail stores, supermarket shops, educational and hospital institutions, artisans and professional services and paid employees in selected urban cities, semi-urban towns and the rural communities. A total of six hundred questionnaires were thus administered to the respondents in the study. However, five hundred questionnaires were returned completed constituting 83.3% (eighty three point three per cent) success rate. Based on the assertion by Moser and Kalton that the result of a survey could be considered as biased and of little value if the return rate was lower than 30 – 40%, the return rate of 83.3% is considered adequate.

The respondents rated each preposition on a four point Likert scale. The scale was then transformed to relative important index for each of the prepositions. The completed and returned questionnaires were analysed using simple percentages and Relative Important Index (R.I.I) based on the work of Lim and Alum (1995).

$$R.I.I. = (4n_4 + 3n_3 + 2n_2 + n_1)/4N$$

Where $n_4$ = Very adequate/Efficient
$n_3$ =Adequate/Efficient
$n_2$ = Not adequate/Efficient
$n_1$ = Not very adequate/Efficient
N = Number of respondents.

The R.I.I. rate of 0.80 and above is considered significant to suggest that the cashless policy is working efficiently and the infrastructures are adequate for the operations of the system.

## 5.0 RESULTS

**Table 1:** Usage of bank products

| S/N | STATEMENTS | POS | % | Mobil | % | ATM | % | Direct Cash | % | Total |
|---|---|---|---|---|---|---|---|---|---|---|
| 1 | Your frequent method use in daily transactions | 40 | 7% | 20 | 4% | 270 | 47% | 240 | 42% | 570 |
| 2 | Most common payment method use in daily transactions | 0 | 0% | 10 | 2% | 200 | 38% | 310 | 60% | 520 |

**Source:** Field survey (2016)

**Table 2:** Cashless policy in Nigeria, Myth or reality?

| S/N | STATEMENTS | Very adequate | % | Adequate | % | Not adequate | % | Not very adequate | % | Total |
|---|---|---|---|---|---|---|---|---|---|---|
| 1 | There is adequate ATM machines in the locality | 20 | 4% | 140 | 28% | 270 | 54% | 70 | 14% | 500 |
| 2 | The ATMs are very functional in the locality. | 20 | 4% | 130 | 26% | 290 | 58% | 60 | 12% | 500 |
| 3 | The Cashless system has provided effective and efficient service delivery since its introduction. | 30 | 6% | 140 | 28% | 260 | 52% | 70 | 14% | 500 |
| 4 | The telecommunications systems in the locality are efficient and effective in driving the cashless payment system. | 60 | 12% | 100 | 20% | 280 | 56% | 60 | 12% | 500 |
| 5 | There are enough functional ATM machines to service customers in the locality. | 40 | 8% | 70 | 14% | 280 | 56% | 110 | 22% | 500 |

**Source:** Field survey (2016)

**Table 3 (using RII):** Cashless policy in Nigeria, Myth or reality?

| S/N | STATEMENT | 4 | 3 | 2 | 1 | Total | RII |
|---|---|---|---|---|---|---|---|
| 1 | There is adequate ATM machines in the locality | 20 | 140 | 270 | 70 | 430 | 0.65 |
| 2 | The ATMs are very functional in the locality. | 20 | 130 | 290 | 60 | 500 | 0.56 |
| 3 | The Cashless system has provided effective and efficient service delivery since its introduction. | 30 | 140 | 260 | 70 | 500 | 0.57 |
| 4 | The telecommunications systems in the locality are efficient and effective in driving the cashless payment system. | 60 | 100 | 280 | 60 | 500 | 0.58 |
| 5 | There are enough functional ATM machines to service customers in the locality. | 40 | 70 | 280 | 110 | 500 | 0.52 |

## 6.0 DATA ANALYSIS

From the findings, 480 (96%) of the respondents in the study own bank accounts in various bank in the locality. Of this number 470 (94%) claimed to have knowledge of cashless payment system while 30 (6%) of the respondents claimed ignorance of the system.

110 (22%) of the respondents accepted being influenced into opening their bank accounts due to the awareness for the cashless banking system while 390(78%) of the respondents stated that they were not influenced by the introduction of the cashless policy into opening their personal accounts. 300(62.5%) of the respondents opened their accounts over 10 years ago, 140(29%) opened their accounts above 5 years and 40(8%) of the respondents opened their accounts within the last 5 years.

From the analysis of the data, while 40(7%) respondents affirmed frequent use of POS on their daily business transactions, 20(4%) respondents affirmed frequent use of Mobil banking facility. Similarly, 270(47%) respondents affirmed frequent use of ATM while 240(42%) respondents affirmed frequent use of cash transactions in their daily business transactions. Therefore, 510(89%) of the respondents effectively use physical cash in their daily business transactions. On the question of the most common payment method used in the locality in the daily business transactions, while 10(2%) respondents stated the use of Mobil banking facility, 200(38%) respondents stated the use of ATM and 310(60%) respondents' stated direct physical cash as the most common payment method in use in the daily business transactions.

On the adequacy of ATMs machines in the locality: 20(4%) respondents are of the opinion that they are very adequate, 140(28%) respondents are of the opinion that they are just adequate for the locality. However, 270(54%) respondents are of the opinion that the machines are not adequate while 70(14%) respondents are of the opinion that the machines are grossly inadequate for the locality. This has a relative important index rate of 0.65 far below the acceptable significant minimum rate of 0.80.

On the investigation to ascertain the functionality of the ATMs installed in the localities: 20(4%) respondents are of the view that the machines are very functional and efficient while 130(26%) of the respondents are of the view that they are just functional. In the contrary, 290(58%) of the respondents are of the view that the machines are not functional and not efficient while 60(12%) respondents are of the view that the machines are not very functional and are very inefficient in performance and functionality. This preposition has a relative important index of 0.56 which is below the acceptable minimum rate of 0.80 considered significant.

On the preposition on whether the newly introduced cashless policy has provided effective and efficient service delivery in business transaction in the country: 30(6%) respondents are of the opinion that it has greatly enhanced service delivery while 140(28%) of the respondents are of the opinion that the policy has enhanced service delivery generally. In contrast, 260(52%) respondents are of the opinion that the policy has not produced the expected objective of enhancing seamless business transactions in the country. Similarly, 70(14%) of the respondents are of the opinion that the policy has completely failed in accomplishing the objective for its implementation. This has a relative important index of 0.57 which again is below the significant minimum rate of 0.80.

On the functionality of the telecommunications facilities in the locality studied: 60(12%) of the respondents are of the opinion that the facilities are very adequate to support the policy while 100(20%) of the respondents are of the opinion that the facilities are just adequate and need further improvement to support the policy. In the contrary, 280(56%) of the respondents are of the view that the infrastructural facilities are not adequate in supporting the programme, 60(12%) of the respondents are of the view that the facilities are very inadequate in supporting the cashless policy programme in the locality. This preposition has a relative important index of 0.58 far below the significant and acceptable minimum rate of 0.80. Similarly, 40(8%) of the respondents on the study are of the view that the functional ATM machines deployed in the localities studied are very adequate to service the population while 70(14%) of the respondents are of the view that the functional ATMs are just adequate for the localities studied. However, 280(56%) of the respondents are of the view that the functional ATMs are not adequate to service the customers in the area as long queues of users is a common sight in the banks. In the same vain, 110(22%) of the respondents are of the view that functional ATMs are very inadequate. That even where there are installed ATMs, many are not functional and so long queues are built every day of the week. The functionality of the ATM machines has a relative important index rate of 0.52 which is below the significant minimum rate of 0.80.

## 7.0 RESULT AND DISCUSSION

From the study although 94% of the respondents claimed to be aware of cashless policy, only 22% of account holders were influenced to open their bank accounts through the awareness campaign of the cashless policy. The study also revealed that 92% of bank customers opened their banking relationship before the introduction of the cashless policy in 2012. Considering the fact that one of the cardinal objectives for the cashless policy was to drive development and modernization of our payment system in line with Nigeria's vision 2020, an 8% increase in the bankable public within 5 years is questionable.

The study revealed POS utilization of 7%. It is evident that the intended POS penetration in the economy is not actualised as many retail shops both in urban, semi urban and rural communities still do not operate the POS. In fact none of the filling stations visited operates a POS in the sale of their products. It also revealed Mobile banking services of 4% as against 47% ATM utilization and 42% physical cash transaction negates yet again one of the CBN cardinal objectives for the policy which is to reduce the amount of physical cash circulating in the economy and encouraging electronic based transactions as the respondents affirmed the use of the ATMs for cash collection only. It is evident that the literacy level of Nigeria has a direct relationship with the cashless policy penetration in the economy as many customers from the study who are given ATM cards only used the cards for cash withdrawals which is not in the real sense of it cashless system. There is therefore still high demand for physical cash for day to day business transactions. This is evident as there are constant long queues at ATM Cash points. The respondents claimed they seldom use the ATMs for internet banking and or cash transfers. The study revealed the most common payment method in the day-to-day business transactions to be physical cash at 60% as against 2% usage of Mobile banking facility. All the filing stations visited in the locality sell on cash as well as most of the super markets and petty traders. This daily business transactions based on physical cash has a direct impact on the demand for ATM services in the locality prompting long queues in all ATM locations with attendant risk factors. This is in agreement with the survey carried out by Global FINDEX 2011 that stated that, around one-third of Brazilians and South Africans with debit cards use e-payments, compared with one in ten Nigerians. And that the 2% of Nigerian adults who currently make e-payments represents a small fraction of the 19% holding debit cards (which is likely to provide e-payment functionality). Similarly, data from EFInA's Access to Financial Services in Nigeria 2012 survey (A2F 2012) highlighted Nigerians' limited adoption of electronic payments and services to date, with less than 2.5% using mobile phones for their banking transactions, 0.8% of banked adults using the internet, and 0.7% of banked adults using POS terminals (EFInA, 2012). This is so because ATM transactions are largely still cash withdrawals (EFInA, 2013). This is contrary to Adewoye (2013) and Morufu and Taibat (2012) who stated that the e-banking services has improved banking efficiency in rendering services to customers in the form of transactional conveniences thus minimising inconveniences, saving of time, quick transaction alert and savings on service costs. There is no minimisation of convenience for a customer to queue long under the sun for the sake of cash withdrawal in an ATM point. The study revelation of inadequacy on the number of ATMs confirms the findings of Ajayi (2014) who stated that limited no of electronic channels continue to be a challenge for the implementation of the cashless policy in Nigeria. Similarly, the study revealed the non-functionality of most of the ATM machines in use. This non-functionality contributes directly to the persistent long queues noticed in the ATM centres. Though, Morufu and Taibat (2012) stated that bankers perceived electronic banking as a tool for minimising inconveniences, reducing transaction cost and customers queuing time and thus saving waiting time in the banking hall, the agony and inconvenience of waiting is transferred from the banking hall to the ATM cash point. It is observed that in most Cash Points, out of 7 ATM machines only two may be functional. The study revealed the inadequacy of social infrastructure like power and telecommunication facilities to drive the cashless policy process. This collaborate the study of Ajayi (2014) who observed that social infrastructure, technology, security and limited number of electronic channels continue to be a challenge and problem mitigating cashless policy of the CBN.

## 8.0 CONCLUSION AND POLICY IMPLICATION

The result from the analysis reveals that the twin policy objectives of the CBN investigated were partially achieved as payment systems in Nigeria have undergone some significant progress in the past few years, though some business transactions are still cash dominated. Therefore, more work need to be down for Nigeria to be among the 20$^{th}$ developed economies by the year 2020.

Social infrastructures in power and telecommunications need improvement and expansion, as the major challenges that impede smooth development of e-payment and e-commerce is due to these infrastructures. There is the need to create more awareness in the populace to encourage the unbanked to embrace banking culture and the benefits of cashless policy in business and daily operations. It is also recommended that the banks be more proactive in their IT architecture as instances abound that the available ATMs are either none functional due to network problems, breakdown and or power outages.

Therefore, there should be vigorous investments by the CBN and the banks on cyber security to stem the fear of cybercrimes as some bank customers who registered for the mobile banking services have been defrauded by fraudsters through the service. Also, efforts should be made to strengthen internet protocols and controls in the banks to give their customers the assurances to apply and use the services. It is also recommended that relevant legislative laws curbing cybercrimes be promulgated by the National Assembly as proactive measures by government. This will create confidence in the minds of the masses.

Finally, since there is a high rate of illiteracy in Nigeria, and there is desire that all people be brought into the system, the banks in collaboration with the CBN should design special enlightenment programmes for the non-literate population using probably signs and symbols to educate this segment on how to operate the cashless system.

## REFERENCES

Adewoye, J. O. (2013). Impact of mobile banking on service delivery in the Nigerian commercial banks. *Int. Rev. Manage. Bus. Res.* 2(2): 333-344.

Ajayi, L. B. (2014). Effect of cashless monetary policy on Nigerian banking industry: Issues, prospects and challenges, *International Journal of Finance and Business Management Research*, 2, 29-41.

Ajayi, S. I. and Ojo, O. O. (2006). *Money and banking*: Analysis and policy in the Nigerian context. Ibadan Daily Graphics

Akhalumeh, A. A. and Ohioka, F. (2012). Nigeria's cashless economy: the imperatives, *International Journal of Management and Business Studies*, 2(2), 31-36

Claudia, C. and Grauwe, P. (2001). *Monetary policy in a cashless society*, Brussel CEPR Discussion Study.

CBN (2015). *The cashless Nigerian project*, Retrieved from: http//www/cenbank.org/cashless/ on August 30, 2015.

EFInA (2012) *Access to Financial Services in Nigeria 2012 survey*, key findings available via www.EFInA.org.ng

EFInA, (2013) *What does the CBN's Cash-less policy mean for financial inclusion in Nigeria?*, Enhancing Financial Innovation and Access, Bankable Frontier Associate (BFA).

Emecheta GN. (2012). *The cashless policy of the Central Bank of Nigeria: Its implications in the management of higher education in Nigeria.* A paper delivered at the Committee of Bursars Meeting, Cross River University of Technology, Calabar, Nigeria

Global FINDEX 2011, World Bank

Humphrey, D. B. (2004). Replacement of cards by cashless in U.S consumer payments, *Journal of Economics and Business*. 56: 211- 225.

Humphrey, D. B.and Berger, A. N. (1990). *Market Failure and Resource Use: Economic Incentives to Use Different Payment Instruments*, New York. Monograph Series in Finance and Economics.

Humphrey, D. B, Pulley, L. B. and Vesala, J. M. (1996). Cash, study and electronic payments: A cross-country analysis. *Journal of Money, Credit and Banking*, 28: 914-939.

James, A. O. (2012). The acceptance of e-banking by customers in Nigeria. *World Rev. Bus. Res.* 2(2):6-8.

James, A. O. (2013). Going cashless: Adoption of mobile banking in Nigeria. *Arab. J. Bus. Manage. Rev.* (Nigerian Chapter). 1(2):9-17.

Jatau, V. S. and Dung, K. L. (2014). The Central Bank of Nigeria's cashless policy: A major panacea for eliminating corruption and enhancing sustainable development in Nigeria, *African Research Review*, 8(4), S/N. 35, 198-205.

Lim, E. C, Alum, J. (1995). Construction Productivity issues encountered by contractors in Singapore, *International Journal of Project Management, 13(1); 51-8*

Marco, A. and Bandiera, L. (2004). *Monetary policy, monetary areas and financial development with electronic money*, IMF Working Study, IMF

Moser, C. A and Kalton, G. (1971). *Survey methods in social investigation*. UK; Heineman Educational.

Morufu, O and Taibat, A. (2012) Banker's perceptions of electronic banking in Nigeria: A review of post consolidation experience. *Research Journal of Finance and Account*. 3(2):5-6.

News Letter (2013, March). Enhancing financial innovation and access, *EFLnA*).

Okoye, P. V. C. and Ezejiofor, R. (2013). An appraisal of cashless economy policy in development of Nigerian economy, *Research Journal of Finance and Accounting*, 4(7), 237-252.

Olajide, V. C. (2012). Cashless banking in Nigeria and its implications, *Munich Personal RePEc Archive (MPRA)*, 38096, 1- 20. Retrieved online on 23/06/2013. Available online at: http:mpra.ub.uni-muenchen.de/38096/

Osazevbara, H. O. and Yomere, G. O. (2015). Benefits and challenges of Nigeria's cashless policy, *Kuwait Chapter of Arabian Journal of Business and Management Review*, 4 (9), 1-10.

The Nation (2013). *CBN's cashless policy begins in six states today*, The Nation Newspaper.

Woodford, M. (2003). *Interest and prices*: Foundations of a Theory of Monetary Policy, Princeton University Press.

Yaqub, J. O; Bello, H. T.; Adenuga, I. A. and Ogundeji, M. O. (2013). The cashless policy in Nigeria: prospects and challenges, *International Journal of Humanities and Social Science*, 3(3), 200-212

# 5

# Tax Stories from South Anatolia

**Mesut Sert**[1]

**ABSTRACT**

In this research, the data obtained from the oral history interviews with both sides – tax payer peasants and tax collectors – are used to interpret how tax relations work and how this process is perceived by the tax payer. Based on the idea that nicknames might offer a more realistic framework in this sense, the nicknames given to tax collectors, such as Rıza of the Cliff (Uçurumlu Rıza), Mustafa the Angel (Melek Mustafa), the Slender Tyrant (İnce Zalım), and the Black/Yellow Hell (Kara/Sarı Cehennem), are believed to be a representative of the relationship between both parties. Never published before in another medium, the story of Süleyman, the Butcher (Kasap Süleyman) is also hereby introduced into field literature.

Keywords: Fiscal sociology, fiscal history, oral history, tax collector.

---

## 1.0 INTRODUCTION

After the proclamation of the Turkish Republic, all imperial methods of revenue collection, including *iltizam* (tax farming) were abolished, and the guiding principle in revenue collection became the individual collection of the revenues by government officials. Because the majority of the country's population resided in rural areas during the early days of the republic and considering the difficulty concerning transportation then, the mounted tax collector proved to be quite significant in the process. However, with the recent improvements in banking transactions and transportation, mounted tax collectors gradually died out in the 1980s. Today, tax collectors work under district revenue departments, and the methods of collection and transportation they use differ greatly from those used in earlier days of the republic. The duty of the tax collector focuses more on notification than on collection today, and they tend to use motorized vehicles.

In this research, the way tax relations function and how the process of tax collection is perceived by tax payers are studied by using oral history method.

[1] Department of Public Finance, Akdeniz University, Turkey. Email: msert@akdeniz.edu.tr

## 2.0 METHODOLOGY

Oral history in short, can be defined as the method which uses the memory as a source for historical research. Although "it was the first kind of history" (Thompson, 2000, p. 25), it especially came in to question after the Great Depression in USA as a method of historical research. Its scope has been expanding to cover almost all social sciences and there are literatures both to introduce and how methodology is used – i.e. (Perks & Thomson, 1998; Danacıoğlu, 2010; Neyzi, 2009).

As a method, Oral History mainly relies on the narrative text which formed with the interviewer and interviewee. After recording videotapes or audiotapes, interview is decoded and interpreted by interviewer with also literature and other source of material to explain research question.

In this research it is interviewed sixteen people at different places and times as shown in following table.

**List of Interviewees**

| Name | Age | Place | Qualification | Date of Interview |
|---|---|---|---|---|
| Osman Aydın | 79 | Manavgat | Tax Collector | August 30, 2012 |
| Mustafa Çakmak | 86 | Gazipaşa | Tax Collector | October 20, 2012 |
| Mustafa Tomruk | 82 | Kaş | Tax Collector | December 22, 2012 |
| Hulusi Oğuz | 58 | Gazipaşa | Tax Collector | October 21, 2012 |
| Necla Duru | 79 | İbradı | Tax Collector Daughter | August 31, 2012 |
| Cazibe Kurt | 69 | Kaş | Tax Collector Daughter | December 22, 2012 |
| Ali Kocaer | 100 | Kalkan | Tax Payer | December 22, 2012 |
| Ali Canbaş | 87 | İbradı | Tax Payer | August 31, 2012 |
| Vahdettin Barut | 86 | İbradı | Tax Payer | August 31, 2012 |
| Hüseyin Gerçek | 87 | İbradı | Tax Payer | September 2, 2012 |
| Ahmet Uysal | 85 | Gazipaşa | Tax Payer | October 20, 2012 |
| Şevket Tanç | 86 | Kalkan | Tax Payer | December 22, 2012 |
| Emin Necati Kırca | 79 | Kalkan | Tax Payer | December 23, 2012 |
| Mehmet Kocasarı | 85 | Kalkan | Tax Payer | December 23, 2012 |
| Sadık Yılmaz | 62 | Kalkan | Tax Payer | December 23, 2012 |
| Yusuf Ustaali | 90 | Kalkan | Tax Payer | December 23, 2012 |

In order to build a more comprehensive framework, the interviews were carried out with not only tax collectors but also their tax payers. The interviewed tax collectors were selected from among those who are still alive, and when this was not possible, the tax collector's children were interviewed. Whereas four of the tax collectors resided in Manavgat, Gazipaşa, and Kaş, the children of the two other were based in İbradı and Kalkan. As a result of a preliminary survey carried out in where ten of our interviewees lived, it was decided that only those between eighty-ninety years of age who have experienced, and thus still remember, tax-related problems be elected.

After the information regarding their place and date of birth, family origins, level of education, marital and military service statuses was obtained, the interviewed tax collectors were asked to provide information on how they got into the business of tax collecting, where and when they started work, what type of taxes they collected, and significant work-related memories. They were also asked whether they were called names/nicknames by the natives. On the other hand, the interviewed tax payers were also asked to provide similar information on their family origins, their affiliated tax collector, the problems, if any, they encountered while taxpaying, their relationship with the tax collector, and whether they called their tax collector names.

In the following sections, the findings obtained from the interviews are summarized[2].

[2] A more comprehensive analysis of the findings is available in the author's previous article.

## 3.0 RELATION BETWEEN TAX COLLECTOR AND PEASANTS: WE LOVE EACH OTHER (DON'T WE?)

Considering the fact that the peasant's main connection to the state is that of tax connection, the relationship between the tax collector and the tax payer is also a reflection of the way the peasant perceives the state.

Based on the interviews, the general feeling from the perspective of the tax collector is that peasants are honest and trustworthy people, which yield a smooth and uneventful communication between the parties. Tax collector Osman Aydın from Manavgat compares the county to the village and says:

> There are some who argue against taxes here [*in the city*], but nobody objects to anything in the village. Peasants are more demure, more alert, and yet more humane. They obey the laws of the state. They wouldn't fox another.

Similar ideas were communicated also by the other tax collectors. Mustafa Çakmak from Gazipaşa shares his ideas as follows:

> ...the people of this district, Gazipaşa... I've always known them and worked with them for a long time. These people are naïve; not well off, but middle-income, let's say. They were never bad debtors. They wouldn't stab you in the back.

Although he does not deny the existence of certain problems, Hulusi Oğuz, from Gazipaşa, in a manner to emphasise the power of the state, says:

> There are always a couple of problems in a flock, but this must not be generalised. If only one out of a hundred creates the problem, then this must not be taken into account. No matter how much one objects to it, the state always gets what it is entitled to get. Otherwise, legal proceedings will be commenced.

It is significant that the tax collectors also paid considerable attention to good relations with tax payers; in fact, they even did them small favours by overlooking certain problems. Mustafa Çakmak, underlining that he sometimes turned a blind eye to small things during stocktaking, says:

> Well, that's between you and me. You have to condone certain things. You count ten [*goats*] but record seven or eight. That's alright. I used to say to the tax payer, 'There you go, I'm doing you a favour and record eight animals, but I can't just erase it all'.

Mustafa Tomruk also mentions avoiding late fees sometimes and says:

> Late fees do not really function when it comes to accrual. Well, there is this man in the village. I look at him. I can see he is poor and penniless. I just condone the late fee, and that's it. My heart just sinks. I have always been on the side of the peasant because I know what being a peasant is. The state is rich. "*Its wealth is like the sea*...[3]"

The answer to the question whether peasants are afraid of the tax collector - who, in a way, is identified with the state itself – is negative from the tax collector's perspective, as would be expected. Almost every tax collector conveys that he was well liked by the peasants and that peasants were not afraid of them. What Mustafa Çakmak, and the tax collector's daughter from İbradı Necla Duru say in this context is almost a summary of the general relationship:

> They used to like me. No, I mean, they trusted me. No, they were not afraid of me. They trusted me.
>
> ...My father was dear to the peasants of his time. Everybody knew his name and called him Necip *Ağa* (Agha/Master).

[3]This is an idiom in Turkish to emphasize richness of state. Whole of idiom is that "*government property is like a sea, people who don't eat is a pig*"

From the tax payer peasant's perspective, the most forthright statement probably belongs to Mehmet Kocasarı:

> ...Of course, we were afraid. When the tax collector's arrival was announced... the tax collector, the gendarme... It was either the gendarme or the tax collector who came to the village, and, yes, I swear, we were afraid.

Although with a different justification, tax payer peasant Yusuf Ustaali relates similar thoughts:

> We were afraid; of course, we were... How can we not be? The man never left the village without taking our money. He [*tax collector*] used to say, 'I'm not here to visit you as a neighbour.' See? That's it. He was here to collect money and he would say it out loud

## 4.0 THE NICKNAME AS AN INDICATOR OF THE COLLECTOR-PAYER RELATIONSHIP

Another field where the collector-payer relationship can be observed is the nicknames given to the tax collectors in villages. It is also legitimate to say that the nicknames are even better at revealing the true nature of the relationship.

Doubtless a tax collector will avoid talking about it if the nickname is not an innocent one. In this regard, Mustafa Çakmak shares his ideas as follows:

> They used to call me Mustafa, the Tax Collector [*Tahsildar Mustafa*] in the village. They still do.

On the other hand, Hulusi Oğuz says:

> They used to call me the Tax Collector [*Tahsildar*], or "the one with the bag."That was the nickname. Because we often had a bag with us.

Only Cazibe Kurt, the daughter of tax collector Ali Rıza Öncü, confirmed and explained, though controversially, why his father was called Rıza of the Cliff (*Uçurumlu Rıza*). The tax collector's friend, Mustafa Tomruk says:

> (Laughs) Well... What should I say? (Laughs) People used to call him Rıza of the Cliff; that's it. (Laughs)

On the other hand, his daughter Cazibe Kurt notes:

> My father used to be an agile, hardworking man. Yes, they used to call him *Uçurumlu*. (Laughs). It was his nickname. He was given the nickname because he was always hardworking.

Thus, it can be asserted that the determinant of the nicknaming process is the relationship built between the tax payer and the tax collector. In this regard, although the nickname might be related with the collector's surname or physical peculiarities, it was mainly influenced by the tax collector's attitude towards peasants.

In the example of Mustafa, the Angel (*Melek Mustafa*), it is seen that the tax collector's surname is the inspiration. Tax payer peasant Ahmet Uysal relates his memories as follows:

> ...*Melek* used to be here. *Melek* Mustafa. He was also a tax collector. His surname was Melek. They called him *Melek*, though. He was known to be *Meleğin Oğlu*[son of the angel], also.

And here is what a peasant says about the nickname:

> This *Melek* never smiled. For God's sake. (Laughs). He never ever smiled... Never smiled. He always kept a straight face. Never would he smile when he was face to face with the debtor. Always kept a straight, solemn face...

Another nickname the Slender Tyrant (*İnce Zalım*), on the other hand, shows how physical appearance influenced the nicknames. The Slender Tyrant worked as a tax collector in Gazipaşa district during the 1940s. Here is how he is described by a peasant Ahmet Uysal:

> The tax collector. He was from Alanya and was known as the Slender Tyrant by almost everyone. That was his nickname, yes. I don't know his name. He was a man, just like we are...He wasn't evil or something. He used to come over and chat with us. He went around collecting the money, and he only did if he could. We would offer him food with might and main, and he was kind enough to stay and eat with us. Then he would leave. All in all, nothing unusual.

Another tax collector, Mehmet Bozca is reported to be called by the names of either *Sarı Cehennem* (The Yellow Hell) or *Kara Cehennem* (The Black Hell) in different accounts. His story seems to clarify why he was called these names. Tax collector Mustafa Tomruk speaks of him and says:

> Mehmet Bozca... He was blonde, but an ugly one... (Laughs). That's the problem with him. A bit grizzly. He used to be called The Yellow Hell down here. He used to go to this village called Palamut, and he gathered people and took out the receipt book. The peasants had to go there when he called them. They had to. The opposite would be unimaginable. There was nothing beneath the receipt, no carbon copy. How much is your tax? When it was three liras, he took five. But then he wrote down two on the receipt. See?.

Before Mr. Tomruk finishes his sentence, another peasant Emin Necati Kırca adds:

> The Black Hell... *Boşça*[4] Boşça The Black Hell Boşça... He was the tax collector. He was old. Someone always announced the Black Hell's coming. He was a tough man; that's what people said. He was tough with the collection, too; people used to be afraid of him, yes. He even slapped people! That's what we used to hear from the others.

*Gene Memet* (Memet, the Mite) the tax collector from the Akseki/İbradı district, has the strangest story of all. A peasant, Ali Canbaş, about the tax collector's nickname, says:

> ...People used to call him Gene Memet...They called him *Gene*; he was known to be quite faithful to his job. Because he was good at his job and took it seriously, people gave him the nickname *Gene*.

On the other hand, Necla Duru, the daughter of one of Gene Memet's friends, cannot remember much about him and says:

> He was from Akseki. I don't think I've ever heard his surname. I don't know why they called him this nickname, though. That's all I remember.

However, Hüseyin Gerçek gives us detailed information and narrates an interesting story as to the origins of *Gene Memet*'s nickname:

> There was a guy called Gene Memet, from İbradı. He often came, and I knew him...He was about 1.73-1.75 cm tall. I am 171 cm tall. He was about my size. He wasn't thin. His face was like that of a gibbon. Sometimes he wore a flat cap, and sometimes a trilby. Because he was from İbradı, we also used to frequent the borough – İbradı used to be a borough, not a town. So, that's how I know Gene Memet. He used to come with a stock book. He was a bit old, I think, or was he visually impaired? Not sure, but he wore glasses, I remember that. He wore his glasses and wrote the receipts... Whenever he was here, he stuck like glue[5].(Laughs) That's why he was called Gene Memet. That's what I know. There used to be an elderly man here named Mehmet. He is long gone now. One day, as he was going home, someone said "Gene Memet is coming". *Gene* is not something nice, once it clings onto your skin, it won't leave you. And this other Mehmet, son of Ömer, takes the announcement personally and files a defamation lawsuit against this person who had announced the coming of *Gene* Memet. However, at court, the defendant defends himself by

[4] The collector's surname in local dialect

[5] As a Turkish idiom, "kene gibi yapışmak" is translated as "stick like glue" into English; however, a literal, word-for-word translation would be "stick like a mite;" "mite" is "kene" [it is *gene* here in the local accent], hence the nickname.

saying that what he meant was that "Mehmet was coming *again.*[6]" The defendant was acquitted. Can you believe that? Yes, I did witness this incident.

## 5.0 THE STORY OF SÜLEYMAN, THE BUTCHER

The intriguing story of Süleyman, the Butcher (*Kasap Süleyman*) that was encountered during the interviews carried out for the purposes of this research in the Kalkan district is unique and has never been published in a written source before. In addition to its novelty, the story also provides a significant example in terms of the way local tax collection functions.

The story of Süleyman, the Butcher who wandered along with the tax collector when the cattle tax (*ağnam vergisi*) was still in effect has been confirmed and verified by almost every interviewee. The first person to narrate this story is Emin Necati Kırca:

> ...There used to be a Sucu [ *Waterman*] Memet Efendi... He always came here with a butcher. If you possess cattle, you'll pay the tax. The guy was called Süleyman, the Butcher. He, Süleyman, the Butcher, was always with the tax collector. His full name was Süleyman Belli, I guess.

Another account that supports this version of the story belongs to Yusuf Ustaali:

> Yes, yes, I know him. I know him, too. They used to go around together. You possess goods and not pay the tax? Süleyman, the Butcher was always with the tax collector. When the debtor failed to pay his taxes, the butcher guy purchased their animals. That's how it worked. I know them.

Sadık Yılmaz also tells us a similar story:

> Süleyman, the Butcher was always with this tax collector man. The butcher purchased debtors' goats and gave the money to the collector.

As to the way this mechanism functions, Emin Necati Kırca adds the following to his story:

> The collector comes to receive the tax, but there is no money. Once, he came to me. I had the cattle, but I didn't have the money. The butcher bought my cattle and took them away. He gave the money to the tax collector. That's how it worked.

Mehmet Kocasarı, on the other hand, says:

> When I had 100 goats in the fold, I used to hide 50 of it. All you needed was to find a shepherd. Then, these guys came to collect taxes. The butcher said "Give me that one and that one, and that." He paid for them to the tax collector. And we were done.

Süleyman, the butcher seems to have underpriced the cattle, which was verified to a large extent in the interviews. Emin Necati Kırca comments on the butcher as follows:

> Yes, he bought them. Of course, he did. Who else had the money to buy those cattle? Whatever price Süleyman, the Butcher gave was okay. It had to be.

Here, He also emphasises the desperation of peasants and how difficult it is for them to question certain things.

> Nobody knows him.(Laughs). Because nobody dared to ask him anything. Nobody could. When the gendarme comes for you, you cannot question them. They just come and get you. It was the same with the butcher.

Mehmet Kocasarı's account is even more desperate:

> ...This man comes on horseback and commands you to gather the goats. He sets aside four of the goats. You have to obey. He never dismounts his horse.

---

[6]The Turkish words for 'mite' and 'again' are quite similar; respectively *kene* (*gene* here) and *yine* (also *gine* in colloquial Turkish).

Complementary to the narrated story, Sadık Yılmaz comments on the relationship between the tax collector and the butcher as follows:

> I heard that they worked together. I think they did.

Mehmet Kocasarı, however, says that such collaboration is out of question and adds that the butcher once talked to him. He notes:

> No. No. No way. No way. There were no such rumours then. But we were happy when the tax collector came. We sent him word so he would come. What would you give the man? We need goats; we need money. We always sold our goats to pay our debts. Fortunately, we had goats or calves to sell. We had to sell something. What else could we do? See?

Although last two narratives are in contradiction and it cannot be easily said that collector and butcher work in agreement, it is true that Süleyman, the Butcher was a rich man and his richness seem to come from buying cheaper.

## 6.0 CONCLUSION AND OVERALL ASSESSMENT

It is well known that one of the fundamental relations between lord and peasants in ancient regime and state and citizens in modern nation state is surplus extraction or tax levy. The other type of relation is recruitment, associated with it, and both are problematical. There has been always a tension between ruler and subject and this tension lead to great upheavals or sometimes revolution as easily found in the history of nation state formation.

In his works Mann (1992; 1986) made a difference between despotic and infrastructural power and state power evolves from the first to the latter in a historical context. Although the parameter of the first type is violence, state try to find and put into practice more sophisticated way of extraction which can also be said rely on consent in second type.

From this perspective, results gathered from the interviews justify this evolution in Turkish case. In consideration of their ages, period which our respondents remembered is 1940s. This era can be characterized as despotic power and it can be said that practices of government under single party rule mostly rely on violence. When it is considered with Second World War conjuncture, it is expected that complain about taxes is in common as can be traced from whole of the tax payer's narratives.

After the 1950 election, oldest and founder party of the republic The Republican People's Party (CHP) lost its hegemony and Democratic Party (DP) came into power, it can be said that new era started. The sign of this new era which partly characterized as infrastructural power can be followed from narratives. Almost all tax payers' narratives, after complaining about heavy taxes, ended expression like "Democratic Party set our free". The fear which become concrete in nicknames is also related the period. It can be said that the condition of the period led to increase the fear although still in case especially in rural area.

## REFERENCES

Danacıoğlu, E. (2010). Geçmişin İzleri: Yanıbaşınızdaki Tarih İçin Bir Klavuz, İstanbul: Tarih Vakfı Yurt Yayınları.

Mann, M. (1986). Source of Social Power Vol. 1: A History from Beginning to A.D. 1760, Cambridge: Cambridge University Press.

Mann, M. (1992). States, War and Capitalism, Oxford: Blackwell.

Neyzi, L. (2009). Ben Kimim: Türkiye'de Sözlü Tarih Kimlik ve Öznellik, İstanbul: İletişim Yayınları.

Perks, R., & Thomson, A. (1998). The Oral History Reader, London and New York: Routledge.

Thompson, P. (2000). The Voice of the Past, Oxford: Oxford University Press.

# 6

# Political Globalization and Foreign Direct Investment Inflows in Turkey

**Cem Doğan[1], Ünal Arslan[2]**

**ABSTRACT**

This article examines the impact of political globalization on foreign direct investment inflows to Turkey. Existence of foreign missions in a country, membership in international organizations, participation in U.N. Security Council Missions, and International Treaties are all seen as indicators political globalization. Using different econometric techniques, this study aims to find out whether any empirical relationship between political globalization and FDI exists. The analysis in this article covers the period in Turkey between 1970-2012. The results of cointegration analysis provide no an evidence of a long-run or short run any relationship political globalization and FDI.

Keywords: Cointegration, FDI, Pesaran bound test, political globalization,

---

## 1.0 Introduction

Foreign direct investment is accepted as one of the most important sources of economic development, particularly so after 1980s. FDI has indeed grown at a phenomenal rate since the early 1980s. Therefore many researchers in finance and economics try to find the factors that affect the FDI (Haksoon, 2010: 59). According to the UNCTAD report (1998), for example, the determinants of FDI could be classified into 3 main categories. These are politic factors, business facilitation and economic factors.

The basic aim of this article is to demostrate the impact of political globalization of Turkey on FDI. It is analyzed with four main sources. According to the our results, ceteris paribus, investors from different

[1] Mustafa Kemal University Faculty of Economics and Administration Science, E-mail: cemdogan@mku.edu.tr
[2] Mustafa Kemal University Faculty of Economics and Administration Science, E-mail: uarslan@mku.edu.tr

countries are likely to invest in Turkey. Thus the relation between political globalization and FDI into Turkey is positive.

The stock of FDI in Turkey was only $ million in 1971, and up until 1980 the avarage annual inflow of FDI was only $ 90 million. As Balasubramanyam (1996) shows, this was far less than other comparable countries, and FDI did not increase significantly for most of the 1980s (Loewendhal and Ertugal, 2000: 3).

This article contains six sections. In section two we give Literature Review of FDI and political globalisation. In section three Turkey and Foreign Direct Investment. In section four empirical Analysis that the realtionship between FDI and political globalisation is examined. In the last section we present empirical results and then conclude the results.

## 2.0 Literature review

In recent years hundreds of theoreretical and empirical studies have tried to explain these kind of questions; what drives decisions on where to invest? How do countries, especially developing and under developed countries attact foreign direct investment and which conditions are conveinent for FDI.

The findings are related with these kind of questions presented in the literature that several factors could facilitate or hinder foreign direct investment inflows. So modeling FDI is a complicated task because so many variables are involved (Mohsin and Zurawicki, 2002: 291). However, several studies have analysed the relationship between FDI and many things. Coughlin, Terza and Arromdee (1991) found for 1981 – 1983 within the United States that states with higher per capita incomes and higher densities of manufacturing activity attracted relatively more foreign direct investment Habib and Zurawicki (2002), in their article analysed the impact of corruption on foreign direct investment. The results showed that although their perceived high corruption China, Brazil, Thailand and Mexico attract large flows of FDI, Belgium, which is smilarly rated on corruption (by Transparency International) attracts substantial FDI.

Brewer (1993), indicated that, the effects on FDI of government policies, morover depend on the relative cross – national changes in policy as well as the cross – national differences in the levels of policies. Busse and Hefeker (2005), using different econometric techniques for a data sample of 83 developing countries and the period 1984 to 2003, explained that investment conflict, ethnic tensions and democratic accuntability are important determinants of FDI flows.

Kenyon and Margalit (2014), they have analyazed the emprical relationship between treaty signing and FDI inflows. They showed that signing of intenational economic treaties can help boost foreign investment inflow via its direct effect on the opportunities to benefit from expanded commerce.

Kilmek (2015) in his article examined the relationship between quality of instituonal enviroment and FDI inflows. Using cross – sectional and panal data techiniques, he found that quality of instituonal enviroment plays important role in the process of capital abroad in the form of FDI for 125 economies across 7 geographic regions over the period of time 1996–2011. Anghel (2004), argues that countries whose governments are hishing ranked according to various indices tend to do better in attracting foreign direct investment. According to the findings of her research countries with corrupt, less efficent governments tent to be less attractive for foreign investors. Madeni and Nobakth (2014), in their article accounted for the political determinant of foreign direct investment inflows for 31 Upper – Middle – Income Countries (UMCs) over the period of 1990 – 2011. The main findings of the emprical analysis are that democracy enhances FDI toward UMCs.

On the Contrary Castro (2014), found that there is no relationship between democracy and FDI. He claimed that Although lagged FDI is statistically significant and positively correlated with FDI inflows, democracy is not statistically signifcant and it has a limited effect on FDI.

Hakro and Ghumro (2011), in their article analysis the determinants of FDI flows and to quantify relevent policy shocks for Pakistan economy, by using dynamic econometric VAR model. Their analysis showed that the investment enviroment improving factor statistically significant not only in short run but also in long run. Krifa and Matei (2010), explained by applying two panel models : a fixed effect model and a dynamic panel model (the Arellano – Bond GMM estimator) for a data sample of 33 developing countries covering the period 1996 – 2008 that reduced levels of political risk, are associated with an increase in FDI inflows and the business operation conditions appear as an important determinant of the FDI.

Büthe and Milner (2008), explained by focusing on a particular type of international institution that international institutions increase the credibility of government commitments and these institutions affect FDI by giving foreign investor access to markets for inputs and outputs

Nuno Carlos Leitao (2012), in his article argued and provided that globalization has positive effect on FDI. Using static and dynamic panel data techiques he showed that market size, globalization, openness trade and urban population are important for the countries selected are members of OECD in between 1990 – 2008. Caroline Witte et al., (2015) in their article analyazed what drives MNEs to select low income Sub – Sahran Africa countries. They found that poltic conflict has a negative effect on propensity of a MNE to invest a location. Using a unique dataset comprised of grenfield FDI in low income Sub- Sahran they also showed that the coefficent of colony variable is positive and higly significant, indicatng that MNEs from former colonizer are more likely to invest in a location. Coupet and Mayer (2005), based their study on the relationship between FDI and instititional determinants. They found that institutions mater independently of GDP per capita. According to the their empirical results, for a sample 52 countries, public efficiency in broad sense as a major determinant of invard FDI. Brunetti and Woder (1998), by using large number of uncertainty varaibles in a standardized data set, showed that there is negative association between political violance and FDI. Biglaise and De Rounen (2006), they have analyzed the determinants of FDI inflows in Latin America for 14 countries between 1980 and 1996. By using panal data techinique, they found that most economic reforms have limited effect on FDI flows. They also pointed out that international capital liberalization and privatization are unlikely to attract foreign interests and regime type seems to have little impact on foreign investors.

## 3.0 Turkey and foreign direct ınvestment

Although liberalization programme and export oriented strategy of development initiated in the early 1980s, Turkey was one of the lowest recipents of FDI among the developing countries until 2000s. During the 1980s cummulative inflows of FDI was about $0,168 billion or 0,86 % of gross domestic invertment (Vural and Zortuk, 2011:15). Because of the unstable political scene, Turkey was not able to utilise its economic growth in 1990s (Demir, 2013). Thus, in terms of international capital with the cumulative FDI/ GNP ratio and the per capita cumulative FDI was well below the avarage (17.3%) for Turkey (4.4%). Morover this ratio was 28 % in developing countries (Akgüç and Ucal, 2003: 9).

In Conclusion, although Turkey shifted to free market economy gradually, FDI flows and export volume remained at low levels during the period 1980 – 2001 because of the financal crises and political instability (Bayar, 2014: 26). Come to 2000s a key feature of the Turkish economy over the last decade has been the robust economic growth with an average annual rate of 5 percent. This remarkable performance of growth together with prudent fiscal policies and major structural reforms has integrated the Turkish economy into the globalized world, while transforming Turkey into one of the major recipients of FDI in its region. Turkey has become the 13th most attractive FDI destination in the world by $123 billion of FDI in the past decade (Dalgıç, at al., 2012: 10).

## 4.0 Empirical analysis

The co-integration relationship between globalization and foreign direct investments in Turkey has been analyzed in the empirical part of this work, using annual data for 1970-2012. Foreign direct investment data has been obtained from UNCTAD . KOF index has been used as political globalization data. It is first necessay to perform unit root tests in order to determine whether any relationship exists between FDI and political globalization.

**Table 1: Unit Root Test Results**

| Variables | Model | Mackinnon Critical Values (5%) | Augmented Dickey-Fuller test statistic | Results |
|---|---|---|---|---|
| FDI | I** | -2.943427 | -7.905179 | I (0) |
| | II *** | -3.520787 | -9.285521 | I (0) |
| | III **** | -1.951000 | -3.987709 | I (0) |
| | IV ***** | | | |
| POLGLB | I** | -2.933158 | -0.769667 | I (1) |
| | II *** | -3.520787 | -1.966761 | I (1) |
| | III **** | -1.948886 | 1.866934 | I (1) |
| | IV ***** | -2.935001 | -7.994112 | I (1) |

For this purpose, stationarity of variables were done using Augmented Dickey Fuller (ADF) test. Augmented Dickey Fuller (ADF) test contains three different regression equations.

$$\Delta Y_t = \mu Y_{t-1} + \Sigma_{i=2}^{p} \beta_i \Delta Y_{t-i+1} + u_t \quad (1)$$

$$\Delta Y_t = \alpha_0 + \mu Y_{t-1} + \Sigma_{i=2}^{p} \beta_i \Delta Y_{t-i+1} + u_t \quad (2)$$

$$\Delta Y_t = \alpha_0 + \alpha_{2t} + \mu Y_{t-1} + \Sigma_{i=2}^{p} \beta_i \Delta Y_{t-i+1} + u_t \quad (3)$$

τ, τμ and τx statistics are used for the testing of $\mu = 0$ (Dickey and Fuller (1981). To test joint hypothesis on the coefficient provide three additional F-statistics that name are $\Omega_1$, $\Omega_2$ and $\Omega_3$. The null hypothesis $\mu = \alpha_0 = 0$ is tested by equation $\Omega_1$ using statistics. $\Omega_2$ is tested by taking a time trend in regression, -i.e. by using (4.3) - joint hypothesis $\alpha_0 = \mu = \alpha_2 = 0$ statistics. Finally $\mu = \alpha_2 = 0$ joint hypothesis is tested using statistics $\Omega_3$ (Enders, 1995: 221-222). Within the scope of these regressions, FDI stability and POLGLB variables have been tested and the results were shown in Table 1. According to the results of the unit root tests, it can be said that the FDA data is constant, while POLGLB data contains a unit root and is first-degree cointegrated. Therefore, Peseran, et al., (2001) test has been used to determine the co-integration relationship.

## 4.1 Co-integration test

Once it has been established that FDI series is stationary and, POLGLB series is cointedgrated in the first order, an unconstrained Vector Autoregression (VAR) model has been developed to determine the optimal level of delay to be employed in co-integration. Optimal lag number was determined as 1 using, LR test statistic (Likelihood Ratio), Final Prediction Error (FPE), Akaike Information Criterion (AIC), Schwarz Information Criterion (SC), Hannan-Quinn Information Criterion (HQ).

Through the bounds test developed by Peseran, et al., (2001), cointegration relationship can be investigated regardless of whether the series are I(0) or I(1). For this purpose, firstly an Unrestricted Error Correction Model (UECM) was developed. Adopted version of this model for our study is as follows.

$$\Delta FDI_t = \alpha_0 + \alpha_1 t + \sum_{i=1}^{p} \alpha_{2i} \Delta FDI_{t-i} + \sum_{i=0}^{p} \alpha_{3i} \Delta POLGLB_{t-i} + \alpha_4 FDI_{t-1} + \alpha_5 POLGLB_{t-1} + u_t$$

F test is calculated for detecting the presence of the co-integration relationship. The basic hypothesis for the F-testing is, $H_0: \alpha_4 = \alpha_5 = 0$. Calculated F test statistics is compared against the lower and upper critical values of Peseran, et al., (2001). If the F statistic is smaller than the Peseran, lower critical value than it is concluded that no co-integration relationship exists. If the F statistics is between the lower and upper values, than no-conclusive comment can be made about the existence of a co-integration relationship. Finally, if the F statistic is above the upper value, this indicates the presence of a co-integration relationship.

**Table 2: Unrestricted Error Correction Model**

| k | F-statistics | Test Critical Values (level 5%) | |
|---|---|---|---|
| 1 | | lower limit | Upper Limit |
| 1 | 3.095177 | 4.94 | 5.73 |

Critical values were obtained from table C (iii) in Peseran, et al., (2001:300) wherein . k is the number of independent variables.

Results obtained from the Unrestricted Error Correction model are shown in Table 2. According to these findings, as a result the analysis performed for the period between 1970 and 2012 in Turkey it was concluded that no co-integration relationship exists between Foreign Direct Investment and Political Globalisation.

## 5.0 Conclusion

The term "globalization" came into popular usage in the second half of the 1980s in connection with the huge surge of foreign direct investment (FDI) by multinational corparations (Gilpin, 2001:7). Meanwhile many indicators shows that FDI's are determined not only by multinational corparations or firms, but also by culture, historical connection, and political regime in which economic operations are embedded. For this reason FDI's are strongly affected by social and political climate.

Because of the foreign direct investment is accepted one of the most important source of economic development many researchers try to find the factors that affect the FDI. The main theoretical determinants of FDI can be summarised as market access, transport costs, size of the host market, factor costs, trade barriers or openness and investment climate. However, empirical analysis for Turkey between the years of 1970-2012 indicate no cointegration relations between political globalisation and FDI.

## Reference


Alıcı, A. and Meltem, Ş. U., (2003). FDI Exports and Output Growth of Turkey : Causalty Analysis. Paper to be Presented at the European Trade Study Group (ETSG) Fifth Annual Conference 11 – 13 September 2003 in Madrid

Anghel, B., (2004). Do Institutions Affect Foreign Direct Investment. http://www.webmeets.com/files/papers/SAE/2005/217/paperFDI.pdf (Second Version 2005) (Date accessed; 08.04. 2016).

Bayar, Y., (2014). Effects of Economşc Growth and FDI Inflows on Unemployment in Turkey. Investment Management and Financal Innovations, 11 (2), 20 – 27.

Bigliase, G., and Rounen, K. De (2006). Economic Reforms and Inflows of Foreign Direct Investment in Latin America. Latin America Research Review. 41 (1), 51 – 75.

Brewer, T. L., (1993). Government Policies, Market Imperfections, and Foreign Direct Investment. Journol of International Business Studies. 24 (1 ) , 101 – 120.

Brunetti, A., and Beatrice W., (1998). Investment and Instituonal Uncertainty A Comparative Study of Different Uncertainty Measures. Weltwirtschafliches Archive, 134 (3), 513 – 533.

Busse, M., and Hefeker, C., (2005). Political Risk, Institutions and Foreign Direct Investment. HWWA Discussion Papers 315.

Büthe, T., and Helen V. M., (2008). The Politics of Foreign Direct Investment into Developing Countries: Increasing FDI Throught International Trade Agrements. American Journal of Political Science, 52 (4), 741- 762.

Carlos, L. N., (2012). Foreign Direct Investment and Globalisation. Actual Problems of Economics, (4).

Castro, D., (2014). Foreign Direct Investment and Democracy. Honors Projecst in Economics Paper 18.

Cletus C. C., Terza, J. V. and Vachira A., (1991). State Characteristics and the Location of Foreign Direct Investment within the United States. The Review of Economic and Statistics. 73 (4), 675 – 683.

Dalgıç, B., and Fazlıoğlu, B. and Gasiorek, M., (2015). Export Spillovers from Foreign Direct Investment: Evidence from Turkey. Turkish Economic Association Discussion Paper. 2015/8.

Demir, O., (2013). FDI Attractivenness: Turkey and the BRIC Countries. The European Financal Review December (29).

Dickey, A. D., and Wayne A. F., (1981). Likelihood Ratio Statistics for Autoregressive Time Series With Unit Root. Econometrica. 49 ( 4).

Enders, W.,, (1995). Applied Econometric Time Series, John Willey and Sons inc., U.S.A. Canada,

Gilpin, R., (2001). Global Political Economy: Understanding the International Order. Princten University Press.

Habib, M., and Leon Z., (2002). Corruption and Foreign Direct Investment. Journal of Business Studies. 33 (2), 291 – 307.

Hakro, A. N., Ikhtiar A. G., (2011). Determinants of Foreign Direct Investment Flows to Pakistan. The Journal of Developing Areas, 44 (2), 217-242.

Haksoon, K., (2010). Political Stability and Foreign Direct Investment. International Journol of Economics and Finance. 2 (3).

Kenyon, T., and Margalit, Y., (2014). Does Joining International Treaties Attract Foreign Investment? Experimental Firm - Level Evidence . http://www.columbia.edu/~ym2297/KenyonMargalit_March_2014.pdf(Date accessed; 18.03.2016).

Kilmek, A., (2015). Institutions and Outward Foreign Direct Investment" International Journal of Management and Economics 46, 101 – 119.

Krifa, Hadjila–Scneider and Iuliana M., (2010). Pollitivcal Risk and FDI in Developing Countries ; Evidence from Panel Data" International Journal of Economics and Finance. 2 (5).

Loewendhal, H., and Ebru E.L., (2000). Turkey's Performance in Attracting FDI: Implications of EU Enlargment. Centre for European Policy Studies Working Document No. 157.

Madani, S., and Mahya N., (2014). Political Regimes and FDI flows : Empirical Evidence from Upper Middle Income Countries. Science and Education Publishing Journal of Finance and Economics. 75 – 82.

Mohsin H., and Leon Z., (2002). Corruption and Foreign Direct Investment. Journal of Business Studies. 33( 2) , 291-307.

Pesaran, M.H., Shin, Y., Smith, R.J. (2001). Bounds Testing Approaches to the Analysis of Level Relationships. Journal of Applied Econometrics, 16, 289- 326.

Quere, B. A., Coupet, M. and Mayer, T. (2005). Instituonal Determinants of Foreign Direct Investment. CEPII, Working Paper No 2005-05.

UNCTAD, (1998). World Investment Report Trends and Determinants. United Nations Conference on Trade and Development.

Vural, İ. Y., and Mahmut Z., (2011). FDI as a Determining Factor in Turkey's Export Performance. Euroasian Journal of Business and Economics. 4 (7), 13 – 23.

Witte, C., Martijn B., Enrico P., (2015). The Effect of Historical Connections on FDI in Conflict Areas in Sub- Saharan Africa http://www.etsg.org/ETSG2015/Papers/458.pdf (Date accessed; 13.03. 2016).

# 7

# Chinese Economic Development in the Next 20 Years

**Liang-Xin Li**[1]

**ABSTRACT**

In this paper, Chinese economic development is discussed in detail. The 5 major strategies are investigated thoroughly: 1) Speed-maintaining strategies. In this strategies, China must hold a suitable high speed economic growth rate in order to fully use Chinese manpower and world economic opportunities; 2)Healthy economy strategy. By designing and making all effective policies, China must strive to keep Chinese economy in a healthy and controllable status. 3) Competiveness strategy. For this strategy to be effective, China have to push up the RD mechanism to pave the way for technology innovation and encourage companies to use and invent new skills and products to develop a higher level living conditions for Chinese people. 4) People's quality enhancement. To make Chinese economy a high speed and competitive for a long run, it is vital to enhance Chinese people's scientific knowledge and skills, especially the modern information technology skills, in this way, Chinese population will be a huge pool for the innovation not the obstacles. 5) Balanced development strategy. All economic related factors must be balanced for a sustainable growth. In the context, the detail procedures and methods are outlined and discussed.

Keywords: Chinese economy, competitiveness, economic growth, reform, strategies.

---

## 1.0 INTRODUCTION

It is a well-known fact that China has made an economic miracle for the past 30 years with an average more than 9.8% GDP growth rate. Now China is the second largest economy which past Japan in 2010. But still China is a developing country with the average GDP per capita 6747$ of 2 thirds of the average GDP per capita of the world which ranked as 84 in the world. China has a very long way to go for its completion of the modernization era. The key success strategies for the past 30 years for China are: 1) Free its economy. China has been striving to reshape its economic system to fulfill the free market requirements by reducing government controlled planning economy; forming all kinds of merchandise, capital and financial markets; releasing human resource potential; and enhancing people living standards, etc. Now China is recognized by most of the countries of the world as a free market system. 2) Participation the international markets. By integrating Chinese economy to the international economy for foreign investors and traders, China keep exchange its goods and services for foreign investments to

[1] Business school, Hunan International Economics University, Hunan, Changsha 410205, China. Email: apolo1@sina.com.

enhance its economic modernization level. As a matter of fact China now is the largest FDI country. 3) Political system modernization.

Chinese government is striving to raise its governing efficiency by restructuring its government systems although it is very long way to change for Chinese political system to be fully supportive for the modernized free economy. 4) Information super high way revolution. By building up the high speed information network, China can achieve two major goals: 1) Make its economic system more efficient, 2) Open up people's understanding the Chinese role in the world. This is a major way to keep Chinese people up to the frontier of the fast changing world. With all this efforts for the past 30 years, now China is the second largest economy in the world, but the bigger challenges are lying ahead: 1) The bigger the economy, the harder the GDP grows. This year Chinese GDP growth rate is just 6.9% along the trends of last year low growth rate of 7.4% which is lowest rate for the past 25 years, although it is still one of the fastest economy in the world big economies. What are those key strategies for China to grow as fast as it should be? 2) The system reform. Concentrating on the economic aspects, free economic reform must keep pushing to the center part of the economy and all economic aspects. 3) With the oversaturation of low level manufacturing industry and low growth rate of its population, Chinese needs more driving forces to grow its economy. 4) Chinese people's quality cannot sustain its economic growth for the long run due to its low level education, culture, scientific and all other aspects of the its people's quality. How to sustain Chinese economic high growth for a long run is a huge challenge facing 1.3 billion Chinese people and the world. This paper is striving to answer all these challenges.

The structure of this paper is as follow: the second part is to detail the strategies; the third part is the conclusions.

## 2.0 THE STRATEGIES

### 2.1 SPEED-MAINTAINING STRATEGIES

In order to be successfully complete its run for the modernized economy, China must be able to maintain a high growth rate [Figure.1]. The reasons are: 1) To release the potential of the biggest human resources of the world, China needs to maintain a high level employment rate which needs Chinese economy to grow a high speed around 7% at least. 2) The world is changing very fast, in order to grasp the best opportunities since world II, China has to move fast before the world shifts its conditions. 3) To compete for the world resource utilization, Chinese economy must be attractive to the foreign investors and international resources, and the key is to keep Chinese economy as fast as it can be for the best return of the foreign investments. 4) There are other big economies which are developing fast which will put a pressure on Chinese economy to hold on a high speed growth rate in order to be a winner instead of a loser of the century. The following are the objective approaches for this strategies.

**Figure 1:** Chinese GDP growth rate for the past 1978-2014 years with the average growth rate 9.8% per year. There is an obvious slow down after 2008.

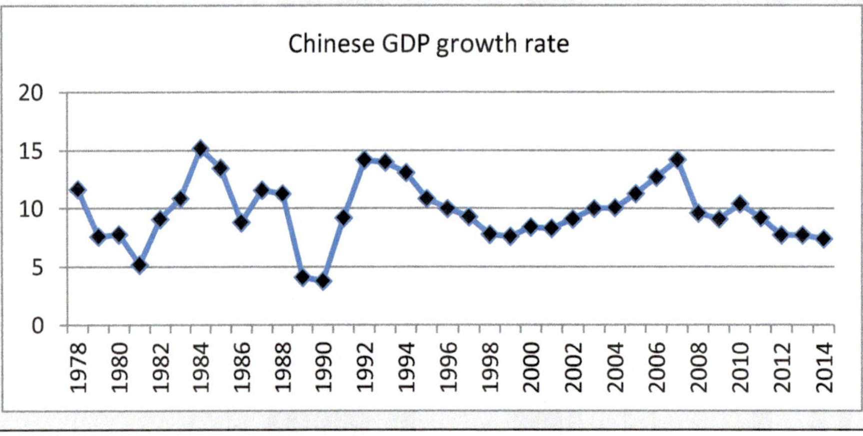

### a) MID-WEST-HOMOGENOUS

Due to historic reasons, Chinese eastern part is moving faster than its mid and western provinces. In average, Chinese eastern part is 10 years ahead of the mid part of China and the mid part is 10 years ahead of western part in the modernization level. But now Chinese eastern part is slowing down because its completion of its infrastructure and information network. Also, the relative bigger GDP scope leads to the eastern part growth rate slowing. To maintain the high speed, China must put more emphasis on mid part of the country for the next 10 years which will compensate for the loss of the speed of the eastern provinces. Also for the healthy growth of the whole economy, this is necessary. After mid provinces 10 years, the western part will provide another 10 years' growth speed compensation to hold on China for at least 20 years high growth rate around 8%. The eastern part can shift its low level manufacturing to the mid and western with its concentration to the field for attracting more advanced foreign investments, high tech manufacturing and services, and technology innovation markets.

### b) COUNTY-LEVEL MANAGEMENT

After 20 years mid-western high speed development, the key growth point for Chinese economy will shift to the county-level regional enhancement of the modernization for the next 40 years starting now. Historically, China is a farmer-dominated country. Although eastern-mid-western can reach the same level of the living standard after 20 years, but the countryside economy is still very much lagging behind. In order to raise 0.8 billion Chinese farmers to the modern level of living conditions, China must use its huge accumulated capital and technology power to complete industrialization of its countryside economy and modernization of farmers' living conditions. In this strategy, all counties can be regarded as big cities, and all resources in each county must be coordinated and industrialized for the big city people's life and work. This will take China another 40 years starting from now. After 40 years, China will be fully developed as a modernized country. The eventual goal is toward a homogenous prosperity for all Chinese people.

### c) TECHNOLOGY DRIVING MECHANISM

As all we know, 60% growth for the world economy is from technology innovation, and the rest is from the capital and labor growth. Chinese economy is mostly in the first phase of expansion by manufacturing others 'high tech products to earn a high growth rate. But with the modernization completion level moving higher, it will be very hard to grow a high speed in that way. China needs to develop its own research and development (RD) mechanism to create new markets to expand its economy further. Chinese government must push all its universities to become research oriented institutions; encourage all industries to form their own RD centers; facilitate the corporation between universities, RD centers and enterprises,; protect people's innovation; market RD resources; attract international innovation resources; build up the solid engagement between Chinese and foreign high tech integration; educate its people to higher level forming the pool of innovation.

### d) INFRASTRUCTURE MODERNIZATION

Chinese infrastructure investment is a vital way to push its GDP growth rate to a higher level. But still Chinese infrastructure is still not as good as it should be. For example, China can still make enormous investment to build up the high speed train network between 340 big cities, construct airfield for all 3400 counties, complete its highway network for all 340000 villages and towns, finish all household information super high way for 1.3 billion people, modernize all water flow channel networks and reservoirs, building more better schools and hospitals, etc. Altogether, China has a huge investment job to do for the next 20 years.

## 2.2 HEALTHY ECONOMY STRATEGY

To be sustainable for next 20 years or more, Chinese economy must be put into a healthy condition constantly. To be healthy, the economy must be a suitable speed around 8-7%; controllable CPI around 1-3%;unemployment rate sound around 3-5%;consumption, investment and export in suitable ratio[Figure 2]; all resources with a safe stock level. All other economic indicators must be good for the economy to grow for a long run. In order to be heathy, Chinese economy must take the following procedures:

**Figure 2:** Chinese economic structure for 2012. The investment and consumption occupies around 50% each with investment little bigger. China's goal is to increase the portion of the consumption to 60% around in next 20 years.

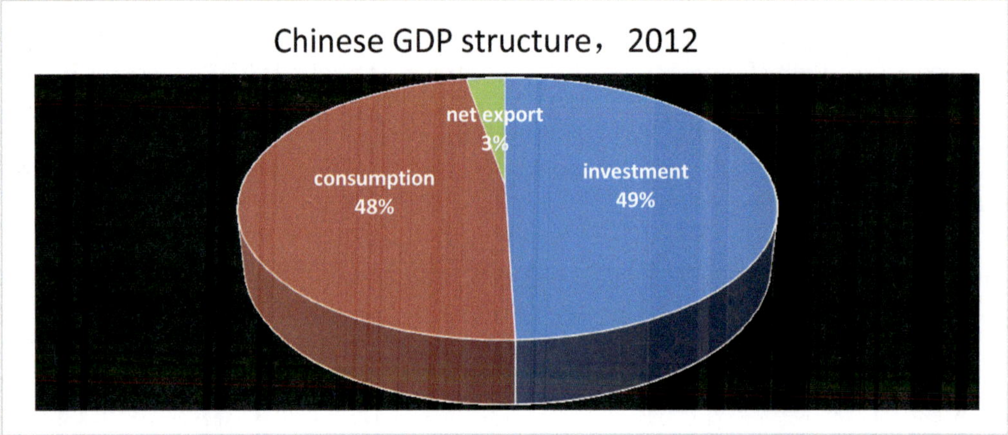


## a) COMPLETE LAWS FOR FREE ECONOMY

To protect a free economy, China needs to legalize all the rules for the economy, for example, antimonopoly, anticorruption, prevent government control, protect private enterprises, protect the free capital flows, facilitate international corporation, protect copyright and patent right, etc.

## b) REDUCE GOVERNMENT INTERVENTION

Chinese economy is reformed from the government controlled planning economy, still now all level governments are playing a big role in the country's economy. How to reduce the government intervention is still a challenge reforming task for China to complete. For example, the central government enterprises are still in different positions from private enterprises in loaning, pricing, competition, and management. How to wipe out these differences are the major direction for the economic reforms. The house industry is another example to be free. Also, the government still controls too many production factor prices which should be free to the market mechanism, such as oil, electricity, gas, interest rates, exchange rates and so on. It is still a long way to go to modernize Chinese market-oriented economy.

## c) WIPE OUT CORRUPTIONS

How to wipe out all kinds of corruption in Chinese economy is vitally important for China to be successful for this century. Corruption causes many problems for the economy to be efficient, such as abuse powers, wrong decisions, stupid investments, waste of the national resources, failure managements, etc. Corruptions are mostly from the governing power monopoly due to old style Chinese governing mechanism. One way to control corruptions is to go transparency of all money flows, another way is to report personal properties to the supervision institutions. Although these are still a goal for China but it has to be completed in order to control the corruption to the minimum level for a healthy economy.

## d) ENTERPRISE MANAGEMENT ENHANCEMENT

Healthy Chinese economy needs all enterprises to be healthy. Obviously, all enterprises must be managed well. China should learn from all other advanced countries for the high level enterprises management. The education and training system must be enhanced for obtaining qualified management personnel; the enterprise management selection process must be transparent and efficient; Chinese enterprise management structures must be modernized to the level of the advanced country, such as USA; The international competition must be encouraged and protected. Chinese enterprises should be able to compete on the stage of the world eventually without any protection from the government.

### e) DIVERSIFICATION

Chinese economy must be diversified through: 1) Encouraging foreign investors to participate Chinese economy;2) Attracting all high level human resources from other countries; 3)Absorbing all other countries' advanced management ideas, thoughts, theories, etc. 4)Respect foreigners' living styles, languages, habits, cultures. 5) Facilitate the exchange of students with foreign countries. The diversification can generate creative ideas and innovations. It will keep pumping new things into Chinese economy for it to be energetic.

### f) INTERNATIONAL ENGAGEMENT

International engagement is another way to keep China from lagging behind again. From history, each every time China closes to the outside, Chinese people will lag behind the world and eventually get into huge problems. China must form the engagement mechanism not just some examples. It is vital for China to keep in the frontier of the world not the opposite. The engagement should include: 1) Education and research exchange mechanism. By exchanging scholars and students, China can learn from other countries. 2) Enterprise engagement. Attracting foreign capitals and human resources to China, at the same time, China invest in foreign countries, which will lead the economic benefits to both sides and the international competition. Especially, the latter should put pressures on those who are lagging behind and wants to stop progressive movements. 3) People engagement. China should open to the foreign people visit and living in China. Foreigners will bring new culture and thoughts to China which will be heathy to Chinese economy development.

### g) SUPPORTIVE CULTURE

Chinese culture is very old. It is supportive for old Chinese economic systems. But now, with modernization， Chinese culture is lagging behind. Its ways of thoughts and innovations are not efficient. China should look around the world, especially those advanced countries for the direction to modernize its cultures, such as religions, science, habits, foods, learning, thoughts, relationships, communications, movies, ideas, openness, and so on. China should absorbing other countries supportive culture for innovation and openness, and rebuild a modernized new culture from its lovely old culture for a new century.

If China can fulfil all these strategies, China economy will be very sustainable for a long high speed growth in the next 20-40 years.

## 2.3 COMPETIVENESS STRATEGY

To compete on the world stage as the second largest economy, China must prepare itself as a strong innovation center not just a manufacturing center of the world. Following methods are vital for this goal.

### a) RD MARKETIZATION

To market RD, China is able to use the market mechanism to stimulate the RD growth. By marketing, RD resources will be able to trade in the market, and RD products and technologies can be exchanged through market. The first step is to make policies to force or encourage all enterprises to build up their RD centers, and encourage all colleges to be integrated into enterprises. Therefore, through the capital and human resources free flow, the RD resources will be raised and used to become the major way to drive Chinese economy to a higher level.

### b) INFORMATION TECHNOLOGY BREAK THROUGH AND POPULARIZATION

The information technology is the new revolution for this century. It changes the ways of living and the thinking styles of humankind. To be competitive in this century, China should be able to generate breakthroughs and occupy a center role in the information technology field all the way for the whole century. Also, Chinese people must be educated to handle and utilize the new information technology for the enhancement of their life, work and business.

### c) NEW TECHS

Besides information technology, there are all other technologies which are or become very important, such as biotechnology, life technology, environmental technology, material technology, space technology, etc. with enormous population in the world, China is sufficient to make big contributions to all these new techs and use them to drive Chinese economy with a suitable speed ahead.

### D) POOL OF HUMAN RESOURCES FORMATION

To be sustainable for a long run in the new century, China must form its own human resource pool, such as college students, scholars, RD population, management personnel. Of course, through expanding the old education system, reforming the universities to research oriented institutions, exchanging people with foreign countries, attracting foreign scholars, China is going to build up sufficient human resources for the completion of its modernization process for the new century.

## 2.4 PEOPLE'S QUALITY ENHANCEMENT

Most of Chinese people are farmers. Their education level is too low in average. In China, only one college student for every 20 people. But in the United States, it is 1 for three people. It is almost 10 times lower than USA. Not to say, the education system are too much lagging behind USA. People's quality will decide a nation's potential for a long run growth of its economy. In order to raise the level of Chinese people's average quality, the following ways should be used.

### a) SCIENTIFIC KNOWLEDGE EDUCATION AND POPULARIZATION

The most important part of a people's quality is the master of the scientific knowledge. To enhance Chinese people's scientific knowledge, the expansion of the education system must be taken. Although, in China, the public funding universities are growing slow due to the shortage for the funds, but the private schools can grow faster due to the sufficient funds for the private sectors. As a matter of the fact, in the United States, the private universities are the most important part of USA education systems which takes account of 60% of the college-level institutions. But in China it is only 5% from zero. Also, by building up the popularization mechanism for the science, more and more people will get the scientific knowledge for their living and working.

### b) LEGAL HABITS FORMATION

Another important quality factor for Chinese people is the law knowledge. Most Chinese people are using the old ways, such as power, relationships, relatives, etc. to protect their interests instead of laws. To popularize law knowledge, such as, how to make laws, how to use laws, what law to use, where to get help for law protection, people can be more rational and more orderly for their life and works. The country will be more stable. The economic efficient will be higher and will lower risk. It will take a long time to form the legal habits instead of the irrational ways for protection of rights.

### C) CULTURE MODERNIZATION FOR OPENNESS AND INNOVATION

The third major factor for people's quality is the openness and innovation ability. To form an environment for openness and innovation, China should seek the culture modernization. Through the information super high way, and all level exchanges of the people with foreign countries, business engagements, and participation in the international organizations, such the UN, APEC, AIIB, and G20, etc., Chinese people should learn how to be open and innovative. Through long term diversification procedure as above section, China will eventually form a new culture to support for the new era.

### 2.5 BALANCED DEVELOPMENT STRATEGIES

In order to grow Chinese economy with a suitable high speed for a long term, China must take a balanced development strategy: 1) Balance the urban and farming area development. The modernization difference between this two areas must be balanced to be controllable. 2) Balance the income between the poor and rich [Figure 3]. Policies must be made to raise the income of poor to narrow the gap between this two. 3) Balance the culture and the economy. The culture should be modernized gradually to be supportive for the economic development; 4) Balance the political system and economic system. Political system also should be reformed to release the potential of the Chinese economy. 5) Balance the openness and the national reform. The economic reform should be controllable and openness are compatible with the national economic reform. ; 6) Balance the people's quality and the country modernization speed. Raising people's quality is a long term task and it should be balanced with the nation's modernization steps in order to make a smooth movement to the modern era.

**Figure 3:** Chinese Gini coefficient, it shows Chinese income inequality is getting smaller although it is still very big. The goal is to reduce the Gini coefficient to 0.35 or below in next 20 years.

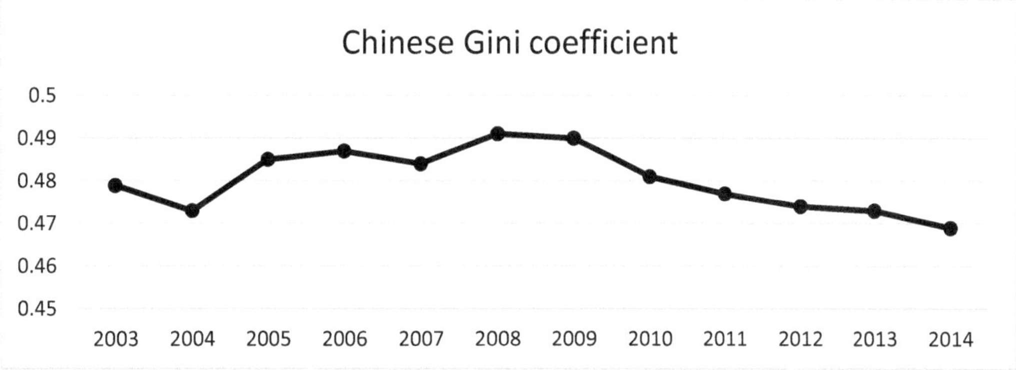


## 3.0 CONCLUSIONS

China is determined to be a completely modernized nation in the new century. The key for the goal to be successful is that Chinese economy must be able to take a fast and healthy way to grow to the new level-the innovation driving level. In about 10 years, China will become the world No.1 economy, but still there is a long way to go for China to become the top real quality driving engine as discussed above. For the next 20 years, the above strategies will lead China into a brand new level of its modernization era, although in about 40 years, Chinese economy will have many jobs to finish. But as the world economic leading engine, China should continue to exhibit a huge impact to the world economy in next 40 years.

## REFERENCES

All data are from Chinese state bureau of statistics with http://www.stats.gov.cn/.

Liang-Xin Li. A Theoretical Approach to the Quantitative Dynamic Structure of Shocks in Macroeconomic Business Cycle. Book: Progress in Economics Research. August 2015, PP133-150. Nova Science Publisher, Inc., New York.

Liang-Xin Li. The Chinese economy after the global crisis. Book: Recession and its aftermath, August 2008, PP81-112. Springer.

Liang-Xin Li. Chinese economic outlook after global crisis, Journal of applied financing and banking, 2011, Vol.1, No.3, P73-81

# 8

# Macroeconomic Determinants of Migrants' Remittances: Evidence from a Panel of Developing Countries

**Safaa Tabit[1], Charaf-Eddine Moussir[2]**

**ABSTRACT**

This work aims to assess the various macroeconomic determinants of migrants' remittances for a panel of 22 developing countries highly dependent observed over the period 1990 to 2014. The results underline the importance of the origin country's GDP, the host country's GDP, inflation, financial development and institutional quality as major determinants of personal remittances. However, the migrant stock, the official exchange rate and the real interest rate in the country of origin do not have a significant influence on remittances received by the panel considered.

Keywords: Developing countries, international migration, panel data, remittances.

---

## 1.0 INTRODUCTION

The consequences generated by international migration arouse considerable debate, both in the migrants' countries of origin and the host countries. This is due to its multidimensional character, which affects several aspects. The fact that the majority of international migrants are from developing countries doesn't make migration a North-South phenomenon. In fact, nearly half of reported migrants move from one developing country to another. In 2014, according to the World Bank's estimates, 3 per cent of the world's population lived outside their country of origin and transferred approximately $493 billion[3]. Developing countries deserve special attention since they receive more than 70 per cent of remittances' flows.

---

[1] Department of Economics, Mohammed V Rabat –Agdal University, Faculty of Juridical, Economic and Social Sciences, Morocco. E-mail: safaa.tabit@gmail.com

[2] Department of Economics, Mohammed V Rabat –Agdal University, Faculty of Juridical, Economic and Social Sciences, Morocco. E-mail: charafmoussir92@gmail.com

[3] 2014's migrant remittances by areas are reported in appendix A

Today, we are witnessing a growing awareness of remittances' benefits in terms of contribution to the economic development of migrants' countries of origin at local, regional and national levels. By way of background, it wasn't until the early 21st century that this question has actually gained visibility within international organizations such as Organization for Economic Cooperation and Development (OECD), International Monetary Fund (IMF), International Organization for Migration (IOM) and the World Bank.

In recent years, migrants' remittances surpassed Official Development Assistance (ODA) received by a lot of countries. However, they are not considered as a substitute for this help, but rather as an alternative source of development finance in many developing countries. (Wanner, 2008). These transfers have also the particularity of being distributed to a large number of people. According to an estimate of the International Fund for Agricultural Development (IFAD), they concern one person out of ten in the world.

Remittances can be defined as interpersonal transfers between migrants and their families remained in the country. According to IMF's Balance of Payments Manual, migrants' remittances include three categories[4]:

i) Compensation to employees comprises wages, salaries, and other remuneration, in cash or in kind, paid to individuals who work in a country other than where they legally reside.
ii) Workers' remittances refer to current transfers by migrants who are employed in new economies and considered residents there and
iii) Migrants' transfers refer to capital transfers of financial assets made by migrants as they move from one country to another and stay for more than one year (IMF, 2009; Straubhaar & Vadean, 2006).

This paper aims to contribute to the literature of migrants' remittances and intends to further understanding of this phenomenon. It analyzes the key macroeconomic determinants that might be responsible for the variation in remittance inflows. Thus, we use a panel of 22 developing countries heavily dependent on remittances over the period 1990-2014.

The rest of the paper is structured as follows: section 2 reviews the existing literature on the determinants of remittances; section 3 presents the data and describes the methodology; section 4 discusses the main empirical findings. The last section concludes with policy implications.

## 2.0 MACROECONOMIC DETERMINANTS OF REMITTANCES: RELATED LITERATURE

Understanding the determinants of remittances and their impacts particularly on economic growth represents a major macroeconomics' research field and a central element of Economic Policy's analysis. In what follows, we propose a range of theoretical and empirical literature related to the topic.

Migrants' remittances represent an external source of capital, for developing countries, steadily increasing (Straubhaar & Vadean, 2006). These transfers take the form of a multitude of relatively small-scale transactions (each migrant transfers to his/her family a varying portion his/ her income). However, once all these transactions are aggregated, we realize how remittances are a significant source of capital for recipient countries.

Understanding the potential role of remittances in the development of countries of origin requires knowing the reasons behind the migrants' decisions to remit. A seminal paper by Lucas and Stark (1985) provides three main motives that drive remittances' decisions: pure altruism, pure self-interest and tempered altruism or enlightened self-interest[5].

---

[4]The categories used by the IMF include only official remittances, they don't capture transfers through informal remittance systems.

[5] For a more detailed explanation, see Hagen-Zanker J. & Siegel M., (2007). The determinants of remittances: A review of the literature. Maastricht Graduate School of Governance.

According to the altruistic model, migrants care about the well-being of those who remained in the country. From a macroeconomic point of view, a deterioration of the economic situation in the country of origin, accompanied by strong frictions on labor market encourage labor force to migrate to high income countries seeking a better life. Given the strong social link existing between the migrants and their families, they would transfer more funds to the latter in order to meet their needs and thus, increase their consumption. Therefore, in times of economic recession, high inflation, unstable exchange rate and constraints in the credit market in the country of origin, migrants are expected to remit more money regularly to their families (Vargas-Silva & Huang, 2006).

In contrast to the altruistic motive, pure self-interest motive underlying the flow of migrant remittances, which is closely related to the theory of portfolio choice, implies that the welfare depends on the migrant only. The latter might transfer money with having as perspective the inheritance of a part of the family's wealth or the desire to see parents take care of his/her property. For instance, an improvement in economic conditions in the country of origin compared to the host country is considered by the migrant as a positive signal for a better return on investment. Thus, a migrant who had decided not to return home might consider a possible return and therefore increase his/her savings at home (Adenutsi, 2014)

However, from a theoretical point of view, Lucas and Stark (1985) argue that remittances can be driven by mixed motives rather than pure altruism or pure self-interest. Hence, tempered altruism or enlightened self-interest presents a less extreme motive. Remittances are viewed, in this case, as an outcome of "implicit family loan agreement" or "implicit co-insurance agreement" (Agarwal R. & Horowitz A., 2002). At first, the migrant plays the role of the insured and the family the role of the insurer (the family finances the initial cost of the migration project). The second step sees the migrant becoming an insurer for the family members left behind.

Note that the various individual or family motives might be the source of migrants' remittances. In fact, remittances might be driven by all these motives together. As Drapier & al. (1997) point out, the empirical validation of each of these motives remains difficult. Although, theoretically, remittances can be analyzed from the altruistic and the self-interest perspectives at the micro level, the macroeconomic models, however, are formulated from a mixed viewpoint combining both pure altruistic motive and pure self-interest motive (Adenutsi, 2014; Mouhoud et al., 2008).

Although migrants' behaviors and individual motivations might explain a part of microeconomic remittances' flows, the economic activity of the host country and the country of origin could explain another. Thus, remittances at the aggregate level can be compared to other key macroeconomic variables of recipient countries. Empirical studies on macroeconomic determinants of remittances' inflows focus on socio-demographic, economic and institutional factors as macroeconomic determinants of remittances (Rahman & Abdul Wadud, 2014; Hagen-Zanker & Siegel, 2007).

The migrant stock in the host country is considered as a crucial determinant of remittances: the higher the volume of workers in the host country is, the greater the volume of remittances would be (Hagen-Zanker & Siegel, 2007).

In addition, various empirical studies (Adenutsi, 2014; Singh et al., 2010; Freund & Spatafora 2008; Vargas-Silva & Huang, 2006; Aydaş et al., 2005; and Lianos, 1997) show that the income gap between the home country and the host country, exchange rate fluctuations, deposit interest rates, political risk and the level of financial development affect the volume and frequency of remittance flows.

In this sense, Chandavarkar (1980) offers one of the first empirical studies on the macroeconomic determinants of remittances (towards Yugoslavia, Turkey, Portugal, Yemen, India and Pakistan), between 1973 and 1977. He highlights the positive impact of the exchange rate on remittances' inflows as well as the importance of a stable institutional environment. Straubhaar (1986) finds, over the period 1963-1982, that only the economic situation of the host country (the level of wages in Germany) is significant, exchange rate and interest rate have no significant impacts on the amounts transferred. El

Sakka & McNabb (1999) show that the differential of exchange rate and the differential of interest rate have an impact on remittances received by Egypt. The remittances sent are invested in real and financial assets, they are not used to improve the consumption of those left behind. Other works such as Shahbaz & Aamir (2009) on Pakistan and Gupta (2005) on India find a negative relationship between remittances and the economic situation of the origin country. These papers which support the hypothesis of an altruistic motive underlying remittances' flows conclude about a counter-cyclical effect of remittances. In other words, a decline in the GDP of the country of origin leads to an increase in migrants' remittances.

Bouhga-Hagbe (2004), Faini (1994) and Elbadawi & Rocha (1992), interested in remittances towards five countries (Morocco, Portugal, Tunisia, Turkey and Yugoslavia) highlight that remittances' flows are driven by altruism. Bouhga-Hagbe (2006) also shows that remittances to Morocco, Tunisia, Egypt, Jordan and Pakistan are motivated by altruism since they increase when agricultural GDP decreases. Similarly, Coulibaly (2009) supports the hypothesis of altruist motive behind remittances. Using 16 Latin American countries data, he finds that remittances' flows respond positively to a deterioration of the economic situation of the home country.

## 3.0 METHODOLOGICAL APPROACH AND EMPIRICAL MODEL

This section provides an empirical evaluation of the macroeconomic determinants of remittances of migrants for a panel of 22 developing countries heavily dependent on remittances over the period 1990-2014. The selection of countries was apprehended by a dependency ratio **Rem / GDP**. Studies such as Danzer & Ivaschenko (2010), Ratha (2006) and the Migration Policy Institute (2006) also suggest this criterion. They define the dependency to remittances as the situation where remittances, as percentage of GDP, are superior to the average. Out of the 104 developing countries, as classified by the World Bank, are selected countries for which data are available for the period considered. 69 countries were selected in the first step. By applying the average dependency ratio which is equal to 4.58%, only 22 countries stand out above average.

**Table 1:** List of 22 countries having a dependency ratio superior to the average

| Country | Dependency ratio | Country | Dependency ratio |
|---|---|---|---|
| Bangladesh | 5.99 | Lesotho | 44.67 |
| Cape Verde | 14.61 | Morocco | 6.64 |
| Dominica | 5.52 | Nigeria | 4.71 |
| Dominican Republic | 7.25 | Philippine | 9.04 |
| Egypt | 6.33 | Samoa | 19.74 |
| El Salvador | 14.51 | Senegal | 6.21 |
| Grenada | 7.42 | Sri Lanka | 7.10 |
| Guatemala | 6.58 | St. Vincent and the Grenadines | 4.66 |
| Honduras | 10.60 | Togo | 5.61 |
| Jamaica | 12.10 | Vanuatu | 5.36 |
| Jordan | 17.65 | Yemen | 13.21 |

Source: calculation of dependency based on WDI data

Our model is based on the empirical literature on the topic. More specifically, it is based on the work of Adenutsi (2014), Rahman & Abdul Wadud (2014) and Singh et al., (2010).

We consider the following specification[6] :

$$\mathbf{R_{i,t}} = \alpha_0 + \alpha_1 \mathbf{LYPH_{i,t}} + \alpha_2 \mathbf{LYPO_{i,t}} + \alpha_3 \mathbf{INF_{i,t}} + \alpha_4 \mathbf{MIGPOP_{i,t}} + \alpha_5 \mathbf{OER_{i,t}} + \alpha_6 \mathbf{TIRD_{i,t}} + \alpha_7 \mathbf{DF_{i,t}} + \alpha_8 \mathbf{QI_{i,t}} + \varepsilon_{i,t}$$

As:

$R_{i,t}$ : Migrant remittances received as a percentage of GDP;

$LYPH_{i,t}$ : The host country's GDP per capita in its logarithmic form[7] ;

$LYPO_{i,t}$: The home country's GDP per capita in its logarithmic form;

$INF_{i,t}$: The home country's inflation rate;

$MIGPOP_{i,t}$: The number of migrants to the home country's population;

$OER_{i,t}$: The home country's official exchange rate;

$TIRD_{i,t}$ : The home country's real interest rate;

$DF_{i,t}$ : Domestic credit to private sector as a percentage of the home country's GDP;

$QI_{i,t}$ : Index of political stability of the home country (institutional quality);

The empirical model is estimated through fixed and random effects estimation methods. The fixed effects model is the estimator of the transformed model using deviations from individual average that eliminate the persistent differences between individuals. This method emphasizes the intra-individual variability. It also has the advantage of being able to identify and measure effects that are not directly observable in cross section. The random effects model assumes, meanwhile, that the individual-specific effects are random. In other words, the error term - which takes into account these effects- and the explanatory variables are uncorrelated. To determine whether a fixed or random effect model is most appropriate, we compute the Hausman test.

## 4.0 MAIN FINDINGS

Fixed effects model and random effects model provide more or less similar results. However, the Hausman test shows that fixed effects model is preferable.

The inspection of results highlights several facts. Indeed, macroeconomic conditions in the host countries and countries of origin are crucial determinants of migrants' remittances. They seem to play a role in absorbing shocks. The coefficient associated with GDP per capita of the home country ***(LYPO)*** is negative and significant. This suggests that when adverse economic shocks affect income in the country of origin, migrants would be willing to remit more in order to protect the well-being of their families. In light of this result, it can be argued that migrants' remittances are motivated by altruism. Likewise, the coefficient of GDP per capita of the host country ***(LYPH)*** is positive and significant, which means that countries with a large Diaspora attract more funds. In other words, the more migrants' communities are in rich countries the more remittances will be important.

As for the number of migrants relative to the home country's population ***(MIGPOP)***, it is positively correlated with the level of remittances, which means that the growing migrant stock abroad contributes to increase flows towards the recipient country. This result is consistent with the findings of Singh et al., (2010) and Barua et al., (2007). However, the fact that the coefficient is not significant is probably due to the selected panel. Furthermore, inflation rate ***(INF)*** affects positively and significantly remittances. This indicates that inflation is not perceived by migrants, as an indicator of economic instability in their countries and could be victims of a monetary illusion. Another way to interpret this result would be an increase in prices of the recipient country makes the situation of remaining households more difficult, leading to a necessity to remit more funds.

[6] The source and description of variables are reported in Appendix B.

[7] Appendix C presents the list of the host countries selected.

**Table 1:** Estimation results

| Endogenous variable: R | Fixed Effects model | Random Effects model |
|---|---|---|
| LYPO | -409597.29* | -8995.6788 |
| | (-2.25) | (-0.06) |
| LYPH | 1350289.3** | 718100.27** |
| | (5.78) | (4.00) |
| MIGPOP | 3.63e+07 | -2.07e+07 |
| | (0.66) | (-0.72) |
| INF | 35800.78* | 33667.481* |
| | (2.13) | (2.14) |
| DF | -23184.951** | -23624.167** |
| | (-6.66) | (-6.39) |
| TIRD | 33115.289 | 27108.703 |
| | (1.87) | (1.59) |
| OER | 43.037081 | 239.41392 |
| | (0.11) | (0.58) |
| QI | 57999.041** | 40053.498* |
| | (3.04) | (2.02) |
| Constant | -9299465.6** | -5735869.2** |
| | (-6.94) | (-5.21) |
| R-squared | 0.47 | 0.43 |
| F test | 14.71** | |
| Wald chi2 | | 84.62** |
| HAUSMAN TEST | | 14.30* |

*, ** significance at 5% and 1% respectively.

The coefficient associated to credit to the private sector as a percentage of GDP ***(DF)*** as an index of financial development is significantly negative, in contrast to other works (Singh et al., 2010; Freund & Spatafora 2005). For the migrants of the panel considered, a less developed financial system of the home country corresponds to higher costs of remittances, which will negatively affect the share of transfer funds through formal channels. Thus, migrant population tends to transfer money via informal channels.

The official exchange rate ***(OER)*** doesn't significantly affect remittances received by our panel of countries. However, our results suggest that remittances don't react significantly to an appreciation of the exchange rate, in contrast to the results presented by Yang (2008) or Chami & al. (2008) but corroborate those found by Singh et al., (2010). The positive sign of this coefficient indicates that investment and insurance motivations aren't the dominant motivations to remit. The real interest rate in the country of origin ***(TIRD)*** is positive but insignificant. An increase in the latter has no effect on the amount of remittances sent by migrants. In this case, for the panel considered, migrants wouldn't be motivated to send more remittances home for investment. This corroborates the results found by Bouhga-Hagbe (2006, 2004), Faini (1994) and Elbadawi & Rocha (1992). The non-significance of the real interest deposit rate allows the rejection of the selfish behavior.

Finally, the coefficient of institutional quality ***(QI)*** is positive and highly significant. It shows that countries with better institutions and / or a more stable political system would receive more remittances. The institutional quality, political rights and governance could be considered as factors that should influence the amount of remittances (Rahman & Abdul Wadud 2014; Singh et al., 2010).

## 5.0 CONCLUSION AND POLICY IMPLICATIONS

This paper intended to identify the key macroeconomic determinants of migrants' remittances of 22 developing countries heavily dependent. The empirical estimation conducted on panel data over the period 1990 - 2014 shows that the home country income, the host country income, inflation, financial development and institutional quality are the main determinants of migrants' remittances of the panel considered. The empirical results suggest that migrants react to macroeconomic conditions at home. This suggests that remittances in these developing countries are mainly driven by altruistic motive which is indicated by significant negative coefficient of domestic per capita GDP. Likewise, the macroeconomic situation of the host countries is crucial as far as remittances are concerned. To this extent, the location of migrants' communities matters, the wealthier the country where migrants are located, the higher the remittances they send back home. Our findings propose, also, that well-functioning domestic institutions seem to be better at unlocking the potential for remittances to contribute to faster economic development in these countries.

Furthermore, as to their economy-wide consequences and because other motives of remittances only become important after altruism, a labor-exporting country will receive more remittances on a regular basis if there is an investment-friendly macroeconomic environment. In order to attract more remittances, policymakers in the developing countries should think more about implementing stable and pro-growth policies. It is, therefore, recommended to devise strategies aimed at achieving a higher and sustained rate of economic growth, improved financial market development and exchange rate stability.

As any research work, this paper could still be improved and extended into various directions. Data availability represents the main limit. A study incorporating more countries would increase, possibly, variables' variability and therefore lead to more accurate results. In addition, it would be appropriate to consider a dynamic modeling rather than static modeling.

## REFERENCES

Adenutsi Deodat E. (2014). Macroeconomic Determinants of Workers' Remittances and Compensation of Employees in Sub-Saharan Africa. The Journal of Developing Areas, 48(1), 337-360.

Agarwal R., Horowitz A. (2002). Are International Remittances Altruism or Insurance? Evidence from Guyana Using Multiple-Migrant Households. Journal of Development Economics, 30(11), 2033-2044.

Aydas O.T., Neyapti B., Metin-Ozcan K. (2005). Determinants of Workers' Remittances: The Case of Turkey. Emerging Markets Finance and Trade, 41(3), 53-69.

Barua S. M., Alauddin M., Akhtaruzzaman M. (2007). Determinants of Workers' Remittances in Bangladesh: An Empirical Study. Policy Analysis Unit. Bangladesh Bank, No. WP, 713.

Bouhga-Hagbe J. (2004). A Theory of Worker's Remittances with an Application to Morocco (No. 4-194). International Monetary Fund.

Bouhga-Hagbe J. (2006). Altruism and Workers' Remittances: Evidence from Selected Countries in the Middle East and Central Asia (No. 6-130).International Monetary Fund.

Chami R., Barajas A., Cosimano T., Fullenkamp C., Gapen M., Montiel. P. (2008). Macroeconomic Consequences of Remittances (No. 259). International Monetary Fund.

Chandavarkar A. B. (1980). Use of Migrants' Remittances in Labor Exporting Countries. Finance and Development, 17(2), 36.

Coulibaly D. (2009). Macroeconomic Determinants of Migrants' Remittances: New Evidence from a Panel VAR. Centre d'Economie de la Sorbonne.

Danzer A.M., Ivaschenko O. (2010). Migration Patterns in a Remittances Dependent Economy: Evidence from Tajikistan during the Global Financial Crisis. Migration Letters, 7(2), 190.

Drapier C., Jayet H., Rapoport H. (1997). Les motifs des migrations et des transferts associés. Une revue de littérature sur les conséquences attendues pour les pays en développement. Région et Développement, 6, 41-65.

Elbadawi I., Rocha R.R. (1992). Determinants of Expatriate Workers' Remittances in North Africa and Europe, (No. 1038). World Bank Working Paper.

El-Sakka M., McNabb R. (1999). The Macroeconomic Determinants of Emigrant Remittances. World Development, 27(8), 1493-1502.

Faini R. (1994). Workers' Remittances and the Real Exchange Rate: A quantitative Framework. Journal of Population Economics, 7(2), 235-245

Freund C.L., Spatafora N. (2008). Remittances: Transaction Costs, Determinants and Informality. Journal of Development Economics, no 3704.

Gupta P. (2005). Macroeconomic Determinants of Remittances: Evidence from India. IMF Working Paper, WP/05/224.

Hagen-Zanker J., Siegel M. (2007). The determinants of remittances: A review of the literature. Maastricht Graduate School of Governance, MGSoG/2007/WP003.

IMF. (2009). Balance of Payments and International Investment Position Manual (Sixth Edition). International Monetary Fund, Washington D.C.

Lianos T. P. (1997). Factors Determining Migrant Remittances: The Case of Greece. International Migration Review, 72-87.

Lucas R.E.B., Stark O. (1985). Motivations to Remit: Evidence from Botswana. Journal of Political Economy, 901-918.

Marshall Monty G., Jaggers K. (2011). Polity IV Project: Political Regime Characteristics and Transitions, 1800-2009. Dataset Users' Manual. Center for International Development and Conflict Management, University of Maryland.

Migration Policy Institute. (2006). Immigration and America's Future: A New Chapter. Geo. JL & Pub. Pol'y, 5, 473.

Mouhoud E.M., Oudinet J., Unan E. (2008). Macroeconomic Determinants of Remittances in the Southern and Eastern Mediterranean Countries. Working Paper 7115. Paris, France: CEPN.

Parsons C.R., Skelden R., Walmsey T., Winters L.A. (2007). Quantifying International Migration: A Database of Bilateral Migration Stocks. World Bank Policy Research Working Paper, (4165).

Rahman A., Abdul Wadud M. (2014). Macroeconomic Determinants of Remittances in South Asian countries: A Dynamic Panel Study. Bangladesh Economic Association.

Ratha D. (2006). Trends. Determinants and Macroeconomic Effects of Remittances. Global Economic Prospects 2006: Economic Implications of Remittances and Migration, 85-115.

Sevestre P. (2002). Econométrie des données de panel. (pp. 109-152). Paris: Dunod.

Shahbaz M., Aamir I.I. (2009). Determinants of Workers' Remittances: Implications for the Poor People of Pakistan. European Journal of Scientific Research, 25(1), 130-144.

Singh R.J., Haacker M., Lee K.W, Le Goff M. (2010). Determinants and Macroeconomic Impact of Remittances in Sub-Saharan Africa. Journal of African Economies, 20(2), 312-340.

Straubhaar T., Vadean F. P. (2006). Les transferts de fonds internationaux des émigrés et leur rôle dans le développement. OCDE. Migrations, transferts de fonds et développement, Paris, 13-40.

Vargas-Silva C., P. Huang. (2006). Macroeconomic determinants of worker's remittances: Host versus home country's economic conditions. The Journal of International Trade, Economic Development, 15(1), 81-99.

Wanner P. (2008). L'apport des migrants au développement : une perspective économique. Annuaire Suisse de politique de développement, 27(2), 121-131.

Yang D. (2008). International Migration. Remittances and Household Investment: Evidence from Philippine Migrants' Exchange Rate Shocks. The Economic Journal, 118(528), 591-630.

## APPENDICES

**Appendix A:** Migrants' remittances by region (% of GDP)

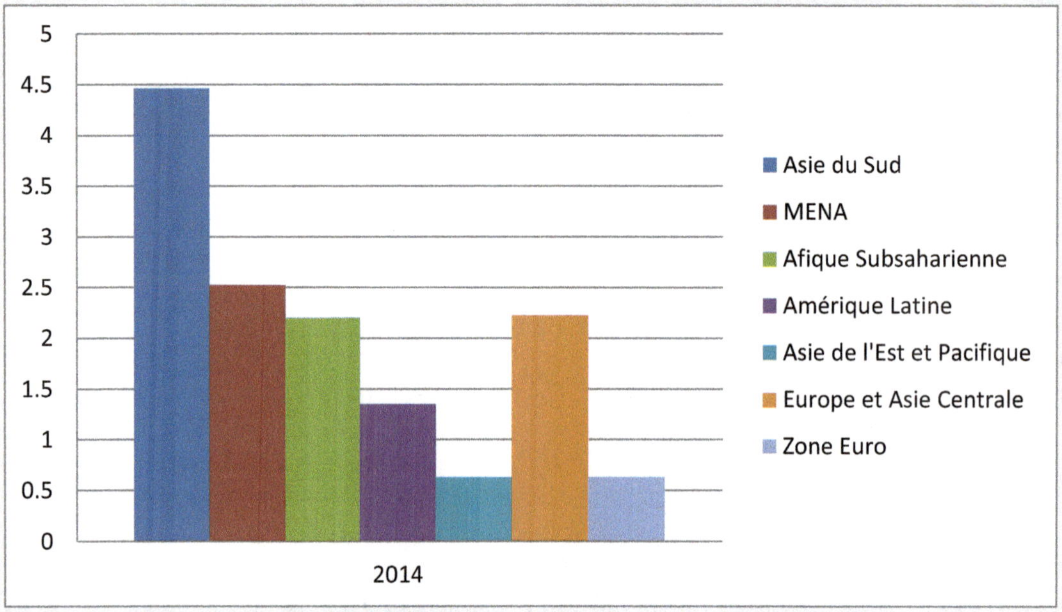


Source: Calculation made based on World Bank data

**Appendix B:** Source and description of variables

| Variables | Description | Source |
| --- | --- | --- |
| $R_{i.t}$ | The sum of the two sections of the balance of payments: personal transfers and compensation of employees (% of GDP) | |
| $LYPH_{i.t}$ | GDP relative to the population of the home country | World Development Indicators (WDI) |
| $LYPO_{i.t}$ | GDP relative to the population of the host country | |
| $INF_{i.t}$ | measured by change in the consumer price index | International Financial Statistics (IFS) |
| $MIGPOP_{i.t}$ | Number of migrants relative to population of the country of origin | Calculation based on WDI data; Parsons , al. (2007) |
| $OER_{i.t}$ | Annual average of the national currency against the US dollar | IFS |
| $TIRD_{i.t}$ | Deposit interest rate minus inflation | Calculation based on WDI data |
| $DF_{i.t}$ | Total credit to private sector ( % of GDP) | WDI |
| $QI_{i.t}$ | polity2: Index used to capture the quality of governance and institutions. it varies between -10 for a weak governance and 10 otherwise. | Marshall , Jaggers (2011) |

**Appendix C: List of host countries of the 22 selected countries**

| *Country of origin* | Major host countries 1 | 2 | 3 | *Selected host country* |
|---|---|---|---|---|
| Bangladesh | Pakistan (PAK) | India (IND) | Saudi Arabia (SAU) | Pakistan |
| Cape Verde | Portugal (PRT) | United States of America (USA) | Mozambique (MOZ) | Portugal |
| Dominica | United States of America (USA) | Great Britain (GBR) | U.S. Virgin Islands (VIR) | United States of America |
| Dominican Republic | United States of America (USA) | Spain (ESP) | Germany (DEU) | United States of America |
| Egypt | Saudí Arabia (SAU) | Jordan (JOR) | United States of America (USA) | Saudí Arabia |
| El Salvador | United States of America (USA) | Canada (CAN) | Pakistan (PAK) | United States of America |
| Grenade | United States of America (USA) | Trinidad and Tobago (TTO) | Great Britain (GBR) | United States of America |
| Guatemala | United States of America (USA) | Mexico (MEX) | Belize (BLZ) | United States of America |
| Honduras | United States of America (USA) | Nicaragua (NIC) | Salvador (SLV) | United States of America |
| Jamaica | United States of America (USA) | Grande Bretagne (GBR) | Canada (CAN) | United States of America |
| Jordan | Palestine (PSE) | Saudi Arabia (SAU) | United States of America (USA) | Palestine |
| Lesotho | Mozambique (MOZ) | Zimbabwe (ZWE) | South Africa (ZAF) | Mozambique |
| Morocco | France (FRA) | Spain (ESP) | Germany (DEU) | France |
| Nigeria | Sudan (SDN) | United States of America (USA) | Great Britain (GBR) | Sudan |

| | | | | |
|---|---|---|---|---|
| Philippine | United States of America (USA) | Malaysia (MYS) | Canada (CAN) | United States of America |
| Samoa | American Samoa (ASM) | United States of America (USA) | New Zealand (NZL) | American Samoa |
| Senegal | Gambia (GMB) | France (FRA) | Italy (ITA) | Gambia |
| Sri Lanka | India (IND) | Saudi Arabia (SAU) | Canada (CAN) | India |
| St. Vincent and the Grenadines | United States of America (USA) | Canada (CAN) | Trinidad and Tobago (TTO) | United States of America |
| Togo | Nigeria (NGA) | Benin (BEN) | Burkina Faso (BFA) | Nigeria |
| Vanuatu | Wallis and Futuna (WLF) | Austria (AUS) | France (FRA) | Wallis and Futuna |
| Yemen | Saudi Arabia (SAU) | Israel (ISR) | Jordan (JOR) | Saudi Arabia |

Source: Parsons et al., (2007)

# 9

# The Effects of Oil Price Volatility on the Economic Sectors of Libya

**Nagmi M. Moftah Aimer**[1]

**ABSTRACT**

Fluctuations in oil price and its impact on economic development is an important issue facing a growing number of world economies. A simple changes in oil prices lead to negative or positive effects on all the economic sectors. This paper seeks to investigate the impact of oil price volatility on economic sectors in the Libyan economy context on the basis of annual data spanning from 1968-2012. The Johansen based Co-integration technique is applied to examine the sensitivity of economic sectors to volatility in oil prices in the long-run. And the short-run relationship is tested by Vector Error Correction Model. Through examining the results, that there is a long-term relationship of oil prices on the agriculture, construction, manufacturing and transport sectors. Finally, this study concludes that increases in oil price did not significantly affect the manufacturing sector in aggregate terms. Moreover, the negative impact on the sector of manufacturing and agriculture. Thus, this study has a significant impact in the Libyan economy in policy development on oil prices. The Libyan government needs to control the price to make sure that price volatility will not harm the manufacturing, agriculture, construction and transport sectors.

Keywords: Economic sectors, granger causality, Libyan economy, manufacturing, oil price volatility, VECM.

---

## 1.0 INTRODUCTION

Crude oil is one of the world's most heavily traded commodities. Oil still remains the main source of energy for economic sectors. So, the volatility of oil prices may impose a significant impact on the economic conditions in the various countries. Crude oil prices change because of the interaction between the forces of supply and demand in the global commodity markets.

We can see that from the past recent years, oil prices have been quite volatile, there is a strong likelihood that sometimes oil prices will increase again, in addition to, many issues have emerged due to rising crude

[1] Social Sciences Institute, Department of Business Administration, Kastamonu University, Turkey. E-mail: najmimuftah@gmail.com

oil prices throughout the world. According to Moradkhani et al. (2010) that higher energy prices lead to other prices increase, such as crude oil, which plays an important role in determining the other goods. Also, the rise in oil prices caused the production costs increase, leading to a decline in production. In addition to, the rise in oil prices leads to increased productivity which negatively affects the economic performance. Several previous studies have proved that an increase in oil price can cause a slowdown in GDP (Husain et al., 2015). The subsidy is typically provided to mitigate such problems and eschewal an economic crisis.

Many economic sectors, such as manufacturing, agriculture, transportation, construction, and use oil to produce outputs. Thus the falling price of oil is a reflection of weak economic sectors. According to Aimer (2016) say that 10% rise in oil prices leads to a 54% increase in GDP of Libya. Furthermore, at the industrial level, low oil prices may not only bring down business expenditures for the manufacturing industries, such as logistic companies and aviation industries, but also affect prices on agricultural products as well.

The slowdown in the agriculture sector as a result of higher oil prices, as this agriculture sector inevitably consumes oil to run activities the field of agriculture. Thus, the high price of oil is causing increased expenditures for the agriculture sector, can trigger increased machinery costs and hardware that agricultural producers have to bear (Dhuyvetter and Kastens, 2005). In the context of the construction sector, oil prices high can also affect this sector as it pushes to the height the costs of raw materials.

Suppliers inevitably increase prices of raw material to contractors to cover the high costs of transport. It also caused higher prices higher shipping costs. In the construction sector, and the increase in oil prices leads contractors for higher raw material costs (Copiello, 2016). Similarly, the manufacturing sector is influenced an oil price increase through high production costs. This leads to a decline in the amount of production, which increases the price of products, thus reducing the demand for consumer goods. Rising oil price may impact on the quantity and cost of raw materials purchased principally for producers (Ee et al., 2015), The transport sector is very energy intensive and thus the impact of rising oil prices translated into higher fuel prices is important. It is generally believed that demand for transport is very rigid and thus should be expected only minor modifications. According to Seth et al. (2016) explained that as oil price increases, transportation costs are affected, thus reducing transport demand.

According to some economists Syed (2010), Ito (2008), and Mallik and Chowdhury (2011) Indicates that if economic growth is not affected fluctuations in the price of oil on economic growth prices policies are not necessary. But these researchers were not considering any nominated sector of the economy for policy making. Before any policy on oil prices, it should first be seen various economic sectors. Torul and Alper (2010), Hanson et al. (1993) Which sectors of the economy were taken into account had done so only to achieve the effects of one or two sectors. The manufacturing, agriculture, construction, and transportation sectors are the main economic sectors that substantially contribute to Libyan GDP. For that, this study is trying influence of oil price fluctuations on manufacturing, agriculture, construction, and transportation sectors.

Movements in oil prices, An important factor in the production process, affecting the financial performance and cash flows of the companies, in turn, influencing firms dividend payments, retained earnings, and equity prices (Benli, 2008).

Also are important steps in this regard, for example, in Taiwan "renewable energy development plan" of the installed capacity of solar power generation capacity planned between the years 2002-2020 in accordance with the aimed to reach 10 percent (Kizgin et al., 2013). Due to the expansion of financial derivative instruments, which have often been held accountable for giving rise to the financial crisis in 2008 (Ulusoy, 2011). According to costs Erdoğan (2011) businesses seeking capital, uncertainties affecting the cost of capital are beneficial because it eliminates and reduces compliance costs. Marketable securities, which can be considered as an indicator of accounting standards increase refers to temporary investments that are bought or sold for companies, the evaluation of the fair value method of marketable securities is another important issue (Erdoğan et al., 2016). Hierarchical structure may be useful in the detection of the theoretical description of financial markets and in the search of economic factors affecting special groups of stocks (Ulusoy et al., 2012). The figure 1 shows the annual series of the prices of crude oil (WTI) from 1986-2015.

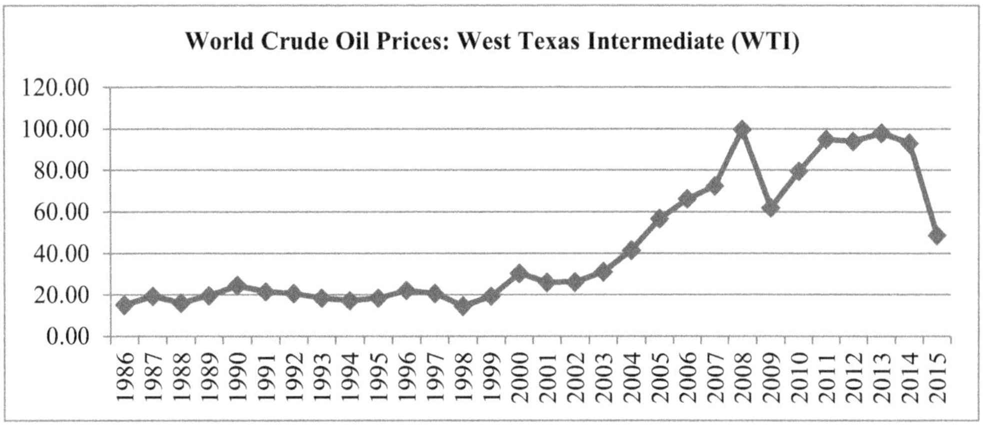


Figure 1: Trends of the annually, world crude oil price US dollars,
Source: US. Energy information administration.

Libya is heavily dependent on crude oil exports, thus volatility in crude oil prices is a cause for concern. Leading to, any particular shock in oil prices can have a significant effect on government revenue and the Libyan economy. Thus, this will negatively affect the competitiveness and growth of the non-hydrocarbon economy. This paper seeks to empirically analyze the impact of crude oil price on the manufacturing, agriculture, construction and transportation sectors in Libya. To fill out the gap in the literature that is examining the consequences of oil price shocks on this sectors using annual data from 1986 to 2012, the secondary data were used for the empirical analyses which were derived from the energy information administration. The rest of this paper is structured as follows: The second section provides an overview of the literature review. The third section presents the econometric methodology. While section four describes results and discussion. It concludes with the final section of the paper with the study results.

## 2.0 LITERATURE REVIEW ON METHODOLOGY

The issue of fluctuating oil prices, many researchers to investigate the harmful effects of fluctuations in oil prices on the economy have attracted. Consequently, there are many models that have been used by previous research to study the effects of oil prices.

Guidi (2009), this study examined the effect of oil prices changes on the manufacturing and services sector in the UK, using a VAR model, found that positive impact of changes in oil prices on the manufacturing sector. In addition, the positive changes in oil prices determine the continued contraction in manufacturing. Negative changes in oil prices, showing that manufacturing output does not increase significantly despite the lower oil prices. The services sector is much more affected by oil prices decreases than increases. They found that the manufacturing sector is much more affected by changes in oil prices from the services sector.

Torul and Alper (2010), examined the relationship between oil price and the manufacturing sector in the Turkish economy, using the VAR model for Turkey from 1988 to 2006 data. They conclude that increases in oil price did not significantly affect the manufacturing sector in aggregate terms, some sub-sectors are adversely affected. Fukunaga et al. (2010), analyze the influence of oil price changes on industrial output of the economies of the United States and Japan, the results provided evidence that the inverse impact of oil price changes on industrial output seems in most of the cases with varying degrees, both in the oil industry-intensive industry or not. Shaari et al. (2013), explore the effects of oil price shocks on economic sectors in Malaysia, using the Co-integration model, and the results indicated that the long-term effects of oil prices on the agriculture, construction, manufacturing, and transportation sectors. In addition, the researcher found that the construction sector depends on the fluctuations in oil prices.

Taghizadeh Hesary et al., (2015) the impact of volatility in oil prices on economic sectors in Japan. Using employ a VAR model by using quarterly data from Q1: 1990 until Q1: 2014. The researchers found that industrial and transport sectors were strongly sensitive to the drastic oil prices volatility. Moreover, The researchers concluded that after the Fukushima disaster in 2011, which led to the shutdown of nuclear power plants in Japan, because of greater reliance on oil imports, the sensitivity of most sectors to volatility declined in oil prices. Riaz et al. (2016), investigate the impact of the uncertainty of oil prices on manufacturing sector of Pakistan. Using the analysis an EGARCH model. Results revealed that manufacturing production is non-linearly related oil price uncertainty, as initially manufacturing production in Pakistan increases with an increase in uncertainty of oil prices but after a threshold level manufacturing production starts declining with the increase in oil price uncertainty. Moreover, impulse response function is shown short run effects of oil price uncertainty contractionary effects on industrial production.

Mahboub and Ahmad (this study examined the effects of oil price shocks on the manufacturing sector in Saudi Arabia during the quarterly period 2002–2014. Using estimate a VAR model. The study showed that there is no long run effect of oil price shocks on the manufacturing sector. The results show that oil price shocks do not affect the manufacturing sector in the short run, and it may have an effect on the manufacturing sector after the tenth quarter.

Although oil prices plays a key role in industrial production and social and economic development of countries, many studies have focused on the existence of a causal relationship between oil price volatility and production. This paper will contribute to the existing knowledge through the study of the impact of oil price volatility on the manufacturing industry, agriculture, and construction sector. In addition, this paper is important because it is the first of its kind in Libya in terms of a more robust estimation technique. It would be interesting to discover whether the conclusions concerning the effects of oil prices shocks on output in the economies of oil exporting also apply to a country such as Libya. The aim of our study is to investigate the effects of oil price volatility on the economic sectors of Libya using Johansen co-integration test and vector error correction model (VECM) for a yearly time series data over the period 1986 to 2012.

## 3.0 METHODOLOGY

In this part of the paper, the impact of oil price volatility on economic sectors through Vector Error Correction Model (VECM) using time series methods of co-integration and Granger Causality techniques. For this purpose, the data set will be determined, thereafter time series properties of the series will be tested. This empirical analysis and focuses on variables (crude oil prices, agriculture, manufacturing, construction and transportation sector) in Libya by the annual time series data from 1986 and 2012. Where:

### 3.1 DATA ANALYSIS

The five variables used in this analysis are comprised of the crude oil price and the four economic sectors, all in logarithmic terms. Table 1 shows the symbols and definitions of these variables.

GDP gross domestic product by economic sector 1986-2012 (At current factor income and in millions of LYD). All the data used were extracted from the statistic of Central Bank of Libya (2015) and Ministry of Planning. Table 2 shows the regression result for oil price shock and economic sectors in Libya. As both time series are non-stationary, we examine the interdependence between their annual logarithmic returns, which fulfill the condition of stationarity. The annual logarithmic returns are expressed by the equation: $r_t = \log(\frac{x_t}{x_{t-1}})$ (1)

Where, χ is the average annual value of the variable at time t or (t-1).

Table 1: Variables and definitions

| Variable | Definition |
|---|---|
| Log (OIL) | In of crude oil prices: West Texas Intermediate (WTI). |
| Log (MAN) | In of manufacturing sector's gross domestic product. |
| log (Prospects) | In of building and construction sector's gross domestic product. |
| log (AGR) | In of agriculture, hunting, forestry and fishing sector's gross domestic product. |
| log (TRAN) | In of transport, storage and telecommunications sector's gross domestic product. |

Source: Authors' compilation.

Table 2: The regression results for oil price shock and economic sectors in Libya

| Variable | Coefficient | Std. Error | t-Statistic | Prob. |
|---|---|---|---|---|
| C | -0.581667 | 0.533471 | -1.090345 | 0.2874 |
| LNTRAN | 1.082613 | 0.137819 | 7.855351 | 0.0000 |
| LNMAN | 0.008647 | 0.137006 | 0.063116 | 0.9502 |
| LNCON | 0.349226 | 0.142414 | 2.452192 | 0.0226 |
| LNAGR | -0.924212 | 0.144369 | -6.401724 | 0.0000 |
| R-squared | 0.950173 | | Mean dependent var | 3.442291 |
| Adjusted R-squared | 0.941114 | | S.D. dependent var | 0.642763 |
| S.E. of regression | 0.155976 | | Akaike info criterion | -0.712651 |
| Sum squared resid | 0.535229 | | Schwarz criterion | -0.472681 |
| Log likelihood | 14.62078 | | Hannan-Quinn criter. | -0.641295 |
| F-statistic | 104.8821 | | Durbin-Watson stat | 1.914313 |
| Prob(F-statistic) | 0.000000 | | | |

Source: Computed from Appendix 1, using Eviews7.

Table 2 shows that the oil price shock has small opposite impact on the agriculture. In other words, Increased oil prices by 1% leads to a decline of $0.92 agriculture sector. Increased crude oil prices by 1% leads to increased manufacturing industry, construction and transport of $0.008, $0.34 and $1.08 respectively.

The R square value in the Linear Regression equation described that the independent variables describe the dependent variable oil price by almost 84%. The remaining portion of oil price is impacted through other macro-economic variables which is only 16%. The results are described by the following equation

$$LNWTI = 1.08LNTRAN + 0.008*LNMAN + 0.34LNCON - 0.92LNAGR - 0.58$$

The VECM model provides long-term relationship and also short-term dynamics of the variables. This model shows the achievement of long-term equilibrium and the rate of change in the short term to achieve equilibrium. In the long run, endogenous variables must converge to their co-integrated relations. To determine the characteristics of time series for each of the variables in the model, the modeling strategy adopted for this paper passes through three stages.

Must be estimated the stationary of time series. Further steps of modeling are: Firstly, determine the order of integration of variables via Augmented Dickey Fuller test (ADF). Secondly, if the variables are integrated in the same order, by the Johansen test of co-integration, technique which serves to find long-term relationship and short-term dynamics. Based on the theoretical derivation of VECM mode, we determine:

### 3.2 STATIONARY TEST

The first step, natural logarithms of the data have been taken before passing to the analysis process. Then, stationarity tests have been performed for each variant. We must test each of the series in the levels and in the first difference. All variables were tested in levels using the Augmented Dickey-Fuller (ADF) test. Consider the equation below:

### 3.3 CO-INTEGRATION TEST

The Johansen co-integration test (Johansen & Juselius, 1990) is applied to study the long-run equilibrium relationship between the variables. This test reveals whether non-stationary series at the level act together in the long run. In case of determination of co-integration relationship (co-integration vector) that shows the presence of the long run relationship between variables.

$$x_t = c + \sum_{j=1}^{p} \Gamma_j \, \Delta x_{t-j} + u_t \qquad (2)$$

There are two types of Johansen test, namely; Trace and Maximal Eigenvalue statistics, both commonly use to ascertain the number of Co-integration rank or in determining the number of Co-integrating vectors. Both tests might not always indicate the same number of Co-integrating vectors. A Co-integrating vector is attained when obtained critical values are more the values for trace and maximum Eigenvalue statistics.

### 3.4 THE VECTOR ERROR CORRECTION MODEL

This is based on a vector autogressive framework; where an error correction term is incorporated into the model. The reason for the error correction term is the same as with the standard error correction model, it measures any movements away from the long run equilibrium and measures the speed of adjustment of the short run dynamics to the long run equilibrium time path. The coefficient is expected to be negatively signed, statistical significant and lie between zero and one.

Moreover, the VECM model treats all series endogenously thereby allowing the predicted variable to explain itself using its own lags, lags of independent variables, the error correction term and the residual. The VECM can be expressed as;

$$\Delta Y_{1t} = \alpha_0 + \sum_{j=1}^{k} \alpha_{1j} \, \Delta Y_{1t-j} + \sum_{j=1}^{k} \alpha_{2j} \, \Delta Y_{2t-j} + \lambda_1 ECT_{t-1} + \varepsilon_{1t} \qquad (3)$$

$$\Delta Y_{2t} = \beta_0 + \sum_{j=1}^{k} \beta_{1j} \, \Delta Y_{1t-j} + \sum_{j=1}^{k} \beta_{2j} \, \Delta Y_{2t-j} + \lambda_2 ECT_{t-1} + \varepsilon_{2t} \qquad (4)$$

$ECT_{t-1}$ is the lagged value of the error correction model. Coefficients $\lambda_1$ and $\lambda_2$ show the equilibrium ratio. When Cointegration is considered, $\alpha_{1j}$ from the equation 6 and $\beta_{1j}$ from the equation are tested whether they are significant in group of F-test and also coefficients of the error correction model $\lambda_1$ and $\lambda_2$ are tested whether significant or not.

### 3.5 GRANGER CAUSALITY TEST

Causality is a kind of statistical feedback concept which is widely used in the building of forecasting models. The Co-integration tests only give an indication of whether there exists a long- run relationship between oil price and economic sectors. However the direction of this relationship is of important. The Granger Causality test is then performed to determine the direction of the relationship between the variables used in the model (Granger, 1980).

Granger (1980) described one variable ($X_t$) to granger cause another variable ($Y_t$) if the lagged values of $X_t$ can predict $Y_t$ and vice-versa. The test is based on the equation below:

$$Y_t = \Upsilon_0 + \sum_{z=1}^{p} \Upsilon_z Y_{t-z} + \sum_{i=1}^{q} \lambda_i X_{t-1} + u_t \qquad (5)$$

$$X_t = \emptyset_0 + \sum_{z=1}^{p} \delta_z X_{t-z} + \sum_{i=1}^{q} \Psi_i y_{t-1} + v_t \qquad (6)$$

Testing the null hypothesis of $H_0$: $\lambda_1 = \lambda_2 = ..... = \lambda_z = 0$, is a test that X does not Granger-cause Y. Similarly, testing the null hypothesis of $H_0$: $\Psi_1 = \Psi_2 = ..... = \Psi_z = 0$, is a test that Y does not Granger-cause X. In each case, a rejection of the null hypothesis implies there is Granger causality.

## 4.0 EMPIRICAL RESULTS

### 4.1 UNIT ROOT TEST

Tables 3 and 4 presents empirical results of the unit root tests and indicate that the natural logarithms of the variables are all I(1) processes at 5% significance level. The null of unit root can therefore be rejected for the first differences of all variables. Tables 2 and 3 report the results of tests of Co-integration.

Table 3: Augmented Dicky Fuller test results

| Variable | At Level | | | First Difference | | | Order of Integration |
|---|---|---|---|---|---|---|---|
| | Non | Intercept, Trend | Intercept | Non | Intercept, Trend | Intercept | |
| lnWTI | 1.510<br>(0.9640) | -1.918<br>(0.6165) | -0.384<br>(0.8981) | -5.262<br>(0.0000)** | -5.723<br>(0.0005)** | -5.633<br>(0.0001)** | I(0) |
| lnAGR | 0.588<br>(0.8370) | -0.8083<br>(0.9518) | -1.779<br>(0.3819) | -4.782<br>(0.0000)** | -5.201<br>(0.0016)** | -4.770<br>(0.0008)** | I(0) |
| lnCON | 0.7870<br>(0.3815) | -1.935<br>(0.6073) | -1.422<br>(0.555) | -4.962<br>(0.0000)** | -4.942<br>(0.0006)** | -4.942<br>(0.0006)** | I(0) |
| lnMAN | 0.805<br>(0.8803) | -3.862<br>(0.0289)*** | -1.520<br>(0.5070) | -7.330<br>(0.0000)** | -7.702<br>(0.0000)** | -7.614<br>(0.0000)** | I(0) |
| lnTRAN | 4.211<br>(0.9999) | -1.593<br>(0.7679) | -0.699<br>(0.8298) | -2.946<br>(0.0049)** | -4.134<br>(0.0168)** | -4.224<br>(0.0031)** | I(0) |

Note: *, ** and *** indicates the rejection of the null hypothesis of non-stationary at 1%, 5% and 10% Significance level.

Table 4: Phillips & Perron test results

| Variable | At Level | | | First Difference | | | Order of Integration |
|---|---|---|---|---|---|---|---|
| | Non | Intercept, Trend | Intercept | Non | Intercept, Trend | Intercept | I(1) |
| D(lnWTI) | 1.679<br>(0.9740) | -1.881<br>(0.6353) | -0.292<br>(0.9134) | -5.258<br>(0.0000)** | -5.739<br>(0.0005)** | -5.639<br>(0.0001)** | I(1) |
| D(lnAGR) | 0.585<br>(0.8364) | -0.848<br>(0.9472) | -1.780<br>(0.3812) | -4.782<br>(0.0000)** | -5.202<br>(0.0016)** | -4.770<br>(0.0008)** | I(1) |
| D(lnCON) | 0.3884<br>(0.7888) | -2.211<br>(0.4638) | -1.426<br>(0.5537) | -4.962<br>(0.0000)** | -5.027<br>(0.0023)** | -4.942<br>(0.0006)** | I(1) |
| D(lnMAN) | 1.161<br>(0.9322) | -3.863<br>(0.0289)*** | -1.2946<br>(0.6164) | -7.272<br>(0.0000)** | -7.681<br>(0.0000)** | -7.592<br>(0.0000)** | I(1) |
| D(lnTRAN) | 3.932<br>(0.9999) | -1.797<br>(0.6767) | -0.699<br>(0.8299) | -2.818<br>(0.0068)** | -4.129<br>(0.0169)** | -4.220<br>(0.0031)** | I(1) |

Note: *, ** and *** indicates the rejection of the null hypothesis of non-stationary at 1%, 5% and 10% significance level. Note: D refers to first differences. Source: Computed by using Eviews 7.

## 4.2 CO-INTEGRATION RELATIONS TEST (JOHANSEN CO-INTEGRATION TEST)

The results of the previous section suggest that a long term relationship may exist between oil price and economic sectors which are of the same integration order. Therefore, Johansen Co-integration tests are performed to test the existence of the Co-integration relationship between the variables. The results are shown below:

Table 5: Co-integration relations test

| Hypothesis | | Max-Eigen | Critical Value | Trace Statistic | Prob |
|---|---|---|---|---|---|
| $H_0$ | $H_1$ | Statistic | (Eigen) at 5% | | |
| r =0 | r ≥ 1 | 0.844436 | 69.818 | 108.100* | 0.0000 |
| r ≤ 1 | r ≥ 2 | 0.706868 | 47.856 | 61.583* | 0.0016 |
| r ≤ 2 | r ≥ 3 | 0.519100 | 29.797 | 30.904* | 0.0371 |
| r ≤ 3 | r ≥ 4 | 0.384035 | 15.494 | 12.602 | 0.1302 |
| r ≤ 4 | r ≥ 5 | 0.019344 | 3.841 | 0.488 | 0.4847 |

Trace test indicates 3 Co-integrating eqn(Guidi) at the 0.05 level. * denotes rejection of the hypothesis at the 0.05 level. Source: Computed by using Eviews 7.

According to the Trace test statistics in Table 4, that both of the trace statistics and the maximum-Eigen value statistics were statistically significant to reject the null hypotheses r=0, r≤1 and r≤2 is rejected by 5% against the alternative hypotheses r≥1 and r≤2. This indicates exists the long-run equilibrium relationship between oil price and all the variables used in the model. According to the Table above, there are three Co-integration relation between variables (the manufacturing industry - construction - Transportation - Agriculture - Oil prices) in the long run.

## 4.3 VECTOR ERROR CORRECTION MODEL (VECM)

Premised on the results of the Johansen Co-integration test which suggests the existence of a long run Co-integration among variables and coupled with the I(1) order condition in the series, we further employed VECM estimation to analyze the long-run dynamics in the variables. Consequently, Table 6 below provides the results of oil prices impact on economic sectors.

Table 6: Results of vector error correction model

| Dependent Variable: DLNY | | | | |
|---|---|---|---|---|
| Variable | Coefficient | Std. Error | t-Statistic | Prob. |
| C | -0.013907 | 0.050610 | -0.274792 | 0.7863 |
| DLN (agriculture sector's) | -0.947877 | 0.328811 | -2.882743 | 0.0092 |
| DLN(construction sector's) | 0.374208 | 0.173503 | 2.156778 | 0.0434 |
| DLN(manufacturing sector's) | -0.058940 | 0.113567 | -0.518989 | 0.6095 |
| DLN(transportation sector's) | 1.453051 | 0.607049 | 2.393632 | 0.0266 |
| U(-1) | -0.022071 | 0.004812 | -4.586461 | 0.0002 |
| R-squared | 0.603711 | | Mean dependent var | 0.070479 |
| Adjusted R-squared | 0.504639 | | S.D. dependent var | 0.222851 |
| S.E. of regression | 0.156847 | | Akaike info criterion | -0.667918 |
| Sum squared resid | 0.492020 | | Schwarz criterion | -0.377588 |
| Log likelihood | 14.68293 | | Hannan-Quinn criter. | -0.584313 |
| F-statistic | 6.093654 | | Durbin-Watson stat | 1.949973 |
| Prob(F-statistic) | 0.001388 | | | |

Source: Computed by using Eviews 7.

DLN (Oil Prices) = -0.013 - 0.947DLN(agriculture sector's) + 0.374DLN(construction sector's) - 0.058 DLN(manufacturing sector's) + 1.453DLN(transportation sector's) - 0.022U(-1)

From the above error correction model, the effects of oil price volatility on the agriculture sector's are found to be negative. That is, a percentage increase in the agriculture sector's will induce a 0.94%

decrease in the crude oil price and vice versa. The effects of oil price volatility on the manufacturing sector's are negative, which satisfies a priori expectation.

Thus, a 1% increase in crude oil prices will cause about a 0.058% decrease in manufacturing sector's. This affirms the conventional inverse relationship between crude oil prices and manufacturing sector's. In addition, the relationship between the construction sector's, the transportation sector's and the crude oil price is positive which confirms that oil price is also being driven by the growing demand from the emerging economies and from all other demanders of crude oil. Thus, a percentage increase in the construction sector's will trigger a 0.37% increase in the crude oil price. The $R^2$ shows that 60% variation in the crude oil price is captured in the model while the F-statistics shows the joint significance of all the explanatory variables in explaining the crude oil price.

The estimation of this model shows the existence of a long-term relationship between oil prices and economic sectors. This is explained by the fact that the coefficient of error correction is negative and significant in the model. There is relationship in the short term between oil prices and the sectors of agriculture, transport and construction. In addition, there is a positive relationship between oil prices and the construction sector and agriculture sectors. And that the industry and the agriculture sector is linked to a negative relationship with oil prices. which means that Libya is very vulnerable to external shocks, particularly the fall in oil prices. Due to the high dependence on oil and the weakness of the economic base.

We can deduce that oil price volatility have contributed enormously to the economic sectors volatility in Libya, These results are consistent with evidence found by the (Kandil, 2000) for the Arab States, (Torul and Alper, 2010) who all demonstrated that changes in oil price had a significant effect on the economic sectors .

## 4.4 GRANGER CAUSALITY TEST

When there is a Co-integration relationship between the model variables, there must be at least one way causal relationship among this variables. The null hypothesis of the first part is "Crude oil prices does not Granger cause each of the economic sectors (the agriculture, construction, manufacturing and transport) and the alternative hypothesis states all of the economic sectors does not Granger cause the crude oil prices". Table 6 provides the causality test results employ (VECM) model in Table 7.

Table 7: The results of pairwise Granger causality test

| Null Hypothesis | Obs | F-Statistic | Prob |
|---|---|---|---|
| Crude Oil Prices does not Granger Cause Agriculture sector's | 24 | 3.78988 | 0.0412 |
| Agriculture sector's does not Granger Cause Crude Oil Prices | 24 | 1.29931 | 0.2959 |
| Crude Oil Prices does not Granger Cause Construction sector | 24 | 4.03228 | 0.0347 |
| Construction sector does not Granger Cause Crude Oil Prices | 24 | 0.65841 | 0.5291 |
| Crude Oil Prices does not Granger Cause Manufacturing sector's | 24 | 2.53740 | 0.1055 |
| Manufacturing sector's does not Granger Cause Crude Oil Prices | 24 | 0.27759 | 0.7606 |
| Crude Oil Prices does not Granger Cause Transportation sector's | 24 | 3.24718 | 0.0612 |
| Transportation sector's does not Granger Cause Crude Oil Prices | 24 | 0.03845 | 0.9624 |

Note: *, and ** denote statistical significance at the 1%, and 5% level, respectively.
Source: Computed by using Eviews 7.

Table 7 shows the Granger Causality between the oil price volatility and manufacturing sector, agriculture, construction, and transportation. The Granger causality test was performed on the four economic sectors with oil prices. There was a demonstrated evidence of economic sectors on oil prices for the four economic sectors. These results were in line with the established theoretical framework as postulated by (Hamilton, 2008). The results of the Granger causality test show that the crude oil prices Granger cause the agriculture and Construction sector. Besides, that a unidirectional causality runs from oil prices to each of agriculture and construction sectors. However, the results of the Granger causality test showed that crude oil prices does not Granger cause the manufacturing and transportation sectors. This result is consistent with economic theory.

## 4.5 IMPULSE RESPONSE FUNCTION (IRF)

The study uses an impulse response function as an additional check of the Co-integration test findings. The response of variables to a shock or impulse from one of the other variables can be analyzed through impulse-response function. Therefore, the impulse-response function provides an avenue to estimate other variables' responses to the shocks that may occur in the future. Impulse response functions are shown in Figure2.

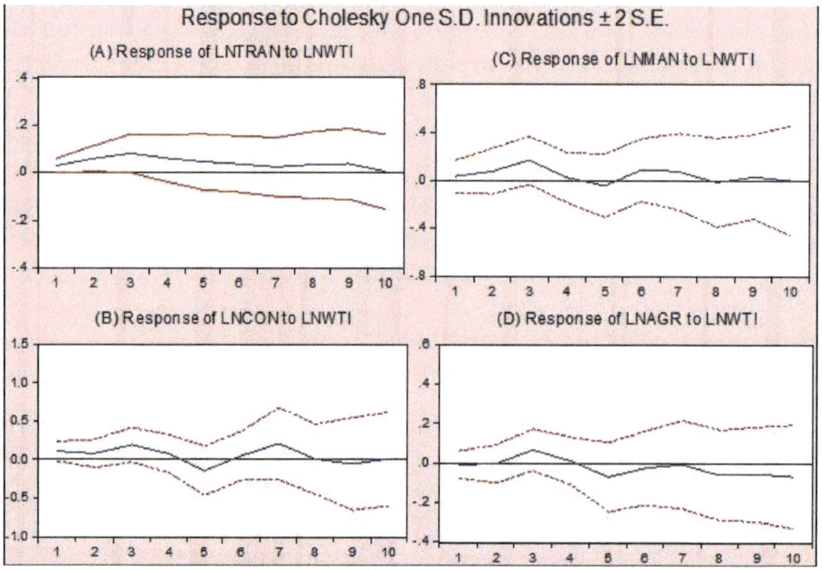


Figure 2: Response of Libya's economic sectors to an oil price volatility, 1986–2012

Based on the graph in (Figure 2) leads us to conclude that oil prices has positive effect on the transportation sector during the next 10 Periods. Interestingly, that a one standard deviation shock to the oil price variation increase the manufacturing sectors 3 years after the shock and returns to decreases it weakly after this date. The similar pattern can be observed in a one standard deviation shock to the oil price variation increase the construction sector 3 years after the shock and returns to falling 5 years and returns to increase 7 years, and returns to falling, afterwards the effects disappear. Also, oil prices has positive effect on the construction sector during the first four years, then became negative

## 5.0 CONCLUSION

This study sought to examine the impacts of oil price volatility on economic sectors in Libya using a sample of observations from 1986 to 2012 by using a vector error correction methodology. To this end, a unit root test was conducted, in which data were shown to be non-stationary in all levels, and stationary in the first difference for all variables. Furthermore, the co-integration model was applied, and the results indicated that one co-integrating equation exists, suggesting the long-term effects of oil prices on the agriculture, construction, manufacturing, and transportation sectors. Based on the Granger causality test, oil price volatility can affect agriculture. Oil price instability also influences the performance of the agriculture sector. In addition, the construction sector was found to be dependent on oil prices. Our study found results that are similar with those of Torul and Alper (2010), (Mehrara and Sarem, 2009). Based on the results of this study, this study has an important implication for the Libyan economy in formulating policies on oil price volatility. The Libyan government must policies take that grow dramatically and diversify their economic base. This should go hand in hand with measures needed to enhance their capacity to withstand adverse external shocks and reduce their exposure to the fluctuations, reduce dependence on oil.

## REFERENCES


AIMER, Nagmi. Moftah. (2016). The impact of oil price fluctuations on the exchange rate in Libya. *Imperial Journal of Interdisciplinary Research (IJIR)*, Vol-2, Issue-12, 2016, ISSN: 2454-1362, http://www.onlinejournal.in, 599-609

BENLI, T. 2008. *Mali Tablolar Analizi*, 1-28.

COPIELLO, S. (2016). Economic implications of the energy issue: Evidence for a positive non-linear relation between embodied energy and construction cost. *Energy and Buildings*, 123, 59-70.

DHUYVETTER, K. & KASTENS, T. (2005). Impact of rising diesel prices on machinery and whole-farm costs. *Manhattan, Kansas: Kansas State University.(Accessed:).*

EE, C. Y., GUGKANG, A. S. & HUSIN, N. H. (2015). The Effect of Oil Price in Malaysia Economy Sectors. *Labuan Bulletin of International Business and Finance (LBIBF)*, 13, 1-9.

ERDOĞAN, M. (2011). *VUK'ndan TFRS'na GEÇİŞ REHBERİ, MUMEYEK Vakfı Yayını:01, İstanbul.*

Erdoğan, M., K. İbrahim, (2016).And G. Salih, *Transferıng Marketable Securıtıes Account Group Of Tucoa To Opennıng Fınancıal Statements Accordıng To New Turkısh Trade Code As Of Tfrs.* Kastamonu Üniversitesi, İktisadi Ve İdari Bilimler Fakültesi Dergisi, 11.181-232.

FUKUNAGA, I., HIRAKATA, N. & SUDO, N. (2010). The effects of oil price changes on the industry-level production and prices in the US and Japan. National Bureau of Economic Research,V.20, 1-23. http://www.nber.org/papers/w15791.

GRANGER, C. W. (1980). Testing for causality: a personal viewpoint. *Journal of Economic Dynamics and control*, 2, 329-352.

GUIDI, F. (2009). The economic effects of oil prices shocks on the UK manufacturing and services sector, MPRA Paper No. 16171, posted 12. 1-35. http://mpra.ub.uni-muenchen.de/16171/

Hanson, K., Robinson, S. & Schluter, G. (1993). Sectoral effects of a world oil price shock: economywide linkages to the agricultural sector. *Journal of Agricultural and Resource Economics*, 18(1), 96-116.

Husain, M. A. M., Arezki, M. R., Breuer, M. P., Haksar, M. V., Helbling, M. T., Medas, P. A. & Sommer, M. (2015). *Global implications of lower oil prices*, International Monetary Fund, 1-41.

ITO, K. (2008). Oil price and the Russian economy: A VEC model approach. *International Research Journal of Finance and Economics*, 17, 68-74.

Kandil, M. (2000, October). Macroeconomic Shocks and Dynamics in the Arab World. In *7th Annual Conference of Economic Research Forum (ERF),"Trends and Prospects for Growth and Human development", Amman, Jordan.*

Kizgin, Y., Karaosmanoglu, K., Hiz, G. & Benli, T. (2013). A Field Study on the Determination of the Credit Card Users' Awareness of the Products/Services Offered with Credit Cards: Turkey Case. *International Journal of Business and Management*, 8, 13.

MAHBOUB, A. A. & AHMAD, H. E. The Effect of Oil Price Shocks on the Saudi Manufacturing Sector, 18(2), 185-200.

MALLIK, G. & CHOWDHURY, A. (2011). Effect of inflation uncertainty, output uncertainty and oil price on inflation and growth in Australia. *Journal of Economic Studies*, 38, 414-429.

Mehrara, M., & Sarem, M. (2009). Effects of oil price shocks on industrial production: evidence from some oil-exporting countries. *OPEC Energy Review*, 33(3-4), 170-183.

Moradkhani, N., Rashid, Z. A., Hassan, T., & Nassir, A. M. (2010). The impact of increasing energy prices on the prices of other goods and household expenditure: Evidence from Malaysia. In *Paper Submitted for the 18th International Conference On Input-Output Techniques, Sydney, Australia. Available from: http://www. Iioa. Org/Files/Conference-1/91_20100424051_Sentone. 28feb. Doc.[Last accessed on 2010 Oct 21].*

PROSPECTS, G. E. (2016). Divergences and Risks, A World Bank Group Flagship Report, JUNE 2016.

RIAZ, M. F., SIAL, M. H. & NASREEN, S. (2016). Impact of Oil Price Volatility on Manufacturing Production of Pakistan. *Bulletin of Energy Economics (BEE)*, 4, 23-34.

SETH, D., GIRIDHAR, B. S. & KRISHNASWAMI, S. (2016). Impact of Crude Oil Price Changes on Select Indian Industries. *International Journal of Social Sciences and Management,* 3, 87-92.

SHAARI, M. S., PEI, T. L. & RAHIM, H. A. (2013). Effects of Oil Price Shocks on the Economic Sectors in Malaysia. *International Journal of Energy Economics and Policy,* 3, 360.

SYED, N. I. (2010). Measuring the Impact of Changing Oil Prices and other Macro Economic Variables on GDP in the Context of Pakistan's Economy. *International Research Journal of Finance and Economics,* 52, 40-49.

TAGHIZADEH HESARY, F., RASOLINEZHAD, E. & KOBAYASHI, Y. (2015). Oil price fluctuations and oil consuming sectors: An empirical analysis of Japan, 539,1-17.

TORUL, O. & ALPER, C. E. (2010). Asymmetric effects of oil prices on the manufacturing sector in Turkey. *Review of Middle East Economics and Finance,* 6, 90-105.

Ulusoy, T., (2011) *Financial Power Analysis Of Countries: Transmitters (Adsorbents),* Setters And Unresistants African Journal Of Business Management, 2011. Bahar Döneminde Yayında, 9088-9108.

Ulusoy, T., Et Al.,(2012). *Complexity Of Major Uk Companies Between 2006 And 2010: Hierarchical Structure Method Approach.* Physica A: Statistical Mechanics And Its Applications, 391(21): P. 5121-5131.

# 10

# Natural Resources and FDI in GCC Countries

**Mohamed Elheddad**[1]

**ABSTRACT**

Natural resources are a blessing for some countries to attract FDI but cursed for others. Existing literature argues the suggestion that resource-rich countries attract less FDI because of resource (oil) price volatility. This study examines that natural resources discourage FDI in GCC countries (the FDI-Natural resources curse hypothesis), using panel data analysis for six oil dependent countries during 1980-2013 and applying several econometrics techniques. The main findings of this paper is that natural resources measured by oil rents have a negative association with FDI inflows; this negative impact is robust even when other FDI determinates of FDI are included. FDI inflows decreased between 0.15 and 0.92% when oil rents increased by 1%. In addition, the empirical results show that trade openness and labour force are the main factors that encourage FDI, while political instability and corruption deter FDI inflows into GCC countries.

Keywords: Economic growth, endogeneity, FDI, GCC region, natural resources, panel data.

---

## 1.0 INTRODUCTION

In recent years, Foreign Direct Investment (FDI) has been considered as a crucial way of transforming technologies, boosting economic growth and reducing poverty worldwide. Therefore, policy makers in both developed and developing countries have introduced policies to attract more FDI. According to the United Nations Conference on Trade and Development (UNCTAD), foreign capital inflows are important to the host country, as inward FDI contributes to economic growth through providing new knowledge, job creation, and supporting competitiveness (Asiedu, 2013).

However, recent literature has observed that some resource-abundant countries attract less FDI than other countries which are resource-poor countries (Asiedu, 2013; Poelhekke & Van der Ploeg, 2010, 2013). These studies also noted that FDI inflows to resource countries concentrated on resource sectors such as oil, diamonds, gas or gold. Investing in these industries could generate unbalanced development in the host countries and tend not to create positive spill-over of FDI. In other words, the resource sector

[1] University of Hull, Hull Business School (HUBS), United Kingdom

crowds out non-resource sector investment. A more specific case is GCC countries. In Qatar, resource FDI constitutes for more than 65% of total FDI, and FDI in the resource sector in Saudi Arabia stands at about 70% of total FDI.[2] In this light, FDI can be seen as an additional vehicle curtailing economic growth under the concept of natural resources curse.

To provide more understanding about this issue, Figure1 depicts the trend of FDI broken down into primary, manufacturing and service sectors. It shows that FDI as a percentage of GDP in the mining sector has exhibited a decreasing trend since 2003; its share in total FDI inflows ranged from 4.29% to 19%. While the share of manufacturing and service sectors have witnessed dramatic shifts during the same period averaged between 46% and 43% at the same time, FDI as absolute values (Millions of Dollars) manufacturing and service divisions have absorbed a large share compared with primary sector.

**Figure 1A:** FDI inflows by sectors in the world (2003-2014), percentage of total FDI

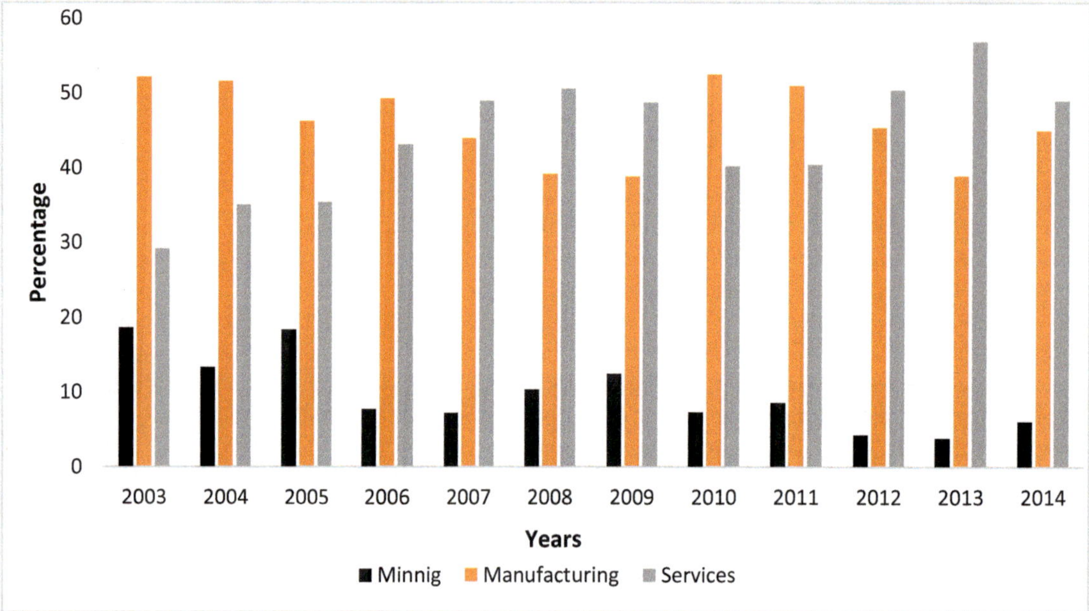


**Figure 2B:** FDI inflows by sectors in the world (2003-2014), in millions of dollars

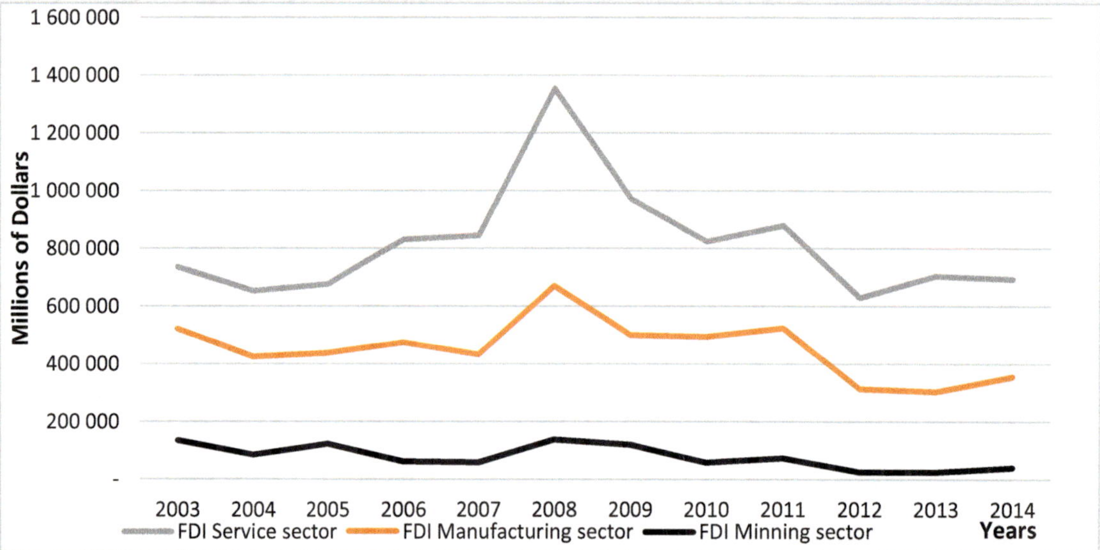


**Source:** Author's work depending on data from World Investment Report 2015 (UNCTAD, 2015)

[2] Author's calculations depending on the dataset of FDI intelligence

For GCC countries, figure 2 plots the correlation between the natural resources measured by oil revenues as a percentage of GDP and FDI inflows. This graph indicates that there is a significant negative correlation between these two variables during 1980-2013, with a correlation coefficient of -0.35%. This figure may raise a question about the relationship between natural resources and FDI in this region and suggests the likelihood of FDI-natural resource curse thesis in GCC countries.

The purpose of this paper is to identify the impact of a natural resource on the amount of FDI in Gulf Cooperation Council countries during the period (1980-2013).The paper contributes to the literature in two aspects. First, it investigates the natural resource impact on FDI movement in the context of the resource curse. Second, this paper is the first empirical work using recent oil revenues data as a proxy for natural resources in the GCC region.

**Figure 2:** Scatter plots FDI and Oil Revenues in GCC countries during (1980-2013)

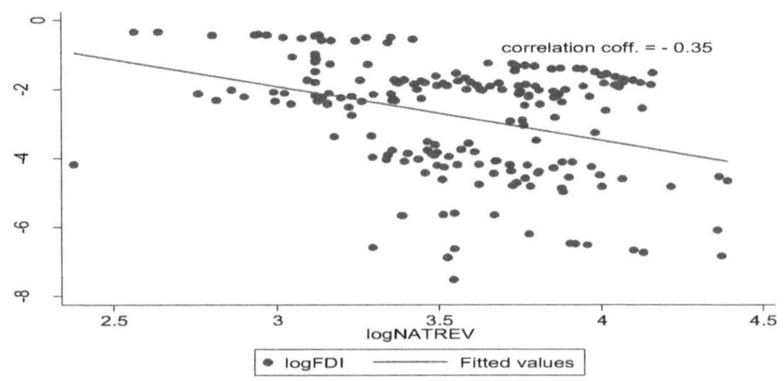


**Source:** STATA output, Author's work depending on data from UNCTAD and World Bank (World Bank, 2015).

## 2.0 REVIEW OF LITERATURE

There is a widespread idea that countries rich in natural resources such as oil, gas, diamonds or gold, motivate more FDI, but this is not always the case. The impact of natural resources on FDI is still a controversial issue, with evidence of inducing positive and negative effects. WDI (2013) noted that " countries that rely on heavily on extractive industries have seen large increases in natural resource rents, but their growth will not be sustainable unless they invest in productive assets" (Bokpin, Mensah, & Asamoah, 2015)

The effect of natural resources can be investigated from two perspectives. First through growth channel and the demand side (determinants). Alfaro (2003) raised the question whether FDI in primary, manufacturing and services sectors yield different effects on a country's growth. Alfaro applied panel data for 47 countries from different regions during (1981-1999) using FDI inflow to all sectors as independent variables and Average real annual per capita growth rate as the dependent variable. Alfaro noted that foreign capital in primary sectors causes a negative impact on economic growth, while FDI in manufacturing and service sectors encourage economic growth. The results show that one unit increase in primary sector FDI leads to a (0.17-0.32) unit fall in economic growth. Regarding GCC region, Mina (2007) looked at the location determinants of FDI for the period 1980-2002 using panel data analysis. Mina's results indicate that natural resources measured by oil reserves have a remarkably negative impact on FDI flows. Also, human development is negatively associated with FDI flows to the Gulf area. Nevertheless, the literature on determinants of FDI inflows reported that natural resources is one of the most attractive factors of MNCs. Asiedu (2006) pointed out that the mineral and oil exports-total exports ratio as a proxy of natural resource has a significant role in attracting FDI inflows, taking 22 African countries as a sample during (1984-2000) and using panel data analysis. The results of Aseidu's study show that one standard deviation increase in natural resources results a 0.65% rise in FDI ratio. In the same line, in 45 African countries, Hailu (2010) examined the demand side factors affecting foreign capital inflows over the period 1980 and 2007. Hailue found that natural resource (mineral depletion as a share in GNI) is positively and significantly correlated with FDI ratio. A One per cent increase in natural resources results in impact between 0.500 and 0.19 per cent. Further, Kinoshita & Campos (2003) investigated the determinants of FDI inflows to 25 transition economies between 1990 and 1998 using unique panel data; this study concludes that natural resources are the key factor for attracting FDI to this area along with institutions, openness and agglomeration.

Recent literature has focused on the specific relationship between FDI inflows, outflows, and natural resources. These studies considered the crowding effect, "Dutch Disease", through FDI channels. Poelhekke and van der Ploeg (2010) among the earliest works has tried to shed light on this issue. They examine whether natural resources attract FDI, covering outflows FDI from Dutch firms to 183 countries for the years 1984-2002 applying a gravity panel data model. By differentiating between FDI outflows to resource sectors and non-resource sectors, they established two econometric models one for resource FDI and another for non-resource FDI. Their estimations showed that subsoil assets as a proxy of natural resources induce an adverse impact on non-resource FDI, but have a positive effect on resource FDI. Also, they found that the net effect of resource abundance on total FDI quickly becomes negative using a simulation exercise (FDI become negative four years after shock in Australia whereas it became negative two years after shock in Norway). One of the surprising results is that institutional quality and trade openness have no significant effects on FDI in the non-resource sector while the institutional quality does have a positive role on resource FDI.

These results are further explained in Poelhekke and van der Ploeg (2013) with the same sample in the same period. They reported that in previously non-resource countries, discovering resources led to non-resource FDI to decreasing by 16% in the short term and by 68% in the long term. In addition, for resource countries, a doubling of resource rents causes a 12.4% decline in resource FDI, and total FDI falls by 4% if the resource rents are doubled.

Additionally, Asiedu (2013) evidence that contradicts her earlier study in 2002, Asiedu (2013) revealed a negative connection between natural resources (defined as the share of fuel exports in total reports and oil rents-GDP ratio). She used the GMM method to regress net FDI inflows-GDP ratio on natural resources, institutional quality and some control variables like trade openness, inflation and GDP per capita in 99 developing countries during 1984-2011. The results of this study illustrate that natural resource have a negative effect on FDI by 0.05.This result was consistent with Poelhekke and van der Ploeg (2010, 2013), but Asiedu (2013) concluded that high quality of institutions could mitigate the adverse influence of natural resources and criticised Poelhekke and van der Ploeg conclusions by using a variety of different measures of institutional quality. Asiedu described this negative relationship as a crowding out effect. Kinoshita & Campos (2003) investigated the determinants of FDI inflows to 25 transition economies during 1990-1998 using unique panel data. They found that natural resource abundance attracted more FDI to these countries.

The main hypothesis of this study is that there is a negative relation between FDI and natural resource in GCC countries as a result of oil price fluctuations which means a high risk, foreign investors are not interested to invest in these market. Also this study tries to investigate the impact of other institutional and political factors on FDI.

## 3.0 DATA, MODEL, AND METHODOLOGY

In the standard literature, the ratio of FDI to GDP is commonly used as a proxy of FDI (Asiedu 2013) Our independent variables are constrained by the availability of data. For instance, data for taxes and real wages are not available in developing countries, in particular, GCC countries. This may explain the scarcity of studies in this area.

To test the validity of FDI-Natural resources curse, this study focuses on two main variables: FDI and natural resources. It also considers some control variables.

Our empirical analyses utilize panel data of 6 oil-dependent developing countries over the period 1980-2013. Data have been collected from different sources as follows: trade openness and Oil revenues collected from the World Bank, FDI, inflation rate and GDP per capita collected from UNCATD and political instability and corruption perception index from the ICRG dataset.

As a natural resource proxy, we employ oil rents as a share of GDP as a measure of resource dependence (Asiedu 2013; Poelhekke and van der Ploeg 2013) It is worth mentioning that a high/low Oil rents/GDP ratio indicates the high/low diversification of the country. We hypothesize a negative relationship between natural resources and aggregate FDI. This argument is based mainly on the puzzle of the resource curse.

Our hypothesis relies on the idea that resource boom tends to lead to appreciation of country's currency, as a result of that, non-tradable exports will be less competitive. By this means the resource sector crowds out non-resource sectors regarding FDI (Poelhekke and van der Ploeg 2010, 2013). Also, natural resources, especially oil, is more fluctuated which makes the country more vulnerable to external shocks. At the end of the day, FDI flies from the oil sector to the non-resource sector, but this non-resource sector is less competitive in the world market. This can be an additional channel of the resource curse.

Following the previous literature, we examine the determinants of FDI inflow to GCC countries.
The expected model is as follows

$$\left(\frac{FDIinfl}{GDP}\right)_{it} = \beta 1 + +\beta 2\ Oil - reveues_{it} + \beta 3\ X_{it} + \varepsilon_{it} \qquad \text{Eq. (01)}$$

Where FDI inflow is real FDI inflows to GCC countries, GDP is real Gross Domestic Product constant 2005, $X_{it}$ is the vector of control variables including: trade openness, Market size, Labour force, Political instability and corruption.

The hypothesis of this study is that if $\beta 2 < 0$ this refers to FDI-Natural resource curse (crowding-out), but if $\beta 2 > 0$ means that there is a crowding-in effect.

The descriptive statistics of the variables are reported in Table 1

**Table 1:** Descriptive statistics

| | (1) | (2) | (3) |
|---|---|---|---|
| Variables | N | mean | Std. Dev. |
| Log(FDI) | 203 | -2.766 | -2.766 |
| Log(openness rate) | 204 | -0.337 | -0.337 |
| Log(oil-revenues/GDP) | 198 | 3.564 | 0.378 |
| Log(Labour Force) | 204 | 6.818 | 6.818 |
| Log(GDP per capita) | 204 | 10.03 | 10.03 |
| Political Instability | 178 | 2.690 | 2.690 |
| Corruption perception Index | 178 | 3.459 | 3.459 |
| Inflation rate | 204 | 2.777 | 2.777 |
| Number of N | 6 | 6 | 6 |

## 4.0 RESULTS AND DISCUSSION

This paper uses long panel data for the period 1980- 2013 (T=34, N=6). Thus, the first stage in evaluating the empirical results is to check for spurious regression. This can be done by applying panel data unit root tests. This paper uses four different panel unit root tests. They are Im, Pesaran and Shin (IPS), Levin, Lin and Chu (LLC), Augmented Dicky Fuller (ADF) and Phillips-Perron (PP)[3]. Appendix B presents the results

[3] Null hypothesis is unit root in common sample and individuals.

of stationarity tests, these results confirm that all variables are stationary at the first difference. As a result of that we apply panel co-integration tests in order to make sure that there is a long-run relationship between the variables of the model. Appendix C gives the results of Kao test and Johansen-Fisher panel co-integration, which means there is an association between variables in the long run.

The second step is to check other econometric problems. The main issue is the endogeneity problem; there is a possibility that unobserved variable may affect both FDI and natural resources. (Asiedu & Lien, 2011). This problem can be mitigated by using GMM and an instrumental variables estimator as it is discussed later in section 4.1. The second problem is the correlation between time-invariant country and explanatory variables. This can be solved by applying a fixed effect model.

First, we depart from analysing natural resource and FDI relationship using Panel correction standard error(PCSE) because our sample is long panel data (T=34 greater than N=6). Hence, this method is more suitable than POLS (Cameron, 2010), We then apply a fixed effects model (FE) and Random effect model. The second part re-estimates the same model taking into account the issue of endogeneity and the impact of business cycle fluctuations through using the GMM method, instrumental variable estimator, and averaging data in 5 years.

Table2, column1, PCSE results show that in GCC countries, high dependence on oil (natural resources) hampers FDI inflows. An increase in the oil revenues ratio by one percent leads to 0.97% decrease in FDI inflows; this impact is significant at the1% level.

Afetr checking the Hausman test, it shows that the fixed effect model is appropiate for this estimation. The fixed effect model controls for the expected heterogeneity between countries. The results show the negative relationship between natural resources and FDI still holds, but is not significant. The coefficient of natural resources is -0.28.

Furthermore, we find that the usual determinants of FDI, such as Labour Force and trade openness significantly attract FDI inflows, while corruption and political stability in the host country deter FDI inflows. A high level of corruption mitigates the FDI inflows to GCC countries by 1%. This result is consistent with previous literature. In the same way, high political instability will depress foreign capital to GCC countries.

## 4.1 ISSUE OF ENDOGENEITY

So far the estimations have not considered the problem of endogeneity. It is important to note that the regression might be biased. There is a possibility that unobserved variables may affect both FDI and natural resources (Oil-GDP ratio). Therefore, we apply two different techniques to eliminate the existence of endogeneity.

The first is GMM method (System and difference) (Arellano & Bond, 1991) and (Blundell & Bond, 1998).

The second is the instrumental variables approach and using the GDP share of oil in total GDP lagged one year as an instrumental variable because it is argued that this variable is strongly exogenous. Its exogeneity can be rationalized as follows: oil production is usually extracted by foreign firms in GCC countries and using their technologies, making oil production relatively independent of unobserved development indicators. Also, lagged values are arguably exogenous.

In order to increase the results credibility, let us now test the FDI-natural resources curse using different estimators. According to GMM results, the coefficient estimated on oil revenues remains negative and significant at 5 and 10%. This negativity ranges between 0.26 and 0.35 for system and difference GMM respectively. The Hansen test for over-identification restrictions confirms the validity of the instrumental variables. These kind of results give the model more robustness.

**Table 2:** The relationship between FDI and natural resources: Benchmark estimations

| | (1) | (2) |
|---|---|---|
| Variables | Panel Correction Standard Error | Fixed Effect model |
| Dependent variable: Log(FDI) | | |
| **Log(oil revenues)** | **-0.973*****<br>**(0.222)** | **-0.287**<br>**(0.207)** |
| Log(openness) | 0.631***<br>(0.0496) | 0.448***<br>(0.105) |
| Log(Labour Force) | 0.635***<br>(0.0802) | 0.916***<br>(0.146) |
| Log(GDP Per Capita) | -0.358**<br>(0.155) | 1.526***<br>(0.272) |
| Political Instability | -0.332***<br>(0.0472) | -0.0889**<br>(0.0433) |
| Corruption Perception Index | -1.049***<br>(0.199) | -0.0331<br>(0.109) |
| Inflation Rate | 0.000550<br>(0.0203) | -0.0299*<br>(0.0153) |
| Constant | 4.791*<br>(2.453) | -22.60***<br>(2.930) |
| Observations | 172 | 172 |
| R-squared | 0.536 | 0.652 |
| Number of N | 6 | 6 |

Standard errors in parentheses *** p<0.01, ** p<0.05, * p<0.1

**Table 3:** The relationship between FDI and natural resources: Robustness estimation

| | (3) | (4) |
|---|---|---|
| Variables | GMM | Instrumental Variables |
| Dependent variable: Log(FDI) | | estimator |
| L.log(FDI) | 1.003***<br>(0.0662) | |
| L2.log(FDI) | -0.168***<br>(0.0565) | |
| **Log (Oil revenues)** | **-0.150**<br>(0.108) | **-0.973*****<br>(0.240) |
| Log (openness) | 0.163***<br>(0.0538) | 0.631***<br>(0.0695) |
| Log (Labour Force) | 0.0981<br>(0.0632) | 0.635***<br>(0.113) |
| Log(GDP Per Capita) | -0.0492<br>(0.0999) | -0.358**<br>(0.178) |
| Political Instability | -0.0286<br>(0.0222) | -0.332***<br>(0.0629) |
| Corruption perception index | -0.0311<br>(0.0787) | -1.049***<br>(0.166) |
| Inflation rate | 0.0240***<br>(0.00808) | 0.000550<br>(0.0265) |
| Constant | 0.149<br>(1.276) | 4.791*<br>(2.465) |
| Hansen J test | 185.45 | |
| P-value | 0.51 | |
| Observations | 172 | 172 |
| Number of N | 6 | 6 |

Adopting the IV approach, the argument that natural resources (Oil) deters the foreign investors from involvement to the GCC countries still holds. Table 3 shows that FDI inflows respond adversely to oil dependence degree by 0.89%. In order to control for the effect of the business cycle, we estimate the model again using a five- year mean interval, which reduces the co-movement biases and the effect of measurement error (Acemoglu, Johnson, Robinson, & Yared, 2008; Islam, 1995). The estimation indicates that the impact of natural resources dependence on FDI become bigger compared with annual results and is still negative.

These empirical results are confirmed by small parallel literature on the impact of natural resources on FDI. Previous studies concluded that there is negative relationship between natural resource endowment and foreign firm's decision. Asidue (2013) used oil exports as a proxy for natural resources while Poelhekke and Van der Ploeg (2013) measure natural resources by oil assets. However, our paper uses oil rents as a variable for resource abundance.

The possible reasons behind this negative correlation between FDI and abundance of FDI are; first, the idea that resource booms lead to an appreciation of local currency. As a result the country's exports will be less competitive at world prices, and thereby crowds out investments in non-natural resource tradable sectors. The second explanation is that natural resources, particularly oil, are characterized by booms and busts, leading to increased volatility in the exchange rate (Sachs & Warner, 1995). Additionally, a higher degree of oil dependence implies less trade diversification, which in turn makes a country more vulnerable to external shocks. Lastly, FDI in natural resource endowed countries tends to be concentrated in the resource sector, which creates unbalanced sectoral FDI and increases the crowding out effect.

**Table 4:** The relationship between FDI and natural resources: Business cycle

| | (5) | (7) |
|---|---|---|
| Variables<br>Dependent variable: Log(FDI) | Fixed Effect model | Instrumental Variables estimator |
| **Log(Oil revenues)** | **-0.987**** | **-0.244** |
| | (0.438) | (0.633) |
| Log(openness) | 0.528** | 0.569*** |
| | (0.213) | (0.162) |
| Log(Labour Force) | 1.235*** | 0.902*** |
| | (0.219) | (0.230) |
| Log(GDP Per Capita) | 0.973* | 1.076** |
| | (0.543) | (0.518) |
| Constant | -17.26*** | -18.53*** |
| | (5.380) | (5.460) |
| Observations | 42 | 36 |
| R-squared | 0.726 | |
| Number of N | 6 | 6 |

Standard errors in parentheses
*** $p<0.01$, ** $p<0.05$, * $p<0.1$
**Source:** STATA output

## 5.0 CONCLUSION

This paper has been stimulated by the decline of FDI to the resource sector in the particular the primary sector. In the line with the Dutch disease model of Cordon and Neary (1982) based on the natural resources curse hypothesis (Sachs and Warner,1995). The main hpothesis of this study has been accepted that there is adverse association between FDI and resource abundance in GCC countries. This paper has empirically provide evidence for negative association between natural resources and FDI inflows in six GCC countries using panel data models. The main findings of this paper are that FDI inflow-GDP ratio is negatively correlated with natural resource abundance, which is consistent with the hypothesis of FDI-Natural resource curse (Asidue 2013). This phenomenon can be attributed to the crowding out the effect of resource sector and the impact of oil price volatility. Also, the paper concludes that trade openness and labour force is one of the main factors for attracting Multinational Corporations, while political instability and corruption deter foreign investors from involvment in GCC countries.

The main policy implications of this study for resource-rich economies generally and GCC countries in paricular are as follows; firslty, policy makers should redce dependence on the oil sector. Table (05) indicates that oil GDP constiutes for more than 50% of total GDP in GCC countries(World Bank dataset) (World Bank, 2015). This makes GCC countries more prone to rent-seeking activities and any fluctautions in oil prices will effect negatively on these economies. Secondly, to minimize the negative impact of natural resources on FDI, govenmnets should think about ways to distibute FDI to different sectors such as the financial and trorsim sectors. This may improve the compitiveness of non-oil sectors. GCC countries ranked in the bottom in terms of FDI and techonology tansfer compititveness.

Future research is needed to fully understand the force behind the negative relationship between FDI and natural resources and it would be very beneficial to use sectoral analysis of FDI to reveal the mechanism of this impact. The main limitation of this study could small number of sample; one would expand the region to include MENA or OPEC countries.

**Table 5:** Structure of GDP in GCC countries

| Country | Oil GDP/GDP % (Average of 1980-2013) |
|---|---|
| United Arab Emirates | 43 |
| Qatar | 56.13 |
| Oman | 53.15 |
| Kuwait | 52.96 |
| Bahrain | 32.95 |
| Kingdom of Saudi Arabia | 46.26 |
| **Average GCC countries(1980-2013)** | **47.40** |

**Source:** Author's work depending on data from World Bank

## REFERENCES


Acemoglu, D., Johnson, S., Robinson, J. A., & Yared, P. (2008). Income and democracy. *The American Economic Review, 98*(3), 808-842.

Alfaro, L. (2003). Foreign direct investment and growth: Does the sector matter?. *Harvard Business School*, 1-31.

Arellano, M., & Bond, S. (1991). Some tests of specification for panel data: Monte Carlo evidence and an application to employment equations. *The Review of Economic Studies, 58*(2), 277-297.

Asiedu, E. (2006). Foreign direct investment in Africa: The role of natural resources, market size, government policy, institutions and political instability. *The World Economy*, 29(1), 63-77.

Asiedu, E. (2013). *Foreign direct investment, natural resources and institutions.* Retrieved from London: International Growth Center. http://www.theigc.org/wp-content/uploads/2014/09/Asiedu-2013-Working-Paper.pdf

Asiedu, E., & Lien, D. (2011). Democracy, foreign direct investment and natural resources. *Journal of international economics, 84*(1), 99-111.

Blundell, R., & Bond, S. (1998). Initial conditions and moment restrictions in dynamic panel data models. *Journal of econometrics, 87*(1), 115-143.

Bokpin, G. A., Mensah, L., & Asamoah, M. E. (2015). Foreign direct investment and natural resources in Africa. *Journal of Economic Studies*, 42(4), 608-621. doi:doi:10.1108/JES-01-2014-0023

Cameron, A. C. (2010). *Microeconometrics using stata* (Vol. 2): Stata Press College Station, TX.

Corden, W. M., & Neary, J. P. (1982). Booming sector and de-industrialisation in a small open economy. *The Economic Journal*, 825-848.
Hailu, Z. A. (2010). Demand side factors affecting the inflow of foreign direct investment to African countries: does capital market matter? *International Journal of Business and Management*, 5(5), 104.
Islam, N. (1995). Growth empirics: a panel data approach. *The Quarterly Journal of Economics*, 1127-1170.
Kinoshita, Y., & Campos, N. F. (2003). Why does FDI go where it goes? New evidence from the transition economies.
Mina, W. (2007). The location determinants of FDI in the GCC countries. *Journal of Multinational Financial Management*, 17(4), 336-348. Retrieved from http://ac.els-cdn.com/S1042444X07000151/1-s2.0-S1042444X07000151-main.pdf?_tid=a833e03e-421c-11e6-81cd-00000aacb35d&acdnat=1467660333_1fd6ec187ba04e97215b0dde7e2e221e
Poelhekke, S., & Van der Ploeg, R. (2010). Do Natural Resources Attract FDI? Evidence from non-stationary sector level data.
Poelhekke, S., & van der Ploeg, R. (2013). Do Natural Resources Attract Nonresource FDI? *The Review of Economics and Statistics*, 95(3), 1047-1065.
Sachs, J. D., & Warner, A. M. (1995). *Natural resource abundance and economic growth*(No. w5398).National Bureau of Economic Research http://www.nber.org/papers/w5398
Schwab, K., & Sala-i-Martin, X. (2015). The Global Competitiveness Report. Worl Economic forum
UNCTAD. (2015). *World Investment Report*. Geneva:United Nations
World Bank. (2015). World Economic Indicators. Retrieved on 25-07-2015

## APPENDICES

**Appendix A:** Variable definition and data sources.

| Variable | source |
|---|---|
| FDI inflow stock | United Nations Conference on Trade and Development |
| GDP per capita | United Nations Conference on Trade and Development |
| Oil rents | World Bank |
| Tarde openness | World Bank |
| Inflation rate | World Bank |
| Political instability | International Country Risk Guide |
| Corruption perception index | International Country Risk Guide |

**Appendix B:** Panel unit root

| variable | LLC[4] | IPS[5] | ADF[6] | PP[7] |
|---|---|---|---|---|
| D(1)Log(FDI/GDP) | -1.76*** | -5.61*** | 53.88*** | 117.37*** |
| D(1)Log(Oil Rents/GDP) | -10.93*** | -10.75*** | 112.75*** | 148.60*** |
| D(1)Log(trade openness) | -5.35*** | -7.28*** | 71.20*** | 120.00*** |
| D(1)Log(labour force) | -1.93*** | -2.91*** | 28.30*** | 17.52*** |
| D(1)Log(GDP Per capita) | -5.03*** | -5.69*** | 57.69*** | 67.08*** |
| D(1) (Inflation Rate) | | | | |
| D(1) (Political Instability) | -4.48*** | -4.89*** | 46.68*** | 71.34*** |
| D(1)Corruption | -5.57*** | -4.10*** | 35.14*** | 60.20*** |

[4] Levin, Lin and Chu
[5] Im-Pasaran-Shin
[6] Augmented Dick-Fuller
[7] Phlips-Perron

**Appendix C.** Panel co-integration test

| Kao test | | | |
|---|---|---|---|
| | Kao Statistics | Prob | Decision |
| | -1.86 | 0.03 | Co-integration |
| Johansen –Fisher panel co-integration | | | |
| Hypothesis | Fisher statistics (trace test) | Fisher statistics (max-Eigen test) | Prob |
| Non | 308.6 | 204.3 | 0.0000 |
| At most 1 | 185.4 | 89.45 | 0.0000 |
| At most 2 | 110.3 | 51.55 | 0.0000 |
| At most 3 | 67.59 | 35.14 | 0.0004 |
| At most 4 | 40.60 | 27.23 | 0.0072 |
| At most 5 | 24.24 | 22.95 | 0.0281 |
| At most 6 | 16.50 | 16.50 | 0.1693 |

It is clear that Null hypothesis Ho: unit root in common sample and individuals is rejected in first difference for all variables, which means all variables are stationary at first difference and integrated from the same order I(1). As a result, co-integration may exist between variables. After applying the Kao test and Johansen-Fisher test, it is obvious that there is co-integration between variables, means that there is a long run relationship.

# 11

# Satyam's Manipulative Accounting Methodology Unveiled: An Experience of an Asian Economy

**Madan Lal Bhasin**[1]

**ABSTRACT**

Manipulative accounting practices are perennial and such practices have occurred in all eras, in all countries and affected millions of corporations. Unfortunately, there are few loopholes in accounting and auditing standards, which provide leeway and thus motivate accounting professionals to use aggressively manipulation practices. In fact, manipulative accounting (MA) involves the intentional cooking-up of financial records towards a pre-determined target. Every company indeed maneuvers the numbers, to a certain extent, as formally reported in its financial statements (FS) to achieve budgetary targets and generously reward senior managers. From Enron, WorldCom to Satyam, it appeared that window-dressing leading to MA is a serious problem that is increasing both in its frequency and severity, which undermines the integrity of financial reports and eroded investors' confidence. The responsibility of preventing, detecting and investigating financial frauds rests squarely on Board of Directors and they should adopt preventive steps. Despite the raft of CG, and financial disclosure reforms, corporate accounting still remains murky and companies continue to find ways to play 'hide-and-seek' game with the system. Satyam computers were once the crown jewel of Indian IT-industry but were brought to the ground by its founders in 2009 as a result of financial manipulations in FS. The present study provides a snapshot of how Mr. Raju (CEO and Chairman) mastermind this maze of AM practices? Undoubtedly, Satyam scam is illegal and unethical in which computers were cleverly used to manipulate account books by creating fake invoices, inflating revenues, falsifying the cash and bank balances, showing non-existent interest on fixed deposits, showing ghost employees, and so on. Satyam fraud has shattered the dreams of investors, shocked the government and regulators and led to questioning of the accounting practices of auditors and CG norms in India. Finally, we recommend that "All types of MA practices should be legally recognized as a serious crime, and accounting bodies, law courts and regulatory authorities must adopt exemplary punitive measures to prevent such unethical practices."

Keywords: Corporate governance, forensic accounting, financial statements, Manipulative accounting, India.

---

[1] Professor, School of Accountancy, College of Business, Universiti Utara Malaysia, Sintok, Kedah Darul Aman, Malaysia.
E-mail: madan.bhasin@rediffmail.com

## 1.0 INTRODUCTION

Corporate financial reporting (henceforth, FR) is intended to serve a number of user groups, with diverse and sometimes conflicting interests, such as, shareholders, creditors, lenders, labor leaders, and governments. A number of perspectives are, therefore, associated with FR but all tilt towards magnifying its importance in resolving the 'principal-agent' conflict occasioned by 'asymmetric' information available to the two parties. One perspective considers FR as the way by which company managers' give account of their 'stewardship' by preparing their financial statements (henceforth, FS) to their owners and other stakeholders. Other considers FR as the 'communication' of FS information to shareholders and all other users, who have interest in a company for making 'useful' economic decisions. In a perfect world, of course, investors, board members, and executives would have full-confidence in companies' FS. They could rely on the numbers to make intelligent estimates of the magnitude, timing, and uncertainty of future cash flows, and to judge whether the resulting estimate of value was fairly represented in the current stock price. Accordingly, they could make 'wise' decisions about whether to invest in or acquire a company, thus promoting the efficient allocation of capital. Recently, Sherman and Young (2016) stated, "Unfortunately, that is not what happens in the real world, for three reasons. First, corporate FS necessarily depend on estimates and judgment calls that can be widely off the mark, even when made in good faith. Second, standard financial metrics intended to enable comparisons between companies may not be the most accurate way to judge the value of any particular company giving rise to 'unofficial' measures that come with their own problems. Finally, managers and executives routinely encounter strong incentives to deliberately inject error into FS."

Introducing 'cooked-up' accounting images therefore, increases the information 'asymmetry', which influences the functioning of financial markets. However, there are plenty of situations where users can be 'influenced', one-way or another, by presenting 'distorted' accounting images and thus, their behavior can be 'manipulated'. According to the American Institute of Certified Public Accountants (AICPA), "Accounting manipulation may involve acts such as the following: "(a) Manipulation, falsification, or alteration of accounting records or supporting documents from which the financial statements are prepared; (b) Misrepresentation in, or intentional omission from, the financial statements of events, transactions, or other significant information; and (c) Intentional misapplication of accounting principles relating to amounts, classification, manner of presentation, or disclosures." Similarly, Mamo and Alia (2014) defined it as, "Financial information manipulation is a distorted presentation, a misstatement of the financial position/performance, creating a false impression of an organization's financial strength." However, accounting manipulation (henceforth, AM) is also known by several other names, such as, revenue management, income smoothing, creative accounting, aggressive accounting, window dressing, etc., but the essence is the same. It creates a very large asymmetry of information for readers of FS that affect their decision-making.

In fact, manipulative accounting (MA) involves the intentional cooking-up of financial records towards a pre-determined target. Every company maneuvers their financial and operating numbers, to a certain extent, as formally reported in FS to achieve budgetary targets and generously reward senior managers. Factors such as greed, desperation, immorality and bad judgment drive some executives to 'fudge' the FS. Undoubtedly, the nightmare of 'risky' MA is on the increase more specifically in the global corporate sector. In the current economic climate, there is tremendous pressure (and personal financial incentive for managers) to report sales growth and to meet investors' revenue expectations.

According to Securities and Exchange Commission (SEC 2016), "misleading financial reports, especially involving 'game' playing around earnings, are being issued at an alarming rate." Needless to say, it is a nightmare that affects more than CEOs' sleep: the shareholders suffer most. Little wonder that lawsuits related to FR are also on the rise. To avoid such a calamity, shareholders and their representatives on corporate boards should keep their eyes 'peeled' for common abuses in the following six areas: (a) revenue measurement and recognition, (b) provisions for uncertain future costs, (c) asset valuation, (d) derivatives, (e) related-party transactions, and (f) information used for 'benchmarking' performance. If disaster strikes, it will most likely occur in one of these accounting 'minefields'.

Unfortunately, FS manipulation is an ongoing and common problem in the global corporate world. The ten worst corporate MA scandals of all time were: Waste Management, Enron, WorldCom, Tyco, Health South, Freddie Mac, American Insurance Group, Lehman Brothers, Bernie Madoff, and Satyam, respectively. Some of the greatest examples of corporations, who manipulated their accounts, are summarized in Table 1. As Bhasin (2012) stated, "If MA no longer dominate headlines as they did, when Enron and WorldCom imploded in 2001-02, that is not because they have vanished but because they have become routine." For example, Lehman Brothers were cooking the account books far more than we ever imagined. At the height of the financial crisis in 2008, Lehman used 'accounting gimmick' to make it appear as if it had off-loaded risky assets and reduced its debts from balance sheet. In fact, executives had used a 'complicated' transaction that enabled them to remove liabilities from Lehman's balance sheet for a short-time, when results were due, and hide the true level of its debts. The report found that Lehman used this transaction to create a materially misleading picture of the firm's financial condition in late 2007 and 2008. Similarly, keen to project a perpetually rosy picture of the Satyam to the investors, employees and analysts, Mr. Raju (CEO and Chairman) manipulated the account books so that it appeared to be a far bigger enterprise than it actually was. According to the founder's own public confession, Satyam had inflated its reported revenues by 25%, its operating profit margins by over 10 times, and its cash and bank balances by over 1 billion dollars.

Table 1: Some of the greatest financial accounting scandals of world

| Organization | Loss | Modus-Operandi |
|---|---|---|
| Toshiba (2014) | Profits were overstated by more than US$ 1 billion | Toshiba understated its costs on long-term projects. Toshiba CEOs put intense pressure on subordinates to meet sales targets, which pushed certain employees to postpone losses or push forward sales on accounting |
| Olympus (2011) | US$1.7 billion accounting fraud-speculative investment losses | Olympus created a Tobashi scheme to shift losses off the Olympus balance sheet. Companies located in Cayman Islands were purchased via exorbitant M&A fees. |
| Satyam (2009) | Falsely boosted revenue by US$ 1.5 billion | Falsified revenues, margins and cash balance to the tune US$ 1.5 billion. |
| Lehman Brothers (2008) | Hid over US$ 50 billion in loans disguised as sales | Allegedly sold toxic assets to Cayman Island banks with the understanding that they would be bought back eventually. Created the impression Lehman had US$ 50 billion more cash and US$ 50 billion less in toxic assets than it really did. |
| Bernie Madoff (2008) | Tricked investors out of US$ 64.8 billion through the largest ponzi scheme in history | Investors were paid returns out of their own money or that of other investors rather than from profits |
| WorldCom (2002) | Inflated assets by as much as US$ 11 billion, leading to 30,000 lost jobs and US$ 180 billion in losses for investors | Inflated assets by as much as US$ 11 billion, leading to 30,000 lost jobs and US$ 180 billion in losses for investors |
| Enron (2001) | Shareholders lost US$ 74 billion, thousands of employees and investors lost their retirement accounts, and many employees lost their jobs | Kept huge debts off balance sheets |

Source: Grant Thornton and ASSOCHAM, Financial and Corporate Frauds (July 2016)

Galloping number of accounting scams, over the last three decades, has raised a heated debate over 'manipulated' FR systems and their inability to detect accounting 'fabrication' in the FS. Table 2 shows some leading examples of the Indian companies practicing AM from 1996-97 to 2008-09. "Recently, the Satyam scam in India had exposed serious lacunae in FR practices, and inadequacy of audit systems. The

MA scams in all these companies were not the result of a few accounting misstatements. Rather, it was more a culture of widespread AM practices followed-up by the top-level corporate management in these firms that eventually led to full-blown up accounting frauds," said Bhasin (2015). The chairman & CEO of Satyam, Mr. Raju had publicly acknowledged that the accounting books for the entire company was in a complete sham for several years. The tide had gone out and caught Satyam with its pants down. Actually, Satyam had not been wearing any pants for many years. An attempt has been made by the author to provide a brief description about the MA methodology used by the Satyam to commit the fraud in FS. Satyam is certainly a company worth investigating further as a case study and one that will surely be a topic of many business classes in the future.

Table 2: Manipulative and fraudulent reporting practices followed by some Indian companies

| Company Name | Years | Method of Manipulations Applied |
|---|---|---|
| WIPRO Ltd. | 1996-97 to 1999-2000 | Transfer of land to stock creating capital reserve with the fair value and using it to neutralize the effect on profit of reduction of land value. |
| Bombay Dyeing & Manufacturing Company Limited | 2003-04 and 2004-05 | Creating provisions for possible loss on firm purchase contract and subsequent write-back of such provision thereby converting operating losses into operating profit. |
| Larsen & Toubro Limited | 1999-2000 and 2001-02 | Income recognition through transfer of loan liabilities at a lower consideration. |
| Apollo Tyres Ltd. | 2004-05 | Debiting profit and loss account with additional excise duty payable to the government and transferring equivalent amount from general reserve to neutralize the effect. |
| Asian Electronics Ltd. | 2004-05 | Impairment of assets: treatment of deferred tax. |
| Oil and Natural Gas Commission, Mukund Ltd., Torrent Power ACE Ltd. and Tata Motors Ltd. | 2004-05 | Capitalization of interest as well as other intangible assets to show fixed assets value upward and understating revenue expenses. |
| Hindustan Zinc Limited | 2003-04 and 2004-05 | Reclassifying assets in the balance sheet. |
| Tata Motors, Bombay Dyeing, Mahindra and Himachal Futuristic | 2001-02 | Direct write-offs from reserves. |
| Satyam Computer Services Limited | 2008-09 | Fraudulently incorporated a non-existent cash component by inflating the bank balances, fudging bills, accounts receivables, interest, and liabilities. |

Source: Jones, M. (2011) 'Creative accounting, fraud and international accounting standards,' John Wiley & Sons, London.

The situation is still grave in emerging Asian markets. There are many 'motives' for a company to manipulate its FS(s) and dupe the investors of their hard earned money. One of the most lucrative motives is an increase in the 'share price' of the company. We as investors, often tend to pay a higher price for companies that communicate 'higher' earning power. Although the SEC has taken many steps to mitigate this type of corporate malfeasance, the structure of management incentives, the enormous latitude afforded by the Generally Accepted Accounting Principles (GAAP), and ever-present conflict of interest between the independent auditor and the corporate client continues to provide the perfect environment for such activity (Adkins, 2016). Due to these factors, investors who purchase individual stocks or bonds must be aware of the issues, warning signs and the tools that are at their disposal in order to mitigate the adverse implications of these problems. "Law enforcement has crime scene investigators to tell them the significance of a bloody fingerprint or a half-smoked cigarette, but investors are often left to their own devices when it comes to trying to figure out whether an accounting crime has taken place and where the fingerprint might be. Now, more than ever, investors have to become 'forensic' accountants themselves if they want to avoid being burned by unscrupulous accounting in a company's financials," said Bhasin (2016d). Although there are many interesting numbers in a company's financials that allow you to make a quick decision about a company's health, you cannot get the full story that way. Six signals to detect a possible financial manipulation and fraud are: (a) Pricey acquisitions; (b) Large idle cash reserves; (c) Capitalized expenses; (d) Rise in cash and bank balances; (e) Large revenue jumps; and (f) Change in promoter shareholdings.

## 2.0 HOW FINANCIAL STATEMENTS ARE MANIPULATED?

There are three primary 'reasons' why management frequently manipulates the FS(s). *First*, in many cases the compensation of executives/managers is directly tied to the financial performance of the company. As a result, management has a direct incentive to paint a rosy picture of the company's financial condition in order to meet established performance expectations and bolster their personal compensation. *Second*, it is relatively easy to manipulate corporate FS because the Financial Accounting Standards Board (FASB), which sets the GAAP standards, provides a significant amount of latitude in the accounting provisions that are available to be used by corporate management. For better or worse, these GAAP standards afford a significant amount of flexibility, making it very easy for corporate management to paint a favorable picture of the financial condition of the company. *Third*, it is unlikely that financial manipulation will be detected by investors due to the relationship between the independent auditor and the corporate client. While Big Four accounting firms are touted as 'independent' auditors, the firms have a direct conflict of interest because they are compensated by the very companies that they audit. As a result, the auditors could be tempted to bend the accounting rules to portray the financial condition of the company in a manner that will keep their client happy. According to Schilit and Perler (2010), there are seven primary ways in which corporate management manipulates the FS(s) of a company (see Table 3). Let's look at these seven general categories of FS manipulations and the typical accounting processes that facilitate the manipulation.

Table 3: Financial statement manipulations

| | |
|---|---|
| Recording Revenue Prematurely or of Questionable Quality | ▪ Recording revenue prior to completing all services<br>▪ Recording revenue prior to product shipment<br>▪ Recording revenue for products that are not required to be purchased |
| Recording Fictitious Revenue | ▪ Recording revenue for sales that did not take place<br>▪ Recording investment income as revenue<br>▪ Recording proceeds received through a loan as revenue |
| Increasing Income with One-Time Gains | ▪ Increasing profits by selling assets and recording the proceeds as revenue<br>▪ Increasing profits by classifying investment income or gains as revenue |
| Shifting Current Expenses to an Earlier or Later Period | ▪ Amortizing costs too slowly<br>▪ Changing accounting standards to foster manipulation<br>▪ Capitalizing normal operating costs in order to reduce expenses by moving them from the income statement to the balance sheet<br>▪ Failing to write down or write off impaired assets |
| Failing to Record or Improperly Reducing Liabilities | ▪ Failing to record expenses and liabilities when future services remain<br>▪ Changing accounting assumptions to foster manipulation |
| Shifting Current Revenue to a Later Period | ▪ Creating a rainy day reserve as a revenue source to bolster future performance<br>▪ Holding back revenue |
| Shifting Future Expenses to the Current Period as a Special Charge | ▪ Accelerating expenses into the current period<br>▪ Changing accounting standards to foster manipulation, particularly through provisions for depreciation, amortization and depletion |

In the wake of recent MA practices around the world, commentators and regulators have called for stronger corporate governance (henceforth, CG) and board oversight to curb MA and frauds. These calls have led to boards with more outside directors with greater financial expertise. Recent empirical evidence suggests that stronger CG and board oversight is associated with more 'conservative' accounting (Caskey and Laux, 2015). Nearly a decade after the Enron fraud made headlines around the world, the landscape of public company CG in the US and India is profoundly transformed by new regulations and the widespread adoption of sensible organizational safeguards—from the election of more 'independent' boards of directors to the establishment of anonymous 'whistleblowing' procedures. Today, as a result of these developments, boards and their Audit Committees perform a critical role in ensuring that the company avails itself of a thorough system of internal controls and FR compliance. Regulators, lawmakers and accounting professions have considered new rules, regulations and standards but as we see these measurements have not been sufficient to prevent the fraud in the FS.

## 3.0 LITERATURE REVIEW

Several analytical studies, from time to time, have been reported in the global media and majority of these studies were performed in developed, Western countries. Unfortunately, no study has been conducted to (a) examine the modus-operandi of the Satyam, India's largest corporate fraud, and (b) analyze the behavioral aspects of top-level management team in the perpetuation of MA practices in the corporate-sector in the context of a developing economy, like India. Winkler, D. (2010) paper provided an analysis of the Indian scandal that analysts have called "India's Enron." It covered the areas of corporate history of Satyam and also provided an insight into how the $2.7 billion scandal evaded regulators, investors, and the board of directors. He also provided a discussion of who was responsible for the fraud, and also explained the scandal's effect in India and the implications for dealing with future obstacles. Finally, the author discussed the regulatory reform following Satyam and the current status of Indian securities markets. In another research study performed by Bhasin (2013), "the main objectives of this study were to: (a) identify the prominent companies involved in fraudulent financial reporting practices, and the nature of accounting irregularities they committed; (b) highlighted the Satyam Computer Limited's accounting scandal by portraying the sequence of events, the aftermath of events, the key parties involved, and major follow-up actions undertaken in India; and (c) what lesions can be learned from Satyam scam?" To attain the above stated research objectives we applied a "content" analysis to the "press" articles. Niazi and Ali's (2015) paper unfolds Satyam's corporate scandal of inflated financial health, the aroused concerns of investors about the effectiveness of CG framework in India, the long-term effects over Indian stock market resulting from Satyam's scam, and several suggestions from the CG theory and practice that could have helped in preventing this debacle. Thus, an in depth study is conducted to analyze the financial scam from a management's perspective.

Another descriptive study by Pai and Tolleson (2015) examined the capture of government regulators using the case of Satyam Computer Services Ltd., one of India's largest software and services companies, which disclosed a $1.47 billion fraud on its balance sheet on January 7, 2009. The authors reviewed the Satyam fraud and PWC's failure to detect Satyam's accounting shenanigans, and also discussed the societal implications associated with a "too big to fail" mentality and the moral hazard of such a mindset. In addition, the paper provides suggestions to protect the public interest while citing lessons learned from this scandal. Similarly, Bhasin (2015a) performed another research study by applying a questionnaire-based survey among 345 bank employees to know their perception towards bank frauds and evaluate the factors that influence the degree of their compliance level. The study reveals that "there are poor employment practices and lack of effective employee training; usually over-burdened staff, weak internal control systems, and low compliance levels on the part of Bank Managers, Offices and Clerks." However, an exploratory research was conducted by Gupta and Gupta (2015) through a combined mode of structured questionnaires from 346 sample companies and 43 interviews with the corporate professionals, management, investors, government offices and authorities having wide experience. They found that the regulatory system is weak, there is dire need to redefine the role of auditors, coordination among different regulatory authorities is poor, and after every scam, there is a blame game." Recently, Bhasin (2016a) conducted a study using a questionnaire-based survey methodology, wherein14 specific research questions were asked. In all, 120 questionnaires were distributed to the preparers' and users' of the company FS and 85 responses from the participants were collected and analyzed using the percentage and frequencies of respondents. The study revealed that the practice of creative accounting (CA) is always a deliberate attempt to gain undue advantage for accountants, managers and companies. We recommend that "CA practices should be considered as a serious crime, and as such, accounting bodies, law courts and other regulatory authorities need to adopt very strict punitive measures to stop unethical CA practices." Accordingly, the primary objective of this paper is to examine managers' unethical behaviors in documented corporate fraud cases, on the basis of press articles, which constitute an ex-post evaluation of alleged or acknowledged fraud cases. Unfortunately, no study has been conducted to examine behavioral aspects of manager's in the perpetuation of corporate frauds in the context of a developing economy, like India. Hence, the present study seeks to fill this gap and contributes to the literature.

## 4.0 MATERIALS AND METHODS

The main objective of this study is to highlight the Satyam Computer Services Limited's manipulative accounting (MA) scandal by portraying the role played by key players involved in the scam process. This study is primarily based on secondary sources of data, and the nature of the study is primarily qualitative, descriptive and analytical. Best possible efforts have made by the author to provide the latest evidence supporting the case. Satyam is certainly a company worth investigating further as a case study and one that will surely be a topic of many business classes in the future to learn some lessons.

### 4.1 Accounting Manipulation Practices at Satyam Computer Services Limited

"Ironically, Satyam means "truth" in Sanskrit, but Raju's admission of guilt has given the company, the name 'Asatyam, Scandalam'!," says Bhasin (2015). The scam at Satyam Computer Services Limited, the fourth largest company in India's much showcased and fiscally pampered IT-industry has had an unusual trajectory. It began with a successful effort on the part of investors to thwart an attempt by the minority-shareholding promoters to use the firm's cash reserves to buy out two companies owned by them: Maytas Properties and Maytas Infra. That aborted attempt at expansion precipitated a collapse in the price of the company's stock and a shocking confession of financial manipulations and fraud from its chairman, Mr. B. Ramalinga Raju (henceforth, Raju). Disgraced former chairman of Satyam, Raju has confessed before investigators that he manipulated the balance sheet of the company for the last 7-years to attract more business and avoid any possible 'hostile' acquisition. Indeed, recession threw Raju off-guard and closed all his options. "But funnily, even Raju, in his wildest of dreams, did not foresee that he could not possibly go undetected forever for cooking up his balance sheets to the tune of thousands of crores," stated Bhasin (2013). Parallel investigations were carried out by the Central Bureau of Investigation (CBI), the Enforcement Directorate (ED), the Serious Frauds Investigations Office (SFIO) and market regulator Security and Exchange Board of India (SEBI).

The investigation by SEBI revealed that directors and employees of Satyam, namely; Mr. B Ramalinga Raju (Ex-Chairman), Mr. B Rama Raju (Ex-Managing Director), Mr. Vadlamani Srinivasa (Ex-Chief Financial Officer), Mr. G Ramakrishna (Ex-Vice President, Finance) and Mr. V. S. Prabhakara Gupta (Ex-Head Internal Audit) had, since Jan. 2001, connived and collaborated in over-statements, fabrication, falsification and misrepresentation of books of account and FS of Satyam Computers. They had colluded and connived with each other in actively inflating the revenues and understating the liabilities of Satyam by manipulation and fabrication of the books of account and financial statements and falsification of the information presented in the same. As Bhasin (2012) reported, "The FS prepared or caused to be prepared by them did not contain true-and-fair disclosures of the financial position of Satyam. They had deliberately projected a grossly false picture of the financials of Satyam to millions of investors. They also provided false CEO/CFO certification, made various announcements and issued advertisements/ press releases on the basis of falsified and misstated financial position of the company. Being promoters/promoter-group entities of the company, they were fully aware that the books of account of the company were being manipulated over the years. Through multiple routes, involving a large number of related companies and myriad transactions, the promoters of Satyam, led by the company's Chairman, are alleged to have siphoned out a huge quantity of money from the firm." To cover that up, the accounts were manipulated and documents were forged to declare non-existent cash reserves and understate liabilities. "But given the scale of the scam at Satyam, what is surprising is that the transactions did not raise suspicion on the part of Board (including independent directors) and auditors much earlier. This does suggest that the system of corporate governance that has been in place after liberalization does not work. The Satyam scam, which is likened by many to the US's Enron scam, has brought about many corporate governance, disclosure and audit reforms to plug the holes that were manipulated by the tainted former chairman of Satyam, B. Ramalinga Raju and team," concluded Bhasin (2016h).

Though the CBI has won accolades for successful investigation and getting conviction in India's biggest corporate fraud perpetrated by the founders of Satyam, the crucial spade work was done by the Crime Investigation Department (CID) sleuths of united Andhra Pradesh. "The crucial evidence about the fraud came to light only when the CID sleuths analyzed data in the 8th Server (out of the total 9 servers) used at Satyam Computers office in Madhapur. The officers found that in Server No. 8, several invoices were altered by the culprits using a special software tool with exclusive login facility for the Raju brothers. By tracing back the work done through the special software tool, cops stumbled upon forged bank deposits soft copies and hard copies of the same were then seized from the document storage facility," said Bhasin (2016g). The auditors initially feigned ignorance about the commission of the fraud saying that "it was solely done by the Raju's family without their knowledge and they had just affixed their signatures on documents furnished with the banks." However, when CID showed them blunders in the documents, they had to finally agree about their involvement in the fraud. Analysis of the data stored on servers also revealed the fictitious bank accounts and bogus companies floated by the fraudsters, and CBI along with other probe agencies, later gathered further evidence which resulted in conviction of the 10 accused.

When CBI finalized its investigations into falsification of accounts and forgery of documents in the Satyam fraud case, they found that the accounting system was 'manipulated' to inflate the company's sales by Rs. 5,117 crores. Using 'cyber-forensic' techniques, the investigating agency said "it had uncovered the modus operandi used by the accused to show inflated sales by Satyam Computer Services Limited." Further, Bhasin (2016e) added, "Officials at Satyam created a protocol to manipulate software computing man-hours spent on client projects in order to show inflated sales by Satyam to the tune of Rs. 4,746 crores. Through this protocol, the accused bypassed the regular system and created false invoices that were shown only to the company's finance department and not to clients. However, these invoices were generated for the purpose of inflating sales and the amounts pertaining to these false and fabricated invoices were shown as 'receivables' in the books of accounts of Satyam thereby 'dishonestly inflating the revenues' of the company."

## 4.2 Cooked-Up Books of Accounts

Mr. B. Ramalinga Raju would have us believe that all that he did wrong was to get caught up in the corporate rat race. Driven to desperation by a ruthless environment where the slightest slip on a quarterly earnings target would pummel Satyam's share price, Raju began inflating both revenue and profit figures to meet market expectations. In a dramatic letter released on Jan. 7, 2009, he admitted to non-existent cash balances, fake interest proceeds and grossly overstated revenues that totaled $1.4 billion, amongst other things. In it, he also reported a 'real' operating margin of 3%t. Keeping in view the media reports, Bhasin (2016f) is of firm opinion that "Satyam's top management simply cooked-up the company's books by overstating its revenues, profit margins, operating profits, ghost employees etc. for every single quarter over a period of 5-years, from 2003 to 2008. In his letter, Raju admitted to inflating the cash and bank balances of the company by Rs. 5,040 crore. The company's total assets as on Sept. 30, 2008, stood at Rs. 8,795 crore. Of this cash and bank balances stood at Rs. 5,313 crore (which was nearly 60% of the total assets). This was overstated by Rs. 5,040 crore. The company basically had cash and bank balances of less than Rs. 300 crore."

Raju also admitted to fudging the last financial result that the company had declared, for the period of three months ending Sept. 30, 2008. The company had reported revenues of Rs. 2,700 crore, with an operating margin of 24% of revenues (or Rs. 649 crore). According to Bhasin (2016a), "In fact, these numbers were made-up. The actual revenues were Rs. 2,112 crore, with an operating margin of Rs. 61 crore (or 3% of the total revenues). So, Satyam had made a profit of Rs. 61 crore but was declaring a profit of Rs. 649 crore. The difference was Rs. 588 crore. The operating profit for the quarter was added to the cash and bank balances on the balance sheet. Hence, cash and bank balances went up by an 'artificial' Rs. 588 crore, just for the three month period ending Sept. 30, 2008. This was a formula that Raju had been using for a while." First, Satyam over-declared its operating profit. Once this fudged amount of operating profit was moved to the balance sheet, it ended-up over-declaring its cash and bank balances. And this led to a substantially bigger balance sheet than was actually the case. The company had total assets of Rs. 8,795 crore, as on Sept. 30, 2008. Once the Rs. 5,040 crore of cash and bank balances that were simply not there were removed from this, the 'real' total assets fell to a significantly lower level of Rs. 3,755 crore. So, how did Raju manage to boost revenues? Here, Bhasin (2016b) provides an explanation as: "In order to do this, Raju created fictitious clients (to boot sales revenue) with whom Satyam had entered into business deals. In order to record the fake sales, Raju introduced 7,000 fake invoices into the computer system of the company. Since the clients were fictitious, they could not make any real cash payments. Therefore, the company kept on inflating the money due from its fictitious clients (or what Raju called debtors position in his letter).

Further, once fake sales had been recorded fake profits were also made and reported in accounts. Ultimately, the fake profits brought in fake cash, which therefore, needed to be invested somewhere. This led Raju to creating fake bank statements (showing forged fixed deposit receipts), where all the fake (or non-existed) cash that the company was throwing up was being invested. Finally, Raju tried his best to use this "fake cash" to buy out two real-estate companies, called Maytas Properties and Maytas Infra (both promoted by the family members) for a total value of $1.6 billion. The idea was to introduce in company accounts some "real" assets against all the "fake" cash that the company had managed to accumulate, so far. Unfortunately, that did not happen, and after this, Raju had no other way out but to come clean. So, Raju finally confessed about fudging the accounts in his Letter." While the Satyam accounting scam, which involved unethical and illegal CA tactics, was to the tune of Rs. 8,000 crore. Shockingly, the scam had caused an estimated notional loss of Rs. 14,000 crore to investors and unlawful gains of Rs. 1,900 crore to Ramalinga Raju and others.

The balance sheet of Satyam (as on Sept. 30, 2008) carried an inflated (non-existent) cash and bank balances of Rs. 5,040 crore, non-existent interest of Rs. 376 crore, and understated liability of Rs. 1,230 crore. In fact, the balance sheet carried an accrued interest of Rs. 376 crore, which was non-existent. Table 4 depicts some parts of the Satyam's fabricated 'Balance Sheet and Income Statement' and shows the 'difference' between 'actual' and 'reported' finances. Keeping in view the modus operandi successfully used by Satyam, Bhasin (2015b) remarked: "To show excess cash, several banks have to be 'fooled' (or asked to look the other way). They probably were. To show huge fake revenues, everyone, from sales teams to MIS managers to accountants, had to be kept in the 'dark' (or conscripted into the conspiracy). Some probably were. To hide it all from investors and analysts, auditors had to be 'fooled' (or roped in as co-conspirators). Some surely were. It is frightening that such large-scale fraud, which is precisely the kind of thing our various 'watchdogs' are meant to prevent, can be perpetrated so casually by just a few people at the top!"

Table 4: Fabricated parts of balance sheet and income statement of Satyam

| | Actual (Rs.) | Reported (Rs.) | Difference (Rs.) |
|---|---|---|---|
| Cash and Bank Balances | 321 | 5,361 | 5,040 |
| Accrued Interest on bank FDs | Nil | 376.5 | 376 |
| Understated Liability | 1,230 | None | 1,230 |
| Overstated Debtors | 2,161 | 2,651 | 490 |
| Total | Nil | Nil | 7,136 |
| Revenues (Q2 FY 2009) | 2,112 | 2,700 | 588 |
| Operating Profits | 61 | 649 | 588 |

## 4.3 Satyam's Manipulative Accounting Methodology Unveiled

Ramalinga Raju, former chairman of Satyam Computer Services Limited (later merged with Tech Mahindra), had confessed to the Rs. 7,800-crore fraud on Jan. 7, 2009 and accepted he had cooked company's account books and inflated profits over the last several years. He was arrested by AP police on Jan. 9, 2009. The CBI's "Multi-Disciplinary Investigation Team" (MDIT) played a crucial role in unraveling the Satyam scam, which was not only massive in scale but also posed challenge to investigators due to web of transactions and other technicalities. It was a complicated case involving digital evidences, computer techniques, audit procedures, accounting standards, revenue records, source codes, and computer network log, etc. On Dec. 8, 2014, Raju, his bother Rama Raju, Vadlamani Srinivas and former director Ram Mynampati were sentenced to 6-month jail term and fined by the Special Court for Economic Offences in connection with complaints filed by Serious Fraud Investigation Office (SFIO) for violation of various provisions of the Companies Act. The Securities and Exchange Board of India (SEBI) in June 2014 barred Raju and four others from markets for 14 years and asked them to return Rs. 1,849 crore worth of unlawful gains with interest.

Shockingly, how did Raju mastermind this maze of Accounting Manipulation (AM) practices at Satyam? Keen to project a perpetually rosy picture of the company to the investors, employees and analysts, Raju & Team manipulated the account books so that it appeared a far bigger enterprise than it actually was. Here, Bhasin (2015) remarked, "The Satyam scam is clearly a case of MA, in which the accounts were 'cooked-up' by creating fake invoices for the services not rendered, recognizing revenue on these fake receipts, falsifying the bank balances and interest on fixed deposits to show these fake invoices are converted into cash receipts and are earning interest, and so on." This type of MA is both illegal and unethical. In its recent indictment of the former promoters and top managers of Satyam, the SEBI and other investigative agencies in India had finally provided minute and fascinating details about how India's largest corporate scam was committed. An attempt has been made by the author(s), based on the media reports, to provide a description about the methodology used by the Satyam to commit the accounting fraud duly supported by evidence, wherever possible.

**Fake Invoices and Tempered Billing System:** "By using the IT skills in-house and tampering with the invoice management system (IMS) of the company, a software module that was internally developed," says Bhasin (2008). The Central Bureau of Investigation (CBI) has revealed details of the fake invoicing system used by Satyam. Documents released by media reports (for example, Verma and Ramana, 2009) to the general public in India showed how the company's standard billing systems were subverted to generate 'false' invoices to show 'inflated' sales, before its former boss, Ramalinga Raju, admitted to his role in the India's largest-ever corporate scandal. The investigators had used cyber forensics to uncover how in-house computer systems were exploited to generate fake invoices. Regular Satyam bills were created by a computer application called 'Operational Real Time Management (OPTIMA)', which created and maintained information on all company projects. The 'Satyam Project Repository (SRP)' system then generated project IDs; there is also an 'Ontime' application for entering the hours worked by Satyam employees; and a 'Project Bill Management System (PBMS)' for billing. An 'Invoice Management System (IMS)' generated the final invoices.

From the above, an intriguing question that arises here is: "how were the fake invoices created by subverting the IMS?" In the IMS system, there is a mandatory field earmarked 'Invoice Field Status'. Unless this is filled, processing of the order does not go ahead. So, what Raju & Company did was to use two alphabets 'H' (Home) or 'S' (Super) in the Invoice Field Status to process the entry. The invoices, thus created were 'hidden' from the view of those who ran the finance units. There were about 74,625 invoices generated in the IMS between April 2003 and December 2008. About 7,561 invoices out of 74,625 had 'S' marked in their invoice field status. Out of this, 6,603 were also found on the company's Oracle Financials software system, to make it seem like these were actual sales. Entries into this system get reflected straight in the Profit and Loss Statement. The balance of 958 invoices remained in the invoice state, and therefore, within the IMS system—they were not keyed into the Oracle enterprise-ware. The total revenues shown against these 7,561 fake invoices were Rs. 5,117 crore. Of this, sales through the 'reconciled' 6,603 invoices were about Rs. 4,746 crore (Ramana, 2009). The CBI has also found that "sales were inflated every quarter and the average inflation in sales was about 18%. After generating fake invoices in IMS, a senior manager of the finance department (named Srisailam), entered the 6,603 fake invoices into Oracle Financials with the objective of inflating sales by Rs. 4,746 crore. By reconciling the receipts of these invoices, the cash balances in the company's account were shown at Rs. 3,983 crore."

The CBI officers have concluded that "the scandal involved this system structure being bypassed by the abuse of an emergency 'Excel Porting System', which allows invoices to be generated directly in IMS... by porting the data into the IMS." This system was subverted by the creation of a user ID called 'Super User' with "the power to hide/unhide the invoices generated in IMS." By logging in, as Super User, the accused were hiding some of the invoices that were generated through Excel Porting. Once an invoice is hidden the same will not be visible to the other divisions within the company but will only be visible to the company's finance division sales team. As a result, concerned business circles would not be aware of the invoices, which were also not dispatched to the customers. Investigation revealed that all the invoices that were hidden using the Super User ID in the IMS server were found to be false and fabricated. The face values of these fake invoices were shown as receivables in the books of accounts of Satyam, thereby dishonestly inflating the total revenues of the company.

## 4.4 Tunneling Strategy Used by Satyam

As part of their 'tunneling' strategy, the Satyam promoters had substantially reduced their holdings in company from 25.6% (in March 2001) to 8.74% (in March 2008). Furthermore, as the promoters held a very small percentage of equity (mere 2.18%) on December 2008, as shown in Table 5, the concern was that poor performance would result in a takeover bid, thereby exposing the gap. The aborted Maytas acquisition deal was the final, desperate effort to cover up the accounting fraud by bringing in some real assets into the business. When that failed, Raju confessed the fraud. Given the stake the Raju's held in Matyas, pursuing the deal would not have been terribly difficult from the perspective of the Raju family.

Table 5: Promoter's shareholding pattern in Satyam

| Particulars | March 2001 | March 2002 | March 2003 | March 2004 | March 2005 | March 2006 | March 2007 | March 2008 | Dec. 2008 |
|---|---|---|---|---|---|---|---|---|---|
| Promoter's holding (in %-age) | 25.6 | 22.26 | 20.74 | 17.35 | 15.67 | 14.02 | 8.79 | 8.74 | 2.18 |

As pointed out by Shirur (2011), "Unlike Enron, which sank due to agency problem, Satyam was brought to its knee due to tunneling. The company with a huge cash pile, with promoters still controlling it with a small per cent of shares (less than 3%), and trying to absorb a real-estate company in which they have a majority stake is a deadly combination pointing prima facie to tunneling." The reason why Ramalinga Raju claims that he did it was because every year he was fudging revenue figures and since expenditure figures could not be fudged so easily, the gap between 'actual' profit and 'book' profit got widened every year. In order to close this gap, he had to buy Maytas Infrastructure and Maytas Properties. In this way, 'fictitious' profits could be absorbed through a 'self-dealing' process. Bhasin (2013a) concludes, "The auditors, bankers, and SEBI, the market watchdog, were all blamed for their role in the accounting fraud."

## 5.0 INSIDER TRADING ACTIVITIES AT SATYAM

Investigations into Satyam scam by the CID of the State Police and Central agencies have established that "the promoters indulged in nastiest kind of insider trading of the company's shares to raise money for building a large land bank." According to the SFIO Report (2009) findings, "promoters of Satyam and their family members during April 2000 to January 7, 2009 sold almost 3.90 crore number of shares thereby collecting in the process Rs. 3029.67 crore. During this course, the founder ex-chairman Ramalinga Raju sold 98 lakh shares collecting in Rs. 773.42 crores, whereas, his brother Rama Raju, sold 1.1 crore shares pocketing Rs. 894.32 crores." Finding these top managers guilty of unfair manipulation of stock prices and insider trading, SEBI has asked them to deposit their 'unlawful gains' of Rs. 1850 crore, with 12% interest, with the regulator within 45 days. They have also been barred from associating with the securities markets in any manner for the next 14 years.

## 5.1 GAPS IN SATYAM'S EARNINGS AND CASH FLOWS

Through long and bitter past experience, some investors have developed a set of early warning signs of financial reporting fraud. Bhasin (2007) described it as: "One of the strongest is "the difference between income and cash flow. Because overstated revenues cannot be collected and understated expenses still must be paid, companies that misreport income often show a much stronger trend in earnings than they do in cash flow from operations." But now, we can see there is no real difference in the trends in Satyam's net income and its cash flow from operations during 2004 and 2005, as shown in **Figure 1** below.

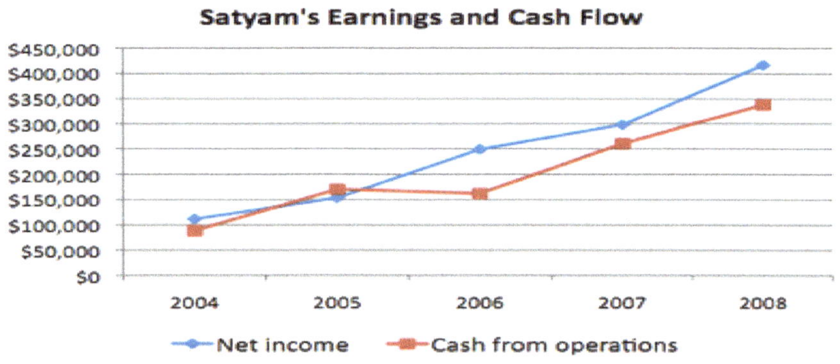


Figure 1: Satyam's earnings and cash flow

Both net income and cash flow lines were almost overlapping each other for 2004 and 2005. That is not because the earnings were genuine; it is because the cash flows were manipulated too. To do that, Raju had to forge several big amount accounts receivables, and simultaneously falsify about their cash collections. Thus, the fake cash flows had led to the bogus bank balances. If cash flow from operating activities of a company is consistently less than the reported net income, it is a warning sign. The investor must ask why operating earnings are not turning into cash. To keep from tripping the income-cash flow alarms, Raju had to manipulate almost every account related to operations. However, wide gaps can be noticed in net income and cash flow from operation during 2006, 2007 and 2008, respectively. "During 2006 to 2008, cash flows were far less than net income due to accounting manipulations. What is even more boggling is that the statement of cash flows seems to be clean as well. This obviously means that not only was the income inflated, but the cash numbers were massaged by a master masseur. Indeed, Satyam fraud was a stunningly and very cleverly articulated comprehensive fraud, likely to be far more extensive than what happened at Enron," said Bhasin (2015a). The independent board members of Satyam, the institutional investor community, the SEBI, retail investors, and the external auditor—none of them, including professional investors with detailed information and models available to them, detected the malfeasance.

## 5.2 FAKE AUDIT AND DUBIOUS ROLE PLAYED BY AUDITOR'S

Many experts cast partial blame for the MA scandal on Satyam's auditor 'Price Waterhouse (PwC)' India, because the fraud went undetected for so many years. In fact, global auditing firm used Lovelock and Lewis as their agent, who audited the Satyam's books of accounts from June 2000 until the discovery of the fraud in 2009. Several commentators criticized PwC harshly for failing to detect the fraud (Winkler, 2010). As Bhasin (2012) stated, "The PwC India signed Satyam's financial statements and hence it, was responsible for the numbers under the Indian law. The fraudulent role played by the PwC in the failure of Satyam matches the role played by Arthur Anderson in the collapse of Enron." However, Mr. S. Goplakrishnan and Mr. S. Talluri, partners of PwC had admitted they did not come across any case or instance of fraud by the company. However, Raju's admission of having fudged the accounts for several years put the role of these statutory auditors on the dock.

The SFIO Report stated that "the statutory auditors instead of using an independent testing mechanism used Satyam's investigative tools and thereby compromised on reporting standards." PwC did not check even 1% of the invoices; neither did they pay enough attention to verification of sundry debtors, which (according to Raju's confession) was overstated by 23% (SFIO report says it was overstated by almost 50%). The Statutory auditors also failed in discharging their duty when it came to independently verifying cash and bank balances, both current account and fixed deposits. Hence, it was required that the auditors (PwC) independently checked with the banks on the existence of fixed deposits, but this was not done for as large as a sum of Rs. 5,040 crore. "The statutory auditors on whom the general public relied on for accurate information not only failed in their job but themselves played a part in perpetrating fraud by preparing a clean audit report for fudged, manipulated and cooked books," concluded Bhasin (2012a). It is shocking to know that "PwC outsourced the audit function to some audit firm, Lovelock and Lewis, without the approval of Satyam."

To be fair, there were probably thousands of Satyam cash accounts that had to be confirmed by the auditor, as the outsourcer has nearly 700 customers (including 185 Fortune 500 companies) in 65 countries. The audits for a company of that size would have been staggered, with millions of dollars of outstanding receivables pouring in to different locations at any given time. As Veena et al., (2014) commented, "The Satyam case focuses on auditors' responsibilities related to obtaining and evaluating audit evidence, particularly as it relates to confirming cash and receivables. It also explores the quality control responsibilities related to audit procedures performed by foreign affiliates of a large international audit firm." One particularly troubling item concerned the $1.04 billion that Satyam claimed to have on its balance sheet in "non-interest-bearing" deposits. Recently, Bhasin (2016d) pointed out, "The large amount of cash should have been a 'red-flag' for the auditors that further verification and testing were necessary. While verifying bank balances, they relied wholly on the (forged) fixed deposit receipts and bank statements provided by the 'Chairman's office'. As to the external auditors, who are supposed to look out for investors, they seem to have been quite a trusting lot. "The forensic audit reveals differences running into hundreds of crores of Rs. between the fake and real statements, as captured by the computerized accounting systems. But for some strange reason, everyone, from the internal auditor to the statutory auditors, chose to place their faith in the 'Chairman's office' rather than the company's information systems," stated Bhasin (2015b). Furthermore, it appears that the auditors did not independently verify with the banks in which Satyam claimed to have deposits. Unfortunately, the PwC audited the company for nearly 9 years and did not uncover the fraud, whereas Merrill Lynch discovered the fraud as part of its due diligence in merely 10 days. Missing these "red-flags" implied either that the auditors were grossly inept or in collusion with the company in committing the fraud.

When scams break out in the private sector auditors too end up on the firing line. The CBI, which investigated the Satyam fraud case, also charged the two auditors with complicity in the commission of the fraud by consciously overlooking the accounting irregularities. On April 22, 2014 "The Institute of Chartered Accountants of India (ICAI)" has imposed a life-time ban on four auditors (Mr. S. Gopalakrishna, Mr. Talluri Srinivas, Mr. V. Srinivasa and Mr. V.S. Prabhakara Rao) involved in the Satyam CA fraud. All of them had been found guilty of gross negligence in discharge of their duties by the Disciplinary Committee of ICAI and they were barred from practicing as a Chartered Accountant. A penalty of Rs. 5 lakh each was also levied on them. Strangely, Satyam's auditor, PwC, got away with a rap on its knuckles.

## 5.3 ABNORMAL AUDIT FEES PAID TO PWC INDIA AGENT

A point has also been raised about the unjustified increase in audit fees. A reference to the figures of audit fee in comparison with total income over a period of time may be pertinent. Table 6 shows that over a period of four years, 2004-05 to 2007-08, the audit fee increased by 5.7 times, whereas total income increased by 2.47 times during the same period. Here, Bhasin (2013) remarked, "Nevertheless, it is difficult to draw any conclusion as to whether the increase in audit fee was justified or not. Suspiciously, Satyam also paid PwC twice what other firms would charge for the audit, which raises questions about whether PwC was complicit in the fraud." Another development that came under investigators lens was that between 2003- 2008, audit fee from Satyam had increased three times. For instance, Satyam's auditor's fee jumped from Rs. 92 lakhs in 2004-05 fiscal to Rs. 1.69 crore the next year. But it was the financial year 2006-07 when PwC's auditing fees shot phenomenally to Rs. 4.31 crores. The Chairman of the AC's in the relevant years should have been interrogated by the investigators as to what justification did the AC have for recommending such a hike?

Table 6: Satyam's total income and audit fees (Rs. in Millions)

| Year | 2004-05 | 2005-06 | 2006-07 | 2007-08 |
|---|---|---|---|---|
| Total Income (A) | 35,468 | 50,122.2 | 64,100.8 | 83,944.8 |
| Audit Fees (B) | 6.537 | 11.5 | 36.7 | 37.3 |
| % of B to A | 0.0184 | 0.0229 | 0.0573 | 0.0444 |

(Source: Annual Reports of Satyam, Percentage computed)

The Price Waterhouse received an annual fee of Rs. 37.3 million (or Rs. 4.31 crore) for financial year 2007-2008, which is almost twice, as what Satyam peers (i.e., TCS, Infosys, Wipro), on an average, pay their auditors. Bhasin (2015) stated, "This shows that the auditors were being lured by the monetary incentive to certify the cooked and manipulated financial statements. Events of such nature raise doubts about statutory auditors' discharging their duty independently." Consequently, on 24th Jan. 2009, two senior partners of PwC, Mr. S. Gopalakrishna (was due for retirement by March 09) and Mr. Srinivas Talluri were booked by Andhra Pradesh CID police on charges of fraud and criminal conspiracy. The PwC has suspended the two partners, who signed on Satyam's balance sheet and are currently in prison. The SFIO report also states that "PwC outsourced the audit function to some audit firm, Lovelock and Lewis, without the approval of Satyam."

## 5.4 WEB OF COMPANIES

A web of 356 investment companies was used to allegedly divert funds from Satyam. Under Ramalinga Raju, Satyam floated 327 companies and published inflated financials. "Through multiple routes involving a large number of related companies and myriad transactions, the promoters of Satyam Computer Services, led by the company's Chairman Ramalinga Raju, are alleged to have siphoned out a huge quantity of money from the firm. To cover that up, the accounts were manipulated and documents were forged to declare non-existent cash reserves and understate liabilities. These front companies purchased 6,000 acres of land, taken loans of Rs. 1,230 crore from these companies, which were not even accounted in books," says Bhasin (2016h). The CID investigation also revealed that Satyam had executed projects in the name of 7 non-existent companies: Mobitel, Cellnet, E Care, Synony, Northsea, Autotech and Hargreaves. All these companies had several transactions in the form of inter-corporate investments, advances and loans within and among them. One such 'sister' company, with a paid-up capital of Rs. 5 lakh, had made an investment of Rs. 90.25 crore, and received unsecured loans of Rs. 600 crore.

According to reports, the Registrar of Companies has found that "Satyam's annual report reveals several transactions with subsidiaries and other group companies by way of investments, purchase of assets and other receivables" that point to the concealed transfer of funds out of the company. Bhasin (2016a) remarked, "About Rs. 1,425 crore, out of Rs 1,744 crore loans obtained from non-banking finance companies were transferred to the bank accounts of Satyam by 37 entities as loans between November 17, 2006, and October 30, 2008, to meet the expenses of the company. Of this amount Rs. 194 crore was returned by the company between October and November 2008 to 15 out of the 37 companies. That left an outstanding liability of Rs. 1,231 crore—the sum Raju says He infused into the company." The key puzzle the CBI was trying to solve was also about the claims of Raju, as per Jan.7, 2009 letter, infusing Rs. 1,230 crore into the company.

## 5.5 FALSIFICATION OF BANK'S FIXED DEPOSITS

The promoters of Satyam regularly used to generate monthly bank statements to be fed into the bank books. Similarly, they also used to generate confirmations of bank balances, at the end of every quarter, against non-existent fixed deposit receipt (FDRs) and interest earned/due thereon. As Bhasin (2013b) commented, "From the records of Satyam, as well as, the books held with the auditors, it was noted that two sets of letters of confirmation of balances of FDRs were available with the auditors. These two sets included confirmations actually sent by banks directly to the auditors (the genuine ones) in the prescribed format, and confirmations through forged letters purportedly sent from various bank branches, but forged." Thus, as on 30 Sept. 2008, while the actual FDs balances with various banks was just under Rs. 10 crore, fake FD receipts shown to the auditors totaled over Rs. 3,300 crore. At HDFC Bank, for example, Satyam claimed Rs. 704 crore in deposits without having a single rupee parked with the bank branch concerned. With Citi Bank, it reported Rs. 613.32 crore of FDs when it actually had just Rs. 1.32 crore. And so on. Providing an explanation, Bhasin (2016c), described the motto and rationale for the process as, "Fake FDs had to be generated since fake business had to be shown to the stock markets, which meant the creation of fake customers and fake invoices from these businesses. Fake businesses generated fake revenues which, in turn, created the illusion of fake profit margins, and, finally, fake cash in the bank. Satyam apparently was very poor on its business fundamentals—with margins being low in many quarters, including negative margins in some quarters."

Indeed, falsification with regards to fixed deposit have been done since 2001-02 till 2007-08 and also for the quarter ended June 2008 and Sept. 2008. Further, Bhasin (2016f) observed, "All the misleading actions of window-dressing and camouflaging created a larger than life picturesque image year-after-year in the minds of millions of gullible investors whose fate underwent a depressive spin." Satyam's balance sheet (as on Sept. 7, 2008) carried an accrued interest of Rs. 376 crore, which was non-existent. These figures of accrued interest were shown in balance sheets in order to suppress the detection of such non-existent fixed deposits on account of inflated profits. The company had created a false impression about its fixed deposits summing to be about Rs. 3,318.37 crores, while they actually held FDRs of just about Rs. 9.96 crores. Many experts cast partial blame for the scandal on Satyam's auditor Price Waterhouse (PwC) India, because the fraud went undetected for so many years.

## 5.6 SHOWING FAKE AND UNDERUTILIZED EMPLOYEES

To quote Bhasin (2012), "One of the biggest sources of defalcation at Satyam was the inflation of the number of employees. Founder chairman of Satyam, Raju claimed that the company had 53,000 employees on its payroll. But according to investigators, the real number was around 43,000. The fictitious/ghost number of employees could be fabricated because payment to the remaining 13,000 employees was faked year-after-year: an operation that evidently involved the creation of bogus companies with a large number of employees." The money, in the form of salaries paid to ghost employees, came to around $4 million a month, which was diverted through front companies and through accounts belonging to one of Mr. Raju's brothers and his mother to buy thousands of acres of land. Making up ghost employees might sound complicated, but investigators said it was not that difficult. "Employees are just code numbers saved in Satyam computer system; anyone can create any amount of them by creating bogus employee IDs, with false address, time-sheets, opening bogus salary accounts with banks, and collecting payments through a local known accomplice," Bhasin (2012a) sums up the process.

Interestingly, the charge-sheet filed by the investigators is of the view that Satyam employees remained underutilized. For instance, the utilization level shown in the latest investor update by the company is about 74.88% for offshore employees. However, the actual utilization was 62.02%. This clearly shows that the bench strength was as high as 40% in the offshore category. Further, as a result of underutilization, the company was forced to pay salaries to associates without jobs on hand, which increased the burden on company's finances. Even in the onshore category, the bench strength was around 5% (of total staff).

## 5.7 LAX BOARD OF DIRECTORS

The Satyam Board was composed of "chairman-friendly" directors, who failed to question the management's strategy and use of leverage in recasting the company. Moreover, they were also extremely slow to act when it was already clear that the company was in financial distress. Here, Bhasin (2011) observed, "The directors acted as mere rubber stamps and the promoters were always present to influence the decision. The glue that held the board members together was Mr. Ramalinga Raju (Chairman). Each of the board members were there on his personal invitation and that made them ineffective. The Board ignored, or failed to act on, critical information related to financial wrong-doings before the company ultimately collapsed." It was only when Raju in the Dec. 2008 announced a $1.6 billion bid for two Maytas companies (Maytas Infra and Maytas Properties) and while the share market reacted very strongly against the bid and prices plunged by 55% on concerns about Satyam's CG, that some of the independent directors came into action by announcing their withdrawal from the Board, by than it was too late.

Satyam board's investment decision to invest 1.6 billion dollars to acquire a 100% stake in Maytas Properties and in 51% stake in Maytas Infrastructure (the two real estate firms promoted by Raju's sons) was in gross violation of the Companies Act 1956, under which no company is allowed, without shareholder's approval to acquire directly or indirectly any other corporate entity that is valued at over 60% of its paid-up capital. "Yet, Satyam's directors went along with the decision, raising only technical and procedural questions about SEBI's guidelines and the valuation of the Maytas companies. They did not even refer to the conflict of interest in buying companies in a completely unrelated business, floated by the chairman's relatives," remarked Bhasin (2016f). Indeed, one of the independent directors, Krishna Palepu, praised the merits of real-estate investment on Satyam's part.

**Unconvincing Role of Independent Directors:** With regard to the role of the 'independent' directors (IDs) at Satyam, we should understand: how 'independent' they actually were? It was seen that all the non-executive directors (NEDs) at Satyam have been allotted significant stock options at an unbelievable low strike price of Rs. 2 per share, and apart from this, all the NEDs have also earned handsome commissions during 2007-08, as reflected by Satyam's audited results. Table 7 shows the details of number of Stock options and commission given to different NEDs, as per Satyam's audited results for 2007-08.

Table 7: Satyam's sumptuous gift to its non-executive directors

| | No. of Options | Commission (in Rs.) |
|---|---|---|
| Krishna Palepu | 10,000 | 1.2 millon |
| Mangalam Srinivasan | 10,000 | 1.2 million |
| T R Prasad | 10,000 | 1.13 million |
| V P Rama Rao | 10,000 | 0.1 million |
| M Ram Mohan Rao | 10,000 | 1.2 million |
| V S Raju | 10,000 | 1.13 million |
| Vinod Dham | 10,000 | 1.2 million |

Source: Satyam's Balance Sheet for 2007-08, Satyam Computer Services Limited, Hyderabad.

Naturally, a basic question that arises here is: "how can directors who had enjoyed such a huge largesse from the Company's promoters, had been beneficiaries of stock options given at an unbelievable strike price of Rs. 2 per share (against the ruling price of Rs. 500 per share in 2007- 08) and who had received such high commissions could be expected to be 'independent'? According to Bhasin (2016), "The idea of giving stock options to the independent directors, was perhaps, an intelligent ploy by Raju to successfully implement his plot at Satyam, with little resistance from the so-called independent directors, to whom, he was supposed to report to. It sounds ridiculous to listen to some of the independent directors at the Press interviews post-scandal that they were not aware of what was going on at Satyam." Furthermore, it is very disturbing that highly respected persons like T. R. Prasad and Dr. Rammohan Rao, both received stock options and commissions from Satyam, without wondering how this was acceptable to their status of independent directors. Take the case of another independent director, the well-known Prof. Krishna Palepu. Prof. Palepu accepted more than $200,000 in total compensation along with 10,000 stocks (equivalent to 5000 ADR) and getting paid a fabulous fee of Rs. 9.2 million for conducting training programs for Satyam employees on CG principles and their compliance, even if not expressly forbidden statutorily, will still place him as one having a vested interest in accepting the unethical policy of the management as a quid pro quo. As an 'independent' director, he should not have accepted any consulting assignment from Satyam. "Satyam scam is one more proof that the mere compliance of SEBI's rule of the minimum number of independent directors does not guarantee ethical practices. Corporate history of the past decade has more than clearly shown that independent directors have not served their purpose," stated Bhasin (2013a).

Notwithstanding Raju's confession, the Satyam episode has brought into sharp focus the role and efficacy of "independent" directors. The SEBI requires the Indian publicly held companies to ensure that independent directors make up at least half of their board strength. The knowledge available to independent directors and even audit committee members was inherently limited to prevent willful withholding of crucial information. The reality was, at the end of the day, even as an audit committee member or as an independent director, I would have to rely on what the management was presenting to me, drawing upon his experience as an independent director and audit committee member. As Bhasin (2010) pointed out, "It is the auditors' job to see if the numbers presented are accurate. That is what the directors should have been asking... Like the dog that did not bark in the Sherlock Holmes story, the matter was allowed to slide. Even if outside directors were unaware of the true state of Satyam's finances, some 'red' flags should have been obvious." The closely-held structure of many Indian companies suggests a need for improved transparency and accountability for independent directors. Apart from improving disclosure standards, re-auditing norms, and greater shareholder activism, there is also a need to counter corruption.

### 5.8 QUESTIONABLE ROLE OF THE AUDIT COMMITTEE

As Bhasin (2016d) strongly observed, "Surprisingly, the failure to detect the Satyam fraud is 'unimaginable' because it involves violating basic audit procedures. Auditing cash is so basic that people do not think twice about accepting the number, never thinking to ask questions about it." Still, a basic question arises: "Where was the Audit Committee (AC)?" As an AC member, we understand that board members are not responsible for re-auditing financial statements. However, the directors have access to the auditors and the right and responsibility to question the audit. For instance, in the case of seeing an accumulated $1 billion on the books, the AC should have raised questions about what the company planned to do with the cash, or how much it was earning on the money, and so on. It also has been suggested that the Public Committee on Accounting Oversight Board (PCAOB)—the U.S. entity charged with auditing firm oversight—bears some responsibility for the alleged poor performance of Price Waterhouse India. Unfortunately, one possible culprit that escaped blame for the Satyam scandal is the accounting rules used by the company. Satyam used both U.S. GAAP and IFRS to report its financial results, which means that one set of accounting standards did not trump the other with respect to shedding light on the fraud. Moreover, Bhasin (2016f) observed that "the timely action on the information supplied by a whistleblower to the chairman and members of the AC (an e-mail dated December 18, 2008 by Jose Abraham), could serve as an SOS to the company, but, they chose to keep silent and did not report the matter to the shareholders or the regulatory authorities."

## 6.0 CONCLUSION

Mr. B. Ramalinga Raju (Chairman of Satyam) had been fudging and cooking up the books of accounts of Satyam quietly from 2001 to 2008 by planting electronically created fictitious order receipts and sales invoices. Then, Raju and his accomplices forged letters from banks to external auditors. As Bhasin (2016) added, "Raju would have us believe that all that he did wrong was to get caught up in the corporate rat race. Driven to desperation by a ruthless environment where the slightest slip on a quarterly earnings target would pummel Satyam's share price, Raju began inflating both revenue and profit figures to meet market expectations. In fact, shareholders are beguiled by high stock prices, since they buy into the idea that high and rising stock prices are a sign of both good performance and good management. When accounts are manipulated and revenues and profits inflated, the stock market performance of the company improves, and that improvement serves to conceal the fraud that is under way."

The CBI has termed Satyam case as one of the biggest corporate frauds in independent India, having international ramifications. It was a complicated case involving digital evidences, computer techniques, audit procedures, accounting standards, revenue records, source codes, and computer network log etc. It raised a number of questions about the survival of Satyam, CG compliance, government's ability to handle corporate fraud, and possible failure among others. In many ways, it was a test for India Inc. and the regulators. "The conviction of Raju and nine of his associates on charges of criminal conspiracy, cheating, forgery and breach of trust by a special CBI court brings closure to India's biggest corporate MA fraud case. However, the sentence of 7-years imprisonment and fine of Rs.5 crores imposed on each of the convicts is light, considering the hefty punishments imposed by the US, which places a high premium on honesty in CG," says Bhasin (2016d). Earlier, market regulator SEBI had found the top management of Satyam guilty of unfairly manipulating stock prices and insider training and imposed a fine of Rs. 1,850 crores.

Satyam, a global IT-company based in India, has just been added to a notorious list of companies involved in fraudulent financial reporting practices. Satyam CEO & Chairman, Mr. B. Ramalingam Raju, took responsibility for all the accounting improprieties. "This leads one to ask a simple question: How does this keep on happening for five years, without any suspicions? So, while Raju ran his fraud, the auditor slept, the analysts slept, and so did the media. To be fair, finally, the media and a whistle-blower did an excellent job of exposing Raju and his many other "shenanigans" after he had confessed" asked Bhasin (2016g). In his letter (of Jan.7, 2009) addressed to board of directors of Satyam, Raju showed the markers of this fraud 'pathology'. Now, more than six years later, the final decision in the Satyam scam has been made and all accused charge-sheeted in the case have been awarded punishment by the Court.

The Satyam fraudulent financial reporting scam is a glaring example of 'abuse' of accounting, in which the account books were cooked up. Recently, Bhasin (2016h) lucidly pointed out that "the culture at Satyam (especially dominated by the board) symbolized an unethical culture." This scam brought to light the role of CG in shaping the protocols related to the working of Audit Committee and duties of Board members. Now, it is amply clear that the Satyam scam was plotted at the top and driven by Ramalinga Raju and his brother. They were the key players in the plot to falsify the accounts and hide the bottom-line truth from everyone. It is also clear that all the culprits—from Raju down to the finance guys—did everything possible to give SEBI and other investigative agencies a run-around and delay the verdict. This is what explains, why it took more than five-and-a-half years to close an open-and-shut-case. It took nearly 2 years, involvement of multitude of investigation agencies, and over 200 experts to assess the total damage of the scam perpetrated by Raju. Now, the final figure is a shade under Rs. 8,000 crore. A special CBI Court in Hyderabad on April 9, 2015 finally, sentenced all the 10 people involved in the multi-crore accounting scam found guilty of cheating, forgery, destruction of evidence and criminal breach of trust. At last, almost the six-year-old case has reached its logical conclusion. Undoubtedly, the Indian government took quick actions to protect the interest of the investors, safeguard the credibility of India, and the nation's image across the world.

According to Mr. Chopra (2011), President of ICAI, "The Satyam scam was not an accounting or auditing failure, but one of CG. This apex body found the two PwC auditors 'prima-facie' guilty of professional misconduct." The CBI also charged the two auditors with complicity in the commission of the fraud by consciously overlooking the accounting irregularities. As Krishnan (2014) pointed out, "Yet both Satyam's internal as well as statutory auditors did not bring it to anyone's notice. Well, the internal auditor hauled up by SEBI has frankly admitted that he did notice differences in the amounts billed to big clients, such as Citigroup and Agilent, when he scoured Satyam's computerized accounts. But when he flagged this with Satyam's finance team, he was fobbed off with the assurance that the accounts would be 'reconciled'. Later, he was 'assured' that the problem had been fixed." Thus, the Satyam episode is not just the result of individual greed. It is also the product of the celebration of profit making irrespective of magnitude, of the belief in markets and the discipline they impose, and of regulatory dilution and regulatory failure. It is this which raises the possibility that Satyam may not be an isolated bad apple, but an instance of something that could recur. "As corporate India absorbs the implications of Raju's actions, business leaders need to push for stricter—yet sensible—accounting practices and CG regulations that keeps an effective checks and balances on companies. Thank God, lot of change has been made, more specifically about CG, corporate disclosure norms, audit committees, independent directors, etc.," suggests Bhasin (2016e). Raju in his letter confessed that doctoring the books over the years was akin to riding a tiger, not knowing how to get off without being eaten. If effective prescriptions are not found, it is more than just Raju and Satyam, who will be consumed in the following year. Finally, we recommend that "Fraudulent FR practices should be considered as a serious crime, and as such, accounting bodies, law courts and other regulatory authorities in India need to adopt very strict punitive measures to stop such unethical practices."

## REFERENCES

AICPA (2002), Consideration of fraud in a financial statement audit. Statement on Auditing Standards No.99, NY.

Adkins, T. (2016), Financial Statement Manipulation: An Ever-Present Problem for Investors. Available at http://www.investopedia.com.

Asif, M.K., Rehana, F. and Mamunur, R. (2011), Cosmetic Accounting Practices in Developing Countries: Bangladesh Perspectives, World Journal of Social Sciences, 1(3), July, 1-15.

Bhasin, M.L. (2007). Forensic Accounting: A New Paradigm for Niche Consulting. *The Chartered Accountant*, Jan., 1000-1010.

Bhasin, M.L. (2008). Corporate Governance and Role of the Forensic Accountant. *The Chartered Secretary*. 38(10), Oct., 1361-1368.

Bhasin, M.L. (2010). Corporate Governance Disclosure Practices: The Portrait of a Developing Country. *International Journal of Business and Management*. 5(4), April, 150-167.

Bhasin, M.L. (2011). Corporate Governance Disclosure Practices: The Portrait of a Developing Country. *International Review of Business Research Papers*. 7(1), Jan., 393-419.

Bhasin, M.L. (2012). Corporate Accounting Frauds: A Case Study of Satyam Computers Limited. *International Journal of Contemporary Business Studies*. Oct., 3(10), 16-42.

Bhasin, M.L. (2012a). Audit Committee Mechanism to Improve Corporate Governance: Evidence from a Developing Country. *Modern Economy*. 3(11), Nov. 856-72.

Bhasin, M.L. (2013). Corporate Accounting Scandal at Satyam: A Case Study of India's Enron. *European Journal of Business and Social Sciences*. 1(12), March, 25-47.

Bhasin, M.L. (2013a). Corporate Accounting Fraud: A Case Study of Satyam Computer Limited. *Open Journal of Accounting*. April, 2(2), 26-38.

Bhasin, M.L. (2013b). Corporate Governance and Role of the Forensic Accountant: An Exploratory Study of an Asian Country. *Amity Business Review*. 14(1), Jan-June, 48-71.

Bhasin, M.L. (2015). Forensic Accounting: Perspectives and Prospects. *Pakistan Accountant*. Oct.-Dec., pp. 44-48.

Bhasin, M.L. (2015a). Menace of Frauds in Banking Industry: Experience of a Developing Country. *Australian Journal of Business and Management Research*. 4(12), April, 21-33.

Bhasin, M.L. (2015b). Creative Accounting Practices in the Indian Corporate Sector: An Empirical Study. *International Journal of Management Science and Business Research*. 4(10), 35-52.

Bhasin, M.L. (2016). Debacle of Satyam Computers Limited: A Case Study of India's Enron. *Wulfenia Journal KLAGENFURT*. 23(3), March, 124-162.

Bhasin, M. L. (2016a). Survey of Creative Accounting Practices: An Empirical Study. *Wulfenia Journal KLAGENFURT*. 23(1), Jan., 143-162.

Bhasin, M.L. (2016b). Unethical Creative Accounting Culture at Satyam Computers Limited: A Case Study of India's Enron. *International Journal of Business and Social Research*. 6(7), 24-48.

Bhasin, M.L. (2016c). Strengthening Corporate Governance through an Audit Committee: An Empirical Study. *Wulfenia Journal*. 23(2), Feb., 2-27.

Bhasin, M.L. (2016d). Contribution of Forensic Accounting to Corporate Governance: An Exploratory Study of an Asian Country. *International Business Management*. 10(4), 479-492.
Bhasin, M.L. (2016e), The Challenge of Improving Corporate Governance by Creating Effective Audit Committees, *International Journal of Management Sciences and Business Research*, 5(8), 25-46.
Bhasin, M.L. (2016f), Perspectives and Prospects of An Audit Committee in An Asian Economy: An Empirical Study, *International Journal of Management Sciences and Business Research*, 5(8), 1-14.
Bhasin, M.L. (2016g), Creative Accounting Scam at Satyam Computer Limited: How the Fraud Story Unfolded?, *Open Journal of Accounting*, 5(4), 57-81.
Bhasin, M.L. (2016h), Unethical Accounting Practices in Connivance with Top Management: A Case Study of Satyam, *International Journal of Management Sciences and Business Research*, 5(9), 5-19.
Caskey, J. and Laux, V. (2015), Corporate Governance, Accounting Conservatism, and Manipulation. Available at SSRN: http://ssrn.com/abstract=2251378.
Chopra, A. (2011). Satyam fraud, not an accounting failure. *Business Standard*. 25 January. Available at http://www.business-standard.com.
Gupta, P.K. & Gupta, S. (2015) Corporate frauds in India: Perceptions and emerging issues. *Journal of Financial Crime*, 22(1):79-103.
Grant Thornton and ASSOCHAM (2006), Financial and Corporate Frauds, July. Available at www.grantthornton.in.
Hayat, U. (2014), The Sherlock Holmes of Accounting: Howard Schilit Explains the Mystery of His Art, 4 March. Available at https://blogs.cfainstitute.org.
ICAI (2009). ICAI finds ex Satyam CFO, Price Waterhouse auditors guilty. www.outlook India.com.
ICAI (2014). The Institute of Chartered Accountants of India has imposed a life-time ban on four auditors, April 22.
Jones, M. (2011). Creative accounting, fraud and international accounting scandals, John Wiley & Sons Ltd. London.
Kaul, V. (2015). Satyam scam: Ramalinga Raju, the man who knew too much, gets 7 years in jail, April 10.
Krishnan, A. (2014). Finally, the truth about Satyam, *The Hindu Business Line*, July 18.
Mamo, J. and Aliaz, A. (2014), Accounting Manipulation and its Effects in the Financial Statements of Albanian Entities, Interdisciplinary Journal of Research and Development, 1(2), 55-60.
Niazi, A. and Ali, M. (2015), The Debacle of Satyam Computers Ltd.: A Case Study from Management's Perspective, Universal Journal of Industrial and Business Management, 3(2), 58-65.
Pai, K. & Tolleson, T.D. (2015). India's Satyam Scandal: Evidence too Large to Indict Mindset of Accounting Regulators is a Global Phenomenon. *Review of Business and Finance Studies*. 6(2), 35-43.
Ramana, K.V. (2009). 7,561 fake invoices=Rs.5,117 crore Sales. April 15, Daily News Analysis. Available at http://www.dnaindia.com.
SEC (2016), Business and Financial Disclosure Required by Regulation S-K, available at https://www.sec.gov/rules/concept/2016/33-10064.pdf
Schilit, H.M. and Perler, J. (2010), Financial Shenanigans, Third Edition, Tata McGraw-Hill Education Limited, New Delhi.
SFIO (2009). Special Fraud Investigation Office Report published in the Pioneer. New Delhi, May 4, 1-10.
Sherman, H.D. & Young, S.D. (2016), Where Financial Reporting Still Falls Short, *Harvard Business Review*, July–August.
Shirur, S. (2011). Tunneling vs. Agency Effect: A Case Study of Enron and Satyam. *Vikalpa*. 36(3), 9-20.
Veena L. Brown, Brian E. Daugherty, & Julie S. Persellin (2014). Satyam Fraud: A Case Study of India's Enron. *Issues in Accounting Education*. August, 29(3), 419-442.
Winkler, D. (2010). India's Satyam Accounting Scandal. Feb.1. Available online at http://blogs.law.uiowa.edu.
Wharton (2009). Scandal at Satyam: Truth, Lies and Corporate Governance. Available at knowledge@wharton website.

# 12

# The Effect of Hot Money Flow on Pre-Crisis Indicators of Current Accounts and Real Sectors in Turkish Economy[1]

**Ömer Uğur Bulut[2], Sadık Rıdvan Karluk[3]**

**ABSTRACT**

We investigate the impact of the hot money movements on current account and real sector leading crisis indicators under VAR (Vector Autoregressive) framework using quarterly data for a long period of 1991-2014. Our findings show that hot money movements have negative impact on current account deficit and foreign trade deficit pre-crisis indicators. We further show that they lead to instability in growth and inflation pre-crisis indicators.

Keywords: Hot money movements, pre-crisis indicators, Turkish economy, VAR model.

---

## 1.0 INTRODUCTION

The hot money flow is an important part of the financial liberalization policies, applied during the 1980s in world economy. This concept, revealed its affect with the abolition of the restrictions on capital movements and the permission given to the residents to access to the financial markets. As suggested by (McKinnon, 1973) and (Shaw, 1973) in their financial liberalization hypothesis; the financial pressure policies such as restricting the movement of capital could contribute to the economic development and cause more effective distribution of the resources. Between the years of 1980 and 1990, affected by these ideas, many countries have applied the financial liberalization policies. However, except in some of the South-East Asia countries, in most of the countries, these policies became unsuccessful (Williamson, Mahar, 2002). Hence, the increase in the global saving pools means the increase of risk and uncertainty in the foreign capital, which is flowing to the countries.

From the 1980s, the liberalization programs supported by International Monetary Foundation (IMF) paved the way for foreign capital which hot money flow has an important part in. However, as in Latin America and South East countries this caused crisis also in Turkey. The foreign capital inflow is

---

[1] This article has been written by benefiting from the "Financial Liberalization and Pre-Crisis Indicators Analysis" named doctoral dissertation which has been written with the dissertation consultant Prof. Dr. S. Rıdvan Karluk

[2] Philosophy of Doctorate, E-mail: bulut.o.u@gmail.com
[3] Professor (retired), E-mail: rkarluk@anadolu.edu.tr

important for countries, which are continuing their industrial development but its negative effects leads up to economic and financial crisis. As emphasized by some researches -such as Kaminsky, Lizondo and Reinhart's research on KLR approach which is the widely-used method in economy literature about pre-crisis indicators- the pre-crisis indicators bear the qualification of signaling in predicting the crisis. There are other studies includes (Frankel, Rose 1996) and (Corsetti, Pesenti & Roubini, 1998). Considering the number of studies and meaningful number of statistical results, the current accounts and real sector pre-crisis indicators are prominent. On the other hand, in studies related to hot money movement in economy literature includes (Corbo, Hernandez 1996), (Yeldan, 1996) and (Rodrik, Velasco 1999) show that the meaning of this concept has not been defined clearly. It is often defined within the short-term capital movement. The number of empirical studies is also low.

By assessing these results in literature, in our study, the positive and negative effects of hot money on the current account and real sector indicators and its usability as a political tool have been studied with vector autoregressive model (VAR). By using the VAR model the effect of hot money movement in pre-crisis indicators of current accounts and real sector in Turkish economy, after year 1991 is analyzed. The sample and data used in econometric analysis section were chosen by considering the performances of pre-crisis indicators in the study of (Kaminsky, Lizondo & Reinhart, 1998) and collected from the web sites of Turkish Central Bank (TCB), Turkish Statistical Institute (TSI) and International Financial Statistics (IFC). The results will provide important hints and opinion to the policy makers on the efficiency and usability of one of the important parts of financial liberalization policy; the hot money flow policy tool, in management of the Turkish economy. The financial liberalization policy of the Turkish economy will be able to directed against hot money movements. Within this purpose, the hot money flow in Turkey is discussed firstly. And then, after expressing the review of literature and pre-crisis indicators, the econometric model application is reported.

## 2.0 THE HOT MONEY FLOW IN TURKISH ECONOMY

Before the 1980, the Turkish economy faced; macroeconomic instability, the problem of financing of balance of payments deficit, the high inflation and high foreign debt (important part of it being short-term), the imports bottleneck and stagnation of exports. During 1970s it has highly been affected by the global crisis and there had been disruption in macroeconomic indicators and problems in foreign debt payments. This situation caused the criticism of import-substitution policies and lead to the search for alternative policies. Thus, with the 24$^{th}$ January 1980 dated Decisions, the foreign financial liberalization policies put in effect. The Turkish economy completed its financial liberalization period with the foreign trade liberalization in 1980 and the abolition of restrictions on the foreign capital movement in 1989. At the end of this period, in which the final steps been taken to be in harmony with the global economy, many crises occurred with different reasons and results.

The movement of capital occurs when; the resident individuals or institutions of one of the country transfer funds to the resident individuals or institutions of another country (Uzunoğlu, Alkın & Gürlesel, 1995). The permission of freedom of movement of capital in Turkey occurs when foreign residents move the actively in financial markets of Turkey buying stocks and bonds in Turkey, and similarly, the residents of Turkey having the right to perform the same transactions in foreign countries.

The movement of capital can be classified as short-term or a long-term based on the time frame that the capital stays in the country for the development purposes, technical purposes, defense and commercial purposes. The movement of capital provides financial and technological resources to the country, by lending, investment or by joining to the process of production.

The movement of capital can be seen in capital account section of balance of payment of countries. The abolition of restrictions on these movements means the liberalization of the capital account. The movement of capital in Turkey reveals its effect with hot money flow.

In 1989, because of the financial liberalization, the freedom of movement of capital and the increasing need of borrowing brought up the topic of hot money flow and it is one of the important part of the movement of capital in Turkish economy. Turkey faced the negative effects of abolition of restrictions on movement of capital firstly, in year 1994. In 1994 and after, in global crisis of November 2000, February 2011 and 2008, a huge amount of hot money out flowed the country (Karluk, 2014).

In economy, there is no general definition of hot money. It is one of the short-term capital movements. However, since the hot money inflows rapidly for profit purposes and outflows in a minor negativity in economy, compared to short term capital, it is vague, speculative and have a high potential of risk. The concept of hot money can be explained as a capital investment which rapidly reacts to the changes in expected income rate and risks (Oktar, 1995). According to another definition, the hot money is the short-term capital flow which have speculative, short term, risk and mobilization components and is a short-term capital movement investing with factors of high risk and income arising from the difference between interest and foreign currency rates in the national markets (Yeldan, 1996). In other words, the hot money, is the short-term money, flowing to the country except by exports, tourism or foreign direct investment, and flowing from two windows; the short-term lending and portfolio investments.

The Turkish economy became vulnerable to economic crisis with the abolition of restrictions on movement of foreign capital. The hot money inflow based on arbitrage about income, the interest rates and expected foreign currency rates, leads the economy into crisis. After 2002, the floating exchange rate system was not able to prevent the outflow of hot money because of the elasticity provided by the forward foreign exchange market (Boratav, 2009).

As can be seen in Table 1, most of the economic crises occurred because of the rapid slowdown of capital inflow or the opposite. The period after the liberalization of capital movement, as revealed in Table 2, the fundamental reason behind the fluctuation in growth is the foreign originated capital movement. In each of periods that the capital inflow slowed down or move oppositely (1994, 2001) the growth rate declined and became negative. As can be seen in Table 2, the positive average growth rate of which is more than 5% caused the current deficit growth and more foreign capital inflow occurred to finance the deficit. Hence, in the years when the capital movement was controlled the foreign capital inflow been used to finance the current deficit.

The period after 1989, in which the movement of capital been liberalized, the reason of short term expansion, in other words the increase in growth, was the increase in foreign capital, which largely includes hot money movement. After The period of 1998-2001, which includes the years of recession and depression, the most effective variable initiating the years of expansion was foreign origin capital inflow (Boratav, 2009). The foreign capital inflow initiates the expansion of demand in any condition. As can be seen in Table 2, triggered by the reasons mentioned, the expansion of demand or short term growth causes the increase in current account deficit starting from the foreign trade balance.

**Table 1:** The foreign capital movement in pre-crisis and crisis years

| The Crisis Years | The Foreign Capital Inflow one year before the Crisis (Million USD) | The Foreign Capital Inflow In the year of Crisis (Million USD) |
|---|---:|---:|
| 1994 Crisis | 12079 | -3925 |
| 2000/2001 Crisis | 15726 | -3837 |
| 2008 Crisis | 75684 | -10894 |

As stipulated in Table 2, after 2001 crisis, the high rate of capital inflow ended with 7,2% growth rate, the current account deficit, increased up to 6%. In 2001 crisis an opposite situation occurred. The foreign capital increased in high rate, compared to the year before the crisis and caused -9,5 growth rate, which was the lowest after the second World War. However, the current deficit occurred 2,6% more, compared to the pre-crisis years. The increase in current deficit became chronic in 2000s. The appreciation of Turkish Lira, the effects of Customs Union and the transformation of structure of industry towards external dependence have influence on this situation (Boratav, 2009). On the other hand, as can be seen in Table 2, between the years of 2002-2007 the high increase in inflow of foreign capital became most effective factor in current deficit financing. Rapidly growing foreign debt is the common reason of the negative relation of current deficit and growth and the effect of foreign capital on them. In Table 2, during 2000s, since the current deficit increased in relation to the growth, the foreign inflow of capital increased more in 2000s compared to 1990s.

**Table 2:** The foreign capital movement, the current deficit and growth (%)

| Year | Foreign Capital Movement/ GDP | Current Deficit / GDP | Growth Rate |
|---|---|---|---|
| 1984–1988 | 2,2 | -0,8 | 6,2 |
| 1989–1993 | 3,3 | -1,2 | 5,0 |
| Crisis: 1994 | -4,8 | 2,0 | -6,08 |
| 1995–1997 | 3,4 | -1,4 | 7,7 |
| 1998–1999 | 3,0 | 0,3 | -1,2 |
| 2000 | 8,1 | -4,9 | 6,3 |
| Crisis: 2001 | -1,7 | 2,6 | -9,5 |
| 2002–2007 | 9,8 | -5,8 | 7,2 |

Table 3 reveals that, when the inflow of foreign capital is compared in years of 1994, 2000 ,2001 and 2008, both before and after the years of crisis, it can be seen that; the foreign capital act reversely (the sign of - reveals the outflow). This Table also stipulates that the Turkish economy dragged into unsteady growth period in the years (1989-2007) that the liberalization of foreign capital started. While the economic growth was -9,5% in year 2001, it was 7,2% on average, in the period of 2002-2007. (Table 2 and Table 3). These two data demonstrate the unsteady growth of capital in Turkish economy and the dependency to the foreign capital movement between the years of 1989-2007. While Turkey grows 3,6% on average, the sharp up and down cycle that is experiences, increased the negative expectations on uncertainty, risk in investments and growth in relation to future.

In 2008 crisis, the foreign capital movement has affected the economy as in the crisis of 1994, 2000-2001. If we compare the intensity of the effect, in the 2008 crisis the foreign capital outflow was higher compared to the other crisis. As can be seen in Table 3, during the 12 months before the year 2008, the foreign capital inflow was 76 billion USD. On the other hand, the foreign capital inflow before the crisis in years of 1994 and 2011 was approximately 28 billion USD. The high foreign capital inflow that occurred in year before the 2008, compared to the years before the other two crisis years caused higher rate of capital outflow in the months of crisis. In relation to the its effect on growth rate of Turkey if we compare the 2008 crisis with other crisis that occurred, we can see that 2001 crisis has the heaviest effect. In relation to growth, the 1994 crisis negative effect was 6,08% and 2008 crisis negative effect was 4,8% however, in 2001 crisis the Turkish economy downsized by 9,5%.

**Table 3:** The foreign capital movement in 1994, 2000-2001, 2008 global crisis and pre-crisis years

| Crisis Years | The Foreign Capital Inflow One year before the Crisis (Million USD) | The Foreign Capital Inflow In the year of Crisis (Million USD) | Net Foreign Capital (Million USD) | The Growth in Years of Crisis (%) |
|---|---|---|---|---|
| 1994 Crisis | 12079 | -3925 | 8154 | -6,08 |
| 2000/2001 Crisis | 15726 | -3837 | 11889 | -9,5 |
| 2008 Crisis | 75684 | -10894 | 64700 | -4,8 |

As can be seen in the Table 4, the main indicator of crisis in Turkey is the outflow of foreign capital and it is 5,4 billion USD net in October 2008, as in 1994 and 2000-2001 crisis. Compared to the 1,654 billion USD net inflow in October 2007, in year 2008 there is a back flow of approximately 7 billion USD. When we analyze the net capital movement, the foreign net inflow realized but compared to the previous year it dropped to 1,142 billion USD in October 2008.The reason of net capital movement being in surplus is the approximately 7,4 billion USD unrecorded capital inflow from an unaccredited source.

The other prominent indicators in Table 4 are; national capital and hot money. In October 2008, 851 million USD national capital, approximately 3 billion USD national hot Money and 5,6 billion USD foreign hot Money outflow was realized. In total, approximately 7,6 billion USD net hot money outflowed from Turkish economy. The decline of foreign capital not only affected the slowdown of national income but also contributed to the decrease of national income. The increase in outflows leads to financial crisis even if there is unrecorded capital inflow (Boratav, 2011).

**Table 4:** The foreign capital movement, October 2007 – 2008 (Million USD)

| | October 2007 | October 2008 |
|---|---|---|
| Foreign Capital | 1654 | -5390 |
| National Capital | 2510 | -851 |
| Unrecorded Capital | -1046 | 7383 |
| Net Capital | 3118 | 1142 |
| Foreign Hot Money | -358 | -5558 |
| National Hot Money | 3053 | -2016 |
| Net Hot Money | 2695 | -7574 |

In 2008 crisis, the net capital movement decreased while the foreign capital outflow occurred in high rate. As can be seen in Table-4, the 7,4 billion USD unrecorded capital inflow compensated the outflow of foreign capital. In that reason, there is a "decline" in the net capital movement and not a "net outflow". As can be seen at Table 5, until October 2008, in economy, the foreign capital inflow continued in an increasing way despite the global crisis. In October 2008, approximately 5,4 billion USD outflow occurred. As can be seen from the data of November 2008 and November 2009, the outflow of foreign capital from Turkish economy continued until November 2009. After in October 2008 the reverse cycle (the conversion of foreign capital from inflow to outflow) ended.

In Table 5, it can be seen that, the foreign capital; from its 4,4 billion outflow in November 2008, changed into 786 million USD inflow in 2009. The net capital increased by 993 million USD. From the 2009 November data laid out in Tablo-5, it can be seen that, the external shock caused by the October 2008 capital movement ended in November 2009.

The Table 3, Table 4 and Table 5 reveals that, after the year 1989, in which the capital movement is liberalized in Turkey, the expansion of economy in Turkey became dependent on the foreign source inflow. When the capital inflow standstills, the contraction occurs and when the inflows changes into net outflow, the financial crisis comes up. The Tables in this section presents the dimensions of the external shocks arising from the capital outflow.

**Table 5:** The foreign capital movement: October 2007, October 2008, November 2008 and November 2009 (Million USD)

| | October 2007 | October 2008 | November 2008 | November 2009 |
|---|---|---|---|---|
| Foreign Capital | 1654 | -5390 | -4357 | 786 |
| National Capital | 2510 | -851 | 3379 | -743 |
| Unrecorded Capital | -1046 | 7383 | 1064 | 1036 |
| Net Capital | 3118 | 1142 | 86 | 1079 |

After the abolition of restrictions on the foreign capital, the markets in Turkey started to be controlled by the short term speculative foreign capital. As an effective crisis indicator; the hot money that bear the risk of leaving the country in any minor negativity, entered into the economic environment which already has important macro-economic instabilities such as current deficit and high inflation and the hot money played an important role in economic problems encountered after 1989. In addition to the macroeconomic instabilities and political uncertainty; the environment where the state intervention is minimized, the stability of the economy dangerously been risked by the speculative movement of foreign capital inflow and outflow [10]. After the liberalization of movement of capital, the Turkish economy became vulnerable to crisis. The crisis which have been experienced after 1989, such as the crisis of 1994, 2000-2001 and 2008 are the known examples of this situation. In an already negative environment the regulation of liberalization, lead up to the increase in crisis.

## 3.0 THE REVIEW OF LITERATURE

The idea of "hot money movement creating instability in economies of countries", lead to the performance of studies on this subject. The studies on the short term capital movement which the hot money flow is part of, (Corbo, Hernandez 1996), (Yeldan, 1996) ile (Rodrik, Velasco 1999) defended that; the short term capital inflow causes instability and crisis in economy and should be restricted when necessary. In their study on the effects of movement of capital on fundamental macro-economic indicators on the period of years between 1989 and 1999 in Turkish economy, (İnsel, Sungur 2003), with the real and financial indicators revealed that the movement of capital causes instability in economy. (Altıntaş, Öz, 2007), in their study on the 1994 and 2001 Turkish economy crisis, by using the signaling approach, presented that the capital outflow can be used as a pre-crisis indicator. In their study, (Mercan, Peker, 2013) used portfolio investments and capital inflow as representing the financial openness, although these indicators found to be affecting the growth in positive way, they were found to be statistically meaningless.

There are also some other studies focusing on pre-crisis indicators of Turkish economy including the current accounts and real sector indicators performed. (Üçer, Rijckeghem & Yolalan, 1998), in order to analyze the 1994 crisis, applied the KLR test. In the study, they presented that the export/import, short-term foreign debt/ GDP, short term advances/ GDP, reserves/M2Y+debt stock and M1 indicators found successful in predicting the financial crises. (Gerni, Selçuk & Değer, 2005), in their study on the Turkish economy crisis, with their pre-indicator approach, reached to the conclusion that the overvaluation of national money is a pre-crisis indicator. (Avcı, Altay 2013), in their study, they used the monthly data of 1990-2009 and the Markov Regime Switching Model and Regression Tree Models and they proved that the inflation and foreign trade balance indicators are successful in predicting financial crisis.

In our study, we aimed to analyze the effect of hot money on the current account and real sector pre-crisis indicators. For this purpose, the objectives can be expressed as follows: (1) How are hot money movements affecting the current account and real sector pre-crisis indicators? (2) How is the efficiency of hot money movements on current account and real sector pre-crisis indicators?

## 4.0 PRE-CRISIS INDICATORS

In the studies performed to assess the economic and financial crisis, the change in the macroeconomic indicators such as; the decline in international reserves, real interest rates, the increase in short term debt, national inflation, current deficit and the imbalance of foreign trade, the decrease of growth rate signals the financial crisis. (Frankel, Rose 1996), (Kaminsky, Lizondo, Reinhart, 1998), and (Corsetti, Pesenti & Roubini, 1998) try to determine the crisis with indexes calculated by using different methods (Seyidoğlu, Yıldız, 2006). This approach for the economic and financial crisis caused others to focus on the studies related to the pre-crisis indictors.

Among the studies on determination of these indicators, the most important and comprehensive one is the approach of (Kaminsky, Lizondo & Reinhart, 1998) which is called KLR approach and performed by using the signaling method. The mentioned study has been performed by using the monthly data of years between 1975 and 1995 of fifteen developing and five developed countries. According to KLR study, when one of the macroeconomic indicators is above the threshold, it is a sign that indicates a possible financial crisis in the following 24 months (Karaçor, Alptekin, 2006). As a pre-crisis indicator of current account, the current account deficit, the foreign currency rate and foreign trade balance and as a pre-crisis indicator of real sector; growth rate and inflation have been designated as important crisis indicators (Kaminsky, Lizondo & Reinhart, 1998).

The fundamental goal of the pre-crisis indicator approach is to assess the crisis before they occur. For this purpose, the signals of designated variables are analyzed within a certain period. The crisis signal occurs when, one of the variables designated as a crisis indicator is above the set threshold (Çeviş, 2005). The study which is named as KLR approach in literature, can be seen on Table 6, where the current balance and real sector pre-crisis indicators performance has been analyzed (Kaminsky, Lizondo & Reinhart, 1998).

In our study; the pre-crisis indicators used in econometric analysis section were chosen by considering the performances of pre-crisis indicators in Table 6 chosen in the study of (Kaminsky, Lizondo & Reinhart, 1998). In relation to the current accounts and real sector pre-crisis indicators, we have considered the studies quantity being excessive and statistical meaning of them. In that manner, as a pre-crisis indicator of current account, the foreign currency rate, the current account deficit, and foreign trade balance deficit and as a pre-crisis indicator of real sector; growth rate and inflation have been used.

The decrease in foreign currency rate is an indicator of change of value of national Money. The overvaluation of national money destabilizes the current accounts. These valuations cause the outflow of capital from the country hence it is expected to increase before the crisis (Avcı, Altay, 2013). The overvaluation of national money increases the probability of occurrence financial crisis (Turgut, 2007). The increase in exports is a sign of loss of completion in international markets, the decrease in exports may be the result of overvaluation of national money. The foreign currency assets can cause risks for the banks that are in breach of their obligations. The increases in imports occur in line with the weak foreign markets and overvaluation of national money and is one of the reasons of money crisis (Altıntaş, Öz, 2007). The deterioration of trade balance increased the expectation of devaluation so it's expected to decrease before the crisis (Avcı, Altay, 2013).

**Table 6:** The economic pre-crisis indicators and their performances

| Sector | Variables | The Number of Studies Analyzed | Statistically Meaningful Results |
|---|---|---|---|
| Current Accounts | Foreign currency rate | 14 | 2 |
| | Current account balance Trade | 7 | 2 |
| | Balance | 3 | 2 |
| | Export | 3 | 2 |
| | Import | 2 | 1 |
| | Terms of Trade | 3 | 2 |
| | Export Prices | 1 | - |
| | Savings | 1 | - |
| | Investment | 2 | - |
| | Currency rate Expectations | 1 | - |
| Real Sector | Inflation | 5 | 5 |
| | Real GDP growth or level | 9 | 5 |
| | Output Gap | 1 | 1 |
| | Employment/ Unemployment | 3 | 2 |
| | Change in Bond Prices | 1 | 1 |

The current account having a negative value in a country means that the exports cannot meet the imports and this leads the country to use borrowing to clear this deficit. The increase in borrowing and capital outflow, in relation to the sustainability of the debt may deepen the current account deficit problems of the country (Altıntaş, Öz, 2007).

The decline of the growth rate is also a Real sector pre-crisis indicator and it increases the vulnerability in economy (Avcı, Altay, 2013). Before the crisis, the decline of growth rate is expected (Kaminsky, Lizondo & Reinhart, 1998). The inflation moves parallel to the high nominal interest rates and by negatively affecting the economy, it increases the vulnerability in economy. Hence, the increase of inflation is also expected (Avcı, Altay, 2013).

## 5.0 THE ECONOMETRIC MODEL APPLICATION

The data for our econometric application been collected from the web sites of Turkish Central Bank (TCB) Turkish Statistical Institute (TSI) and International Financial Statistics (IFC). The Eviews 8.0 packaged software been used. In that manner, the three-month-data used and application made for the years between 1991-2014. Since the foreign capital inflow increased in high rate in 1991 in Turkey, that year has been used for beginning.

The VAR model is an appropriate model since it can designate the efficiency and usability of the indicators as a policy tool. The designation of most effective variance on the macro-economic indicators is determined with the variance decomposition and the efficiency and usability of this effective variance as a policy tool is determined by cause and effect functions (Sevüktekin, Nargeleçekenler, 2010).

In order to clear the seasonality effect on the time series of variables, "Tramo Seats" and "Moving Average" method been use and the time series of variables has been transferred into logarithmic form. However, since the cab, hmm and open variables became negative in some periods, their logarithmic transformation have not been performed. In the following phase, the Zivot-Andrews unit root test has been applied to determine whether the variables are stable or not. At this point the classical unit root tests such as ADF is criticized since these tests have tendency to find unrealistic unit root when there is structural breaks. (Zivot, Andrews 2002) developed the Zivot-Andrews test, which designates the structural breaks in the predicted period, and perform the unit root test. Zivot-Andrews test designates the structural breaks of variables internally.

Zivot-Andrews unit root test results are presented in Table 8. According to the results in Table 8 in the model including stable and trend in the 5% significance level, the values of cab, hmm, open levels are high so they are stable. In the light of these results; based on the Zivot and Andrews unit root test results, the pre-crisis indicators of real sector which are growth (rgdp) and inflation (inf) will be in VAR model with their first differences. Also, based on the Zivot-Andrews unit root test results the pre-crisis indicators of current account which are current account (open), foreign trend deficit (open) with their level values and foreign currency exchange rate (e) with its first difference will be in VAR model. The hot money movement (hmm) also with its level value will be in VAR model.

**Table 7.** The ındicators used in econometric application

| The Real Sector Pre-crisis Indicators | The Current Account Pre-crisis Indicators | Capital Movement Pre-crisis Indicators |
|---|---|---|
| The Growth (rgdp) | Curent Account Balance (cab) | Hot Money Movement (hmm) |
| Inflation (inf) | Foreign Currency Exchange Rate (e) | |
| | Foreign Trade Deficit (open) | |

In the VAR model after determining the stability of the variables (whether they are stable or not) the other test that should be applied is the appropriate test to designate the lag-length. After that, it is important to apply variance and autocorrelation test and examine the characteristic roots, in order to determine whether the VAR model is stable or not. The lag-length test results based on the VAR model information criteria are presented in Table 9. The optimal lag lengths can be designated with Akaike, Schwarz and Finite Prediction Error information criteria (Gujarati, 2003). As long as there is no structural problem in the model (such as changing variance and autocorrelation) the leg-lengths that these kind of information criteria refer are used in general.

**Table 8:** The results of zivot – andrews unit root test

| The Variables | Break in Stable and Trend[a] | Stability |
|---|---|---|
| Current Account Balance (cab) | -5.46 (2001Q1) | I (0) |
| Foreign Currency Exchange Rate (e) | -4.63 (2001Q1) | I (1) |
| Foreign Trend Deficit (Open) | -5.14 (2001Q1) | I (0) |
| Growth (rgdp) | -3.74 (2002Q1) | I (1) |
| Inflation (inf) | -3.91 (2003Q3) | I (1) |
| Hot Money Movement (hmm) | -5.21 (2010Q1) | I (0) |

a. For the break in stability in 1%, 5% and 10% significance level are (in order) -5.34, -4.93 and -4.58. The values in break in trend are (in order) -4.80, -4.42 and -4.11. The break in stability and trend are (in order) -5.57, -5.08 and -4.82. The dates shown in parenthesis show years of the break.

In Table 9 the according to LR, FPE and AIC the lag-length is 4. In this lag-length, there is no change in variance and autocorrelation and all the roots are within the circle, so there is no structural problem in the model. The VAR (4) model is stable and consistent.

**Table 9:** VAR model designation of lag-length criteria

| Lag | LR | FPE | AIC | SC | HQ |
|---|---|---|---|---|---|
| 0 | NA | 5.66e+54 | 143.1008 | 143.2769 | 143.1715 |
| 1 | 282.4996 | 3.16e+53 | 140.2122 | 141.4449* | 140.7071* |
| 2 | 37.59462 | 4.47e+53 | 140.5454 | 142.8347 | 141.4645 |
| 3 | 46.56811 | 5.32e+53 | 140.6843 | 144.0302 | 142.0276 |
| 4 | 114.1564* | 1.85e+53* | 139.5596* | 143.9621 | 141.3271 |
| 5 | 35.68127 | 2.49e+53 | 139.7380 | 145.1971 | 141.9297 |
| 6 | 42.29703 | 2.81e+53 | 139.6761 | 146.1918 | 142.2921 |
| 7 | 19.01674 | 5.46e+53 | 140.0665 | 147.6389 | 143.1067 |
| 8 | 27.26576 | 8.63e+53 | 140.1183 | 148.7473 | 143.5827 |

* refers the lag-length chosen by information criteria, LR: The likelihood rate; FPE: Finite Prediction Error Criteria AIC: Akaike Information Criteria; SIC: Schwarz Information Criteria; HQ: Hannan – Quinn Information Criteria

In VAR model, the cause and effect functions that are produced with "Cholesky decomposition" method, can be changed based on the order of variables. The order of the variables that are entered into the model should be made starting from external and after internal. The order is designated by the previous knowledge on the variables (Tarı, 2015).

In the cause and effect functions that are designated by using these methods, to define the standard errors the Monet Carlo simulation technique been used and for the point predictions (cause and effect results) the standard errors with 100 iterations are calculated. In Figure 1 the reaction of current account and real sector pre-crisis indicators to the shocks in hot money movement can be seen. The broken lines show the standard errors and the straight lines show the cause and effect results. The results below the zero reveal the negative reactions and the values over the zero reveal the positive reactions.

In order to assess the shocks that will be applied to the hot money flow; the movement of the variables during 10 periods been examined. In Figure 1 the reaction of the pre-crisis indicators of current account and real sector to hot money flow in 1 standard deviation of error terms is given. The results give information on the negative and positive effects of hot money movement on pre-crisis indicators of current account and real sector

In Figure 1 the reaction of the pre-crisis indicators of current account; the current account deficit (cab) and foreign trade deficit (open) to hot money movement (hmm) is negative in the beginning. The negative effect continues during the period. The effect of both cab and open variable to hmm is negative during 10 periods and the approach towards positive after second and sixth period is totally limited. The hot money movement has negative and increasing effect on pre-crisis indicators of current account; the current deficit and foreign trade deficit. The reaction of foreign exchange rate (e) to hmm is (as in other pre-crisis indicators of current account) negative in the beginning, after the fifth period it reacts up and down and after eighth period it returns to negative again. The results in the Figure 1 reveal that the hot money movement affects another pre-crisis indicator current account foreign exchange rate negatively at the end of 10 periods in general. According to VAR (4) model, the hot money movement cannot be used as policy tool for current account pre-crisis indicator because it does not have any positive effect on these indicators.

**Figure 1:** The reaction of pre-crisis indicators of current accounts and real sector to shocks that are generalized one standard deviated hot money movement (± 2 S.E.)

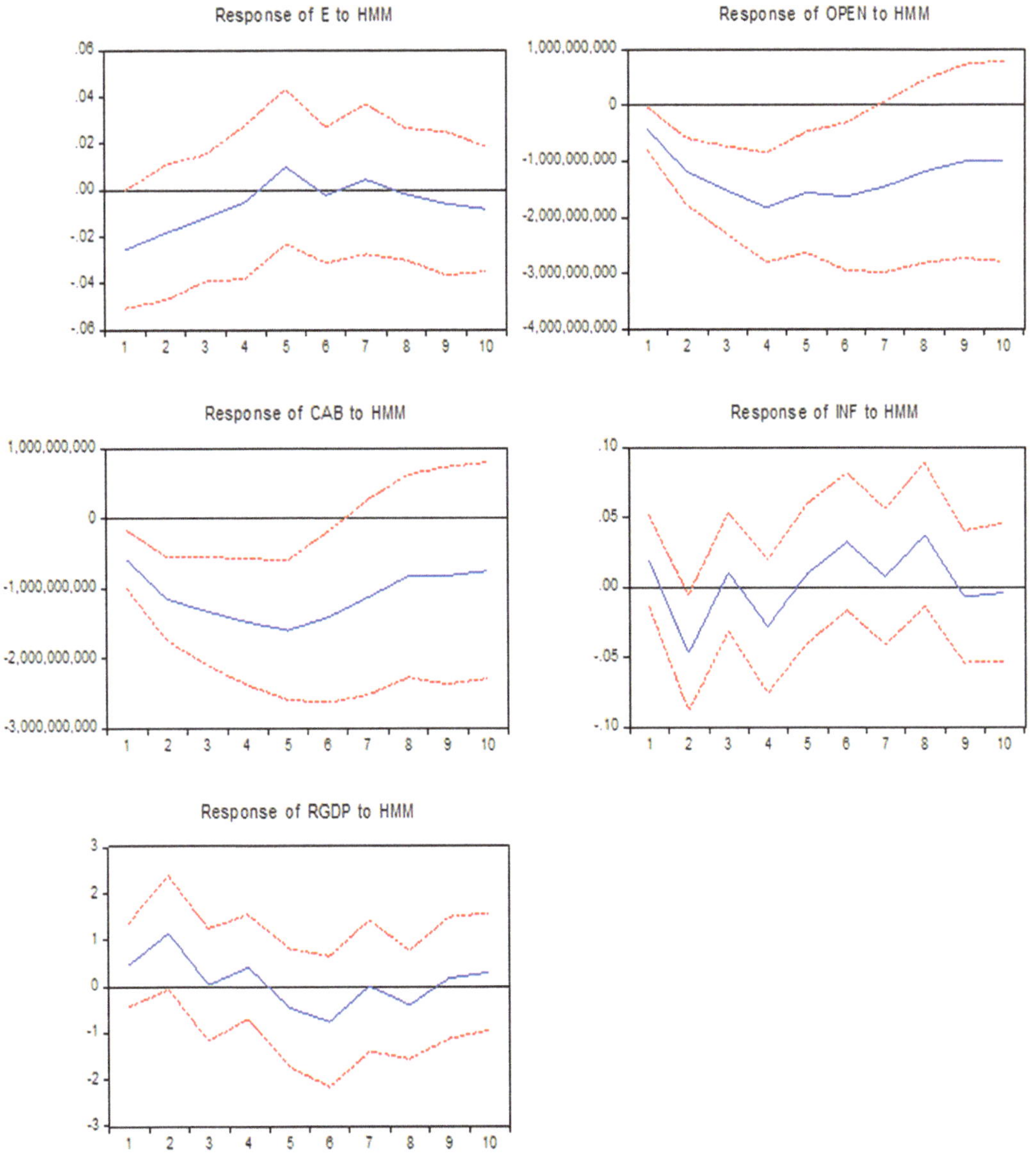

According to Figure 1 (above), the effect of hot money movement on growth (rgdp) is positive in the beginning although this positive effect returns to negative starting from the fifth period, at the end of the tenth period the growth gives positive reaction again. The inflation (inf) between the first and second period, reacts to hot money movement by sharply descending. After that, between the third and fourth period it reacts to hot money movement by increasing sharply. In the fifth period, the inflation reacts to hot money movement positively and in the last period this reaction returns to negative. During 10 periods the reaction of real sector pre-crisis indicators; growth and inflation is up and down and unstable. In 10 periods, the hot money movement effects both the inflation and growth positively and increasingly in general. As a result, the hot money movement causes fluctuation and instability on both of these indicators.

The variance decomposition is an approach that targets to define the relationships of macro-variables. In variance decomposition; the change in variance is examined to define how much of this change (in percentage) occurred by the variance itself and how much (in percentage) of it occurs by the effect of other variances (Tarı, 2015). The fundamental reason of VAR (4) model variance decomposition is to reveal the effect of hot money on current account and real sector indicators.

**Table 10:** Variance decomposition of current account balance

| Period | HMM | E | OPEN | CAB | INF | RGDP |
|---|---|---|---|---|---|---|
| 1 | 8.279522 | 9.335518 | 61.55717 | 20.82779 | 0.000000 | 0.000000 |
| 2 | 20.93126 | 7.640864 | 57.93176 | 12.99184 | 0.332096 | 0.172171 |
| 3 | 29.01176 | 6.869367 | 54.67017 | 9.013945 | 0.287389 | 0.147375 |
| 4 | 37.39657 | 7.359322 | 47.11191 | 7.502390 | 0.431414 | 0.198397 |
| 5 | 44.26402 | 9.999274 | 39.02371 | 6.129474 | 0.407625 | 0.175899 |
| 6 | 48.34712 | 11.21034 | 34.25529 | 5.490665 | 0.482735 | 0.213848 |
| 7 | 50.19279 | 12.02497 | 31.56577 | 5.492102 | 0.464419 | 0.259953 |
| 8 | 50.25701 | 13.40162 | 29.80401 | 5.826622 | 0.458254 | 0.252482 |
| 9 | 50.42848 | 14.92062 | 28.32158 | 5.540955 | 0.506701 | 0.281656 |
| 10 | 50.53192 | 16.06916 | 27.17761 | 5.326901 | 0.617513 | 0.276889 |

When Table 10 and Table 11 is analyzed, at the end of ten period, the changes that occur in the current account balance (cab) and foreign trade deficit (open) variances can mostly be explained by the hot money movement (hmm). In the Variance Decomposition results; the hot money movement is the most effective indicator on the current account balance and foreign trade deficit and this result coincide with the cause and effect results.

In the VAR (4) Model cause and effect results; the negative reaction of the current account deficit (cab) and foreign trade deficit (open) to hot money movement (hmm) in the beginning continues and exists during the period.

**Table 11:** Variance decomposition of foreign trade

| Period | HMM | E | OPEN | CAB | INF | RGDP |
|---|---|---|---|---|---|---|
| 1 | 5.207899 | 14.05958 | 80.73252 | 0.000000 | 0.000000 | 0.000000 |
| 2 | 19.76466 | 12.14884 | 65.79045 | 1.707580 | 0.152981 | 0.435485 |
| 3 | 29.95487 | 11.48049 | 55.85825 | 1.867347 | 0.261513 | 0.577532 |
| 4 | 40.87141 | 10.77494 | 45.67024 | 1.645668 | 0.278266 | 0.759477 |
| 5 | 44.93721 | 12.42225 | 39.24028 | 2.493216 | 0.281017 | 0.626025 |
| 6 | 48.87426 | 14.05159 | 33.67688 | 2.429452 | 0.376496 | 0.591321 |
| 7 | 51.33741 | 15.24147 | 30.18799 | 2.248200 | 0.345863 | 0.639062 |
| 8 | 52.35511 | 16.04600 | 28.10192 | 2.501191 | 0.353942 | 0.641831 |
| 9 | 52.26209 | 17.27567 | 26.46781 | 2.973253 | 0.367380 | 0.653794 |
| 10 | 52.16483 | 18.78914 | 25.08375 | 2.898373 | 0.433999 | 0.629904 |

**Table 12:** Variance decomposition of foreign currency exchange

| Period | HMM | E | OPEN | CAB | INF | RGDP |
|---|---|---|---|---|---|---|
| 1 | 6.513374 | 93.48663 | 0.000000 | 0.000000 | 0.000000 | 0.000000 |
| 2 | 8.885109 | 90.53328 | 0.013082 | 0.392209 | 0.000245 | 0.176077 |
| 3 | 9.724854 | 88.35640 | 0.219251 | 1.126015 | 0.048875 | 0.524608 |
| 4 | 9.443389 | 85.72360 | 2.041992 | 1.796155 | 0.437519 | 0.557341 |
| 5 | 9.851367 | 83.54479 | 2.137000 | 1.729736 | 1.050169 | 1.686938 |
| 6 | 9.717802 | 83.28670 | 2.351503 | 1.868399 | 1.097340 | 1.678255 |
| 7 | 9.674245 | 82.81702 | 2.487258 | 1.871721 | 1.497984 | 1.651767 |
| 8 | 9.588859 | 82.20632 | 2.844633 | 1.894896 | 1.567081 | 1.898207 |
| 9 | 9.629246 | 81.69037 | 3.178423 | 1.858936 | 1.712348 | 1.930676 |
| 10 | 9.980613 | 80.84925 | 3.590698 | 1.960161 | 1.694381 | 1.924896 |

According to Table 12, at the end of 10 periods, the foreign exchange rate (e) -another current account pre-crisis indicator- is mostly affected by hot money movement, after itself. The hot money movement is almost 10% effective on the foreign exchange rate at the end of 10 periods.

**Table 13:** Variance decomposition of growth

| Period | HMM | E | OPEN | CAB | INF | RGDP |
|---|---|---|---|---|---|---|
| 1 | 1.375208 | 29.38429 | 2.077686 | 0.046460 | 0.063577 | 67.05277 |
| 2 | 8.956216 | 26.22195 | 4.212115 | 0.328302 | 0.473091 | 59.80832 |
| 3 | 8.802332 | 25.76167 | 5.812999 | 0.379223 | 0.465601 | 58.77818 |
| 4 | 9.259267 | 25.12433 | 8.434551 | 0.910070 | 0.499941 | 55.77184 |
| 5 | 7.757803 | 32.45887 | 7.981066 | 1.437972 | 0.406249 | 49.95805 |
| 6 | 9.799217 | 31.25885 | 8.360561 | 1.385168 | 0.525596 | 48.67061 |
| 7 | 9.742160 | 31.07744 | 8.413602 | 1.651270 | 0.538785 | 48.57674 |
| 8 | 10.10550 | 30.83144 | 9.155786 | 1.755670 | 0.778082 | 47.37351 |
| 9 | 9.745776 | 31.02109 | 9.216980 | 1.675665 | 0.845192 | 47.49530 |
| 10 | 9.957790 | 30.73702 | 9.409397 | 1.682125 | 0.885199 | 47.32847 |

According to Table 13 and Table 14, the changes that occur in the real sector pre-crisis indicators; growth (cab) and inflation (open) variance can mostly be explained by foreign currency exchange rate (e) after themselves at the end of 10 periods. Variance decomposition results, the effect of hot money on growth and inflation found to be not much. In the VAR (4) Model cause and affect results, the impermanent reaction given by the pre-crisis real sector indicators coincide with this result.

**Table 14:** Variance decomposition of inflation

| Period | HMM | E | OPEN | CAB | INF | RGDP |
|---|---|---|---|---|---|---|
| 1 | 1.761644 | 23.60522 | 7.158460 | 0.002302 | 67.47237 | 0.000000 |
| 2 | 10.67834 | 21.45893 | 11.93011 | 0.109094 | 55.73058 | 0.092938 |
| 3 | 10.66503 | 21.01196 | 13.65588 | 0.151997 | 53.46725 | 1.047868 |
| 4 | 11.79739 | 23.88348 | 12.28750 | 1.391954 | 49.43527 | 1.204399 |
| 5 | 10.47861 | 23.56186 | 10.71728 | 1.261017 | 52.36670 | 1.614529 |
| 6 | 12.97039 | 22.72235 | 10.75673 | 1.271373 | 50.69080 | 1.588350 |
| 7 | 12.92009 | 22.43415 | 10.67681 | 1.341413 | 50.25557 | 2.371967 |
| 8 | 15.20906 | 20.42132 | 9.738398 | 1.531825 | 50.78093 | 2.318468 |
| 9 | 14.90209 | 20.22049 | 9.732792 | 1.489077 | 50.80378 | 2.851761 |
| 10 | 14.86307 | 20.17279 | 9.695797 | 1.499112 | 50.80135 | 2.967880 |

## 6.0 THE CONCLUSION AND DISCUSSION

In Turkish economy, an important rate of hot money inflow occurred after the abolition of restrictions on capital movement in 1989. The outflow of hot money, which causes increase in demand, growth and monetary expansion, caused negative results. The hot money flowing to Turkey caused crisis, in connection with the high arbitrage return between the interest rates and foreign Exchange rates. As in 1994, 2000/2001 and 2008 crisis, the high rate of hot money outflow caused the crisis in the country. (Üçer, Rijckeghem & Yolalan, 1998), (Gerni, Selçuk & Değer, 2005) and (Avcı, Altay 2013) also expressed that hot money flow is an important pre-crisis indicator for Turkish economy.

The VAR (4) model in our study reveals that the hot money movement negatively effects the current account pre-crisis indicators. The hot money movement causes instabilities in real sector pre-crisis indicators. These results from The VAR (4) model cause and effect functions are supported by the variance decomposition analysis. Similar results are stated in the studies of (Corbo, Hernandez 1996), (Yeldan, 1996) and (Rodrik, Velasco 1999).

In conclusion, the hot money movement in Turkey is an ineffective policy tool on the current account and real sector pre-crisis indicators. The economy policy makers should not trust to hot money movement and use alternative policy tools.

In Turkey, after 1989, the year which restrictions on capital movement are abolished, the major problem is insufficient savings. The capital flowing to the country for financing the deficit is short term and speculative hot money movement so it only can create a temporary stability. The sudden outflow of foreign capital from the country can change the short-term stability of the economy to opposite as occurred in 1994, 2000-2001 and 2008 crisis. In that point, the economic decision making mechanisms should consider the policy targets of employment, exports and investments and if necessary interfere to the movement of capital.

In Turkish economy, low level of direct foreign investment is an important problem. After 1989, the year which restrictions on capital movement are abolished the direct foreign investment increased. However, it is examined that this increase was low compared to hot money flow. In that sense, economic decision-making mechanisms should support the direct foreign investment more.

## REFERENCES


Altıntaş, H., Öz, B. (2007). Predicting currency crises with signals approach: The case Of Turkey. *Anadolu University Journal of Social Sciences*, 7(2), 19-44.

Avcı, M.A., Altay, N.O. (2013). Finansal Krizlerin Sinyal Yaklaşımı ile Öngörülmesi: Türkiye, Arjantin, Tayland ve İngiltere İçin Bir Analiz. *Pamukkale Üniversitesi Sosyal Bilimler Enstitüsü Dergisi*, 14(1), 47-58.

Boratav, K. (2009). *Türkiye iktisat tarihi: 1908-2007*. Ankara: İmge Kitabevi.

Boratav, K. (2011). *Bir krizin kısa hikâyesi* (2). Ankara: Arkadaş Yayınevi

Corbo, V., Hernandez, L. (1996). Macroeconomic adjustment to capital inflows: lessons from recent Latin American and East Asian experience. *The World Bank Research Observer*, 11(1), 61-85.

Corsetti, G., Pesenti, P., Roubini, N. (1998). Fundamental determinants of the Asian crisis: a preliminary empirical assessment. *Unpublished manuscript (New Haven, New York, New York: Yale University and University of Bologna, Federal Reserve Bank of New York and NBER)*.

Çeviş, İ. (2005). *Para krizlerine ampirik bir yaklaşım*. Ankara: Sermaye Piyasası Kurulu.

Frankel, J.A., Rose, A.K. (1996). Currency crashes in emerging markets: An empirical treatment. *Journal of International Economics*, 41(1), 351-366.

Gerni, C., Selçuk, E., Değer, M.K. (2005). Erken uyarı sistemleri yoluyla Türkiye'deki ekonomik krizlerin analizi. *Ekonometri ve Istatistik Dergisi*, 2(1), 39-62.

Gujarati, D.N. (2003). *Basic econometrics* (4). McGraw Hill.

İnsel, A., Sungur, N. (2003). Sermaye akımlarının temel makroekonomik göstergeler üzerindeki etkileri: Türkiye örneği-1989: III-1999: IV (No. 2003/8). Discussion Paper, Turkish Economic Association.

Kaminsky, G., Lizondo, S., Reinhart, C.M. (1998). Leading indicators of currency crises. *Staff Papers*, 45(1), 1-48.

Karaçor, Z., Alptekin, V. (2006). Finansal krizlerin önceden tahmin yoluyla değerlendirilmesi: Türkiye örneği. *Celal Bayar Üniversitesi İktisadi ve İdari Bilimler Fakültesi Dergisi*, 13(2), 231-256.

Karluk R.S. (2014). *Türkiye ekonomisi cumhuriyetin ilanından günümüze yapısal dönüşüm* (13). İstanbul: Beta Basın Yayım.

McKinnon, R. (1973). *Money and capital in economic development*. Washington: The Brookings Institution.

Mercan, M., Peker, O. (2013). Finansal gelişmenin ekonomik büyümeye etkisi: ekonometrik bir analiz. *Eskişehir Osmangazi Üniversitesi İktisadi ve İdari Bilimler Dergisi*, 8(1), 93-120.

Oktar S., Dalyancı, L. (2010). Finansal kriz teorileri ve Türkiye ekonomisinde 1990 sonrası finansal krizler. *Marmara Üniversitesi İktisadi ve İdari Bilimler Fakültesi Dergisi*, 29(2), 1-22

Rodrik, D., Velasco, A. (1999). *Short-term capital flows* (No. w7364). National Bureau of Economic Research.

Sevüktekin, M., Nargeleçekenler, M. (2010). *Ekonometrik zaman serileri analizi* (3). Ankara: Nobel Yayıncılık.

Seyidoğlu, H., Yıldız, R. (2006). Ekonomik kriz öncesi erken uyarı sistemleri: Makale derlemesi (1). İstanbul: Arıkan Yayınevi.

Shaw, E. (1973). *Financial development in economic development*. Oxford University Press, New York.

Tarı, R. (2015). *Ekonometri* (11). Umuttepe Yayınları.

Turgut, A. (2007). Türleri, nedenleri ve göstergeleriyle finansal krizler. *TÜHİS İş Hukuku ve İktisat Dergisi*, 20 (4-5), 35-46.

Uzunoğlu, S., Alkın, K., Gürlesel, F. (1995). *Uluslararası sermaye hareketlerinin gelişmekte olan ülkelerde makroekonomik etkileri ve Türkiye*. İstanbul: İMKB Yayınları.

Üçer, M., Rijckeghem, C. V., Yolalan, R. (1998). Leading indicators of currency crises: a brief literature survey and an application to Turkey. *Yapi Kredi Economic Review*, 9 (2), 3-23.

Williamson, J., Mahar, M. (2002). *Finansal Liberalizasyon Üzerine Bir İnceleme*. (Translation: G. Delice). Ankara: Liberete Yayınları.

Yeldan, E. (1996). Kısa vadeli sermaye akımlarının Türk finans piyasalarına olan etkileri üzerine gözlemler. Ekonomide Durum, 4(1), 41-49.

Zivot, E., Andrews, D. W. K. (2002). Further evidence on the great crash, the oil-price shock, and the unit-root hypothesis. *Journal of business & economic statistics*, 20(1), 25-44.

# Institutions and Development: Are some more critical than others? – A Panel Study of 50 countries from 2002 to 2011[1]

**Bertram C.I. Okpokwasili**[2]

**ABSTRACT**

Strong institutions are often viewed as part answers to Africa's development dilemma. But given the resource constraints of many African countries, one would need to be selective as to which institution or institutions to commit scarce resources. An attempt to strengthen all institutions at the same time could be rather daunting. And many questions would remain. First, what is the relative importance of one institution to another? Second, whether all institutions exert an equal impact on comprehensive development as they do on economic growth. This paper on Institutions and Development, first published in 2007 tries to answer these questions. It has been modified (in the 2016 version) for three reasons- 1, to bring the data up to date, 2, to use a different and possibly more accurate econometric model (fixed effect) for the analysis and 3, to assess if the same institutions remain more critical than others, as observed in 2007. Even though the rule of law institution would seem, in this revised version, to have a slightly better impact on GDP/Capita, government effectiveness is still dominant in both non-differenced and differenced models, especially when comprehensive development is considered.

Keywords: Economic development; government effectiveness; infant mortality; institutions; life expectancy.

---

## 1.0 INTRODUCTION

Many African countries, in the 1980's underwent wrenching economic strictures in the name of structural adjustments for economic growth. The results were in the main, disappointing[3].

---

[1] The School of Business and Digital Media, Georgian Court University, Lakewood, NJ. This version of the paper contains corrections from the panel of blind reviewers at IJBSR. I thank them for their insightful comments. I am sure this paper is much better for it. I also thank my wife, Eunice Okpokwasili, for patiently reading and re-reading this paper every time changes were made to it, and finding errors that I could never have seen. This paper is undoubtedly better for such scrutiny. To the extent that the paper has any redeeming quality, the credit goes to the reviewers and to my wife. Any problems or short comings are mine and mine alone.

[2] Georgian Court University, Lakewood, NJ, E-mail: bokpokwasili@georgian.edu

[3] William Easterly and Ross Levine, Africa's Growth Tragedy, A Retrospective, 1960-1989

The primary goal of this revised paper, as was the case in the original paper, is to determine if any of the six institutions (voice and accountability, political stability, government effectiveness, regulatory quality, the rule of law and corruption mitigation efforts) are more critical than the orders, so that efforts directed to the particular institutions would be more beneficial on the whole. One recognizes the need for efficiency in all the institutions for the development of a nation. The problem is that many countries do not have necessary and sufficient resources to move all the institutions forward simultaneously. And even if countries had the necessary resources, these institutions could work together, and some may have the effect of improving others even when those others might not be specifically targeted. An effective governance structure, for instance, could promote less corruption and enable voice and accountability. The rule of law could have an impact on political stability and corruption; it would seem.

In this version of the study, however, we have taken two steps that, in our opinion, would make the study and its findings more reliable.

First, we employed a real panel data, the annual data for each country in the analysis, rather than the averages over the years. Secondly, we used differencing, in Tables 5 and 6, to more effectively address what could be seen as an econometric weakness. This approach would remove the unexplained variable effect on the Ordinary Least Squares (OLS) estimation of the panel data[4]. Such unexplained variable could result in unreliable regression estimates of the relevant parameters. Unfortunately, the differencing had the effect of reducing the panel data by one year.

We tried to include lagged variables for the countries, but abandoned it, since our initial results turned out not to have better confidence than without them. The Log-Log and Log-Linear transformations of the variables seemed to work quite well.

This 2016 analysis found improvement in both life expectancy and infant mortality in all the African countries, all coming from very low levels (in Life Expectancy) and very high levels (in Infant Mortality) relatively. Except for Liberia, per capita income went up for all the countries.

In assessing the importance of institutions on development, it made a difference whether one addressed economic growth or comprehensive development. Surrogates like life expectancy and infant mortality would be used to represent comprehensive development in this revised study, as was the case in the earlier study.

A determination of which institutions would have the greatest impact on development could help shape the policy directions of many developing countries, especially in the African region.

We found in the earlier study that Government Effectiveness (GE) was the institution, which if strengthened, would have the most impact on economic growth and comprehensive development.

The present study re-enforced the 2007 findings, but with some differences. It looked like the rule of law, when log differencing was applied to the stated methodology, was a slightly stronger institution than government effectiveness, in relationship to economic growth. Government effectiveness had much better show about comprehensive development.

The current paper analyzed the relative impacts of institutions on development, using the most recent data from 2000 to 2014. 50 countries were analyzed, most of them (29)[5] from Sub-Sahara Africa.

---

[4] Jeffrey Wooldridge, Introductory Econometrics, page 421

[5] The number of countries as well as the years covered by the statistical analysis are different because of data availability. We depended on the Penn World Tables Data (PWT) for consumption, gross investment, government spending and exports. Unfortunately, the most current PWT was V8.1, and had data through 2011. For consistency, we chose to stay with this source in most of the analyses. Some countries did not have data on TFP (Total Factor Productivity), forcing us to remove them from analysis.

The whole paper is structured as follows. Section 2 reviews the literature. Section 3 defines the variables used in this updated study and the methodology. Section 4 discusses the impact findings. Section 5 concludes the findings of the 2016 study. We list the participating countries in Appendix A

## 2.0 LITERATURE REVIEW

Why the development problems of the continent seemed to defy solutions (Easterly, 1998) has motivated numerous inquiries, many focusing on institutions. The question remained which institution and what development?

Some difficulties existed with the data derived entirely from the African sub-region, as Janine Aron aptly pointed out (Feb. 2000) – "given the very limited variation in the institutional indexes for African countries, often with serious endogeneity problems, there is little to gain on the role of institutions from studies focused solely on Africa", This made it necessary to include data from other developed and developing countries. So this study included countries from Asia, Europe and North America (the list is given in Appendix A).

Fosu (1992) investigated the impact of Political Instability (PI) on economic growth. He concluded that PI had serious implications on economic growth. He argued that PI did not only cause 'brain drain' – the flight of skilled workers to better economic opportunities (human capital reduction), it decreased the willingness of investors to invest and accumulate capital (capital reduction). The reduction in the quantity of capital, physical and human, would result in output reductions. His study was a number of Sub-Sahara African countries, using a modified Cobb-Douglas production function.

Vijayaraghavan and Ward (2006) investigated the impact of each institution on economic growth, using predominantly African countries, and a mix of other developing countries in Asia and South America. They used four institutions, namely: security of property rights, governance, political freedom, and government consumption. The governance measure was a simple average of corruption, the rule of law and bureaucracy.

Using the augmented Solow growth model, in an Ordinary Least Squares (OLS) Regression Analysis, they estimated the impact of these institutions on growth. Vijayaraghavan and Ward (V&W) concluded that the most influential were security and property rights, and government size. Security and property rights were positively related to growth in income. Growth in government consumption was negatively related to income growth.

As in most economic literature looking at institutional impact, V&W resorted to an aggregated measure for governance. One would have difficulty arguing how property rights would exist outside the rule of law. In our study, using the World Bank measure of institutions, the rule of law and property rights would seem to be inseparable.

Government consumption does not mean efficient bureaucracy. Rauch and Evans found in their study of bureaucracy (weberianness score) that it was not the size of government that was the issue, but the structure of the bureaucracy[6]. The dramatic growth of the East Asian 'Tigers' in the 70's and 80's could be attributed to their bureaucracies. Meritocratic bureaucracy would relate positively to economic growth in spite of government size.

Mauro (1995) was one of the first economists to measure the impact of the institution on growth, using a composite of institutional measures, he concluded that corruption deterred private investment, and consequently was detrimental to economic growth. He also determined that bureaucratic efficiency might be, at least, as important for investment and growth, as political stability. Again he measured the impact of aggregated institutional measures.

[6] Evans and Rauch constructed what they called a weberianness scale, of different bureaucracies, and found that this score, in a growth regression analysis, contributed significantly to growth.

Jamison, Jamison, and Hanushek (Oct. 2006), found that education quality (using scores in countrywide tests) was positively related to technological progress and that this was also related to reductions in Infant Mortality. They found a strong association between the quality of education and reduction in infant mortality. They joined the assertion that infant mortality was indicative of overall development, a thought process that Amartya Sen had championed[7].

Janine Aron (2000) pointed out that many studies found the impact of democracy on growth to be inconclusive. On the positive side, she wrote that transparency and accountability would enhance economic growth. On the negative side, the delay introduced in seeking consensus, and interest group lobbies would delay responses to shocks and implementation of legislative mandates.

Just like democracy, there seem to be conflicting research findings on whether political stability has a positive relationship to economic growth or comprehensive development, for that matter. Again what has taken place in Africa since the wave of independence in the 1960's, has prompted numerous studies, to determine if the laggard growth was caused by the many coups d'état, and political assassinations. Mancur Olson (1963) theorizes that economic growth leads to political instability and that political stability, in the long run, would lead to lower economic growth. An attempt by Arthur Goldsmith (1987) to substantiate Olson's theory with data from the less developed countries from 1958 through 1977, failed to prove the negative relationship. However, Jakob de Hann and Clemens Siermann (1996) find that only in Africa was there a mixed support for the view that political instability reduces economic growth. They find that in Asia, political repression and growth are positively related, even though political instability hampers investment.

Janine Aron (2000), finds that when property rights are included in the investment equation, PI (political instability) ceases to be significant. She says that PI, in many cases has no impact on economic growth. The problem with PI is that of endogeneity. Whereas PI could enhance growth, the reverse is also possible. We find a mixed impact. In some cases, PI has an impact. In other cases, its impact is not noticeable. Bayley (Dec. 1966) argued that corruption might not be as bad to development as one would think. He demonstrated that corruption might indeed 'wear two hats' – in fact playing a useful role in transition economies. He argued that corruption played a role, which could, in its absence, be played by another activity which might be more detrimental to the economy. Opportunity for corruption, he theorized, might indeed improve the quality of the civil servants, and could also result in increased allocation of resources from consumption to investment. Even though some studies have pointed to the benefits of corruption, the overwhelming evidence was that corruption was harmful to growth and harmful for infant mortality[8].

## 3.0 DATA DEFINITIONS AND THE METHODOLOGY

This revised study started with a data set of 32 Sub-Sahara Africa countries, 12 from Western Europe & North America, and ten from Asia. The data covered a period of 14 years, from 2002 to 2015. Two factors accounted for whittling these numbers down both regarding countries and years covered, in the most recent study. First was the availability of the required data, and second was the differencing methodology which was applied in some of the models. The World Bank GDP/Capita data for 2015 was available for only very limited countries. The Penn World Table V8.1 had data through 2011. So we used data from 2002 to 2014 from the World Bank, and eventually reduced the years to 2002 to 2011.
The study employed natural logarithms of the components of the Gross Domestic Product (consumption spending, gross investment, government spending, and exports) as independent variables in some of the analyses. The original 2007 paper used the logs of labor and capital.

---

[7] Amartya Sen: Development as Freedom

[8] Mauro (1995) finds that corruption reduces private investment in the economy, resulting in reduced growth in national income. JS Nye in Corruption and Political Development: A Cost-Benefit Analysis (1967) enumerates some advantages of corruption as well as some offsetting disadvantages.

Two other independent variables were used with the differencing models- capital stock accumulation for each country, and TFP (total factor productivity). The two variables were shown to be influential in economic development. Data on capital was available for most African countries. TFP was hardly available for African countries. We found these variables to be of much significance in the log-linear or log-log relationships, with growth especially. They, however, forced some analyses with fewer than the 54 countries we started with.

The second factor was that differencing reduced the data by one year. So that the data used for each country from 2002 to 2014, would be reduced by one year when we subtracted year one from year two, year two from year three and so on. This was the price one paid for seeking a more reliable econometric approach. This was the major difference between the 2007 version and this revised, 2016 version of the paper.

## 3.1 INSTITUTIONS / GOVERNANCE MEASURES

Six governance measures (institutions) were derived from the World Bank Papers[9]. The six are described below.

*(i) Voice and Accountability (INST1)* measures the democracy in a country – the extent of political participation, the freedom of speech, and the freedom of the media. All the institutional scores are standardized. They vary from a low of –2.5 to a high of 2.5, with 0 (zero) as the mean. The higher the score, the better the country is, in the institution of democracy.

*(ii) Political Stability and Absence of Violence (INST2)* measures the likelihood that a sitting government would be thrown out of office by some non-democratic means.

*(iii) Government Effectiveness (INST3)* measures the quality of the bureaucracy. It is a measure of the effectiveness of the civil service, and its insulation from political pressures.

*(iv) Regulatory Quality (INST4) measures* the extent to which government regulations permit and promote private sector development. One would expect a positive relationship with GDP/Capita, and a negative relationship with increases in Infant Mortality (IM).

*(v) Rule of Law (INST5)* measures the quality of, and confidence in, the judicial system and its law enforcement apparatus. This also addresses the ability of the system to protect the physical well-being of individuals and their properties – property rights.

*(vi) Control of Corruption (INST6)* addresses the extent to which government checks the use of public power for private gain. One would think that in the African context, the mitigation of corruption would be a 'cure all.' Our study did not seem to support that.

### 3.1.1 OTHER INDEPENDENT VARIABLES

*(i)TFP (Total Factor Productivity)* refers to measures of a country's productivity, given its major factors of production, labor, and capital. These measures should be positively related to economic growth. It measures changes in production possibilities which would be possible due to the application of technology, human capital and all other resources with which a country is endowed. This could also be a reflection on how changes in the labor force might influence growth. One is the growth of capital/worker, and the other is unemployment. If labor grows without growth in capital investment, there would be a

[9] The data on Governance were compiled by the team of Kaufmann, Kraay and Mastruzzi for the World Bank – Governance Matters IV and v: Aggregate and Individual Governance Indicators for 1996 – 2005, and 1996- 2002- World Bank Working Paper Series #4012, 2006. The most recent data is also from the World Bank- Kaufman, Krey et al at http://papers.ssrn.com/sol3/papers.cfm?abstract_id=1682130

decrease in capital per worker, and a decrease in output per worker. If unemployment increases as labor grow, there would also be a negative impact on output. We do not have unemployment figures available for most of the countries in the study, most of which are in Sub-Sahara Africa. The thinking is that unemployment is unusually high.

We expected a positive relationship with institutions. The signs were properly reflected, but with not much significance in all our measures.

Our data for TPF were derived from the Penn World Table V8 data.

*(ii)Capital Stock* at constant 2005 US $$. Measures the accumulation of plants and equipment used in the production of goods and services. The more capital stock an economy has, the higher their output, and more likely, the higher their economic growth. We had hoped to see positive relationships with institutions in the differenced models. The signs were as expected, and there seemed to be much significance with the measures of growth, much more so than comprehensive development.

*(iii)Private Consumption Expenditures, Gross Investment, Government Expenditures and Exports* at constant 2005 dollars are the expenditure approach to measuring the Gross Domestic Product, except that exports are net, not gross. In the earlier version of this paper, we employed Labor and Capital measures for a country's output of goods and services. This is more like the income approach to GDP since the measures of labor and capital are the primary components of the factors of production. Quite often the expenditure measures are more reliable and more frequent than the income measures. This is why we changed from our previous use of labor and capital – the Solow model. Capital and Labor are implied in the differenced models used in Tables 5 and 6, in the form of capital stock and total factor productivity.

### 3.1.2 DEPENDENT VARIABLES

*(i)Real GDP/Capita and Real GDP/Capita Growth* measure the Gross Domestic Product divided by the population of the country and its change, at a constant 2005-dollar value. It is a measure of how well a country is doing economically. We derived our figures from the latest World Bank Data Series.

*(ii)Infant Mortality.* Data on infant mortality were derived from the World Bank Data[10]. It measures a number of deaths per thousand of under one-year-old babies who were born alive. Infant mortality was the dependent variable for Table 4 in the appendix. Mortality rates, in addition to income levels, are indicators of the well-being of any economy (Jamison et al., 2006). In this paper, we use infant mortality as a surrogate for comprehensive development.

*(iii)Life Expectancy.* Life expectancy at birth indicates the number of years a newborn is expected to live before death, in a country. The more developed a country, the higher the life expectancy. Very low life expectancy is a reflection of poor medical institutions, poor nutritional endowments and overall poverty in the availability of those features which enable citizens of a country to grow without unnecessary afflictions of sickness and death – a combination that Amartya Sen referred to in "Development as Freedom Thesis."[11]

## 3.2 METHODOLOGY

We analyzed in this version of the study, a panel data set, collected for 50 countries for the years 2002 through 2011. By the time we were through, we would be analyzing data for about 50 countries over ten years. That was some 500 data items.

---

[10] Mortality rate, infant (per 1000 live births) World Bank Reports, derived from various United Nations and Country specific sources.

[11] Sen, Amartya, Development as Freedom, Oxford University Press, 2001.

The first set of analyses, reported in Tables 1 to 4, would employ non-differenced panel data. The model used, takes the form of equation (1) below. There are, of course, some statistical problems caused by the possibility of the unobserved independent variable in the model. This could cause problems of heteroskedasticity (non-uniformity of the variances of the error terms), possibly leading to unreliable OLS estimation.

The second model estimated, was a differenced version of equation 1, reported in Tables 5, supposedly corrects for the problem of the effect of unobserved independent variable possible in equation 1. This is equation two below. The log version is reported in Table 6 and gave much better estimates.

$$Yit = \beta_0 + \partial_2 t + \beta_1 (X_1)it + \beta_2 (X_2)_{it} + \text{------} + \beta_k (X_k)_{it} + a_i + \varepsilon_{it} \qquad (1)$$[12]

Where I represent the cross section observation, different countries

--------- t is time, 2002 to 2014

--------- X is independent variables (GDP components and Institution Variables)

--------- Y is dependent variables (GDP/Capita, Life Expectancy and Infant Mortality)

-------- d is dummy variables representing the years

-------- a unobserved constant variable, constant for the years.

-------- ε error term incorporating all uncontrolled for variables independent variables.

We also estimated the differenced form of equation 1 (equation 2), whose results are in Tables 5 and 6:

$$\Delta Ln\ Y_{it} = \beta_0 + + \beta_2 \Delta d + \beta_1 \Delta(Ln.X_1)_{it} + \beta_2 \Delta (Ln.X_2)_{it} + \text{----} + \beta_k \Delta (Ln.X_k)_{it} + \Delta\varepsilon \qquad (2)$$

$\beta_0$ is the intercept. $\beta_1, \beta_2, \beta_3$, and $\beta_4$ are coefficients.

di = Dummy Variables for each year from 2002 to 2014

$\Delta\varepsilon$ = Differences in the error term

$\Delta d$ = Differences in the error term

In the differenced models, X1 and X2 are TPF and Capital Stock.

## 4.0 RESULTS AND IMPACT FINDINGS

Table 1 presents the result by using equation 1 and OLS to determine the impact of the institutions on growth, measured by GDP/Capita, and controlling for the four components of GDP (consumption, investment, government expenditures and exports), and year effects.

The purpose of models 1 through 9 was to estimate the relationships between the institutions and economic wellbeing, represented by Ln GDP/Capita for the different countries. This would be similar to the version we estimated in 2007. We analyzed the model's residuals for compliance with the four basic requirements of OLS[13].

[12] Wooldridge, An Introduction to Econometrics, Chapter 13

[13] A regression model has four basic assumptions that should be satisfied, if we are to have confidence in their estimates. Kalibanoff, Sandroni, Moselle and Saraniti "Managerial Statistics – A Case-Based Approach", 2006, page 181, gives these assumptions as: linearity, constant error of variance, independent errors, and normal errors. Linearity can be checked by plotting the residuals. Constant error of variance (homoscedasticity, violation is heteroskedasticity), we can check with the Breusch-Pagan residual heteroskedasticity test. We can detect lack of independence of the variables by checking the Durbin-Watson statistic of the residuals. The non-normality of the errors can be detected by the use of the Jargue-Bera non-normality test. For the Breusch-Pagan heteroskedasticity (BP) test a score close to 0% would have confirmed that the variances of the residuals were different. For the Jargue-Bera (JB) non-normality test a score close to 0, would indicate non-normality of the residuals. For the Durbin-Watson (DB) test a score of 2 gives perfect no autocorrelation. A score of 0 gives strong negative autocorrelation, and a 4 gives a perfect positive autocorrelation.

**Table 1:** All 50 Countries for 2002 to 2011

LN GDP/ CAPITA VS INSTITUTIONS, LN GDP COMPONENTS and & YEAR DUMMIES

| Variables | | Model 1 | Model 2 | Model 3 | Model 4 | Model 5 | Model 6 | Model 7 | Model 8 | Model 9 |
|---|---|---|---|---|---|---|---|---|---|---|
| intercept | $\beta_0$ | 2.3729 | 0.165 | 3.6586 | 3.446 | 2.842 | 2.219 | 6.823 | 6.4634 | 5.8743 |
| | | (5.128)** | (0.3734) | (9.316)** | (9.058)** | (7.413)** | (5.193)** | (7.281)** | (7.027)** | (5.959)** |
| Ln Cons Exp | X1 | -0513 | -0.1043 | -0.1825 | -0.1509 | -0.1811 | -0.1814 | -0.2231 | -0.1778 | -0.2449 |
| | | (-8.86)** | (-1.7967) | (-3.944)** | (-3.33)** | (-3.88)** | (-3.454)** | (-4.465)** | (-4.09)** | (-4.68)** |
| | | -0.5128* | -0.1042* | -0.1824* | -0.1508* | -0.181* | -0.1813* | -0.2229* | -0.1777* | -0.2447* |
| Ln Gross Invstmts | X2 | | | | | | | -0.3083 | -0.2859 | -0.274 |
| | | | | | | | | (-3.661)** | (-3.485)** | (-3.172)** |
| | | | | | | | | -0.0677* | -0.063* | -0.0602* |
| Ln Govt. Exp | X3 | 0.7378 | 0.57488 | 0.3216 | 0.3181 | 0.3703 | 0.4747 | 0.4113 | 0.3832 | 0.4446 |
| | | (12.98)** | (9.703)** | (6.651)** | (6.714)** | (7.643)** | (8.794)** | (8.19)** | (8.169)** | (8.3969)** |
| | | 0.7540* | 0.5874* | 0.3286* | 0.3250* | 0.3783 | 0.4851* | 0.4202 | 0.392* | .4543* |
| Ln Exports | X4 | 0.3925 | 0.3513 | 0.2861 | 0.2882 | 0.3379 | 0.2947 | 0.2567 | 0.2529 | 0.3124 |
| | | (9.765)** | (8.295)** | (8.427)** | (8.678)** | (9.998)** | (7.619)** | (7.942)** | (7.987)** | (9.24)** |
| | | 0.2132* | 0.1909* | 0.1554* | 0.1566 | 0.1836 | 0.1602* | 0.1395* | 0.1374* | 0.1698* |
| governance1 (voice&acct) | INST1 | 1.211 | | | | | | 0.1463 | | 0.129 |
| | | (24.35)** | | | | | | (1.744) | | (1.548) |
| | | 0.5986* | | | | | | 0.0723* | | 0.0635* |
| governance2 (political stab) | INST2 | | 0.989 | | | | | 0.2588 | 0.27897 | |
| | | | (22.62)** | | | | | (4.554)** | (5.304)** | |
| | | | 0.483* | | | | | 0.126* | 0.1362* | |
| governance3 (govt effectiveness) | INST3 | | | 1.2887 | | | | 0.5237 | 0.4433 | |
| | | | | (32.99)** | | | | (3.431)** | (4.204)** | |
| | | | | 0.7310* | | | | 0.2971* | 0.2515 | |
| governance4 (regulatory quality) | INST4 | | | | 1.3754 | | | 0.6465 | 0.7371 | |
| | | | | | (33.97)** | | | (5.154)** | (6.603)** | |
| | | | | | 0.7163 | | | 0.3367* | 0.3839* | |
| governance5 (rule of law) | INST5 | | | | | 1.2246 | | 0.0159 | | 1.0205 |
| | | | | | | (32.59)** | | (0.0989) | | (9.684)** |
| | | | | | | 0.6823* | | 0.0089* | | 0.569* |

| | | | | | | | | | | |
|---|---|---|---|---|---|---|---|---|---|---|
| governance6 (corruption mitigation) | INST6 | | | | | | 1.0533<br>(27.10)**<br>0.6047* | -0.0975<br>(-1.1654)<br>-0.0560* | | 0.1575<br>(1.975)***<br>0.090* |
| Year Dummies | D1 | -0.00679<br>(-0.511)<br>-.0096* | -0.00902<br>(-0.654)<br>-0.0128* | 0.0159<br>(1.441)<br>0.0225 | -0.00255<br>(-0.2363)<br>-0.0036* | -0.0043<br>(-0.3881)<br>-0.0061 | 0.0010<br>(0.084)<br>0.0015* | 0.00934<br>(0.895)<br>0.0132* | | |
| Coefficient of Det | $R^2$ | 82.83% | 81.44% | 88.21% | 88.68 | 88.01% | 84.81% | 90.05% | 89.94% | 88.45% |
| Adjusted $R^2$ | | 82.66% | 81.26% | 88.09% | 88.56 | 87.89% | 84.66% | 89.83% | 89.80% | 88.29% |
| F statistic | | 476.61 | 433.6 | 738.98 | 773.82 | 725.11 | 551.7 | 401.47 | 628.66 | 538.3996 |
| Degrees of Fr | | (5, 494) | (5,494) | (5, 494) | 5, 494 | (5, 494) | (5, 494) | (11, 488) | (7, 492) | (7, 492) |
| Significance for F, p-value | | 0.0000% | 0.0000% | .00000% | .00000% | 0.0000% | .00000% | .00000% | .00000% | 0.0000% |

** Statistically significant at the 95% confidence level. * beta-weight values- no of standard deviations change in dep. variable if the independent is changed by one standard deviation. *** significant at 90% level

A single asterisk (*) in the variable cells of all the Tables, showed beta weights[14]. Double asterisks (**) indicated statistical significance at the 95% level. Individual coefficients in a statistically significant relationship were estimates of how much the dependent variable would change when the independent was changed by one unit, all other independent variables remaining unchanged. The coefficient of determination $R^2$ indicated how much variability in the dependent variable was explained by the independent variables in the equation.

These four measures advised of how critical the institutions were.

The measures of the beta weights throughout the first six models, showed that INST3 (government effectiveness) was the highest of all six institutions. INST3 had a beta weight of 0.7310. It was followed by INST4 (regulatory quality) at 0.7163, INST5 (the rule of law) was third at .6823, INST6 (corruption mitigation) at 0.6823, with INST1 (voice and accountability) and INST2 (political stability) showing the least impact.

The coefficients of the institutional variables showed that growth would change more per unit change of INST4 and INST3 than with a unit change in any of the other institutional variables.

The coefficients of determination (R2) and its adjusted version showed that INST4 and INST3 were higher than the others, given that the other independent variables controlled for were the same for each of the institutions.

What Table 1 indicated to us was that the two institutions INST3 and INST4 were the most critical on economic growth.

[14] Beta weights are used to assess the relative importance of the variability in each of the independent variables in the model, in helping to explain why the dependent variable varies through the population.

We further checked for the conformance of our models to OLS requirements, and we found a mixed bag. The Jarque-Bera non-normality test at 32.295% was quite good. Our Breusch-Pagan test at 0% was not so good, indicating some heteroskedastic variables. The Variance Inflation numbers for all the variables were within acceptable range of less than 10. The variance inflation would show how much an independent variable was influenced by another.

**Table 2:** Life Expectancy at birth VS Institutional Measures and the Year Dummies.

| Variables | | Model 10 | Model 11 | Model 12 | Model 13 | Model 14 | Model 15 |
|---|---|---|---|---|---|---|---|
| Intercept | $\beta_0$ | 2.9433 | 2.835 | 3.3164 | 3.2531 | 3.4172 | 2.96555 |
| | | (19.48)** | (17.68)** | (26.515)** | (24.78)** | (26.53)** | (21.898)** |
| Ln Consumption | $X_1$ | `-0.0274 | 0.00298 | -0.00437 | -0.0013 | -0.00584 | -0.0023 |
| | | (-3.53)** | (0.3883) | (-0.7179) | (-0.2031) | (-0.951) | (-0.3358) |
| | | -0.2812* | 0.0306* | -0.0449* | -0.0133* | -0.0600* | -0.0235* |
| Ln Gross Invstmts | $X_2$ | 0.8129 | 0.0729 | 0.0640 | 0.06497 | 0.0698 | 0.0823 |
| | | (6.12)** | (5.004)** | (5.862)** | (5.652)** | (4.156)** | (6.812)** |
| | | 0.1835* | 0.1645* | 0.1445* | 0.1467* | 0.1061* | 0.1858* |
| Ln Govt Exp | $X_3$ | 0.0528 | 0.04235 | 0.0183 | 0.0196 | 0.0250 | 0.0308 |
| | | (6.805)** | (5.363)** | (2.844)** | (2.918)** | (4.1563)** | (4.325)** |
| | | 0.5538* | 0.4447* | 0.1917* | 0206* | 0.1061* | 0.3235* |
| Ln Exports | $X_4$ | 0.01146 | 0.00987 | -0.00192 | -1.742 | 0.00228 | 0.0014 |
| | | (2.193)** | (1.768) | (-0.4355) | (-0.0038) | (0.5179) | (0.2826) |
| | | 0.0640* | 0.0551* | -0.0108* | -0.0001* | 0.0127* | 0.0078 |
| governance1 (voice&acct) | INST1 | 0.0926 | | | | | |
| | | (13.42)** | | | | | |
| | | 0.4705* | | | | | |
| governance2 (political stab) | INST2 | | 0.0702 | | | | |
| | | | (10.96)** | | | | |
| | | | 0.3521* | | | | |
| governance3 (govt effectiveness) | INST3 | | | 0.1186 | | | |
| | | | | (22.053)** | | | |
| | | | | 0.6913* | | | |
| governance4 (regulatory quality) | INST4 | | | | 0.1196 | | |
| | | | | | (19.98)** | | |
| | | | | | 0.6401* | | |
| governance5 (rule of law) | INST5 | | | | | 0.1152 | |
| | | | | | | (21.708)** | |
| | | | | | | 0.66*. | |
| governance6 (corruption mitigation) | INST6 | | | | | | 0.0887 |
| | | | | | | | (17.014)** |
| | | | | | | | 0.523* |
| Year Dummies | D1 | 0.00675 | 0.0066 | 0.0093 | 0.00747 | .00763 | 0.00756 |
| | | (3.911)** | (3.622)** | (6.453)** | (4.978)** | (5.287)** | (4.712)** |
| | | 0.0982* | 0.0953* | 0.1352* | 0.1086* | 0.1109* | 0.1099* |
| Coefficient of Determination | $R^2$ | 69.62% | 66.65% | 79.12% | 77.08% | 78.79% | 73.86% |
| Adjusted $R^2$ | | 69.25% | 66.24% | 78.86% | 76.80% | 78.53% | 73.55% |
| F statistic | | 188.25 | 164.18 | 311.307 | 276.273 | 305.252 | 232.215 |
| Degrees of Freedom | | (5, 493) | (6, 493) | (6, 493) | (6, 493) | (6, 493) | (6, 493) |
| Significance for F, p-value | | 0.0000% | 0.0000% | 0.0000% | 0.0000% | 0.0000% | 0.0000% |

** Statistically significant at the 95% confidence level. * beta-weight values- no of standard deviations change in dep. variable if the independent is changed by one standard deviation. *** significant at 90% level

### 4.1: Impact of the Institutions on Life Expectancy (table 2)

Using the Log of Life Expectancy for the various countries as a surrogate for comprehensive development, we employed equation one again in detecting the most critical institutions. The dependent variable was changed to the Log of life expectancy. Our findings are reported in Table 2.

The beta weights showed that INST3 (government effectiveness) was 0.6913, followed by INST5 (the rule of law) at 0.66, then INST4 (regulatory quality) at 0.6401. The position of INST1 and INST2 in these measures should not be a surprise.

Dictatorships and autocratic regimes, many a time, achieved both economic and developmental improvement for their people. In fact, it would seem that many coup d'états happened because somebody thought they could do better than an existing ineffectual government[15].

The statistical coefficients showed a slightly higher value for INST4, at 0.1196, than for INST3 at 0.1186. The coefficients of determination were higher for INST3 than for the other institutions. In fact, INST5 (the rule of law) had a higher coefficient than INST4 (regulatory quality).

With our first surrogate for comprehensive development, INST3- government effectiveness- seemed most critical.

The analysis failed some of the OLS test, showing near zero normality and heteroscedasticity tests. The Durbin-Watson showed positive autocorrelation at 0.2945, and the variation inflation factor showed that government expenditures were influenced by some other independent variable

### 4.2: Assessing the Impact of Institutions on Infant Mortality (Table 3)

The second test for comprehensive development was done with the log. of infant mortality, just as in the 2007 version. The results are shown in Table 3. Consider the beta weights. INST3 (government effectiveness) had a beta weight of -0.7663, negative because as would be expected, the institutions would be inversely related to infant mortality.

The next in order were INST5 (the rule of law) at -0.7222, and INST4 (regulatory quality) at -0.7045. INST6 (corruption) is 4th, INST1 and INST2 5th and 6th. The coefficient of Determination for INST3 was 87.37, higher than all the others.

With the infant mortality analysis, our residuals seemed to comply much better with OLS requirements. The heteroscedasticity test was very much improved for all the institutions, registering numbers very much above zero in all the cases. Same with the non-normality tests. The Durbin-Watson, though not as close to 2 as would be required, was above zero in all cases.

The variance inflation numbers, indicating some dependence existed for some GDP components were above the acceptable number of 10. This did not seem to be unusual, since government expenditures, and consumption figures could influence one another in many areas, such as taxes, transfer payments and the like.

What one continued to observe in these analyses was the superiority of INST3, government effectiveness, as an institution critical to both economic health and comprehensive development.

[15] De Hann and Siermann (1996)

**Table 3:** Infant Mortality VS Institutional Measures, and the Year Dummies.

| Variables | | Model 16 | Model 17 | Model 18 | Model 19 | Model 20 | Model 21 |
|---|---|---|---|---|---|---|---|
| Intercept | $\beta_0$ | 8.399 | 8.1734 | 5.6158 | 6.1752 | 4.9973 | 8.1525 |
| | | (9.0663)** | (8.616)** | (8.3826)** | (8.3147)** | (7.0184)** | (10.412)** |
| Ln Consumption | $X_1$ | 0.19404 | -0.0349 | 0.0162 | -0.0078 | 0.0261 | 0.001505 |
| | | (4.0796)** | (-0.7696) | (.4955) | (-0.2168) | (0.7692) | (0.0382) |
| | | 0.289* | -0.0521 | 0.0241* | -0.116* | 0.0389* | 0.0022* |
| Ln Gross Invstmts | $X_2$ | -0.1525 | -0.00669 | -0.02456 | -0.0364 | 0.0958 | -0.15585 |
| | | (-1.872) | (-0.0777) | (-0.4199) | (-0.5592) | (1.5323) | (-2.2313)** |
| | | -0.0500* | -0.0022* | -0.008* | -0.0119* | 0.0314* | -0.0511* |
| Ln Govt Exp | $X_3$ | -0.3897 | -0.31498 | -0.1254 | -0.1368 | -0.1784 | 0.2204 |
| | | (-8.1995)** | (-6.617)** | (-3.648)** | (-3.598)** | (-5.0141)** | (-5.3496)** |
| | | -0.5941* | -0.4802* | -0.1912* | -0.2086* | -0.2719 | 0.3359* |
| Ln Exports | $X_4$ | -0.1882 | -0.1541 | -0.0871 | -0.01032 | -0.1218 | -0.10877 |
| | | (-5.872)** | (-4.666)** | (-3.675)** | (-3.943)** | (-5.005)** | (-3.788)** |
| | | -0.1525 | -0.1249* | -0.0706* | -0.0837* | -0.0988* | -0.0882* |
| governance1 (voice&acct) | INST1 | -0.7132<br>(-16.847)** | | | | | |
| governance2 (political stab) | INST2 | | -0.6191<br>(-16.35)**<br>-0.4511* | | | | |
| governance3 (govt effectiveness) | INST3 | | | -0.9055<br>(-31.44)**<br>-0.7663* | | | |
| governance4 (regulatory quality) | INST4 | | | | -0.9067<br>(-26.767)**<br>-0.7045* | | |
| governance5 (rule of law) | INST5 | | | | | -0.8689<br>(-29.59)**<br>-0.7222* | |
| governance6 (corruption mitigation) | INST6 | | | | | | -0.6893<br>(-22.86)**<br>-0.5904* |
| Year Dummies | D1 | -0.01888 | -0.01946 | -0.0382 | -0.0241 | -0.0252 | -0.0253 |
| | | (-1.783) | (-1.817) | (-4.948)** | (-2.8348)** | (-3.154)** | (-2.726)** |
| | | -0.0398* | -0.0411* | -0.0806* | -0.051* | -0.0531* | -0.0534* |
| Coefficient of Determination | $R^2$ | 75.92% | 75.40% | 87.37% | 84.53% | 86.33% | 81.58% |
| Adjusted $R^2$ | | 75.63% | 75.10% | 87.22% | 84.35% | 86.17% | 81.36% |
| F statistic | | 259.05 | 251.792 | 568.5884 | 449.1 | 519.087 | 363.94 |
| Degrees of Freedom | | (6, 493) | (6, 493) | (6, 493) | (6, 493) | (6, 493) | (6, 493) |
| Significance for F, p-value | | 0.0000% | 0.0000% | 0.000% | 0.000% | 0.000% | 0.0000% |

** Statistically significant at the 95% confidence level. * beta-weight values- no of standard deviations change in dep. variable if the independent is changed by one standard deviation. *** significant at 90% level

### 4.3: Africa Infant Mortality Analysis (Table 4)

We explored the impact of the institutions on African development. Our results are recorded in Table 4 below. There had been some improvement over the years in infant mortality in the African countries. The same trend that held for the entire group in Tables 1, 2 and 3, also held at table 4, for Africa, South of the Sahara. Effective government (INST3) was the institution of choice, outperforming the rest of them. INST3 is the most critical, followed by INST5 (the rule of law) and INST6 (corruption mitigation). The one noticeable difference is that the coefficients of determination were markedly low. The highest was with INST3 at 56.38%. The residual test for OLS requirements was not met in all cases.

**Table 4:** Africa Alone (29 Sub-Sahara African Countries)
Infant Mortality Measures VS Institutions, GDP components and the Year Dummies.

| Variables | | Model 22 | Model 23 | Model 24 | Model 25 | Model 26 | Model 27 |
|---|---|---|---|---|---|---|---|
| Intercept | $\beta_0$ | 6.8226 | 6.6585 | 4.4584 | 6.0215 | 4.8323 | 6.9478 |
| | | (11.47)** | (10.4)** | (8.402)** | (10.42)** | (8.863)** | (11.422)** |
| Ln Consumption Exp. | | -0.0252 | -0.0617 | 0.0268 | -0.0424 | -0.0224 | -0.052 |
| | | (-0.8273) | (-2.055)** | (1.058) | (-1.5204) | (-0.882) | (-1.73) |
| | | -0.0793* | -0.1944* | 0.0845* | -0.1337* | -0.0707* | -0.1639* |
| Ln. Gross Investments | | -0.2294 | -0.1798 | -0.0376 | -0.1591 | -0.03007 | -0.2176 |
| | | (-4.602)** | (-3.182)** | (-0.8490) | (-3.27)** | (-0.638) | (-4.146)** |
| | | -0.2582* | -0.2024* | -0.0424* | -0.1790* | -0.0338* | -0.2448* |
| Ln Govt. Expenditures | | -0.01005 | -0.0015 | -0.0059 | 0.0324 | -0.00489 | 0.01132 |
| | | (-0.3393) | (-0.0506) | (-0.2464) | (1.1928) | (-0.1963) | (0.3832) |
| | | -0.0327* | -0.0050* | -0.0192* | 0.1056 | -0.0159* | 0.0369* |
| Ln. Exports | | 0.00473 | 0.00166 | -0.02194 | -0.01141 | -0.01985 | -0.012 |
| | | (0.2376) | (0.082) | (-1.3331) | (-0.6075) | (-1.1618) | (-0.5921) |
| | | 0.0120* | 0.0042* | -0.0554* | -0.0289* | 0.0502* | -0.0303* |
| governance1 (voice&acct) | INST1 | -0.2281 | | | | | |
| | | (-7.212)** | | | | | |
| | | -0.3827* | | | | | |
| governance2 (political stab) | INST2 | | -0.1610 | | | | |
| | | | (-6.167)** | | | | |
| | | | -0.3701* | | | | |
| governance3 (govt effectiveness) | INST3 | | | -0.4712 | | | |
| | | | | (-14.397)** | | | |
| | | | | -0.6979* | | | |
| governance4 (regulatory quality) | INST4 | | | | -0.3218 | | |
| | | | | | (-9.562)** | | |
| | | | | | -0.5* | | |
| governance5 (rule of law) | INST5 | | | | | -0.39898 | |
| | | | | | | (-13.10)** | |
| | | | | | | 0.6518* | |
| governance6 (corruption) | INST6 | | | | | | -0.2128 |
| | | | | | | | (-6.4351)** |
| | | | | | | | -0.3555* |
| Year Dummies | D1 | -0.03112 | -0.0308 | -0.0394 | -0.03229 | -0.034 | -0.032 |
| | | (-4.585)** | (-4.436)** | (-6.971)** | (-5.027)** | (-5.829)** | (-4.637)** |
| | | -0.3827* | -0.2177* | -0.2788* | -0.2286* | | -0.2267* |
| Coefficient of Determination | $R^2$ | 36.16% | 33.38% | 56.38% | 42.88% | 52.96% | 34.07% |
| Adjusted $R^2$ | Adj.$R^2$ | 34.81% | 31.97% | 55.45% | 41.67% | 51.96% | 32.68% |
| F statistic | | 26.715 | 23.63 | 60.96 | 35.408 | 53.1 | 24.38 |
| Degrees of Fr | | (6, 283) | (6, 283) | (6, 283) | (6, 283) | (6, 283) | (6,283) |
| Significance for F, p-value | | 0.0000% | 0.0000% | 0.000% | 0.0000% | 0.000% | 0.0000% |

** Statistically significant at the 95% confidence level. * beta-weight values- no of standard deviations change in dep. variable if the independent is changed by one standard deviation. *** significant at 90% level

Models 22-25 use Mortality vs. Inst3, Inst4, Inst5, Inst6; Models 26-29, are the same as 22-25, except that GDP/Capita Growth is the dependent variable. Capital stock and Total Factor Productivity are controlled for. Differencing of the variables is employed.

**Table 5:** Using differences for development and growth vs. selected institutions and the year dummies.

| Variables | | Model 22 Mortality | Model 23 Mortality | Model 24 Mortality | Model 25 Mortality | Model 26 GDP/Cap | Model 27 GDP/Cap | Model 28 GDP/Cap | Model29 GDP/Cap |
|---|---|---|---|---|---|---|---|---|---|
| intercept | Bo | -5.3478<br>(-10.68)** | -5.241<br>(-10.42) | -5.425<br>(-10.85) | -5.026<br>(-9.887)** | -0.6488<br>(-1.15) | -0.5152<br>(-0.91) | -0.647<br>(-1.15)** | -0.5956<br>(-1.0237) |
| governance3 (govt effectiveness) | X3 | -2.993<br>(-2.089)**<br>-0.1041 | | | | -1.175<br>(-0.725)<br>-0.0336* | | | |
| governance4 (regulatory quality) | X4 | | -4.016<br>(-2.63)**<br>-0.1318 | | | | -3.081<br>(-1.729)<br>-0.083* | | |
| governance5 (rule of law) | X5 | | | -2.64<br>(-1.414)<br>-0.0698* | | | | -2.4006<br>(-1.14)<br>-0.0522* | |
| governance6 (corruption mitigation) | X6 | | | | -4.428<br>(-3.448)**<br>0.1743* | | | | -1.0362<br>(-0.705)<br>-0.0335* |
| TPF | X7 | -4.0374<br>(-0.716)<br>-0.0355* | -3.295<br>(-0.584)<br>-0.029* | -4.38<br>(-0.773)<br>-0.0385 | -5.1345<br>(-0.925)<br>-0.0451* | 82.431<br>(12.91)**<br>0.5952* | 83.435<br>(13.08)**<br>0.6024* | 82.72<br>(12.97)**<br>0.597* | 81.99<br>(12.91)**<br>0.5920* |
| Capital Stock | X8 | 3.179E09<br>(0.0107)<br>0.0005 | 1.636<br>(0.0554)<br>0.0027* | -1.338<br>(-0.0450)<br>-0.0022* | -1.02<br>(-0.0348)<br>-0.0017 | -7.157<br>(-2.135)**<br>-0.098* | -7.014<br>(-2.10)**<br>0.096* | -7.25<br>(-2.17)**<br>-0.099* | -7.2058<br>(-2.15)**<br>0.0986* |
| Year Dummies | D1 | 4.405<br>(9.29)**<br>0.4603* | 4.3162<br>(9.075)**<br>0.4510* | 4.52<br>(9.613)**<br>0.4724* | 4.077<br>(8.426)**<br>0.4260* | 0.672<br>(1.253)<br>0.0577* | 0.5372<br>(0.998)**<br>0.0461* | 0.685<br>(1.295)<br>0.0588* | 0.6236<br>(1.126)<br>0,0535* |
| Coeff of Determinatn | $R^2$ | 24.22% | 24.81% | 23.67% | 25.95% | 34.58% | 35.12% | 34.74% | 34.58 |
| Adjusted $R^2$ | Adj. $R^2$ | 23.27% | 23.87% | 22.71% | 25.02% | 33.76% | 34.31% | 33.92% | 33.75% |
| F statistic | | 25.49 | 26.32 | 24.73 | 27.94 | 42.157 | 43.17 | 42.45 | 42.15 |
| Degrees of Fr | | (4, 319) | (4, 319) | (4, 319) | (4, 319) | (4, 319) | (4, 319) | (4, 319) | (4, 319) |
| Significance for F, p-value | | 0.0000% | 0.0000% | 0.000% | 0.0000% | 0.0000% | 0.0000% | 0.0000% | .00000% |

** Statistically significant at the 95% confidence level. * beta-weight values- no of standard deviations change in dep. variable if the independent is changed by one standard deviation. *** significant at 90% level

### 4.4 The impact of institutions on growth per capita, on Life expectancy and on Infant Mortality (using differencing) [Tables 5 and 6]

We used different variables and a different model formulation to produce the analysis reported in Table 5. Differencing was used, to avoid some of the unaccounted for the variable effect that might have existed in our other formulations. The two independent variables added to the institutions were capital stock and total factor productivity (TPF). We tested for the most critical institution using GDP/Capita and Infant Mortality. First without log transforms, and the results are on table 5. Secondly, we differenced the log of all the dependent and independent variables, with the exception of the institutions. We report the results of the log-linear transforms on table-6.

**Table 6:** Using Log Differences for Dependent Development and Growth vs. Selected Institutions

| Variables | | Model 31 Mortality | Model 32 Mortality | Model 33 Mortality | Model 34 Mortality | Model 35 Mortality | Model 36 Mortality | Model 37 GDP/Cap | Model38 GDP/Cap Model | Model39 GDP/Cap | Model40 GDP/Cap |
|---|---|---|---|---|---|---|---|---|---|---|---|
| intercept | $\beta_0$ | -0.055 | -0.0595 | 0.0625 | -0.0567 | -0.054 | -0.0609 | 0.00303 | -0.00075 | -0.00279 | 0.00192 |
| | | (-7.6)** | (-7.1)** | (-9.9)** | (-8.1)** | (-8.8)** | (-8.6)** | (0.7284) | (-0.17) | (-0.8)** | (0.3855) |
| Governance 1 | INST1 | -0.5874 | | | | | | | | | |
| (Voice & Accountability) | (X1) | (-12)** | | | | | | | | | |
| | | -0.34* | | | | | | | | | |
| Governance 2 | INST2 | | -0.1841 | | | | | | | | |
| (Political Stability) | (X2) | | (-5.1)** | | | | | | | | |
| | | | -0.1630 | | | | | | | | |
| governance3 (government | INST3 | | | -0.6512 | | | | 0.4168 | | | |
| effectiveness) | (X3) | | | (-17.5)** | | | | (16.9)** | | | |
| | | | | -0.4101* | | | | 0.2188* | | | |
| governance4 (regulatory | INST4 | | | | -0.6788 | | | | 0.4569 | | |
| quality) | (X4) | | | | (-13.)** | | | | (14.1)** | | |
| | | | | | -0.3527* | | | | | | |
| governance5 (rule of law) | INST5 | | | | | -0.759 | | | | 0.5452 | |
| | (X5) | | | | | (-18.6)** | | | | (23.4)** | |
| | | | | | | -0.4257* | | | | 0.2549* | |
| governance6 (corruption | INST6 | | | | | | -0.5732 | | | | 0.3104 |
| mitigation) | (X6) | | | | | | (-13)** | | | | (10.02)** |
| | | | | | | | -0.3398* | | | | 0.1534* |
| | | -0.2487 | -0.5192 | -0.0810 | -0.0927 | 0.06223 | -0.4438 | 1.1437 | 1.1304 | 0.9909 | 1.403 |
| LN TPF | Ln X7 | (-0.9928) | (-1.784) | (-0.37)** | (-0.3766) | (0.2909) | (-1.809) | (7.901)** | (7.197)** | (8.10)** | (8.189)** |
| | | -0.0264 | -0.0552* | -0.0086* | -0.0099* | 0.0066** | -0.0472* | 0.1013* | 0.1002* | .0878* | 0.124* |
| | | 0.345894 | 0.3648 | 0.3656 | 0.3635 | 0.365 | 0.365 | 0.549 | 0.5512 | 0.5512 | 0.5473 |
| LN Capital Stock | Ln X8 | (26.64)** | (23.91)** | (33.12)** | (29.37)** | (34.12)** | (29.18)** | (75.41)** | (69.8)** | (90.08)** | (62.66)** |

| | | | | | | | | | | | |
|---|---|---|---|---|---|---|---|---|---|---|---|
| | | .7250* | 0.7646 | 0.7663 | 0.7620* | 0.7652 | 0.7652* | 0.9595 | 0.963 | 0.9631 | 0.9564* |
| Year Dummies | D1 | | | | | | | | | | |
| Coefficient of Determination | $R^2$ | 76.73% | 68.47% | 82.25% | 77.85% | 83.32% | 77.33% | 94.63% | 93.73% | 96.21% | 92.32% |
| Adjusted $R^2$ | Adj. $R^2$ | 76.52% | 68.19% | 82.09% | 77.65% | 83.17% | 77.13% | 94.58% | 93.68% | 96.17% | 92.25% |
| F statistic | | 369.36 | 243.27 | 518.87 | 393.61 | 559.3 | 382.1 | 1973.32 | 1675.05 | 2840.86 | 1347.3 |
| Degrees of Fr | | (3, 336) | (3,336) | (3,336) | (3, 336) | (3, 336) | (3, 336) | (3, 336) | (3, 336) | (3, 336) | (3, 336) |
| Significance for F, p-value | | 0.0000% | 0.0000% | 0.0000% | 0.0000% | 0.0000% | 0.0000% | 0.0000% | 0.0000% | 0.0000% | 0.0000% |

** Statistically significant at the 95% confidence level. * beta-weight values- no of standard deviations change in dep. variable if the independent is changed by one standard deviation. *** significant at 90% level

Since our prior analyses, reported in Tables 1 through 4, clearly indicated that two institutions, voice, and accountability and political stability were not the most critical about growth or comprehensive development, we chose to evaluate the other four when we applied both differencing and the log of differencing. We would now go ahead and report the findings with INST3, INST4, INST5 and INST6. We also dispensed with Life Expectancy and used only Infant Mortality and its log in the analyses reported in Tables 5 and 6.

The linear-linear OLS analyses, reported in Table 5, showed a significant relationship between the institutions and comprehensive development even when capital stock and total factor productivity were controlled for. The four institutions, except the rule of law, were significant. Corruption (INST6) was the most relevant, with Regulatory Quality (INST4) coming in second. Government Effectiveness was 3rd in importance. The measurements were the beta weights and the coefficients of determination. When GDP/Capita Growth was measured against the institutions, controlling for the capital stock and TPF, none of the institutions showed any significance. The controlled for variables showed substantial significance with growth. In all these cases, the coefficients of determination were quite low, ranging from 22% to 34%.

On Table 6, log-log analyses were used, and the significance and coefficients of determination were quite impressive, reaching (in the case of coefficients of determination), 96%, when the rule of law (INST5) was regressed against GDP/Capita growth, and capital stock, controlling for TPF. INST3 (government effectiveness) and INST5 (the rule of law) seemed to be the most critical intuitions with comprehensive development as well as GDP/Capita growth. In both cases, INST5 was slightly better than INST3.

## 5.0 CONCLUSION

Government Effectiveness (INST3) demonstrated a clear pattern of superiority in impact on growth and comprehensive development. About growth, INST3 showed the highest impact when we used the linear-linear fixed effect model, (both differenced and non-differenced). When tested against infant mortality, even with Sub-Sahara African data alone, INST3 showed the most impact. In a log-linear and log-log analysis, INST3 was also superior, except that INST5 showed a slightly higher level of importance in the case of log-log differenced models (Table 6). Even then INST3 came in a very close second.

We came to the conclusion early that INST1 (Voice and accountability) and INST2 (Political Stability) were not as critical as the other four institutions. Different institutions could have different impacts, depending on whether growth or comprehensive development is the focus. Government Effectiveness was the most critical institution, followed by the Rule of Law. Government Effectiveness was critical in growth. Its superiority was in comprehensive development. Regarding policy priorities, governments, especially in developing parts of the world, would be well advised to channel their efforts and resources toward improving two institutions, government effectiveness (the civil service) and the rule of law. These two institutions, especially the civil service, have the capacity to improve the lives of the people, in addition to possibly dragging along the other institutions with them. Governments and policymakers in developing countries should pay close attention.

## REFERENCES


Anderson, Sweeney and Williams (2004), *Essentials of modern business statistics, 2e, with Microsoft Excel,* Thomson, South-Western.

Aron, J., (2000), Growth and institutions: a review of the evidence, *The World Bank Research Observer,* 15(1)

Bayley, D., (1966), Effects of corruption in a developing nation, *Political Research Qtly*, 19, pp.719-32

Beck T. and Levine Ross (2003), Law enforcement institutions and financial development, *World Bank, WPS3136.*

Bills, M.,and Klenow P., (2000), Does schooling Cause Growth? *American Economic Review*, 90 (5) 1160-83

Court J., Hyden Goran, and Mease Ken (2003), The judiciary and governance in 16 developing countries, *United Nations University, World Governance Survey Discussion Paper 9.*

Easterly, W. (1998), The quest for growth, *The World Bank Research Papers.*

Easterly W. and Ross Levine (1995), Africa's growth tragedy, *The World Bank Policy Research Working Paper, #1503.*

Evans P., and Rauch James E. (1999), Bureaucracy and growth: a cross-national analysis of the effects of "weberian" state structures on economic growth, *American Sociological Review*, 64(5), pp 748-765

Feenstra, R.C, Robert Inklaar and Marcel P. Timmer (2013), *Penn World Tables Version 8,* available on www.ggdc.net/pwt.

Fosu, A. K.(1992) Political instability and economic growth: evidence from sub-sahara africa, *Economic Development and Cultural Change*, 40 (4), pp.829-841.

Goldsmith, A., (1987) Does political stability hinder economic development? Mancur Olson's theory and the third world, *Research Notes, Comparative Politics: PhD Programs and Political Science,* City University of NY

Hyden G., Court Julius, and Mease Ken (2003), The bureaucracy and governance in 16 developing countries, *Overseas Development Institute, world Governance Survey Discussion Paper 7*

Jakob De Haan, Siermann, C.I.J (1966), *New evidence on the relationship between democracy and economic growth.* Public Choice, 86, pp.175-198.

Jeffrey H., David Hume, Hussein Jillian and Richard Philips (2003) Bureaucratic effects: weberian state structures and poverty reduction"

Jamison, E. A., Jamison, Dean T., Hanushek, Eric A (2006), The effects of education quality on income growth and mortality, *National Bureau of Economic Research, Cambridge, MA.*

Kaufmann D., Kraay Aart, and Mastruzzi, Massimo(2003), Governance matters III governance indicators for 1996-2002", The World Bank, WPS3106.

Kaufmann D., Kraay Aart, and Mastruzzi, Massimo (2005), Governance matters IV governance indicators for 1996-2004", *The World Bank, WPS3630.*
Klibanoff, P., Sandroni Alvaro, Moselle, Boaz, and Serantini, Brett (2006), *Managerial Statistics: A Case – Based Approach,* Thomson- South Western Publishers
Knack, S., and Philip Keefer(1995), Institutions and economic performance: Cross-Country tests, using alternative institutional measures, *Economics and Politics,* 7(3), pp 207-27
Kohli A., (2004), *State – directed development*, Cambridge University Press
Laeven L., and Majnoni Giovanni (2003), Does judicial efficiency lower the cost of credit? *The World Bank,* WPS3159.
Mauro, P., (1995) Corruption and growth, *Quarterly Journal of Economics,* 110 (3) pp 681-712
Messick R. E (1999) Judicial reform and economic development: a survey of the issues, *The World Bank Research Observer,* 14(1).
Okpokwasili B., (2005), Economic growth vs. economic development, a case of nigeria, *Proceedings of the Association of Global Business,* Miami, Florida.
Okpokwasili B., (2007), Institutions and development: are some more critical than others? – A cross-section empirical analysis of 54 countries", *Journal of Business and Public Affairs,* 1(1).
Ojo Oladeji and Temitope Oshikoya (1994), Determinants of long-term growth: some african results," *Journal of African Economics,* 4 (2), pp 163-91.
Olson, Mancur Jr. (1963), Rapid growth as a destabilizing force, *The Journal of Economic History,* 23(4), pp.529-552.
Olson, Mancur Jr.(1998), Mancur Olson on the key to economic development, *Population and Development Review,* 24(2), pp. 369-379
Pinheiro, A.C., 2003, Economics and justice: concepts and empirical evidence
Posner, R.A, (1998), Creating a legal framework for economic development, *The World Bank Research Observer,* 13(1), pp 1-11
Rodrik, D., (2000) Institutions for high quality growth: what they are and how to acquire them *Studies in Comparative International Development.*
Sen, A., (2001), *Development as Freedom,* Oxford University Press.
Sen, A., (2000), "What is the role of law enforcement and judicial reform in the development process. *World bank Law enforcement Conference, Washington DC, June 5,* retrieved, July 27, 2006
United Nations Development Program (UNDP), (1995-2005), *Human Development Reports,* various issues.
Vijayaraghavan, M., and Ward, W. A (2006). *Institutions and economic growth: empirical evidence from cross-national Analysis,* Clemson University.
Wooldridge, J.M., (2000), *Introductory Econometrics, A Modern Approach,* South Western College Publishing
World Bank, (1995-2005), *World Development Reports,* various issues.
World Bank, (1995-2005), *World Development Indicators,* various issues.
World Health Organization (WHO) (1995-2006), *World Health Reports,* various issues.

**APPENDIX A**

**Countries in the Analysis**

| | | | | |
|---|---|---|---|---|
| Benin | Gabon | Namibia | Belgium | Portugal |
| Botswana | Gambia | Niger | Canada | United Kingdom |
| Burkina Faso | Ghana | Nigeria | Denmark | United States |
| Burundi | Guinea | Senegal | Finland | Bangladesh |
| Cameroon | Kenya | South Africa | France | China |
| Central African Republic | Liberia | Tanzania | Germany | India |
| Chad | Mali | Uganda | Greece | Japan |
| Congo Zaire | Mauritania | Zambia | Ireland | Korea, Republic of |
| Congo Brazzaville | Mauritius | Zimbabwe | Italy | Malaysia |
| Ethiopia | Mozambique | | Norway | Pakistan |
| | | | Singapore | Thailand |

# 14

# Impact of Interest Rate in the Economy from the Viewpoints of Banking Managers: Empirical Evidence from Jordan

**Dr. Reem Shaher Al-Araj**[1]

**ABSTRACT**

The research aims at investigating the role, impact and determinants of interest rate in Jordanian economy from view points of banking managers in Jordan. The methodology is descriptive and analytical using mean, standard deviation, t-test and percentages as statistical tools. The study concludes that the role of interest rate in Jordanian monetary policy is restricted by two factors: pegging JD with US$ which limits the effective role of interest rate in Jordanian monetary policy and the dual banking system of traditional and Islamic banks where Islamic banks do not deal with Interest rate. Raising interest rate in Jordan caused higher cost of credit for companies, less competitiveness of exports, less liquidity in the economy, higher profit margin for banks, higher exchange rate of JD and higher inflation. Nevertheless, lowering interest rate in Jordan caused lower cost of borrowing, higher liquidity, better competitiveness of exports and more credit facilities by banks but inflation was much lower. Moreover, the study concluded the determinants of interest rate in Jordan are money supply, demand for money, inflation and economic conditions. In order to have an effective role for interest rate in monetary policy, the researcher recommends pegging JD to a basket of currencies.

Keywords: Economy of Jordan, interest rate, monetary policy, economic impact.

---

## 1. Introduction

There is a controversy among economists and financial analysts on the role of interest rate as a tool for monetary easing and tightening policies and their impact on stimulating economic growth, creation of employment, provision of liquidity, controlling inflation and whether monetary easing policy should be stopped due to its burden on the government budget and public debt which reached more than 14

[1] Assistant Professor, Faculty of Management & Finance, Middle East University. Eamil: reem@ipbaudit.net.

trillion dollar in USA. Since 2008, central banks in USA, Euro Zone, United Kingdom, Japan and China. Several countries used changes in interest rate as a tool for controlling inflation, employment, economic growth and aggregate demand. Since December 2015, US Federal Reserve bank adopted a tightening monetary policy by increasing interest rate gradually to reach 3.5% in a few years started by increasing interest rate by 0.25% to reach 0.50% in USA followed by other countries particularly those which peg their currencies to US Dollar such as Jordan, Jordanian Arabia and other GCC countries. Various scenarios are open to Central Bank in Jordan (CBJ) to change interest rate as a tool of monetary policy to control inflation, stimulate economic growth, generate employment and increase aggregate demand.

The research problem stems from the significance of using interest rate as a tool of Jordanian monetary policy in the light of pegging Jordanian Dinar to US Dollar and the impact of changing interest rate on Jordan's economy. The research problem could be formulated in the following research questions: (1) what is the role of interest rate in Jordanian monetary policy? (2) What is the impact of changing interest rate on the Jordanian economy?

The research objectives are: (1) Investigating the role of interest rate as a tool of Jordanian monetary policy. (2) Shedding light on the impact of changing the interest rates on Jordanian economy during the period 2008-2015.

The research importance stems from the scarcity of research on the role and impact of using interest rate as a tool of Jordanian monetary policy besides the importance of the conclusions and policy implications of the study for decision-makers of monetary policy, financial analysts and economic researchers.

The research methodology is descriptive and analytical of primary and secondary data collected using statistical tools of mean, standard deviation, t-test and percentages. The primary data was collected through a purposive sample of 12 banking directors representing the following six Jordanian banks: Bloom bank, Ahli Bank, Itihad Bank, Capital Bank, Arab Bank and ABC Bank. A questionnaire was designed by the researcher including 34 paragraphs on role, impact and determinants of interest rate in Jordan and the questionnaire was sent to several universities' professors in finance as referees for evaluating its appropriateness and several amendments were made according to the suggested changes.The reliability of the questionnaire was tested by Cronbach Alpha as follows:

Table 1: Reliability test

| Item | Coefficient of Cronbach Alpha |
|---|---|
| Role of Interest Rate | 0.913 |
| Impact of Rising Interest Rate | 0.873 |
| Impact of Lowering Interest Rate | 0.880 |
| Determinants of Interest Rate | 0.903 |
| Total | 0.892 |

Source: Researcher computation

Coefficient of Cronbach Alpha (0.892) of the questionnaire's paragraphs is appropriate for this kind of study (see the Appendix). The secondary data was collected from reports of Central Bank of Jordan, Ministry of Finance besides IMF and World Bank.

The organizational structure of the study includes five sections. Section I: Introduction. Section II: Conceptual Framework of Interest Rate and Previous Studies. Section III: Salient Characteristics of Jordanian Monetary Policy & Macroeconomic Indicators. Section IV: Analysis of the Role, Impact and Determinants of Interest Rate in Jordan. Section V: Conclusions & Policy Implications, besides references and appendix.

## 2. Conceptual framework of interest rate and previous studies

Interest is defined as the rate of return on capital as a factor of production or the price which is paid by borrowers to lenders for the use of their savings. In other words, interest is the price that the consumer asks to compensate him for delaying his consumption for a coming period. Interest rate is the compensation required by the owner of capital for his loans to customers (Ahuja, 2006).

Interest is classified as "nominal rate of interest" which prevails in the market and "real interest rate" which is the nominal rate of interest adjusted for inflation as in the following equation: Real Interest rate= Nominal interest rate –Inflation.

Other types of interest are simple and compound rate of interest where simple interest rate is calculated on the principal amount of loan and compound interest rate is calculated on the principal amount plus interest accrued for loan.

There are three economic theories that explain the determinants of interest rate: First, the "Classical Theory of Interest" which stresses that interest is determined by demand and supply of savings for investment purposes. Second, the "Neoclassical Loanable Fund Theory" which explains the determinants of interest rate by the equilibrium between demand and supply of loanable funds. Third, the "Keynesian Interest Theory" which explains interest rate by the equilibrium between demand and supply of money. Keynesian Theory of Interest is called "Liquidity preference" where money is demanded for transactions motive, for precautionary motive and for speculative motive. John Keynes discussed liquidity trap which results from the fact that central bank cannot increase money supply after the interest rate reaches the minimum level of zero. Liquidity preference theory promoted by John Keynes explains changes in interest rates (Ahuja: 2006).

Other determinants of interest rate include money supply, inflation and discount rate charged by Central Bank when providing loans to banks, the business cycle of recession, boom, prosperity and depression besides whether the monetary policy is expansionary or contractionary. Central bank usually fixes the interest rate as an indicator for the banks' decisions on interest on deposits, loans and interest margin. Other concerns of interest are its impact on saving, investment, credit facilities, bonds' return, discount rate on repos, reverse repos and liquidity for the banking system (Begg etal: 2011).

According to changes in interest rates have an impact on the exchange rate of a currency which in turn affects exports, imports and foreign direct investment in a country where high interest rate leads to currency appreciation and vice-versa in case of low interest.

Raising interest rate is used by the US Federal Reserve Bank in case of "Monetary tightening" while lowering interest is used to get "Monetary Easing" in order to influence aggregate demand, inflation, employment and economic growth. Furthermore, determinants of interest rate in emerging markets include concentration ratio, cost of economic restructuring, direct and indirect monetary policies which have impact on companies profits (Ozdemir and Altinoz 2012).

Based on the economic theory, the equilibrium interest rate is determined by the cross point of money demand and money supply curves. Interest rate will be low when money demand declines and vice versa when demand for money increases. More money supply lowers interest rate and vice versa when money supply decreases (Samuelson & Nordhaus: 2005).

Concerning Monetary School, Milton Freidman, who belongs to Chicago School of Economics, explained how the increase of money supply and cutting down taxes lead to more economic activities and change of prices as specified by the following Quantity Theory of Money (Samuelson & Nordhaus:2005):

**M V=PQ**

Where
M= Money Supply
V=Velocity of Money
P= Price level
Q=Size of economy or output

The equation shows that more money supply leads to higher prices if the velocity of money and output are kept constant. In the light of the International Financial Crisis, the Federal Reserve Bank in the USA adopted the Monetary Easing since 2008 by lowering interest rate to 0.25% and expanding money supply in order to encourage companies to borrow at low cost and get out of the economic recession. Monetary easing was accompanied by purchasing government bonds and encouraging commercial banks to borrow from the Federal Reserve Bank through the Security Lending Facility in order get rid of the liquidity trap which allows banks to borrow with their security guarantees under the so-called Asset Relief Program. In December 2015 the Federal Reserve Bank started Money tightening by raising interest rate to 0.50% after the USA economy achieved progress in economic growth, declining unemployment to 5% and higher inflation which reached less than 2%. Interest rate will be increased gradually to reach 3.5% in 2017 (Yelen: 2015).

As a reaction of increasing interest rate on US dollar, central banks in the EURO zone and in Japan followed the Federal Reserve Bank by increasing their interest discount rates (Edwin: 2009).

In order to fight recession, the Central European Bank has extended the Money Easing policy in the EURO Zone till 2017 with interest rate reaching less than 0.25%. Moreover, the Central Bank of Japan followed monetary easing policy by lowering its interest rate and buying governmental bonds to deal with Japan's recession. China Central Bank has lowered value of Yewan currency and lowered its interest rate from 2% to 1.5% to increase competitiveness (Al-Watan: 2015).

Money Easing is new application different from the traditional monetary policy for dealing with recession (http//en.wikipedia/quantitative easing.com.) US dollar constitutes a high percentage of reserves of international currencies as in Figure1:

Figure 1: Shares of main currencies in international reserves

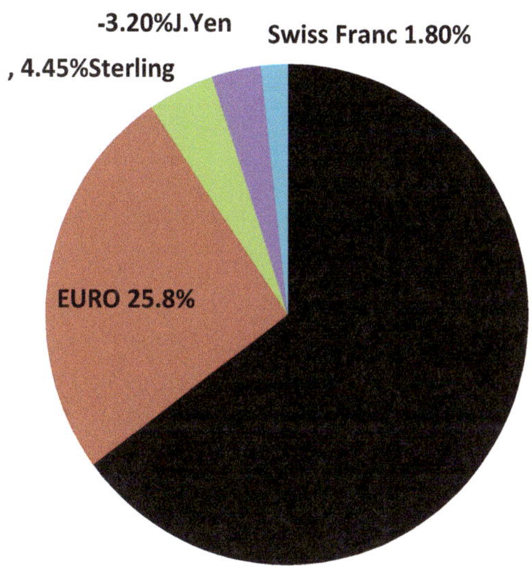


Source: IMF (2015) Financial Statistics. Washington DC.

Moreover, US Dollar plays an important role in foreign trade and global payments System as in Table 2:

Table 2: Role of US $ in foreign traded and global payments system

| Item | Percentage/Value |
|---|---|
| Global Exports in USA Dollar | 50% |
| Share of US $ in International Reserve | 64% |
| Size of Transaction in US $ | 3 trillion USA $ |

Source: IMF (2015) Financial Statistics. Washington DC.

Interest on US $ has fluctuated in the last decade as shown in Table 3:

Table 3: Development of interest rates in USA during 1997-2015

| Year | Interest Rate | Reasoning |
|---|---|---|
| 1997-2000 | 6.50% | Dot Com. Bubble |
| 2001-2003 | 1.0% | Recession |
| 2004-2007 | 5.25% | Mortgage of Housing Bubble |
| 2008-2015 | 0.0%-0.25% | International Financial Crisis |
| December 2015- | 0.25-.50% | Monetary Tightening Policy |

Source: Federal Reserve Bank (2015) Declining and Rising Interest Rates on Federal Funds. Washington

Development of Interest Rates in USA (1997-2015) is shown in Figure2:

Figure 2: Development of interest rates in USA (1997-2015)

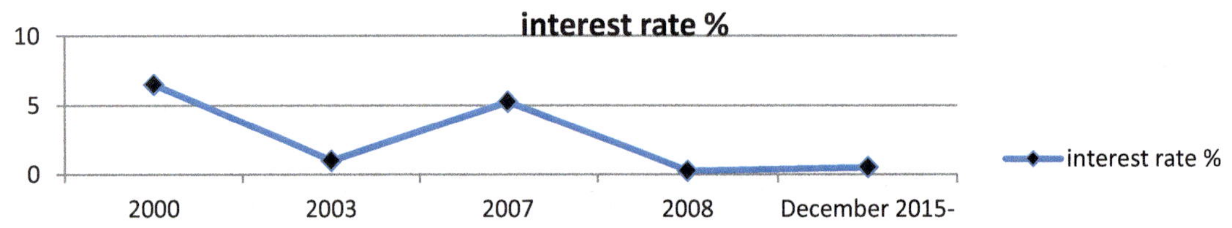


Source: Researcher design

The impact of raising the interest rate in USA is strengthening the Dollar, increasing the value of assets valued in Dollar and raising the values of currencies pegged to US dollar. Higher interest rates have reversed negative impact on consumption and investment as in figure 3 (Begg etal: 2011):

Figure 3: Function of interest rate

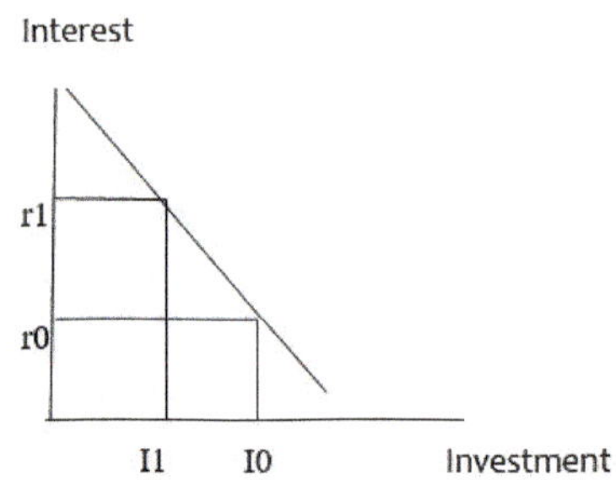


Quantitative Monetary Easing was introduced to overcome the global financial crisis which has the following implications: (1) Collapse of mortgage market. (2) Lack of bank lending. (3) Lower banks' reserves. (4) Lower aggregate demand. (5) Lower capital adequacy ratio. (6) Lower bonds prices. (7) Lower investment and consumption which are parts of aggregate demand. (8) Recession and loweconomic growth.

Review of previous studies is discussed as follows:

- The Study of Henry C. Murphy (1950) Role of Interest Rates in a Changing World: Reappraisal of Easy Money. The study concludes that interest rates have two fold function: the positive relation between interest rate and saving, i.e., the higher the interest, the greater the amount of saving and interest rate has negative relation to investment, i.e., high interest rate discourages real investments. Furthermore, high interest rates curb excessive credit creation; i.e., if the interest rates are too high, banks credit would contract and prices would rise. Moreover, high interest rates have negative impact on capital formation due to the negative impact of interest on investment. The study also concluded that in time of emergency, interest rate is not an appropriate measure to allocate funds between the public and private sectors.

- The Study of Phillip C. James (2014) Sector Rotation and Interest Rate Policy. The study concluded that a sector rotation strategy based on changes in interest rates is one way for investors to maximize their returns. The study used U.S. monthly bank prime loan rate from January 31, 1949 to December 31, 2012 to measure changes in interest rate which were labeled as expansionary or restrictive. Betas to measure portfolio risks were obtained by regressing monthly equally weighted returns against the monthly Dow Jones industrial index. The study concluded that a sector rotation strategy based on changes of interest rate adjustments can improve the performance of investor's portfolio.
- The Study of Nilufer Ozdemir & Cuneyt Altinoz (2012) Determinants of interest rate for emerging market economies: the role of financial market structure. The study concluded that it is essential for central banks to assess whether or not the pass-through from monetary policy rates to credit and deposit interest rates is complete in order to ensure price stability. Emerging market countries lack large panel data sets that are typically available for developed countries which make it hard to analyze the determinants of pass-through coefficients for emerging markets. The findings indicate that competition among banks plays a more important role for emerging market countries than the developed counterparts.
- The Study of Khalil Abdelrahim & Farid Flemban (2009) Economic Feasibility of Pegged Dinar to US Dollar & Options for Adjusting Saudi Foreign Exchange System in Light of Recent Economic Developments. The study concluded that Saudi Arabia Monetary Agency (SAMA) has lost independence of its monetary policy due to pegging the Saudi Riyal (SR) with US Dollar for the last 30 years since 1986 where SAMA was obliged to change its interest rate to match the changes of Federal Reserve Bank of interest rate in USA. The study recommended that in order to increase the control of SAMA on Saudi Monetary Policy, Riyal should be pegged to a basket of currencies of US dollar by (40%), Euro (30%), Sterling Pound (10%) Japanese Yen (10%), Swiss Franc (5%) and Special Drawing Rights (5%).
- The Study of Arab Monetary Fund (2015) Developing Arab Bond Markets. The study concluded that bond return is affected by the level of market interest rate. Bonds markets in the Arab Countries are weak compared with stock markets. The bond market is considered a source of finance in medium and long term. Bonds markets support the role of banks in providing finance to economic sectors particularly long-term financing. Sukuk, which is an alternative to bond, is used as a tool of Islamic Financing which is growing rapidly to reach about 1 trillion dollar world-wide.
- The Study of Mackenzie International Consultative Institute (2015) Saudi Arabia Far Away from Oil Sector. The study concluded that KSA should identify the areas of disequilibrium in Saudi economy and should have a strategy till the year 2030 to diversify its economy away from the share of 90% of oil in the economy to reach 30% in 2030, creation of 6 million jobs for the Saudis, increasing the per capita income by 60% till the year 2030, investment of 1 trillion Dinar during the coming 15 years mostly through private sector, privatization of certain governmental project to raise productivity, increasing training of human resources and attracting more foreign investments.
- The Study of Fahd Ben Abdullah Alhwimani (2015) Impact of the American Monetary Policy upon Saudi Monetary Policy. The study concluded that the changes in US Monetary Policy created challenges to Saudi Arab Monetary Agency (SAMA) due to pegging Riyal to US Dollar since 1986 despite the differences in economic structure between the two countries. Interest on deposits in KSA was lowered to 1.5% when US lowered interest rate to nearly zero leading to more lending by Saudi Banks and when the US Federal Reserve Bank

increased interest rate from 0.25% to 0.50%, SAMA increased the interest rate on reversed repos to 0.50% which led to increase the interest on loans between banks (SIBOR) to 1.3% which caused an increase in the borrowing cost. Such an interest change caused pressure on SR exchange rate which hurts exports.

## 3. Jordan's macroeconomic indicators & monetary policy

Macroeconomic indicators of Jordan in the last decade show increase in unemployment rate, reduction of inflation, increase in consumption, decline in investment, lower growth of GDP, increase in broad money supply, increase in government and private sector debts, fluctuation of interest rate and increase of interest on treasury bills as shown in Table 4:

Table 4: Macroeconomic indicators of Jordan (2010-2015)

| Year | 2010 | 2011 | 2012 | 2013 | 2014 | 2015 |
|---|---|---|---|---|---|---|
| Population number | 6.113 | 6.993 | 7.427 | 8.114 | 8.804 | 9.532 |
| Unemployment Rate | 12.5% | 12.9% | 12.2% | 12.6% | 11.9% | 13.0 |
| GDP at Current Prices (JD) | 18762 | 20476 | 21965 | 21851 | 25437 | 26.289 |
| GDP Growth at constant prices | 2.3% | 2.6% | 2.7% | 2.8% | 3.1% | 2.4% |
| National Income in current prices | 21323 | 23743 | 24774 | 28424 | 30302 | 30.234 |
| Change in Price Index | 4.8% | 4.2% | 4.5% | 4.8% | 2.9% | -0.9 |
| Share of Consumption in GDP | 95.7% | 105.1% | NA | NA | NA | NA |
| Share of Fixed Investment in GDP | 23.6% | 21.6% | NA | NA | NA | NA |
| Share of national Saving in GDP | 4.3% | 5.1%- | NA | NA | NA | NA |
| Money Supply (M2) in JD | 22306 | 24118 | 24945 | 27363 | 29240 | 31605 |
| Government Debt (JD) | 4907 | 6701 | 9461 | 10494 | 10473 | 11386 |
| Net Debt on Private Sector (JD) | 13612 | 14925 | 15953 | 17222 | 17582 | 18704 |
| Re-discount Rate | 4.25% | 4.50% | 5.0% | 4.50% | 4.25 | 3.75 |
| Interest on Treasury Bills | 2.208% | 3.232% | 3.788% | NA | NA | NA |

NA= non available

Source: Central Bank of Jordan, Annual Reports 2010-2015. Research Department

Monetary indicators of Jordan in the last few years show a decline in foreign currency reserves, increase in money supply, increase in credit facilities and an increase in bank deposits as shown in Table 5:

Table 5: Main Monetary indicators of Jordan (2015-2016) JD million and % change

| Monetary Indicators | November 2015 | November 2016 | %Change |
|---|---|---|---|
| Foreign Currency Reserves | 14077 | 12708 | -10.2% |
| Money Supply (M2) | 31366 | 32472 | 2.7% |
| Credit Facilities | 21048 | 22736 | 7.7% |
| Total Bank Deposits | 32433 | 32901 | 0.9% |

Source: Central Bank of Jordan, Annual Reports 2010-2015. Research Department

Interest rate in Jordan economy is structured into interest rate on monetary policy instruments and interest rates on credit facilities of banking institutions. In the last few years Central bank of Jordan followed flexible interest rate policy where the interest rate was mostly reduced to stimulate the economy as shown in Table 6:

Table 6: Structure of interest rate in Jordan (2012-2013) and (2015-2015)

| Interest rate | 2012 | 2013 | 2015 | 2016 |
|---|---|---|---|---|
| Re-discount rate | 5.00% | 4.50% | 3.75% | 3.75% |
| Repurchase agreements overnight | 3.75% | 3.50% | 3.50% | 3.50% |

| | | | | |
|---|---|---|---|---|
| Overnight Deposit window rate | 1.75% | 1.50% | 1.5% | 1.5% |
| Repurchase agreement one month | 2.50% | 2.25% | 2.5% | 2.5% |
| Interest rate on Certificate of Deposit one week | 2.50% | 2.25% | 2.25% | 2.25% |
| Demand deposits | 0.45% | 0.30% | 0.33% | 0.24% |
| Time deposits | 3.73% | 2.96% | 3.13% | 3.04% |
| Discount bills and notes | 8.58% | 7.91% | 9.24% | 10.37% |
| Loans and Advances | 9.38% | 10.06% | 8.27% | 7.90% |
| Over draft | 8.34% | 7.58% | 7.93% | 7.64% |
| Prime lending rate | 8.49% | 8.39% | 8.37% | 8.39% |

Source: Central Bank of Jordan. Statistical Monthly Bulletins 2015-2016. Amman

The Central Bank of Jordan changed the structure of interest rate during (2013-2016) by reducing discount rate from 4.5% to 4.25%%, reduction of interest rate on loans among banks from 4.25% to 4%, reduction of repurchasing agreement (Repos) from 3.5% to 3% and reduction of interest rate on deposit for one night among banks from 3.5% to 2.75% as in Table 7:

Table 7: Change of interest rates on loans, deposits and treasury bills In Jordan

| Interest Rate | 2012 | 2013 | 2014 | 2015 | 2016 |
|---|---|---|---|---|---|
| Weighted Average of interest on loans | 8.95 | 9.03 | 8.84 | 8.24 | 7.91 |
| Weighted Average of interest on Time Deposits | 4.19 | 4.97 | 4.11 | 3.06 | 2.96 |
| Interest Rate on Treasury bills for six months | 3.788 | 3.788 | 3.788 | 3.788 | 3.788 |

Source: Ministry of Finance (2016) public finance bulletin no.4 vol.18 May.Amman

In sum, the monetary policy of Central Bank of Jordan during 2013-2016 was characterized by flexibility as it used quantitative money easing policy first to stimulate the economy and increase credit facilities for the economic sectors followed by quantitative tightening of money since November 2016, the Central Bank of Jordan increased interest rate by 25 points in consistency with the increase of the Federal Reserve Bank of USA due to pegging Jordanian Dinar to US$. However on February 19, 2017 CBJ increased the interest rate in Jordan by 50 points in order to maintain the stability of the economy which was an independent decision of the Central Bank away from the Federal Reserve Bank of USA.

## 4. Analysis and discussion of empirical results on role, impact and determinants of interest rate in Jordan

### 4.1 Characteristics of respondents in the sample

The descriptive analysis of the characteristics of respondents shows that they are selected on purpose from six Jordanian banks in Amman; one forth of them are branch managers, one forth are credit directors, one forth are head of corporation and 16.7% of them executive manager and 8.3% of them are head treasury. Their specializations are accounting 16.7%, finance 58.3%, economics 16.7% and management 8.3%. Five of the respondents are with master degree, four of them are with bachelor degree and three of them are with doctorate degree. The experiences of the respondents are 16- 20 years and more for 41.7% of them, 10years or less for 33.3% of them and 11-15 years for 25% of the respondents as in Table 8:

Table 8: Characteristics of sample's respondent

| Variable | Category | Frequency | Percentage |
|---|---|---|---|
| 1-Job | Head of corp. | 3 | 25.0 |
| | Head Treasury | 1 | 8.3 |
| | Credit director | 3 | 25.0 |
| | Branch Manager | 3 | 25.0 |
| | Executive Manager | 2 | 16.7 |
| | Total | 12 | 100 |

| | | | |
|---|---|---|---|
| 2-Bank | Bloom bank | 3 | 25.0 |
| | Ahli Bank | 2 | 16.7 |
| | Itihad Bank | 1 | 8.3 |
| | Capital Bank | 3 | 25.0 |
| | Arab Bank | 1 | 8.3 |
| | ABC Bank | 2 | 16.7 |
| | Total | 12 | 100 |
| 3-Specialization | Accounting | 2 | 16.7 |
| | Finance | 7 | 58.3 |
| | Economics | 2 | 16.7 |
| | Management | 1 | 8.3 |
| | Total | 12 | 100 |
| 4-Scientific Degree | Bachelor | 4 | 33.3 |
| | Master | 5 | 54.7 |
| | Doctorate | 3 | 25.0 |
| | Total | 12 | 100.0 |
| 5-Experience | 10 years or less | 4 | 33.3 |
| | 11-15 years | 3 | 25.0 |
| | 16-20 years or more | 5 | 41.7 |
| | Total | 12 | 100.0 |

Source: Researcher computation

## 4.2 Analysis and discussion of the role of interest rate in Jordan's economy

Analysis of respondents' points of view on role of interest rate in Jordan economy shows the following: Average of role of interest rate in Jordanian economy was (4.324) which is higher than average 3 at Likert scale. Interest rate role in attracting deposits got the highest rank with a ( mean =4.50) which is statistically significant (t=9.798), followed by interest role in controlling liquidity with a (mean =4.42) which is statistically significant (t=6.708), followed by interest role in controlling credit facilities with a (mean=4.33) which is statistically significant (t=9.978), followed by interest role as a monetary instrument and as stimulating economy against recession with a (mean=4.25) which is statistically significant (t=4.118, t=6.332)), followed by role of interest in controlling profit margin and calculating present value with a(mean=417) which is statistically significant (t=4.714, t=6.091), followed by interest role in controlling discount rate and inflation with a mean (4.08) which are statistically significant (t=3.161, t=3.00), followed by role of interest rate as a cost of capital (mean=4.00) which is statistically significant (t=4.811) as in Table 9:

Table 9: Descriptive statistics and one sample T-Test of role of interest rate

| Role of Interest Rate | Mean | Rank | Std. | t-test | Sig.(2-tailed) |
|---|---|---|---|---|---|
| Interest is an instrument of Monetary Policy | 4.25 | 4 | 1.215 | 4.118 | .003 |
| Interest rate is the cost of capital | 4.00 | 7 | .853 | 4.811 | .001 |
| Interest rate is used as discount rate by Central Bank | 4.08 | 6 | .996 | 3.161 | .012 |
| Interest rate is used to control Inflation | 4.08 | 6 | .996 | 3.000 | .015 |
| Interest rate is used by banks to determine profit margin | 4.17 | 5 | .718 | 4.714 | .001 |
| Interest rate is used to attract more deposits | 4.50 | 1 | .522 | 9.798 | .000 |
| Interest rate is used by banks to control credit facilities. | 4.33 | 3 | .778 | 9.798 | .000 |
| Interest rate is used for controlling liquidity | 4.42 | 2 | .669 | 6.708 | .000 |
| Interest rate is used to calculate Present Value of Cash flows | 4.17 | 5 | .718 | 6.091 | .000 |
| Interest rate is used by central bank to stimulate economy | 4.25 | 4 | .754 | 6.332 | .000 |
| Average of Role of interest rate | 4.325 | | | | |

Likert scale 1=strongly disagree 2=disagree, 3=some what agree, 4=agree, strongly agree=5

Source: Researcher Computation

## 4.3 Analysis and discussion of impact of rising interest rate in Jordan

Analysis of respondents' points of view on impact of rising interest rate in Jordan economy shows the following: Average of impact of rising interest rate in Jordanian economy was (3.845) which is above average 3 at Likert scale. Increase Cost Of Borrowinggot the highest rank with a ( mean =4.25) which is statistically significant (t=23.685), followed by Increase Profit Margin with a (mean =4.00) which is statistically significant (t=18.7628), followed by Incrased Cost Of Production with a (mean=3.92) which is statistically significant (t=17.110), followed by Lower Credit Facilities with a (mean=3.83) which is statistically significant (t=18.501), followed by Reduce Competitiveness Of Export with a(mean=3.75) which is statistically significant (t=17.234), followed by Increase Prices Of Goods And Services with a mean (3.67) which are statistically significant (t=16.316), followed by Raise Exchange Rate with a(mean=3.42) which is statistically significant (t=13.146) as in Table 10:

Table 10: Descriptive statistics and one sample T-Test of impact of rising interest rate

| Impact of Rising Interest Rate | Mean | Rank | Std. | t-test | Sig. (2-tailed) |
|---|---|---|---|---|---|
| Increase Cost Of Borrowing | 4.25 | 1 | .622 | 23.685 | .000 |
| Incrased Cost Of Production | 3.92 | 3 | .793 | 17.110 | .000 |
| Increase Prices Of Goods And Services | 3.67 | 6 | .778 | 16.316 | .000 |
| Lower Credit Facilities | 3.83 | 4 | .718 | 18.501 | .000 |
| Increase Profit Margin | 4.00 | 2 | .739 | 18.762 | .000 |
| Raise Exchange Rate | 3.42 | 7 | .900 | 13.146 | .000 |
| Reduce Competitiveness Of Export | 3.75 | 5 | .754 | 17.234 | .000 |
| Reduce Foreign Exhange | 3.92 | 3 | .793 | 17.110 | .000 |
| Average Impact of Rising Interest Rate | 3.845 | | | | |

Likert scale 1=strongly disagree 2=disagree, 3=some what agree, 4=agree, strongly agree=5
Source: Researcher computation

## 4.4 Analysis and discussion of impact of lowering interest rate in Jordan

Analysis of respondents' points of view on impact of lowering interest rate in Jordan economy shows the following: Average impact of lowering interest rate in Jordanian economy was (3.88) which is above average at Likert scale. Reduce Cost Of Borrowing got the highest rank with a ( mean =4.33) which is statistically significant (t=23.685), followed by Attracting Foreign Investment with a (mean =4.17) which is statistically significant (t=17.234), followed by Improving Competitiveness Of Exports with a (mean=4.08) which is statistically significant (t=18.501), followed by increase of liquidity and credit facilities with a (mean=4.00) which is statistically significant (t=17.110, t=16.316), followed by Reduce Cost Of Production with a(mean=3.83) which is statistically significant (t=13.146), followed by interest Resist Recession with a mean (3.75) which are statistically significant (t=23.635), followed by Reduce Inflation (mean=3.42) which is statistically significant (t=18.762) as in Table 11:

Table 11: Impact of lowering interest rate in Jordan

| Impact of Lowering Interest Rate | Mean | Rank | Std. | t-test | Sig. (2-tailed) |
|---|---|---|---|---|---|
| Reduce Cost Of Borrowing | 4.33 | 1 | .492 | 23.685 | .000 |
| Increase Liquidity Of Banks | 4.00 | 4 | .739 | 17.110 | .000 |
| Increase Credit Facilities | 4.00 | 4 | .739 | 16.316 | .000 |
| Improve Competitiveness Of Exports | 4.08 | 3 | .669 | 18.501 | .000 |
| Reduce Inflation | 3.42 | 7 | 1.240 | 18.762 | .000 |
| Reduce Cost Of Production | 3.83 | 5 | .718 | 13.146 | .000 |
| Attract Foreign Investment | 4.17 | 2 | .718 | 17.234 | .000 |
| Increase Burden Of Burden Of Public Budget | 3.42 | 7 | .996 | 17.110 | .000 |
| Resist Recession | 3.75 | 6 | .866 | 23.685 | 000 |
| Average of Impact of Lowering Interest Rate | 3.88 | | | | |

Likert scale 1=strongly disagree 2=disagree, 3=some what agree, 4=agree, strongly agree=5
Source: Researcher computation

## 4.5 Analysis and discussion of determinants of interest rate in Jordan

Analysis of respondents' points of view on determinants of interest rate in Jordan shows the following: Average impact of determinants of interest rate in Jordan was 3.89 which is above average 3 at Likert scale. Demand for money has positive relation with interest rate with a ( mean =4.17) which is statistically significant (t= 25), followed by Recession has negative relation with interest rate with a (mean =4.08) which is statistically significant (t=21.158), followed by liquidity has negative relation with interest rate rate with a (mean=4.00) which is statistically significant (t=18.762), followed by Economic boom has positive relation to interest rate with a (mean=3.92) which is statistically significant at (t=15.070), followed by money supply has negative relation with interest rate with a(mean=3.83) which is statistically significant (t=18.501), followed by inflation has positive relation with interest rate with a (mean =3.67) which is statistically significant at (12.899), followed by pegging dinar with US$ with a (mean=3.58) which is statistically 99significant at (t=18.567) as in Table 12;

Table 12: Analysis of determinants of interest rate in Jordan

| Impact of Lowering Interest Rate | Mean | Rank | Std. | t-test | Sig. (2-tailed) |
|---|---|---|---|---|---|
| Money supply has negative relation with interest rate | 3.83 | 5 | .718 | 18.501 | .000 |
| Demand money has positive relation with interest rate | 4.17 | 1 | .577 | 25.000 | .000 |
| Inflation has positive relation with interest rate | 3.67 | 6 | .985 | 12.899 | .000 |
| Pegging dinar with US$ | 3.58 | 7 | .669 | 18.567 | .000 |
| Liquidity has negative relation with interest rate | 4.00 | 3 | .739 | 18.762 | .000 |
| Recession has negative relation with interest rate | 4.08 | 2 | .669 | 21.158 | .000 |
| Economic boom has positive relation to interest rate | 3.92 | 4 | .900 | 15.070 | .000 |
| Average of Determinants of Interest rate | 3.89 | | | | |

Likert scale 1=strongly disagree 2=disagree, 3=some what agree, 4=agree, strongly agree=5
Source: Researcher computation

## 5. Conclusions & policy implications

The study aims at investigating the role, impact and determinants of interest rate in Jordan. The limitation of this study is that its coverage is limited to the period of the International Financial Crisis (2008-2015) which is significant period and other periods are not covered.

The conclusions of the study could be summarized as follows: (1) Pegging Jordanian Dinar (JD) to American Dollar has restricted the role of interest rate as a tool of monetary policy in Jordan. Hence, the role of Jordanian monetary policy in the economy is weak compared with the role of fiscal policy which plays a bigger role in the economy. (2) Due to the dual banking system in Jordan, where traditional banks exist side by side with Islamic banks, the impact of fluctuating interest rate in Jordan have affected profitability of traditional banks, while the Islamic banks have not been affected by changing interest rate as they are prohibited by Sharia Law from using interest rate in their operations. (3) Raising interest rate in Jordan caused higher cost of credit for companies, less competitiveness of exports, less liquidity in the economy, higher profit margin for banks, higher exchange rate of JD and higher inflation. (4) Lowering interest rate in Jordan caused lower cost of borrowing particularly for small and medium enterprises, higher liquidity, better competitiveness of exports and more credit facilities by banks but inflation was much lower. Moreover, lowering interest rate caused financial burden on government budget and public debts. (5) The determinants of interest rate in Jordan are: (a) Money supply in Jordan has a reverse relation with the interest rate as more money supply lowers the interest rate. (b) Demand for money in Jordan has positive relation with the interest rate as more demand for money increases interest rate. (c) Inflation in Jordan has positive relationship with nominal interest rate as when nominal interest rate increases, inflation will have tendency to rise. On the other hand, inflation has negative relation with real interest rate as when inflation rises, real interest rate declines. (d) Pegging the Jordanian Dinar with US$ determines to certain extent the rate of interest in

Jordan. (e) The economic condition of economic recession or economic boom determines the level of interest rate in Jordan. In case of recession, interest rate is lowered to stimulate the economy and when there is an economic boom, interest rate is to rise.

The policy implications of the study are: (i) the role of interest rate in Jordanian monetary policy is restricted by two factors: pegging JD with US$ which limits the role of interest rate in monetary policy and the dual banking system where traditional and Islamic banks exist side by side. (ii) In order to have an effective role of interest rate in Jordanian economy, one of the alternatives is to peg JD to a basket of currencies including US$.

The study recommends that researchers could investigate other aspects of the interest rate in Jordan that this research could not tackle such as: the impact of the interest rate in Jordan's economy if the Jordanian monetary authorities decide to peg the Jordanian Dinar to a basket of currencies instead of pegging to US dollar.

## References

Abdelrahim, K. & Farid F., 2009. Economic Feasibility of Pegged Riyal to US Dollar & Options for Adjusting Jordanian Foreign Exchange System. *Taif University Research Journal no. 2, 2009.*

Ahuja. H.L, 2006. *Modern Microeconomics: Theory and Application*. S. Chand & Company LTD. New Delhi.

Alhwimani, Fahd Ben Abdullah, 2015. *Impact of the American Monetary Policy upon Saudi Monetary Policy*. Saudi Economic Society. Al-Riyadh. P.14

*Alwatan, No. 5505 dated October 26, 2015.* Decline of Interest Rate in China. Riyadh.

Arab Monetary Fund, 2015. *Developing Arab Bond Markets*. Institute of Economic Policies. A Conference in December. Abu- Dhabi. P.13

Begg D., Gianluigi, Vernasca, Stanley Fischer, Rudiger Dornbush, 2011. *Economics*, 10th Edition, McGraw-Hill Education.London.

Central Bank of Jordan, *Annual Reports 2010-2015*. Research Department.Amman.

Central Bank of Jordan. *Statistical Monthly Bulletins 2015-2016*. Amman

Edwin. H. Neave, 2009. *Dealing with Global Credit and Liquidity Crisis in Modern Financial Systems: Theories and Application*. John Wiley &Sons Inc. New Jersey.

Federal Reserve Bank, 2015. *Declining and Rising Interest Rates on Federal Funds*. Washington D.C

Henry C. Murphy, 1950. Role of Interest Rates in A Changing World: Reappraisal of The Easy Money. *The Journal of Finance on December 29. P.11.*

http//en.wikipedia/quantitative easing.com.

IMF, 2015) *Financial Statistics*. Washington DC.

*International Advances in Economic Research. 18.4 (Nov. 2012): p397*

James, Phillip C., 2014, *Sector Rotation and Interest Rate Policy*. New York

Mackenzie International Consultative Institute, 2015. *Saudi Arabia Far Away from Oil Sector*. Riyadh p.14.

Ministry of Finance, 2016. Public Finance, *Bulletin No.4 Vol.18 May*. Amman.

Nilufer, O. & Cuneyt, A., 2012. Determinants of interest rate pass-through for emerging market economies: the role of financial market structure.

Samuelson, P., & Nordhaus, W., 2005. *Economics*. 18$^{th}$ Edition. McGraw Hill. New York. PP; 695-697

Yelen, J., 2015. Raising Interest Rate on US Dollar in 2016. *Middle East Journal. No 13491, November 15.*

## Appendix: Questionnaire

Impact of interest rate in the economy from the viewpoints of banking managers: Empirical evidence from Jordan

Part I: Personal data

Job :

Institution :

Specialization :
Scientific Degree :
Years of Experience :

Part II: Select appropriate answer on role of interest rate as a monetary instrument

| Serial No. | Paragraph | Strongly Disagree 1 | Disagree 2 | Some What Agree 3 | Agree 4 | Strongly Agree 5 |
|---|---|---|---|---|---|---|
| 1 | Interest is an instrument of Monetary Policy | | | | | |
| 2 | Interest rate is the cost of capital | | | | | |
| 3 | Interest rate is used as discount rate by Central Bank for lending commercial banks | | | | | |
| 4 | Interest rate is used to control Inflation | | | | | |
| 5 | Interest rate is used by banks to determine profit margin | | | | | |
| 6 | Interest rate is used to attract more deposits | | | | | |
| 7 | Interest rate is used by banks to control credit facilities. | | | | | |
| 8 | Interest rate is used for controlling liquidity | | | | | |
| 9 | Interest rate is used to calculate Present Value of Cash flows | | | | | |
| 10 | Interest rate is used by central bank to stimulate economy and resists recession | | | | | |

Part III: Select appropriate answer on impact of raising interest rate

| Serial No. | Paragraph | Strongly Disagree 1 | Disagree 2 | Some What Agree 3 | Agree 4 | Strongly Agree 5 |
|---|---|---|---|---|---|---|
| 1 | Increase cost of borrowing for small and medium enterprises | | | | | |
| 2 | Increase cost of production | | | | | |
| 3 | Increase prices of goods& services | | | | | |
| 4 | Lower value of credit facilities | | | | | |
| 5 | Increase profit margin of banks | | | | | |
| 6 | Raise foreign exchange of currency | | | | | |
| 7 | Reduce competitiveness of exports | | | | | |
| 8 | Reduction of Foreign Investment | | | | | |

Part IV: Select appropriate answer on impact of lowering interest rate

| Serial No. | Paragraph | Strongly Disagree 1 | Disagree 2 | Some What Agree 3 | Agree 4 | Strongly Agree 5 |
|---|---|---|---|---|---|---|
| 1 | Reduce cost of borrowing | | | | | |
| 2 | Increase liquidity for banks | | | | | |
| 3 | Increase value of credit facilities | | | | | |
| 4 | Improve competitiveness of exports | | | | | |
| 5 | Reduce inflation | | | | | |
| 6 | Reduce cost of production | | | | | |
| 7 | Attract more of foreign investment | | | | | |
| 8 | Increase burden on public budget | | | | | |

| | |
|---|---|
| 9 | Resisting recession |

Part V: Select appropriate answer on determinants of interest rate

| Serial No. | Paragraph | Strongly Disagree<br>1 | Disagree<br>2 | Some What Agree<br>3 | Agree<br>4 | Strongly Agree<br>5 |
|---|---|---|---|---|---|---|
| 1 | Money Supply has negative relation with interest rate | | | | | |
| 2 | Demand for money has positive relation with interest rate | | | | | |
| 3 | Inflation has positive relation with interest rate. | | | | | |
| 4 | Pegging local currency with US $ | | | | | |
| 5 | Liquidity has negative relation with interest rate | | | | | |
| 6 | Recession has negative relation with interest rate | | | | | |
| 7 | Economic has positive relation with interest rate | | | | | |

Source: Researcher computation

# 15

# Threshold Effects of Fiscal Policy on Economic Activity in Developing Countries

**Salma Slimani**[1]

**ABSTRACT**

The aim of this paper is to investigate the relationship between fiscal policy and economic growth for a panel of 40 developing countries for the period 1990 – 2012 with a focus on a comparative analysis between Morocco and the panel. The variables used are real GDP, budget deficit, current government spending, national saving, inflation rate, total investment, public debt and current account balance. The main findings are: *First*, there is evidence of a double threshold effect of the fiscal balance. When exceeding a budget deficit level of 4.8% of GDP or a fiscal surplus level of 3.2% of GDP, economic growth is negatively affected. *Second*, the sign of the relationship between budget deficit and economic growth is conditioned by the level of total investment. For values of total investment higher than 23%, it follows that there is a positive relationship. However, it becomes negative, when investment falls below this threshold. *Third*, from Morocco's perspective, analysis of threshold effects suggested that above 4.8% of budget deficit, average growth rate falls by 2.1%, while median growth falls by 1.5%.

Keywords: Developing countries, economic growth, fiscal deficit, investment, threshold effects.

---

## 1.0 INTRODUCTION

In both theory and evidence, there are controversial thoughts and debates that focus on the impact of fiscal deficit on economic growth. Since the nineties, this subject becomes highly debated in the literature. Barro (1990) is considered as one of the most important pioneers in the field. He suggests a simple endogenous growth model and shows that the share of government spending in GDP may have a significant effect on economic growth. Later, Bertolat and Drazen (1993) point out that this relationship might be non-linear. Starting in the years 2000, it can be observed a significant body of empirical and theoretical work taking into account the non-linearity that can prevail on the relationship between

[1] Ph.D. researcher, Department of economics, Mohammed V Rabat –Agdal University, Faculty of Juridical, Economic and Social Sciences, Morocco. E-mail: slimani.salma11@gmail.com.

growth and budget deficit [Minea and Villieu (2008), Adam and Bevan (2005), Tanimoune, Combes and Plane (2008) and Minea and Villieu (2012)]. These authors try to identify anti-Keynesian effects, which are related to the persistence of high fiscal contractions. However, there is still no consensus about the threshold of fiscal deficit that authorities must not exceed.

The European debt crisis in 2010 shook the global economy when some indebted countries in Euro area, which had been maintaining high levels of debt and fiscal deficit, faced the default on payment of the public debt and on its interest. Even more worrying is the fact that most of the projected deficits in a number of industrial countries are structural and unsustainable [Cecchetti, Mohanty and Zampolli (2010)]. Although the crisis mainly pertained to European countries, the concern of a similar public debt crisis is also shared by other low-income countries, and even more heavily in a context of an economies suffering from macroeconomic vulnerabilities, output below its potential and high levels of unemployment.

The increasing budget deficit and public debt in Morocco during the past four years raises nowadays the concern of politicians as well as researchers. The Moroccan government is convinced of the major role that plays fiscal policy as a stabilization tool, the only remaining question is finding the appropriate threshold that should not be exceeded. Euro convergence criteria in the Maastricht Treaty (1993) outlined that the ratio of the annual general government deficit relative to gross domestic product (GDP) at market prices, must not exceed 3% at the end of the preceding fiscal year. Even though it is hardly justified[2], Moroccan politicians try to bring the deficit near to the 3% threshold. But is it really the most relevant threshold for the Moroccan case?

From within the lineage of recent empirical studies, this research paper tries to provide some possible answers to the question asked through identifying the nature of the relationship between budget deficit and economic growth for a panel of 40 developing countries. Using annual data over the period 1990 – 2012, the paper concludes with the existence of anti-Keynesian effects that are associated to a fiscal deficit exceeding 4.8% of GDP, but also a negative impact of a fiscal surplus on economic growth may occur when exceeding the threshold of 3.2% of GDP. Results show also that the level of total investment is a major determinant in the relationship between the budget deficit and growth: when total investment exceeds the threshold of 23% of GDP, then the budget deficit is positively correlated to economic growth, whereas it is negatively correlated to growth when total investment falls below the threshold. Therefore, countries concerned by the study should set priorities in favour of productive investment and should implement appropriate mechanisms to prevent exceeding the thresholds found. The Moroccan case represents, notably, an effective framework to consider the relevance of previous results. Using data spanning from 1980 to 2010, the findings remain consistent. In fact, the behavior of economic growth varies depending on variations in the budget deficit: when the budget deficit exceeds the 4.8% threshold, median growth falls sharply by 1.5 %, whereas average growth falls even strongly by 2.1%.

This paper is organized as follows: The next section will briefly return to the theoretical and empirical studies around this subject. Section 3 outlines the methodological approach, data employed in the study of the econometric analysis of both linear and non-linear model. The threshold analysis uses the threshold estimation technique outlined by Hansen (1999). Section 4 presents, first, the estimation results of the linear model. The latter allows identifying the economic variables that affect real GDP growth. Second, the threshold analysis was carried out by considering sequentially, the overall fiscal deficit and total investment as threshold variables. Third, From Morocco's perspective, an overview of the historical behavior of fiscal policy and economic growth is presented to further see how Moroccan real GDP growth behaves as the fiscal deficit varies. Section 5 concludes the paper and summarizes its main findings.

---

[2] It has been argued by many economists that the threshold of 3% was set arbitrarily and has no basis but the circumstances as European fiscal deficits in the early 90s were less than 3%. See Buiter, Corsetti and Roubini (1993), and Buiter (2006) for more details.

## 2.0 PRIOR LITERATURE

Before the advent of the Keynesian theory, governments tried to implement every effort to reach the fiscal balance. But with the Keynesian theory, this dogma was questioned. Keynes argued that there is a positive relationship between budget deficit and economic growth. Governments are encouraged to run deficits during recession as it will help to stabilize the economy. On the other hand, there is the liberal theory that argued the opposite. Their main argument is related to the crowding out phenomenon. More recently, Barro[3] (1990) presented an endogenous growth model which is considered now as a fundamental reference. The model highlights an explicit link between government spending and long-run economic growth in the context of endogenous growth, and shows that we can determine an optimal public spending. At this point, any additional expenditure may affect economic growth negatively. Therefore, if public expenditures exceed their optimal level, there will be a negative correlation, and conversely, if public expenditures fall below their optimal level, there will be a positive correlation. However, there are only a few theoretical studies that deal with non-linear effects of fiscal deficits in growth models. By way of example reference, there is Perotti's model (1999) where non-linear effects of fiscal policy are identified, but not in a growth context. Their model shows that government expenditure may have positive "keynesian" effects or reversed effects depending on the initial level of public debt[4]. So, in high-debt contexts, a fiscal consolidation may reduce the risk of defaulting on sovereign debt, thus improving confidence and increasing private consumption. By using Barro's (1990) model, Greiner and Semmler (2000) removed the balanced budget assumption and analyzed different budgetary regimes. They claimed that the impact of deficit financed increase on growth depends on the budgetary regime the government operates within. Thus, governments can generate positive growth effects of a public deficit on the growth rate only for a given debt/capital ratio and if the deficit is used primarily for public investment. Ghosh & Mourmouras (2004) extended the Greiner and Semmler framework to include welfare analysis. Their main objective is to analyze the growth and welfare implications of the golden rule of public finance. They showed that optimal fiscal policy depends on the particular budgetary regime considered.

In Barro's (1990) model, neither public debt, nor public deficits are allowed. Thus, all public expenditures are productive and growth-enhancing. Minea and Villieu (2012) tried to examine the nature of fiscal deficit effects on growth by extending the Barro (1990) endogenous growth model. They introduced productive public spending, public deficit and debt in the model to study non-linear effect of fiscal policy in the short and long run, and showed in their model how the effect of public deficit shifts from one condition to another depending on the multiplicity of balanced growth paths. In the long run, if public deficits are devoted to public investment, we will be in presence of a lower balanced growth path. On the other hand, in the short run, the effect of public deficit depends on both the level of growth's steady states and the initial level of public debt.

Beyond the theoretical debates, the study of the relationship between fiscal policy and economic growth received much attention in the empirical literature. However, it is difficult to provide an unclouded characterization of what the appropriate behavior of fiscal policy should be. Empirical results are quite often inconsistent and sometimes contradictory. This discordance in terms of evaluation and finding are mainly due to multifarious factors such as time dimension, types of governments, methods of analysis as well as econometric methods that are used. By not taking into account the non-linear hypothesis, a large body of empirical literature on fiscal policy falls under the Keynesian theory, while other studies claim that having a balanced budget is more desirable as it will help the economy to grow faster over time. In order to explain the "productivity slowdown" in the 1970s for the United States, Aschauer (1989)

[3] In Barro's model (1990), all public expenditures are productive and goes for public investment increasing marginal productivity of private capital, as for example infrastructure, schools, sanitation, property rights, etc. Investment public spending is financed through income taxes, complement private investments. Thus, since public investments raise the productivity of private investments, higher taxes can be associated with an increase or a decrease in overall growth.

[4] In contrast with Perotti (1999), Giavazzi, Jappelli & Pagano (2000) found no evidence of a small impact of high or rapidly growing public on non-linear effects of fiscal policy, but found instead that during periods of rapidly growing public debt the impact of taxes and government spending on national savings is significantly different.

indicates, by using time series, a positive relationship between government expenditure and economic growth: a 1% increase in the ratio of public to private capital stocks raises productivity by 0.39%. However, the study points out the importance of how the public capital is composed. The core infrastructure (streets, highways, airports, mass transit, sewers, water systems, etc.) is the most important component in determining productivity. Almost same conclusion is derived from the research made by Easterly and Rebelo (1993) for the period going from 1970 to 1988. By using panel data for 28 countries and cross-sectional data for 100 countries, they found that the share of public investment in transport and communication is robustly and positively correlated with growth. Public outlays on infrastructure investment raise growth. Contrariwise, agriculture investment is consistently negatively correlated with growth, while Public enterprise investment has no effect on growth. Based on the research made by Benos (2009), the previous result related to infrastructure spending was again proven to be accurate. The author used panel data on 14 EU countries during 1990-2006 and found also that public expenditures on property rights protection enhance growth, while government expenditures on human capital have no effect on growth.

On the opposite side, other studies agreed with the liberal theory thought, in which fiscal deficits have a negative effect on economic growth. A theory that gives support to the budgetary rule assuming that obtaining a balanced budget is considered as the only way to maintain a sustainable growth over time. Within the same framework, Gupta, Clements, Baldacci, Mulas-Granados (2005) found for a panel of 39 low-income countries during the period 1990 - 2000 that a balanced budget stance leads generally to an increase in economic growth in both short and long terms. The study pointed out also the significant importance that holds the composition of public spending: when wages accounts for a big share of public expenditure, growth falls dramatically, while governments which concentrate their spending on capital and nonwage goods and services are more likely to experience a significant increase in growth. With an emphasis on the causal relationship lying between budget deficit and economic growth, keho's study (2010) focused on the member countries of the West African Economic and Monetary Union during the period 1980 - 2005. The results suggest that for three countries there is no causality link between budget deficit and growth, whereas for the remaining four countries deficits exert a negative impact on growth.

Consistent with the Ricardian equivalence hypothesis[5], other studies claimed that there is neutral relationship between fiscal deficit and growth[6]. From Malaysia's perspective, Abd Rahman's study (2012) gives support to the previous hypothesis. By using an Autoregressive Distributed Lag modeling, it was found that there is no long-run relationship between fiscal deficit and growth, and that only the GDP and productive spending can bring the economy to its equilibrium state in case where the Malaysian economy undergoes a shock.

Differences in terms of results may be due to default in taking into account the non –linearity hypothesis as fiscal deficits may have either traditional Keynesian effects or reversed effects. Nevertheless, more recently, a major importance was given to this hypothesis. There is, for instance, Adam and Bevan's research paper (2005) where the authors try to identify thresholds effects of fiscal deficit on growth for a panel of 45 developing countries for the period 1979 - 1999. The study indicates that fiscal deficits are associated with robust non-linear effects on growth and finds evidence of a threshold effect at a level of the deficit around 1.5% of GDP. When reducing deficits to this level, there appears that governments enjoy faster growth expansion; this effect reverses itself when exceeding the determined threshold. Nearly, the same conclusion was found in a research made by Tanimoune, Combes and Plane (2008) on the pattern of public debt with a focus on the member countries of the West African Economic and Monetary Union during the period 1986 - 2002. The study indicates a threshold effect at a debt level of 83%. There appears to be a growth-shrinking to exceeding debt at this level. As regards for OECD countries, Minea and Villieu (2008) carried out a research to determine if there can be a non-linear effect of fiscal deficit

[5] See Barro (1974) for more details on Ricardian equivalence.

[6] There is, however, an extensive empirical literature that has found evidence against this hypothesis [Feldstein (1986), Kotlikoff, Razin and Rosenthal (1988), Modigliani and Sterling (1990), Dalamagas (1992), Graham (1995), Evans (1993), Cardia (1997) and Banzhaf and Oates (2012)].

on growth, depending on the public debt to GDP ratio. Results confirm that budget deficits are growth-increasing only for low-indebted economies as long as the debt burden may be absorbed by a cut in government consumption. In contrast, for further high debt values, raising deficits are growth-decreasing since government can no longer reduce public consumption and the budget adjustment will inevitably rely on decreasing productive spending. Hence above a certain level of public debt, raising deficits becomes growth-reducing. The study indicates a threshold for a debt level standing at around 90%. This is consistent with the Rogoff and Reinhart's (2010) analysis. It was also claimed that exceeding 90% of public debts will result in impeding the process of economic growth. On the basis of a database covering forty-four countries spanning about two hundred years, the study finds evidence that growth for countries above 90% of public debt is -0.1% on average. A result which has been rectified in Herndon, Ash and Pollin's review study (2013) reporting 2.2% on average real GDP growth, a drop of only a 1% in growth.

These last studies indicate that fiscal deficits are in general associated with strong non-linear effects on growth. In high debt contexts, growth drops off sharply. And inversely, for low debt values, growth remains high. Hence, this paper aims to investigate fiscal policy from the perspective of a non-linearity by using the panel threshold regression technique proposed by Hansen (1999).

## 3.0 METHODOLOGY, DATA AND ECONOMETRIC ESTIMATION

This section empirically evaluates the fiscal policy initially by considering that the relationship between fiscal policy and economic growth is a linear one, and then trying to determine the economic variables that affect growth. Secondly, the threshold effects analysis is conducted assuming a priori that this relationship might be non-linear by considering sequentially the overall fiscal deficit and total investment as threshold variables.

The study covers a panel of forty[7] developing countries for the period 1990 – 2012. The sample selection was made a priori depending on data availability. Indeed, Hansen's method (1999) is valid only for a balanced panel. The choice of period and annual data is determined by their availability since 1990 and the lack of monthly and quarterly data.

### 3.1 LINEAR MODEL ESTIMATION

Appendix B provides a summary of the statistics of the data and defines the variable mnemonics used later in the paper. In this sub-section the following empirical growth model is estimated:

$$GDP_{it} = \mu_i + \alpha_1 GE_{it} + \alpha_2 NS_{it} + \alpha_3 FD_{it} + \alpha_4 INV_{it} + \alpha_5 INF_{it} + \varepsilon_{it}$$

Where (i,t) captures the cross-sectional and temporal dimensions of the panel, $\mu_i$ represents the country-fixed effects and $\varepsilon_{it}$ is a stochastic error term. The econometric model is a fixed effects model where the relationship between the dependent variable and the explanatory variables are supposed to be identical for the countries in question. Using a fixed effects model will enable to take into consideration differences in terms of economic structure and history for each country. Choosing this specification is backed by the Hausman[8] and the Breusch & Pagan[9] test. As a matter of fact, it was concluded that the choice of "Within" estimator is required. Individual-specific means are removed to eliminate the individual effect.

The expected sign for $\alpha_5$ is negative, while for $\alpha_2$ and $\alpha_4$ it is positive:

[7] Details of country coverage, data source and descriptions are provided in Appendix (A and B).

[8] The Hausman test probability is less than 10% (P-value = 0.0002% <10%), implying that the fixed effects model is preferred over random effects model.

[9] This test allows examining the significance of the individual specific effects. It is based on the residues obtained by the OLS. The probability of the Breusch & Pagan statistic showed that fixed effects are significant at the 5% level (P-value <0, 05). And therefore, a fixed effects model is preferred.

$$GDP_{it} = f(\underset{?}{GE_{it}}, \underset{+}{NS_{it}}, \underset{?}{FD_{it}}, \underset{+}{INV_{it}}, \underset{-}{INF_{it}})$$

As regards the domestic saving, classical and neoclassical theories show their importance for economic activity. When allowing for investment financing, savings enable for maintaining productivity growth. Aghion, Comin and Howitt (2006) found that for poor countries, national saving plays an important role in attracting foreign investment and therefore to promote innovations. Thus, local savings matter for economic growth. Hence, a positive sign is expected for this variable. Regarding the fiscal deficit and the government current expenditure, it seems a little equivocal to predict a priori, under the linearity assumption, their impact on economic growth. While Keynesian economies showed their beneficial effect, liberal economies indicated the opposite. Similarly for empirical literature, findings are mitigated and contradictory. Concerning investment, it is, as is well known, a determining factor of growth and productivity, for both the neoclassical and the Keynesian economies. Furthermore, it may generate, in accordance with the endogenous growth theory, positive externalities. As for inflation, Liberals consider it as highly injurious for economic growth. Besides, a wide range of empirical studies indicate a negative relationship between inflation and growth. Khan and Senhadji (2001) claimed the presence of a threshold effect of inflation on growth. Both industrialized and developing countries caught their interest. For the industrialized ones, when inflation exceeds 1-3% it has a negative impact on growth. Whereas, for developing countries, inflation has constantly a negative impact on productivity and it does widen even more when inflation surpasses 11-12%. Therefore, a negative sign for inflation is expected.

## 3.2 THRESHOLD EFFECTS ANALYSIS

Before moving to a more systematic analysis, it is proposed to explore a simple scatter plot visualizing the relationship between budget deficit and GDP growth. The existence of threshold effects assumes implicitly that this relationship is non-linear. Figure 1 illustrates this relation in the form of a cloud diagram. The non-linear function is plotted, as a locally weighted smoothing[10] (lowess smoother) with a "bandwidth" setting of 0.5, to identify graphically the existence of non-linearities.

**Figure 1 :** Fiscal deficit and GDP Growth in 40 developing countries, 1990-2012

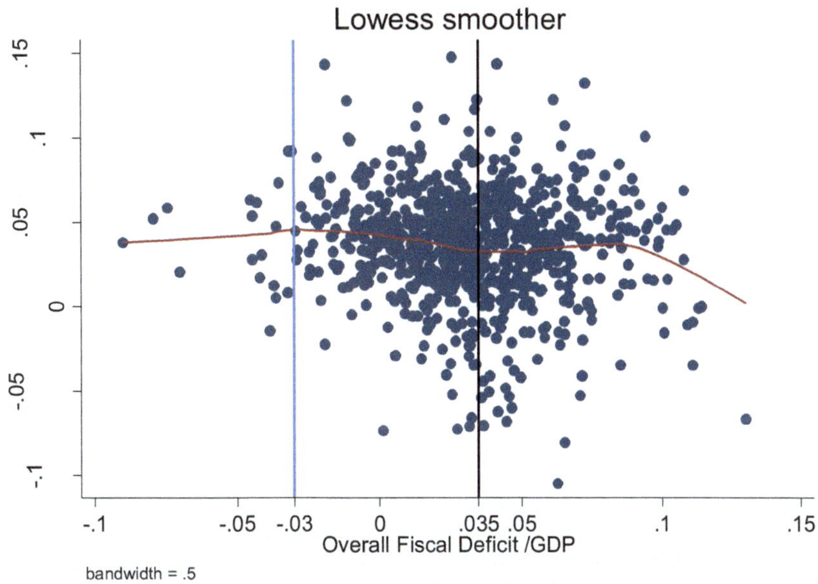


[10] It is a smoothing method that tends to follow the data. Basically, the main idea is to create a new variable, so that each observation in the data may correspond to a smoothed value. The smoothed values are obtained from a regression, growth of GDP in the fiscal deficit. This regression is weighted so that each point receives the highest weight.

It can be drawn from figure 1 that a linear representation may hide important and relevant nonlinearities at many budget deficits' levels. Moreover, it is clear that high budget deficit is associated with a very low GDP growth. However, growth payoffs start as the deficit falls from around 3.5%. The existence of a threshold effect implies not only a variation in the slope of the regression line, but also a sign switch in the relationship. For a budget deficit value below a given threshold, there appears to be a favourable effect on economic activity, this effect inverse itself for higher fiscal deficit values.

Given the high degree of dispersion, as observed in the scatter plot, this attempt to view the data is just preliminary; hereafter the findings are submitted to a more systematic analysis using econometric methods.

## A BRIEF DESCRIPTION OF THE ECONOMETRIC APPROACH: HANSEN (1999)

The panel threshold regression model with individual-specific effects proposed by Hansen (1999) will be used below to characterize the relationship between growth and fiscal policy. Estimating the PTR requires the minimization of the sum of squared errors according to the following equation:

$$y_{it} = \mu_i + \alpha_1 x_{it} I(q_{it} \leq \gamma) + \alpha_2 x_{it} I(q_{it} > \gamma) + \varepsilon_{it}$$

Where $q_{it}$ is the threshold variable[11], $\gamma$ refers to the threshold, I(.) is an indicator function of the "regimes" transition which equals 1 when the condition in parenthesis is satisfied and 0 otherwise. Although, in this model, we have a single threshold where the observations are divided into two regimes depending on whether the threshold variable $q_{it}$ is smaller or larger than the threshold parameter $\gamma$, we can generalize the model to a more larger specification with r thresholds (i.e. r + 1 regimes) as illustrated below:

$$y_{it} = \mu_i + \alpha_1 x_{it} I(q_{it} \leq \gamma_1) + \alpha_2 x_{it} I(\gamma_1 < q_{it} \leq \gamma_2) + \ldots \alpha_r x_{it} I(\gamma_{r-1} < q_{it}) + \varepsilon_{it}$$

Estimating this model is carried out by stages. First, the individual fixed effects $\mu_i$ should be removed by eliminating individual specific means, and then we apply the ordinary least squares procedure. Afterwards, we can compute the sum of squared residuals referred to as $S_1(\gamma)$:

$$S_1(\gamma) = \sum_{i=1}^{N} \sum_{t=1}^{T} \hat{\varepsilon}_{it}^2$$

The threshold parameter $\gamma$ is then estimated by minimizing $S_1(\gamma)$.

$$\hat{\gamma} = Arg\ Min_{\gamma}\ S_1(\hat{\gamma})$$

As Hansen (1999) stresses, the sum of squared error function is a step function with at most *nT* steps. Thus, the minimization problem can be reduced to a search over values of $\gamma$ equal to the distinct values of $q_{it}$ in the sample. The next step consists of testing whether the identified threshold is statistically significant or not. The null hypothesis describes a linear specification and can be writen as: $H_0 : \alpha_1 = \alpha_2$. We use the likelihood ratio test verify this hypothesis:

$$F_1 = \frac{S_0 - S_1(\gamma)}{\sigma^2}$$

Where $S_0$ indicates the sum of the squared residuals of the linear model, $S_1(\gamma)$ is the sum of the squared residuals of the model with a single threshold, and $\sigma^2 = S_1(\gamma) / n(T-1)$. However, Hansen emphasizes that the distribution of this statistic $F_1$ has a non-standard character since that the PTR model contains unidentified nuisance parameters under $H_0$, and propose, in order to resolve this problem, to simulate by Bootstrap the asymptotic distribution of the statistic $F_1$. When a single threshold effect is attested to be significant, the same procedure can be applied to the general model in order to determine the number of regimes. In this case, the new null hypothesis consists of testing a specification with r regimes versus a specification with r+1 regimes. For determining the number of thresholds, Hansen advocates to start

[11] The threshold variable is assumed to not be time invariant, and it cannot be contemporaneous endogenous variable.

by testing one threshold versus two, then two versus three, and so forth. The procedure stops when the null hypothesis is not rejected.

## 4.0 RESULTS AND DISCUSSION

### 4.1 LINEAR ESTIMATION RESULTS

Appendix C reports the estimation results. On the basis of the information criterion[12], the best model is (3). The p-value of the first Fisher test is below 5% (0.000), which attests to the significance of the explanatory variables. The second Fisher test shows the wide heterogeneity of individuals in the form of fixed effect, as the p-value is lower than 5% (0.000). All the variables have the signs that were previously anticipated. The variables FD, INV and INF are significant at a 1% level. GE variable is significant at the 5% level. And finally, the variable NS is significant at the 10% level. Current government expenditure is negatively correlated with growth and thus its increase can hinder the process of growth. A high ratio of national savings to GDP has a favourable impact on economic activity. Fiscal deficit has a negative sign, which means that raising deficit is growth reducing. As for total investment, it has a positive sign and hence a positive effect on GDP growth. And finally, inflation has a negative sign, and thus having high inflation rates have an adverse economic impact, with harmful consequences for growth.

### 4.2 FISCAL DEFICIT AS A THRESHOLD VARIABLE

This threshold least square regression model is specified as follows:

$$GDP_{it} = \mu_i + \alpha_1 GE_{it-1} + \alpha_2 FD_{it-1} + \alpha_3 INV_{it-1} + \alpha_4 INF_{it-1} + \beta_1 NS_{it-1}\, I(FD_{it-1} \leq \gamma_1) + \beta_2 NS_{it-1}\, I(\gamma_1 < FD_{it-1} \leq \gamma_2) + \beta_3 NS_{it-1}\, I(\gamma_2 < FD_{it-1}) + \varepsilon_{it}$$

Where $\mu_i$ represents the country-fixed effects, (i,t) captures the cross-sectional and time dimensions of the panel, and $\varepsilon_{it}$ is a stochastic error term.

In order to determine the number of threshold effects, the model above is estimated by the least squares method, sequentially, for one, two and three threshold effects. The test statistics F1, F2 and F3, set out together with their bootstrap p-values[13] are presented in the table 1. The statistic F1 which made a reference to the test for a single threshold effect is significant at a 5% level with a bootstrap p-value of 0.016. The test for a double threshold effect F2 is even more significant at a 1% level with a bootstrap p-value of 0.006. Finally, the test for a triple threshold effect F3 may be considered as not statistically significant at the 5% level as the bootstrap p-value is equal to 0.050. These tests allow concluding that there are two thresholds effect of fiscal deficit on economic productivity according to the empirical growth regression model. The two thresholds estimated values and their asymptotic confidence intervals 95% are reported in table 2. The point estimates are -0.032 and 0.048. Appendix E, F and G present the likelihood ratio function $LR_1(\gamma)$, $LR_2^r(\gamma)$ and $LR_1^r(\gamma)$, respectively, corresponding to estimates for $\gamma_1$, $\gamma_1^r$ and $\gamma_2^r$. The point estimates are the value of γ at which the likelihood ratio reached the zero axis.

**Table 1 :** Threshold effects tests for the fiscal deficit

| | |
|---|---|
| Test for a single threshold effect | |
| $F_1$ | 16.001 |
| P-Value | 0.016 |
| (10%, 5%, 1% critical values) | (11.714 ; 13.745 ; 18.262) |
| Test for a double threshold effect | |
| $F_2$ | 18.382 |
| P-Value | 0.006 |
| (10%, 5%, 1% critical values) | (11.599 ; 13.175 ; 17.322) |

[12] The AIC (Akaike Information Criterion) outputs for model selection are shown in Appendix C. The BIC (Bayesian Information Criterion) outputs for model selection are shown in Appendix C.

[13] 500 bootstrap replications were used for each test.

| Test for a triple threshold effect | |
|---|---|
| $F_1$ | 14.160 |
| P-Value | 0.050 |
| (10%, 5%, 1% critical values) | (11.850 ; 14.124 ; 18.805) |

**Table 2 :** Threshold estimates for the fiscal deficit

| | Estimate | 95% Confidence Interval |
|---|---|---|
| $\gamma_1^r$ | -0.032 | [-0.032 ; 0.055] |
| $\gamma_2^r$ | 0.048 | [0.017 ; 0.055] |

The point estimates are -0.032 and 0.048. Figures (5, 6 and 7) present the likelihood ratio function $LR_1(\gamma)$, $LR_2^r(\gamma)$ and $LR_1^r(\gamma)$, respectively, corresponding to estimates for $\gamma_1$, $\gamma_1^r$ and $\gamma_2^r$. The point estimates are the value of γ at which the likelihood ratio reached the zero axis. The regression coefficient estimates and their standard deviations are shown in the table 3.

**Table 3 :** Regression estimates for a double threshold effect of the fiscal deficit

| Explanatory Variables | Coefficient estimate | OLS Standard-errors | White-corrected Standard-errors |
|---|---|---|---|
| $INV_{it-1}$ | 0.003 | 0.028 | 0.028 |
| $GE_{it-1}$ | -0.023 | 0.027 | 0.028 |
| $FD_{it-1}$ | **-0.237*** ** | **0.054** | **0.053** |
| $INF_{it-1}$ | -0.00084 | 0.00078 | 0.00061 |
| $NS_{it-1}\ I(FD_{it-1} \leq -0.032)$ | **-0.115*** ** | **0.047** | **0.056** |
| $NS_{it-1}\ I(-0.032 < FD_{it-1} \leq 0.048)$ | **0.056** ** | **0.030** | **0.033** |
| $NS_{it-1}\ I(0.048 < FD_{it-1})$ | **0.148*** ** | **0.035** | **0.037** |

*** Significant coefficient at the 1% level, ** 5% and * 10%.

The Student's t-test[14] served out to test the significance of the non-linear regression slope estimates. The variables FD and NS are the only significant ones. The ratio of the budget deficit / GDP lagged by one period ($FD_{it-1}$) has a negative impact on GDP growth. Results indicate also that when the ratio of budget deficit / GDP approaches 0.048 starting from the highest deficit value of 0.13, domestic savings $NS_{it-1}$ have a positive effect on growth with the coefficient estimate of 0.148. And conversely, domestic savings have a positive impact on growth, but with a smaller coefficient equal to 0.056, only for countries being close from a balanced budget with a deficit lower than 0,048 and a surplus not exceeding 0.032. And finally, if the surplus exceeds the value of 0.032, then domestic savings have a negative impact on growth. The percentages of countries belonging to each of the three defined regimes in each year are reported in the table 4. This distribution allows seeing the countries division per year according to the pension deficit.

**Table 4 :** Percentage of countries per year in each regime of the fiscal deficit

| Regime | | 1991 | 1992 | 1993 | 1994 | 1995 | 1996 | 1997 | 1998 | 1999 | 2000 | 2001 |
|---|---|---|---|---|---|---|---|---|---|---|---|---|
| 1st | $FD_{it-1} \leq -0.032$ | 0 | 3 | 0 | 3 | 0 | 0 | 0 | 3 | 3 | 3 | 0 |
| 2nd | $-0.032 < FD_{it-1} \leq 0.048$ | 90 | 75 | 80 | 78 | 73 | 80 | 70 | 78 | 60 | 75 | 80 |
| 3rd | $0.048 < FD_{it-1}$ | 10 | 23 | 20 | 20 | 28 | 20 | 30 | 20 | 38 | 23 | 20 |

| Regime | | 2002 | 2003 | 2004 | 2005 | 2006 | 2007 | 2008 | 2009 | 2010 | 2011 | 2012 |
|---|---|---|---|---|---|---|---|---|---|---|---|---|
| 1st | $FD_{it-1} \leq -0.032$ | 0 | 0 | 0 | 0 | 3 | 10 | 5 | 5 | 0 | 3 | 3 |
| 2nd | $-0.032 < FD_{it-1} \leq 0.048$ | 78 | 68 | 73 | 88 | 83 | 80 | 80 | 80 | 68 | 68 | 70 |
| 3rd | $0.048 < FD_{it-1}$ | 23 | 33 | 28 | 13 | 15 | 10 | 15 | 15 | 33 | 30 | 28 |

The percentage of countries which fall into the first regime varies from 0% to 10% over the years. The percentage of countries, in the second regime, ranges from 60% to 90%, and finally, in the third regime, it varies from 10% to 33%. It can be observed that most countries fall into the second regime, and this is valid

[14] When Student's t-test statistic is greater than the value read in the student's table (1.96 at the 5% level and 1.64 at the 10% level), the null hypothesis of the non-significance of the parameters is rejected.

for all years. It is interesting to note that the highest number of countries with a budget deficit exceeding the level of 4.8% is observed in 2010.

## 4.3 INVESTMENT AS A THRESHOLD VARIABLE

The following threshold least square regression model will be estimated:

$$GDP_{it} = \mu_i + \alpha_1 GE_{it-1} + \alpha_2 NS_{it-1} + \alpha_3 INV_{it-1} + \alpha_4 INF_{it-1} + \beta_1 FD_{it-1} I(INV_{it-1} \leq \gamma_1) + \beta_2 FD_{it-1} I(\gamma_1 < INV_{it-1}) + \varepsilon_{it}$$

Where $\mu_i$ represents the country-fixed effects, (i,t) captures the cross-sectional and time dimensions of the panel, and $\varepsilon_{it}$ is a stochastic error term.

**Table 5 :** Threshold effects tests for investment

| | |
|---|---|
| Test for a single threshold effect | |
| $F_1$ | 18.687 |
| P-Value | 0.002 |
| (10%, 5%, 1% critical values) | (11.148 ; 12.421 ; 15.649) |
| Test for a double threshold effect | |
| $F_2$ | 3.271 |
| P-Value | 0.876 |
| (10%, 5%, 1% critical values) | (10.446 ; 12.295 ; 16.357) |
| Test for a triple threshold effect | |
| $F_1$ | 2.086 |
| P-Value | 0.968 |
| (10%, 5%, 1% critical values) | (9.062 ; 10.348 ; 12.884) |

**Table 6 :** Threshold estimates for investment

| | Estimate | 95% Confidence Interval |
|---|---|---|
| $\gamma_1$ | 0.236 | [0.212 ; 0.250] |

The same procedure will be adopted. The test statistics F1, F2 and F3, set out together with their bootstrap p-values[15], are presented in the table 5. The statistic $F_1$ which refers to the test for a single threshold effect is the only significant statistic at a 1% level with a bootstrap p-value of 0.002. Both tests for a double threshold effect $F_2$ and for a triple threshold effect $F_3$ are not significant at the 5% level. These tests allow for concluding that there is a single threshold effect for investment. The threshold estimate with its asymptotic confidence interval 95% is reported in table 6.

The point estimate is 0.236. Appendix H presents the likelihood ratio function $LR_1(\gamma)$ corresponding to the estimate for $\gamma_1$. The regression coefficient estimates and their standard deviations are showed in the table 7.

**Table 7 :** Regression estimates for a single threshold effect of investment

| Explanatory Variables | Coefficient estimate | OLS Standard-errors | White-corrected Standard-errors |
|---|---|---|---|
| $NS_{it-1}$ | **0.062*** ** | **0.030** | **0.032** |
| $GE_{it-1}$ | -0.032 | 0.027 | 0.027 |
| $INV_{it-1}$ | -0.024 | 0.029 | 0.034 |
| $INF_{it-1}$ | -0.0008 | 0.0008 | 0.0006 |
| $FD_{it-1} I(INV_{it-1} \leq 0.236)$ | **-0.137*** ** | **0.047** | **0.042** |
| $FD_{it-1} I(0.236 < INV_{it-1})$ | **0.167*** ** | **0.069** | **0.076** |

*** Significant coefficient at the 1% level, ** 5% and * 10%.

[15] 500 bootstrap replications were used for each test.

Similar to the previous analysis, The Student's t-test[16] test the significance of the non-linear regression slope estimates. The coefficient estimates for the following variables NS, FD and INV are significant. Investment is significant just in the case of regimes switching. Gross national savings lagged by one period $NS_{it-1}$ has a significant positive impact on growth. When investment in the previous year is less than or equal to the threshold of 23.6%, then the budget deficit $FD_{it-1}$ has a negative effect on growth with a coefficient estimate of -0.137. And conversely, it has a positive impact on growth with a coefficient estimate of 0.167 as the investment exceeds the defined threshold.

**Table 8 :** Percentage of countries per year in each regime of investment

| Regime | | 1991 | 1992 | 1993 | 1994 | 1995 | 1996 | 1997 | 1998 | 1999 | 2000 | 2001 |
|---|---|---|---|---|---|---|---|---|---|---|---|---|
| 1er | $INV_{it-1} \leq 0.236$ | 55 | 75 | 75 | 70 | 65 | 63 | 63 | 65 | 60 | 73 | 70 |
| 2ème | $0.236 < INV_{it-1}$ | 45 | 25 | 25 | 30 | 35 | 38 | 38 | 35 | 40 | 28 | 30 |
| Regime | | 2002 | 2003 | 2004 | 2005 | 2006 | 2007 | 2008 | 2009 | 2010 | 2011 | 2012 |
| 1er | $INV_{it-1} \leq 0.236$ | 78 | 75 | 80 | 70 | 65 | 65 | 60 | 55 | 73 | 70 | 63 |
| 2ème | $0.236 < INV_{it-1}$ | 23 | 25 | 20 | 30 | 35 | 35 | 40 | 45 | 28 | 30 | 38 |

Table 8 reports that the percentage of countries belonging to the first regime - where the ratio of total investment / GDP is below the threshold of 23% - varies from 55% to 80%. Whereas the second regime - where investment exceeds the threshold of 23% - the percentage ranges from 20% to 45%. Hence, most countries fall into the first regime.

## 4.4 THE MOROCCAN CASE

Since we want to focus on Moroccan growth in response to the increase in the fiscal deficit, it seems useful to undertake a brief review of the historical behavior of economic growth, public debt and fiscal deficit as it will prepare the ground to lead a threshold effects analysis of fiscal policy while relying on results that were obtained previously.

### THE HISTORICAL BEHAVIOR OF FISCAL POLICY PUBLIC DEBT, AND GROWTH

To draw a picture about the economic situation across the country, this sub-section presents the evolution of the following three variables[17]: the general government net lending/borrowing as a percentage of nominal GDP, public debt as a percentage of nominal GDP and real GDP growth over the period 1980-2012. In Morocco, since the 1980s, the public debt increasing issue is one of the major concerns of public authorities. Figure 2 illustrates the variation of public debt (% GDP) since 1990.

**Figure 2 :** Public Debt, Morocco, 1990 - 2012

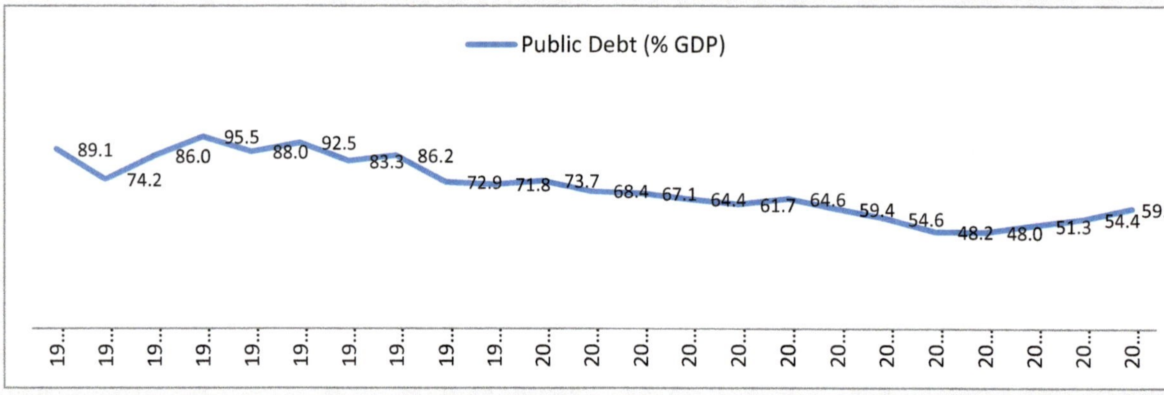


Data source: World Economic Outlook Database April 2013.

[16] When Student's t-test statistic is greater than the value read in the student's table (1.96 at the 5% level and 1.64 at the 10% level), the null hypothesis of the non-significance of the parameters is rejected.

[17] General government net lending/borrowing or the fiscal balance is expressed in current prices, as well as public debt. Data on general government net lending/borrowing are taken from the "Haut-commissariat au Plan" database. Data on real GDP growth are taken from the IMF's "International Financial Statistics (IFS)" database. Data on public debt are taken from the IMF "World Economic Outlook Database April 2013" database and are available only from 1990. Data on nominal GDP are taken from the IMF's "IFS" database.

From figure 2, three separate periods in terms of debt structure can be distinguish: the first period - which can be described as a very high debt period - varies from 1990 to 2000 and indicates a high debt level ranging from 71% to 95% of GDP with a fluctuating nature. In the second period, where it starts in 2001 and terminates in 2009, the debt ratio has declined almost persistently all over the period. The third period of 2009-2012, the public debt registered a continuous enhancement reaching 500.7 billion dirham at the end of the year 2012, which is equivalent to 59.6% of GDP. To ease the burden of the budget deficit, the government has relied on the international financial market. It raised one billion Euros in 2010 and 1.5 billion of dollars in December 2012. The IMF granted Morocco a "precautionary and liquidity line" by an amount equivalent to 6.2 billion dirham.

Figure 3 shows the evolution of both the fiscal balance (% of GDP) and GDP growth (annual %):

**Figure 3 :** GDP Growth and the Fiscal Balance, Morocco, 1980 - 2012

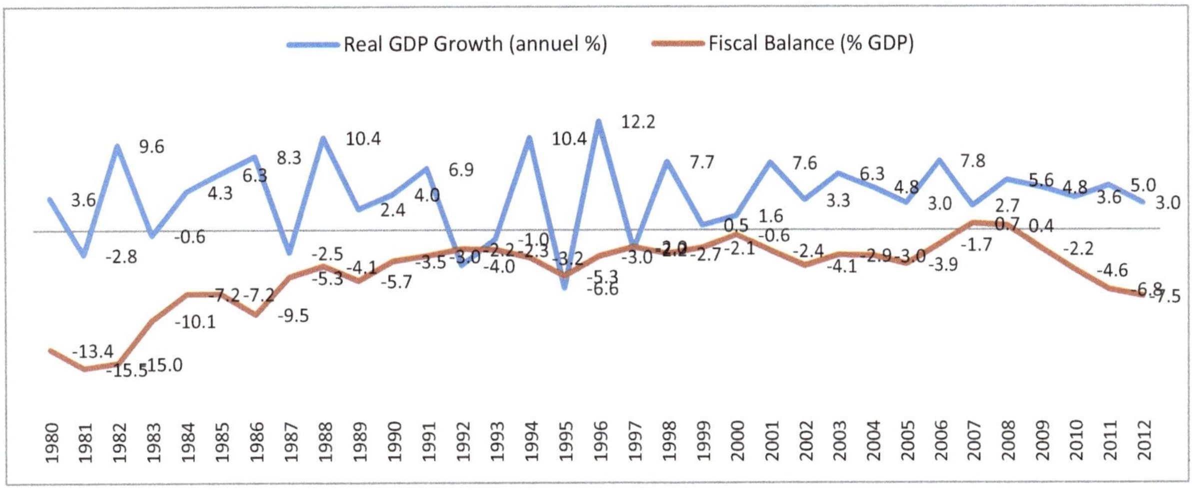


Data source: HCP for the fiscal balance and IFS for Real GDP Growth.

Throughout the review period, Morocco registered frequently fiscal deficits; the only notable exceptions being related to 2007 and 2008 where it is observed surplus positions of, respectively, 0.7 and 0.4. The highest deficit was registered in 1981 (-15.5% of GDP). The chart shows also the chaotic behavior of economic growth, especially during the eighties and the nineties. This behavior tends to abate from 2000 onwards. This is mainly due to periodical droughts in Morocco. According the World Bank database, the Moroccan GDP was divided in 2012 to 15% in agriculture, 30% in industry and 55% in services. This division shows the substantial weight that takes agriculture in Morocco. However, since 2000, GDP growth progresses on a relatively proportional basis with the general government net lending/borrowing.

## MOROCCO'S THRESHOLD EFFECTS ANALYSIS[18]

As a reminder, data varying between 1990 and 2012 were used for the panel estimation. However for Morocco, it seems more accurate to extend the observation period and let it cover 1980 – 2012; as it will reduce the potential for error and to get a better statistical accuracy.

Figure 4 shows the variations of the fiscal balance ratio and real GDP[19] growth with two horizontal lines plotted representing the two threshold levels already found in previous analysis for the fiscal balance ratio, which are 0.032 and -0.048.

[18] Reinhart and Rogoff (2010) approach has inspired me to conduct the threshold effects analysis for Morocco.

[19] The key statistics and data source are provided in Appendix D.

**Figure 4 :** GDP Growth and the Fiscal Balance with a Double Threshold Effect, Morocco, 1980 - 2012

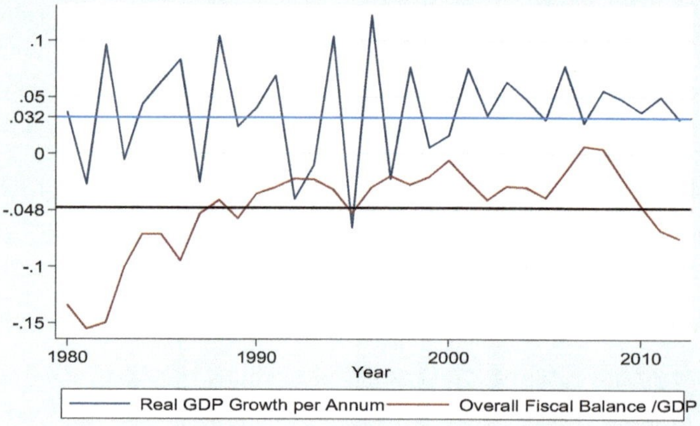


Data source: HCP for the fiscal balance and IFS for Real GDP Growth.

Over the period 1980 – 1987, the budget deficit remains below the threshold level of 4.8 % of GDP but with an exception for the year 1988 where Morocco has recorded a budget deficit of 2.5% of GDP. But one again, Morocco has registered a budget deficit below the threshold during 1995, 2011 and 2012. Besides that, throughout the whole considered period, Morocco's budget balance remains below the threshold of 3.2% of GDP.

**Table 9 :** Real GDP Growth as the Level of Fiscal Balance Varies, Morocco, 1980 - 2012

| Regime | | Obs. | Mean | Median | Standard Deviation |
|---|---|---|---|---|---|
| 1st | FB ≤ -0.048 | 12 | 0.025 | 0.033 | 0.048 |
| 2nd | -0.048 < FB ≤ 0.032 | 21 | 0.046 | 0.048 | 0.042 |
| 3rd | 0.032 < FB | 0 | - | - | - |

Table 12 provides details on the behavior of economic growth as the level of budget balance varies. Morocco has never recorded a budget surplus exceeding the threshold level of 3.2% of GDP over the whole considered period 1980-2012. When the budget deficit exceeds the threshold level of 4.8%, median growth falls markedly by 1.5[20]%, whereas average growth falls even heavily by 2.1%[21].

## 5.0 CONCLUSION

This paper contributes to the fiscal policy literature by re-examining the relationship between the fiscal deficit and economic growth. First, the study identifies, under a linear hypothesis, the impact of five economic variables, namely the fiscal deficit, current government expenditure, national savings, inflation rate and total investment. Results shows that current government expenditure is negatively correlated with growth and thus its increase can hinder the process of growth. Raising deficit is also growth reducing. Investment has a positive sign and hence a positive effect on GDP growth. Second, examining the scatter plot in Figure 1 urged calling into question the nature of the relation between growth and the fiscal deficit as it shows an apparent non- linearity, hence the existence of threshold effects in the relationship between fiscal policy and growth is considered by using the threshold estimation approach as proposed by Hansen (1999) for non-dynamic panels. Two types of non- linearity emerged, one related to the impact of the fiscal deficit on growth, and the other involving the effects of investment. The empirical results strongly suggest the existence of a double threshold effect of the fiscal balance which is robust to their inclusion. A fiscal deficit exceeding 4.8% of GDP drives an anti-Keynesian effect on growth, but also a fiscal surplus exceeding the threshold of 3.2% of GDP impacts negatively on economic

[20] 1.5% is obtained from the difference between the second regime's average growth and the first regime's average growth (4.8% - 3.3% = 1.5%).

[21] 2.1% is obtained from the difference between the second regime's average growth and the first regime's average growth (4.6% - 2.5% = 2.1%).

growth. Results show also that the sign of the relationship between the budget deficit and growth is conditioned by the level of total investment: when total investment exceeds the threshold of 23% of GDP, then the budget deficit is positively correlated to economic growth with a coefficient estimates of 0.167, whereas it is negatively correlated to growth with a coefficient estimates of -0.137 when total investment falls below this threshold. Within this framework, government budget of the countries concerned need to be monitored. These countries are expected to prevent the occurrence of deficits exceeding the thresholds found and to set priorities to reducing government final consumption expenditure in favour of productive investment. Finally, Morocco's threshold effects analysis shows that the behavior of economic growth varies depending on variations in the budget deficit: when the budget deficit exceeds the 4.8% threshold, then median growth falls sharply by 1.5 %, whereas average growth falls even stronger by 2.1%.

While the results are instructive, some caveats are important to bear in mind when interpreting these results. First, the asymptotic distribution of the statistic $F_1$ on the threshold variable has a non-standard character and requires bootstrap methods to compute its significance level. Second, the estimated model does not provide the precise channels through which fiscal policy affects growth. There are also some particular issues related to data which may skew the results. Inflation rate and the current account balance show a high degree of dispersion and heterogeneity within the sample of countries. Strong asymmetry in the inflation distribution was detected as it reveals the presence of a few high values.

Several improvement extensions can be applied to the econometric approach. For future research, we could consider developing other methods where we can introduce dynamic panels in the threshold estimation approach so that one or more lags of the dependent variable "GDP growth" might be included in the model as explanatory variables. This would definitely provide solutions to the problem of omitted variables. It would be also more instructive to give more attention to the issues related to endogenous variables and to the reverse causation between economic growth and fiscal policy.

### ACKNOWLEDGEMENTS

I would like to thank Pr. EL ABBASSI Idriss[22], Pr. TOUNSI Said[23] and Pr. HANSEN Bruce[24] for the very helpful comments and suggestions.

## REFERENCES

Abd Rahman N. H., (2012). How federal government's debt affect the level of economic growth? International Journal of Trade, Economics and Finance, Vol. 3, No. 4.

Adam C. S., Bevan D. L., (2005). Fiscal deficits and growth in developing countries. Journal of Public Economics, No. 89, P. 571– 597.

Aghion P., Comin D., Howitt P., (2006). When does domestic saving matter for economic growth?. NBER Working Papers, No. 12275, National Bureau of Economic Research.

Aschauer D. A., (1989). Is public expenditure productive?. Journal of Monetary Economics, No. 23, P. 177-200.

Banzhaf H. S., Oates W. E., (2012). On fiscal illusion and ricardian equivalence in local public finance. NBER Working Papers, No. 18040, National Bureau of Economic Research.

Barro R., (1974). Are government bonds net wealth?. Journal of Political Economy, No. 82(6), P. 1095-1117.

Barro R., (1990). Government spending in a simple model of endogenous growth. Journal of Political Economy, Vol. 98, No. 5, P. 103-125.

[22] Professor, Department of economics, Mohammed V Rabat –Agdal University, Faculty of Juridical, Economic and Social Sciences, Morocco. E-mail Address: idriss_elabbassi@yahoo.fr.

[23] Professor, Department of economics, Mohammed V Rabat –Agdal University, Faculty of Juridical, Economic and Social Sciences, Morocco. E-mail Address: sadtounsi@gmail.com.

[24] Professor, University of Wisconsin–Madison, E-mail Adress: behansen@wisc.edu.

Benos N., (2009). Fiscal policy and economic growth: empirical evidence from EU countries. MPRA Paper, No. 19174, University of Ioannina.

Bertolat G. and Drazen A., (1993). Trigger points and budget cuts: explaining the effects of fiscal austerity. American Economic Review, Vol. 83, No.1, P. 11-26.

Buiter, W. H., Corsetti G., Roubini N., (1993). Excessive deficits: sense and nonsense in the Treaty of Maastricht. Economic Policy, No. 16, P. 75-100. Reprinted in the Political Economy of Monetary Union, Edited by Paul de Grauwe, P. 297-331.

Buiter W. H., (2006). The 'sense and nonsense of Maastricht' revisited: what have we learnt about stabilization in EMU?. Journal of Common Market Studies, Vol. 44, P. 687-710.

Cardia E., (1997). Replicating ricardian equivalence tests with simulated series. American Economic Review, Vol. 87, P. 65-87.

Cecchetti S. G., Mohanty M. and Zampolli F., (2010). The real effects of debt. BIS Working Papers, No. 352.

Dalamagas B.A., (1992). Testing ricardian equivalence: a reconsideration. Applied Economics, Vol. 24, Issue 1, P. 59-69.

Easterly W., Rebelo S., (1993). Fiscal policy and economic growth: an empirical investigation. Journal of Monetary Economics, No. 32, P.417-458.

Evans P., (1993). Consumers are not ricardian: evidence from nineteen countries. Economic Inquiry, Vol. 31, Issue 4, P. 534-548.

Feldstein M., (1986). The effects of fiscal policies when incomes are uncertain: a contradiction to ricardian equivalence. NBER Working Papers, No. 2062, National Bureau of Economic Research.

Ghosh S., Mourmouras I. A., (2004). Endogenous growth, welfare and budgetary regimes. Journal of Macroeconomics, Vol. 26, Issue 4, P. 623-635.

Giavazzi F., Japelli T., Pagano M., (2000). Searching for non-linear effects of fiscal policy: evidence from industrial and developing countries. European Economic Review Vol. 44, Issue 7, P. 1259-1289.

Graham, F. C., (1995). Government debt, government spending, and private sector behavior: comment. American Economic Review, Vol. 85, P. 1348-1356.

Greiner A., Semmler W., (2000). Endogenous growth, government debt and budgetary regimes. Journal of Macroeconomics, Vol. 22, Issue 3, P. 363-384.

Gupta S., Clements B., Baldacci E., Mulas-Granados C., (2005). Fiscal policy, expenditure composition, and growth in low-income countries. Journal of International Money and Finance, Vol. 24, Issue 3, P. 441-463.

Hansen B., (1999). Threshold effects in non-dynamic panels: estimation, testing, and inference. Journal of econometrics, Vol. 93, Issue 2, P. 345-368.

Herndon T., Ash M., Pollin R., (2013). Does high public debt consistently stifle economic growth? a critique of Reinhart and Rogoff. PERI Working Paper Series, No. 322.

Keho Y., (2010). Budget deficits and economic growth: causality evidence and policy implications for WAEMU countries. European Journal of Economics, Finance and Administrative Sciences, No. 18, P. 99-104.

Khan M. S., Senhadji A. S., (2001). Threshold effects in the relationship between inflation and growth. IMF Staff Papers, vol. 48, No. 1.

Kotlikoff L. J., Razin A., Rosenthal R. W., (1988). A strategic altruism model in which ricardian equivalence does not hold. NBER Working Papers, No. 2699, National Bureau of Economic Research.

Minea A., Villieu P., (2008). Un réexamen de la relation non-linéaire entre déficits budgétaires et croissance économique. Presses de Sciences Po |Revue économique, No. 3, Vol. 59, P. 561-570.

Minea A., Villieu P., (2012). Persistent deficits, growth and indeterminacy. Macroeconomic Dynamics, Vol. 16, P. 267-283.

Modigliani F., Sterling A. G., (1990). Government debt, government spending and private sector behavior: a further comment. American Economic Review, Vol. 80, No. 3, P. 600-603.

Perotti R., (1999). Fiscal policy when things are going badly. Quarterly Journal of Economics, No. 114, P. 1399-1436.

Reinhart C. M., Rogoff K. S., (2010). Growth in a time of debt. American Economic Review, Vol. 100, No. 2, P.573-578.

Reinhart C. M., Rogoff K. S., (2013). Errata, Growth in a time of debt. Harvard University.

Tanimoune N. A., Combes J.-L., Plane P., (2008). La politique budgétaire et ses effets de seuil sur l'activité en Union Economique et Monétaire Ouest Africaine (UEMOA). La Doc. française| Economie & prévision, Vol. 186, No. 5, P. 145-162.

## APPENDICES

**Appendix A:** Sample Countries

Bahamas, Bangladesh, Barbados, Benin, Bolivia, Brazil, Central African Republic, Chile, Colombia, Comoros, Costa Rica, Djibouti, Dominica, Dominican Republic, Ecuador, El Salvador, Fiji, Ghana , Honduras, Hungary, India, Jamaica, Jordan, Kenya, Malaysia, Mexico, Morocco, Mozambique, Namibia, Pakistan, Poland, South Africa, Sri Lanka, Suriname, Saint Vincent and the Grenadines, Syria, Thailand, Tunisia , Uruguay, Vanuatu.

**Appendix B:** Summary statistics, data for 40 developing countries

| Variables | Mnemonic | Obs. | Mean | Standard Deviation | Median | Min. | Max. | Total Variance | Within Variance | Between Variance |
|---|---|---|---|---|---|---|---|---|---|---|
| Real GDP growth | GDP | 915 | 0.036 | 0.034 | 0.040 | -0.119 | 0.148 | 0.001 | 0.001 | 0.000 |
| Ratio of current government expenditure to GDP | GE | 854 | 0.153 | 0.058 | 0.143 | 0.032 | 0.402 | 0.003 | 0.000 | 0.003 |
| Ratio of gross national savings to GDP | NS | 849 | 0.178 | 0.077 | 0.175 | -0.061 | 0.399 | 0.006 | 0.002 | 0.004 |
| Ratio of the overall budget deficit to GDP | FD | 824 | 0.031 | 0.030 | 0.030 | - 0.090 | 0.130 | 0.001 | 0.001 | 0.000 |
| Ratio of total investment to GDP | INV | 872 | 0.215 | 0.063 | 0.211 | 0.047 | 0.466 | 0.004 | 0.002 | 0.002 |
| Inflation rate | INF | 911 | 0.113 | 0.311 | 0.056 | -0.074 | 5.858 | 0.097 | 0.085 | 0.012 |
| Ratio of the general government debt to GDP | GD | 670 | 0.547 | 0.304 | 0.482 | 0.039 | 2.197 | 0.092 | 0.031 | 0.061 |
| Ratio of current account balance to GDP | CCB | 917 | -0.039 | 0.065 | -0.032 | -0.331 | 0.171 | 0.004 | 0.002 | 0.002 |

**Sources**

Data on real GDP growth, gross national savings, overall budget deficit, investment, Inflation, general government debt are taken from the IMF's World Economic Outlook database April 2013.
Data on current government expenditure are taken from the World Bank database.

**Definitions**

Data on current government expenditure, overall fiscal balance, gross national savings, total investment, current account balance and government's total debt are expressed in current local currency as ratios to nominal GDP. Data on inflation are expressed as annual percentages of the average consumer prices. Data on GDP growth are expressed on constant prices.
General government final consumption expenditure includes all government current expenditures for purchases of goods and services (including compensation of employees). It also includes national defense and security outlays, but excludes government military spending.
Overall fiscal balance expresses a net lending (+) or borrowing (–) and measures the extent to which the government is either putting, in the event of a surplus, financial resources at the disposal of the other economic sectors and the rest of the world, or, in the case of a deficit, utilizing the financial resources generated by the other sectors and the rest of the world.
Gross national saving is calculated as gross disposable income minus final consumption expenditure after taking account of an adjustment for pension funds.
Total investment or gross capital formation is measured by the total value of the gross fixed capital formation – Gross fixed capital formation include land improvements (fences, ditches, drains, and so on), plant, machinery, and equipment purchases; and the construction of roads, railways, etc. including schools, offices, hospitals, private residential dwellings, and commercial and industrial buildings – plus net changes in the level of inventories and acquisitions of valuables.
Current account balance is the sum of net exports of goods and services, net primary income, and net secondary income.
General government debt consists of all liabilities that require payment or payments of interest and/or principal by the debtor to the creditor at a date or dates in the future. It includes domestic and foreign liabilities such as currency and money deposits, securities other than shares, and loans.
Inflation rate and real GDP growth are measured on the basis of year-on-year changes; the base year is country-specific.

**Appendix C:** Linear model estimation

| Dependant Variable: Real GDP Growth | | | |
|---|---|---|---|
| The linear models | | | |
| Explanatory Variables | (1) | (2) | (3) |

| | | | |
|---|---|---|---|
| GE | -0.159** | -0.159** | -0.119** |
| | (2.29) | (2.30) | (2.23) |
| NS | 0.099 | 0.080** | 0.053* |
| | (0.84) | (2.41) | 1.88 |
| FD | -0.121** | -0.120** | -0.201*** |
| | (2.14) | (2.13) | 4.18 |
| INV | 0.167 | 0.186*** | 0.164*** |
| | (1.36) | (5.68) | 5.75 |
| INF | -0.034 | -0.034 | -0.042*** |
| | (1.42) | (1.43) | 3.01 |
| GD | -0.006 | -0.006 | |
| | (0.95) | (0.95) | |
| CCB | -0.020 | | |
| | (0.17) | | |
| Constant | 0.017 | 0.016 | 0.020** |
| | (1.20) | (1.20) | 2.06 |
| Fisher Test (1) | F (7.517) = 11.76 | F(6.518) = 13.74 | F(5.666) = 21.62 |
| Fisher Test (2) | F (34.517) = 4.11 | F(34.518) = 4.23 | F(36.666) = 5.23 |
| AIC | -2453.441 | -2455.412 | -3092.999 |
| BIC | -2418.832 | -2425.129 | -3065.624 |
| $R^2$ | 0.14 | 0.14 | 0.14 |
| Number of observations | 559 | 559 | 708 |

*** Significant coefficient at the 1% level, ** 5% and * 10%.
Student's t-values are put between brackets.
Fisher Test (1) checks the significance of the explanatory variables.
Fisher Test (2) is used to examine the significance of the fixed effects.

**Appendix D:** Summary statistics, Data for Morocco

| Variable | Mnemonic | Obs. | Mean | Median | Standard Deviation | Min. | Max. |
|---|---|---|---|---|---|---|---|
| Real GDP growth | GDP | 33 | 0.038 | 0.040 | 0.045 | -0.066 | 0.122 |
| Ratio of the overall fiscal balance | FB | 33 | -0.048 | -0.035 | 0.040 | -0.155 | 0.007 |

Sources: Data on real GDP growth are taken from the IMF's International Financial Statistics (IFS)
Data on Overall fiscal balance are taken from the "Haut-Commissariat au plan" (HCP).

**Appendix E:** Likelihood ratio function 〖LR〗 _1(γ) for a single threshold effect of the fiscal deficit

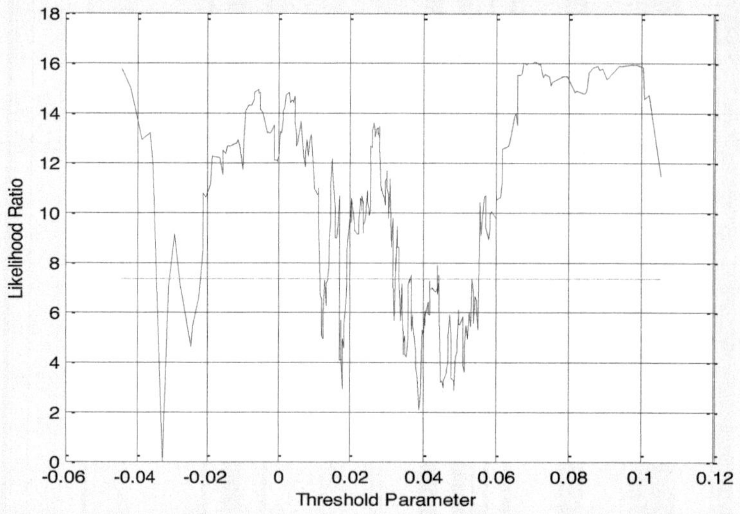

**Appendix F:** Likelihood Ratio Function $LR_2^r(\gamma)$ for a Double Threshold Effect of the Fiscal Deficit

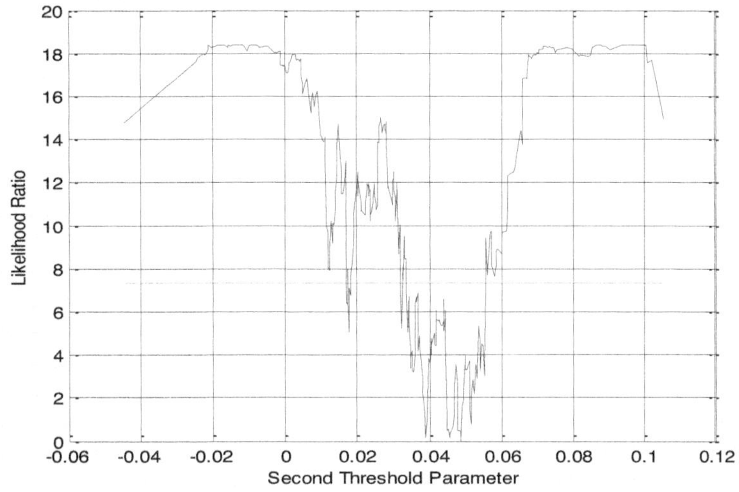


**Appendix G:** Likelihood ratio function $LR_1^r(\gamma)$ for a double threshold effect of the fiscal deficit

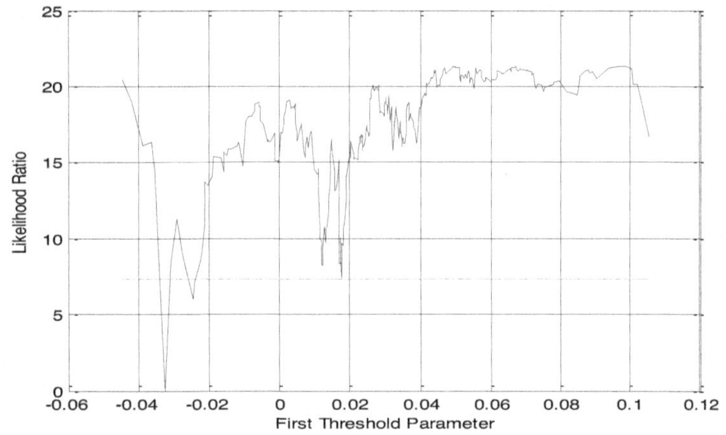


**Appendix H:** Likelihood ratio function 〖LR〗 _1(γ) for a single threshold effect of investment

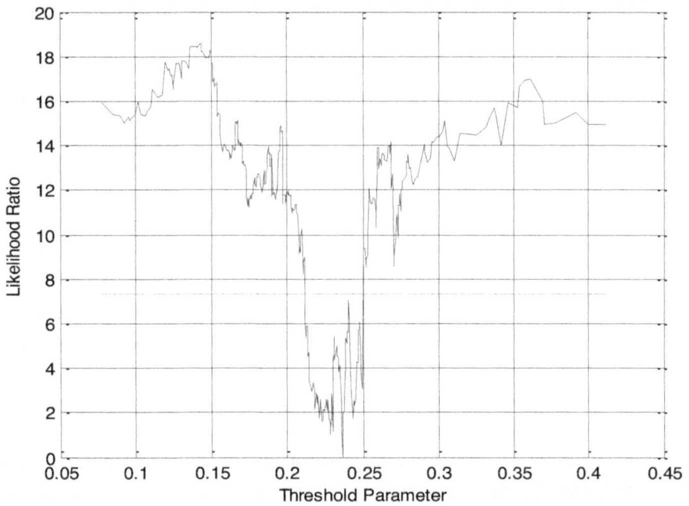

# 16

# Analysis of Fiji's Export and Its Impact on Economic Growth

**Shivneil Kumar Raj**[1], **Priteshni Pratibha Chand**[2]

**ABSTRACT**

Exports are vital for Fiji's economy as it contributes significantly to its gross domestic product (GDP) and economic growth. The export data over the years show very slow growth and is gradually increasing. Fiji's GDP data show that GDP is gradually increasing. Thus, Fiji's economic growth is also increasing at a steady rate. This study aims to measure the relationship between exports and economic growth in Fiji. A regression analysis on data collected for Fiji from 2000-2015 shows that there is a strong positive relationship between exports and economic growth. Thus, when exports increase, economic growth also increases. Potential sectors that can be further developed to boost Fiji's exports are sugar, garment, tourism and agriculture. The government should restrict imports through import quotas, tariffs and embargoes and give subsidies and tax incentives to potential export sectors to boost domestic production and increase exports. The government's motive is to increase export incentives and promote Fiji made products both locally and overseas. Thus, this leads to an increase in exports, improves the trade balance and economic growth. This research article was undertaken to carry out research to investigate the link between Fiji's export and economic growth and highlight ways and potential sectors to increase Fiji's export and reduce imports.

Keywords: Economic growth, exports, GDP (Gross Domestic Product), imports, international trade.

---

## 1.0 INTRODUCTION

The transfer of goods, services and capital crossing foreign boundaries is known as international trade (En.wikipedia.org, 2017). Selling commodities such as sugar produced in one country to citizens of other countries are termed as exports. Exports are not only limited to goods but are also extended to intangible

[1] Assistant Lecturer, School of Business and Economics, The University of Fiji, Lautoka, Fiji. E-mail: shivneilr@unifiji.ac.fj / shivneilraj@yahoo.com

[2] Assistant Lecturer, School of Business and Economics, The University of Fiji, Lautoka, Fiji. E-mail: priteshnic@unifiji.ac.fj / pritychand8@gmail.com

items such as tourism services of which is categorized as an invisible export. International trading requires the countries to pay for the goods and services in the currency of the exporting country. Thus, it is not only exchange of goods, services, and capital but also an exchange of currencies taking place between the trading partners. Trade embodies the major contributor to Gross Domestic Product (GDP) of many economies whether developed of still developing.

According to literature, the association between exports and economic growth has received mixed reviews over the years. Economic growth is stimulated by international trade. And the expansion of exports, in turn, escalates the income of the inputs used in the production process thus increasing the demand for the factors of production to produce more goods and services. This fosters technological change and brings about better opportunities for investment. The higher demand generated by exceeding exports is also likely to spill over to the entire economy (Quddus and Saeed, 2005). Furthermore, through trade, nations have the advantage to access technology from other countries to improve their production processes and to increase economic well-being of their countries. For example, Fiji imports latest communication devices and computers to improve its production processes enabling them to use these tools to bring effective and efficient production. Thus, the overall production increases. The advancement in technology, for example, modern production techniques, together with state-of-art transport structure, efficacious development of industries within a nation and large companies operating internationally have accelerated international trade. (Economywatch.com, 2017).

Moreover, Balassa (1978), Krueger (1978) and Ndulu and Ndungu (1998), suggest that the growth of the export sectors in an economy may lead to an escalation in the capacity of economies of scale as the market size increases and allocative efficiency and competitiveness is enhanced at the firm level. Thus making the export sector more productive compared to non-export sectors when greater incentives enhance investments and upgrade technologies, therefore, having a favorable impact on the economic gross domestic product. Pugel (2007) further adds that the trading across borders has been intensified as a result of the benefits it encompasses and trade is a significant source of earnings for a growing nation. Another important benefit of international trade is that it enhances domestic competitiveness. For example, through trade, domestic producers become more efficient, so they increase their production and the surpluses are exported which earns them higher revenue thus leading to increased sales and profit. Nations take advantage of international trade technology to improve their production processes such as, automation that is using more machines in the production process. This makes production process fast and is cost effective.

Furthermore, nations engage in international trade because nations with strong international trade have become prosperous and have the power to control the world economy. The global trade can become one of the major contributors in the reduction of poverty. David Ricardo, a classical economist, employing his principle of comparative advantage explained how trade can benefit all parties such as consumers, firms, and countries involved in it, as long as goods are produced with the lowest opportunity costs. This leads to specialization, that is, a country focuses on producing those items in which it has a cost advantage. The net benefits from such activity are called gains from trade. This is one of the most important concepts in international trade. Adam Smith, another classical economist, with the use of the principle of absolute advantage, demonstrated that a country could benefit from trade if it has the least absolute cost of production of goods that is per unit input yields a higher volume of output. According to the principle of comparative advantage, benefits of trade are dependent on the opportunity cost of production. The opportunity cost of production of goods is the amount of production of one good reduced, to increase production of another good by one unit. A country with no absolute advantage in any product, that is, the country is not the most competent producer for any goods, can still be benefited from focusing on the export of goods for which it has the least opportunity cost of production (Economywatch.com, 2017).

Nations engage in international trade because nations with strong international trade have become prosperous and have the power to control the world economy. The global trade can become one of the major contributors in the reduction of poverty. David Ricardo, a classical economist, employing his principle of comparative advantage explained how trade can benefit all parties such as consumers, firms, and countries involved in it, as long as goods are produced with the lowest opportunity costs. This leads to specialization, that is, a country focuses on producing those items in which it has a cost advantage. The net benefits from such activity are called gains from trade. This is one of the most important concepts in international trade.

Another benefit to countries engaging in international trade is a higher standard of living. International trade increases standard of living because it enables the country to have access to a wide variety of goods and services. Other reasons to trade internationally are the lack of resources and climatic and geographical conditions. Lack of resources is one of the major reasons for international trade. Most countries have limited natural resources; therefore they will not be able to produce everything they require. For example, Fiji lacks oil reserves so petroleum products are imported from Singapore and Korea. Fiji has abundant of land resources so they carry out more agricultural activities. The agricultural products are exported to earn revenue. Countries may not be able to produce different food items because they do not have the right climate. For example, apples cannot be grown in Fiji as it requires cold climates. Fiji has a tropical maritime climate. It is able to produce tropical fruits and vegetables. Fiji has an open economy that export and import goods and services with many countries. Although trade embodies many benefits to an economy and leads to economic growth and development but some studies indicate otherwise. Studies by Dodaro (1991), Bhagwati (1988), Kunst and Marin (1989) and Henriques and Sadorsky (1996) suggest that the intensity of export growth is dependent on the level of development in an economy.

There are many theories on trade and a few of them will be highlighted here. The principle of Absolute Advantage was first depicted by Adam Smith (1776) using only labor input. It is a theory which emphasizes on a country producing goods in which it has greater productivity and imports the goods with lower productivity. Fiji has absolute advantages in the products that it earns the highest export earnings, such as sugar, agricultural products, and fish and mineral resources. Another economic theory is the principle of Comparative Advantage depicted by David Ricardo (1817). Comparative advantage states that a country should export products in which it has a lower opportunity cost. According to the estimated by The Reserve Bank of Fiji (2017), A study by Prasad (2004) reveals that Fiji has a comparative advantage in products such as sugar, fish, timber, fruits and vegetables, cork and wood, clothing, gold, mineral water, garments, beverages and footwear for the period of 1998-2002.

In addition to this, the Heckscher - Ohlin Theory states countries should export those products that utilize inputs which are abundant in supply in the country. It is a triple comparison of comparative advantage: across countries: across products and: mainly across factors of production. Fiji has in abundance supply of unskilled laborers and abundance of unused land. The combination of the two available factors of productions is most attractive to labor and land intensive production, mainly agricultural and fisheries. The farmers of the agricultural products are not highly skilled but are appropriate for the production of agriculture produces. Fiji lacks high skilled labor thus does not produce high technological products such as automobiles and computers.

Most country's competitiveness increases as a result of international trade but due to some adverse factors, there is a decline in the performance of some export factors. The Dutch disease is a situation where some sector of the country performs poorly but previously they were very productive. Although Fiji has achieved diversification, a closer examination of the mining industry in isolation reveals a downfall due to common pitfalls associated with the natural resource depletion. Another example of Dutch disease is the garment industry in Fiji. This sector declined due to the expiry of tax-free zones. One such example is the sugar industry which was once known as the backbone of Fiji, being the major source of foreign exchange earnings. Sugar production has declined mainly due to the expiring of land leases after 1997.

Thus, due to international trade, export is an important economic variable in determining economic growth. Fiji's various export sectors contribute significantly to Fiji's economic growth. Export is an important variable in the calculation of gross domestic product; therefore an increase in net exports implies an increase in a country's gross domestic product. Thus, this increases the economic growth in the country. Fiji's government is continuously promoting Fiji made products overseas to increase its exports earnings, improve its trade balance and the country's economic growth.

Although various studies have been conducted employing different methods to examine the causality between exports and economic growth and analysts have reached mixed conclusions, unfortunately, no such study exists for the Fiji Islands, in the South Pacific. Thus, there is a need to bridge this gap as sustained economic growth is vital for a developing nation like Fiji. The objective of this study attempts to measure the impact of export growth on economic growth in Fiji and provide recommendations to policy makers on which sectors of the economy to focus on to expand its production possibilities. There are a total of five sections in this paper: the next section focuses on literature review followed by the methodology, data analysis and finally the concluding remarks and policy recommendations

## 2.0 LITERATURE REVIEW

Lin and Li (2001), re-examine the contribution of international trade to economic growth in China for the years 1979 to 2000 using a Two-Stage Least Squares method as the sample size was small. Their argument is that previous studies have not differentiated between the portrayal of imports and exports on economic growth thus failing to describe the relationship between various economic variables. This had led to underestimating the contribution made by international trade. Therefore, they have employed econometric models and observed that a ten percent increase in exports leads to a one percent increase in GDP.

Velnampy and Achchuthan (2013) analyzed the impact of export and import on economic growth in Sri Lanka using data from 1970 to 2010. A time-series investigation using Eviews version 5 statistical software was conducted to establish the impact of the two variables on economic growth. It was discovered that there is a robust positive relationship between exports and imports and both of these economic variables have a significant impact on economic growth.

Shahbaz, Ahmad and Asad (n.d.) use the ARDL bounds test approach to explore the export led growth in Pakistan with data from 1990 to 2008. The study proves that the export is positively interrelated with growth for both the short-run and the long-run period. It further provides evidence that a depreciation in exchange rate hinders economic growth while a running real capital stock fosters it. Another study by Sharma and Dhakal (1994) also examines the association of exports growth and economic growth in thirty developing countries for the years 1960 to 1988. It is evident that international trade increases the level of output and generates more income in a country which assists in stimulating the volume of trade.

A few more studies have been conducted in this area which reveal the same result. Studies by Balassa (1994), Sprout and Weaver (1993) and Lucas (1990) validate the export-led theory based on the neoclassical growth accounting techniques of production function. They conclude that output growth is caused by export growth and not the other way round while other analysts, Holman and Graves (1995), Jung and Marshal (1985) and Bahmani-Oskooee et al (1991) accomplish that there is a significant causality between exports growth and economic growth. Chemeda (2001), utilizes Cobb-Douglas production function to analyze the impact of exports growth on economic growth for the Ethiopian economy for the years 1950 to 1986. The study uses co-integration techniques to examine the causality between the two economic variables. The finding is that there exists a significant long run relationship between export and gross domestic product.

## 3.0 METHODOLOGY

In the first few pages, an introduction to the proposed area of research was presented. This included a description of the study's research problem, several research purposes, rationale or justification of the study, research objectives and research questions that will serve to direct the data analysis and an identification of several key terms to the study. In addition, a review of relevant literature related, established a background of support for the study. The analysis of Fiji' exports and its impact on economic growth have been studied extensively; however it was only carried out on a single research paradigm. This research was an effort to carry out a mixture of research paradigms, that is, a mixture of qualitative and quantitative research methods to assess and analyze Fiji's export and its impact on economic growth. Thus, the "Ontological Position" of this research project was both a mixture of objectivist and subjectivist. The research philosophy will be a mixture of positivist and interpretive view. The study has been conducted mainly on the basis of literature survey, interviews and secondary information. Various journals and research papers, diagnostic study reports and newspaper articles have been surveyed to give validity and viability to this research. Research entails the collection of data and analyzing the collected data into useful information. This underscores the immense role that research plays in academic research as well as in the business environment which cannot be underrated. The research method section of the study introduces major activities – the research strategy and the research design.

## 4.0 DATA ANALYSIS AND RESULT DISCUSSION

### 4.1 OVERVIEW OF THE FIJIAN ECONOMY

This study is based on Fiji, which is a small island nation in the South Pacific with a population close to a million (0.824m) as in 2007. The World Bank (2002) classifies this economy as an upper middle-income country with gross domestic product per capita as $4050 in 2008. The policy makers in Fiji had implemented import substitution policies after its independence which was directed at encouraging consumption to innervate economic growth. Since 1986 Fiji has altered its strategy to export-led growth endorsed by the International Monetary Fund as it preceding policy was ineffective in invigorating constant economic growth (UNDP Pacific Office in Fiji, 2017).

Fiji's economy is an open economy and it trades (exports and imports) in the international market. It has been noticed and highlighted that Fiji's export earnings over the years having been declining and showing slow growth likewise, imports have been seen to continuously rise year over year increasing Fiji's trade deficit and balance of payments According to Rogers (2000) the ratio of imports to gross domestic product has rapidly increased over the last three decades. Export production in Fiji is also declining due to several reasons. Prasad (2000) said that the process of Fiji's assimilation with the world in previous years has been brought by significant developments in its balance of payments. One such development was signs of improvement in the countries' export orientation program, leading to increase in Fiji's exports.

Over the years, export growth in Fiji has been mainly affected by the nature of Fiji's preferential trade arrangements, exchange rate arrangements. Fiji's domestic exports, which mainly consist of agricultural products, faced spiked fluctuations from exogenous and endogenous factors. In most developing nations, the commodity concentration of Fiji's exports has been regarded as a major factor contributing to the short-term variability of Fiji's exports. Instability in global prices for agricultural products poses a significant amount of insecurity about export earnings from one year to the next (Prasad, 2000). A factor, such as the susceptibility of exports to adverse weather conditions has impacted Fiji's export earnings, thus, affecting gross domestic product and economic growth.

Export means that domestic country is selling its goods and services overseas. Some of the commodities Fiji export are, agricultural and forestry products, sugar, timber, gold, fish. The various export sectors in Fiji that contribute significantly to Fiji's economy in bringing export earnings are tourism, sugar industry, dairy, agriculture, fisheries, and forestry. Fiji also has a garment industry that export garment products. However, due to the expiry of tax-free zones, garment industry products in Fiji have significantly declined. Fiji has some garment factories still operating but the production is not on a very large scale.

The major garment factory 'GIMLI' closed its operations in Fiji due to the expiry of tax-free zones. Sugar used to be Fiji's largest export earner but due to many upheavals, tourism has become Fiji's largest foreign exchange earner. Sugar industry still continues to play an important role as an export earner. Other sectors such as agriculture, fisheries, and forestry, continue to play a vital role in Fiji's economy as well as bringing export earnings to Fiji. Some of the countries that buy Fiji goods and services are Australia, New Zealand, America, European Union, Japan and the pacific regions.

Export earnings are important to Fiji's economy. Over the years, Fiji's export earnings have shown very slow growth. From the years 1995 till 2005, export earnings continue to fluctuate and steadily decline. The negative effects relating to Fiji's growth is related to the impulsiveness in the global commodity prices, natural disaster prone environment and decline in the confidence of foreign investors, ongoing declines in the sugar industry and uneven global recovery. Looking at this report of negativity towards its economic structure, Fiji is in high need to at least increase its exports in relation to its Gross Domestic Production.

Fiji is a member of many trade agreements and the most significant one is World Trade Organization (WTO).

WTO offers benefits from increased access to foreign markets, opening up more room for export earnings for a nation. WTO facilitates trade expansion and liberalization of international trade under non-discriminatory, predictable and transparent conditions, with prescribed rules based on General Agreement on Tariffs & Trade (GATT For a small island nation such as Fiji, it brings in huge benefits to be a part of the World Trade Organization. It's trading concerns are protected by the rules set by the international body and provides an equal platform for the smaller economies to trade which have less authoritative power. Fiji is also a member country in PICTA (Pacific Island Country Trade Agreements) and some other pacific and global trade agreements. These agreements help Fiji have duty free access to products; allow free trade and also better access to foreign markets (Foreignaffairs.gov.fj, 2017).

### 4.1.1 FIJI'S ECONOMIC GROWTH TREND (1970 – 2010) AND EXPORTS: FACTORS AFFECTING IT

Fiji's growth performance has been adversely affected by the country's vulnerability to both internal and external shocks. These include political unrest (four coups since 1987), natural disasters (cyclones and floods), global oil and food price shocks, and global financial and economic crises. From 1970 to 1980, the economy experienced moderate rates of economic growth, with the real gross domestic product (GDP) increasing by an average of 6.5% per annum on account of high levels of public investment and increasing exports of sugar and copra. Until 1986, economic policy was marked by a strong emphasis on import substitution, food self-sufficiency, and economic diversification, with the state playing a dominant role in economic activity. In the late 1980s, prior to joining the World Trade Organization (WTO), Fiji embarked on an important policy shift toward a more market-oriented, outward-looking development strategy. Against this backdrop, Fiji gradually liberalized its trade and reduced import restrictions in favor of export promotion. The more open trading approach led to increased opportunities in the economy, creating thousands of jobs in industries like tourism and textiles. Over 2001–2006, the Fiji economy experienced extreme volatility in growth performance. Annual GDP growth fell to 2.7%, on average, while during 2007–2009 the economy contracted at an average rate of –0.4% (Economic Analysis: Summary, 2014).

### 4.1.2 EXPORT SECTORS

One important cause of Fiji's weak growth record beginning in the mid-1990s has been the performance of the merchandise exporting sector. Since 1970, sugar and textile exports drove Fiji's economy, but both have experienced difficulty in competing effectively in deregulating global markets. The sugar industry has suffered from quality concerns, management problems, labour relations issues, non-renewal of land leases, shortages of harvest labour, and most importantly the phasing out of the preferential price agreement with the European Union—due to end in 2017—leading to sugar price reductions of 36% and a decline in sugarcane production. In 2010, the government began implementing industry reforms. These are making an impact, with sugar production increasing by 16.2% in 2013, reversing a contraction of 7.1% in 2012. The textile industry similarly declined following the end of the quota system under the Agreement on Textiles and Clothing and the full integration of textiles into the WTO tariff regime3. Overall, garment exports have declined from 34% of all merchandise exports in 1999 to only 11% in 2013; while sugar exports were 15% in 2013, down from 28% in 1999 (Economic Analysis: Summary, 2014).

More recently, growth has been driven by Fiji's strong tourism industry, which has demonstrated a strong degree of resilience to the setbacks of cyclones and floods occurring in the tourism high season. Some 45% of Fiji's visitors come from Australia, with large numbers also coming from New Zealand, the United States, the United Kingdom, and the Pacific islands. Mining is also an emerging sector with the potential to boost the economy's output significantly. Fiji's second highest foreign exchange earner after tourism is remittances from Fijians residing and working overseas. These have increased in importance and in 2013 were estimated to be equivalent to 3% of GDP (Economic Analysis: Summary, 2014). Thus, exports are important to Fiji's economy. The government of Fiji has been promoting Fiji made products both local and overseas to increase exports earnings and economic growth.

Pie chart 1: Major trading partners of Fiji in 2015

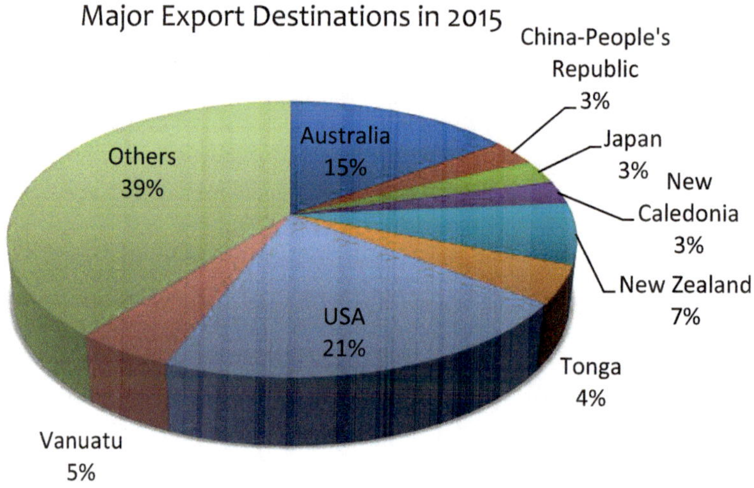


Source: Fiji Bureau of Statistics, 2017

In the year 2015, Fiji exported majority of its commodities to The United States of America (21%), followed by its neighbouring countries Australia (15%) and New Zealand (7%) in 2015.

Pie chart 2: Major export commodities in 2015

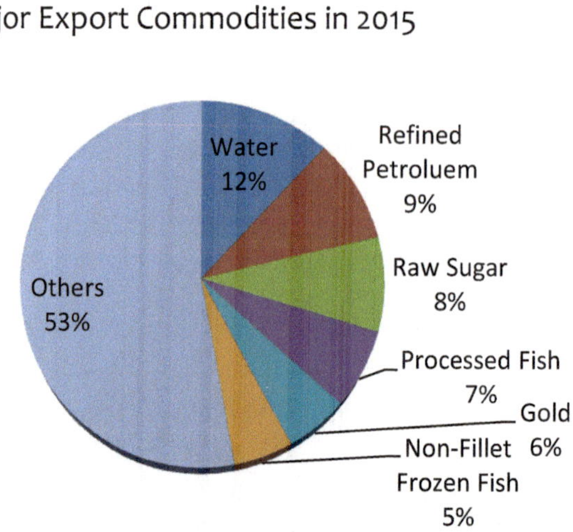


Source: The Observatory of Economic Complexity (OEC), 2017

The commodity Water was the key foreign exchange earner in the year 2015 surpassing the earnings of raw sugar which was considered the major export commodity a decade ago. Water includes artificial or natural mineral water and also aerated water. It does not, include natural or artificial mineral waters and aerated waters. A greater part of the mineral water export went to The United States, followed by Canada. A total of eight percent of raw sugar was exported in 2015 and the exports destinations were United Kingdom, Portugal, Romania Italy and The United States of America. Processed Fish comprises 7% of total exports and The United States, Vanuatu and Papua New Guinea are the main buyers of this product. Fiji exports 9% of Refined Petroleum to Tonga, Kiribati, Nauru, Cook Islands, Wallis and Futuna, New Caledonia and a few other small islands in the South Pacific. The third largest commodity exported by Fiji is raw sugar which is 8% of total exports. The exports destinations are the United Kingdom, Portugal, Romania, Italy and The United States respectively. Fiji sells processed fish mainly to the United States which is 7% of total exports. A total of ninety-seven percent of the gold exports is to Australia. Non-fillet frozen fish has a share of 5% of total exports and countries which import this product are China, Japan, Thailand, other Asian countries, Vietnam, American Samoa, Hong Kong and a few more (Atlas.media.mit.edu, 2017).

## 4.2 STATISTICAL ANALYSIS: STATISTICAL ANALYSIS OF FIJI'S EXPORTS AND ECONOMIC GROWTH

### 4.2.1 FIJI'S EXPORT AND GROSS DOMESTIC PRODUCT (GDP) DATA FROM THE YEARS 2000 TO 2015

A. DATA INPUT

Table 1: Data showing Fiji's exports and GDP for the years 2000 to 2015.

| | | FJD (Millions) |
|---|---|---|
| Year | Exports | GDP |
| 2000 | 1,155 | 4,892 |
| 2001 | 1,221 | 4,985 |
| 2002 | 1,132 | 5,145 |
| 2003 | 1,269 | 5,186 |
| 2004 | 1,206 | 5,466 |
| 2005 | 1,193 | 5,395 |
| 2006 | 1,202 | 5,497 |
| 2007 | 1,210 | 5,448 |
| 2008 | 1,471 | 5,502 |
| 2009 | 1,310 | 5,425 |
| 2010 | 1,605 | 5,588 |
| 2011 | 1,925 | 5,739 |
| 2012 | 2,182 | 5,820 |
| 2013 | 2,120 | 6,095 |
| 2014 | 2,302 | 6,418 |
| 2015 | 2,059 | 6,784 |

Source: Fiji Bureau of Statistics

Eviews is economics statistical software that was being used in conducting statistical analysis of Fiji's exports and economic growth. The ordinary least squares method (OLS) was used to generate the output. For this research paper, only 16 years of recent data from 2000 to 2015 were used to conduct the analysis based on the 2011 base price. Data from 1999 and backwards were not used because the base price had changed. If more data were used, this would have distorted the gross domestic product (GDP) at constant prices, since two base prices would have been used. To be consistent in the analysis, only the data relating to one base price is taken into account. GDP is used as an indicator for economic growth. From the Table 1 above, it can be concluded that from 1995 to 2005, Fiji's exports is gradually increasing however there is some fluctuations over the years as shown in Table 1. As for Fiji's GDP, there is a gradual increase from 2000 to 2015.

Furthermore, for GDP, only real GDP at constant prices were used. Real GDP is the value of all goods and services measured at constant prices and adjusted for inflation. Nominal GDP is GDP that includes inflation and measures goods and services at current prices. Real GDP is used instead of nominal GDP, because of the importance of using actual changes in GDP. An actual change in GDP gives the true picture of Fiji's economic growth. If the nominal GDP was used, it will not show the actual changes in GDP since it includes inflation as one of the basis to calculate GDP. This does not give the true picture of Fiji's GDP as the inflation level varies from time to time. For example, in one year there was very high inflation, thus the GDP at current prices were very high. In another year, inflation was very low, thus GDP at current prices was low. This indicates that fluctuations in inflation will vary GDP at current prices. Therefore it does not reflect the true picture of the economy in terms of the actual changes in GDP. Thus, real GDP is used in the statistical analysis.

B. EVIEWS OUTPUT INTERPRETATION (OLS REGRESSION OUTPUT)

Table 2 shows LNY is the dependent variable and represents economic growth. Economic growth is represented by GDP since GDP is an indicator of Economic Growth. C is a constant. LNX is the independent variable and represent exports. A simple linear regression model was used in the form of: $y=\beta_0+\beta_1 x$. Where y represents dependant variable, $\beta_0$ is a constant, $\beta_1$ is the coefficient which is multiplied by x which is the independent variable. Thus, the following equation was derived based on the model:

LNY = \$4,063.138 + 0.992378*LNX.

Table 2: Table showing the regression output generated from eviews.

Dependent Variable: LNY
Method: Least Squares
Date: 04/07/17 Time: 14:27
Sample: 2000 2015
Included observations: 16

| Variable | Coefficient | Std. Error | t-Statistic | Prob. |
|---|---|---|---|---|
| LNX | 0.992378 | 0.165933 | 5.980590 | 0.0000 |
| C | 4063.138 | 263.8645 | 15.39857 | 0.0000 |
| R-squared | 0.718692 | | Mean dependent variance | 5586.563 |
| Adjusted R-squared | 0.698598 | | S.D. dependent variance | 501.5186 |
| S.E. of regression | 275.3341 | | Akaike info criterion | 14.19032 |
| Sum squared residuals | 1061324. | | Schwarz criterion | 14.28689 |
| Log likelihood | -111.5225 | | Hannan-Quinn criteria. | 14.19526 |
| F-statistic | 35.76746 | | Durbin-Watson stat | 0.781984 |
| Probability (F-statistic) | 0.000034 | | | |

Source: Eviews Econometrics Software Version 10

Full Equation: ECONOMIC GROWTH (GDP in \$) = \$4,063.138 + 0.992378 * EXPORTS (\$)

'$\beta_0$' represents a constant (\$4,063.138, intercept) and $\beta_1$ is the coefficient and represents slope of the line. Since $\beta_1$ is a positive number (0.992378), the regression line is positive. This shows a positive linear relationship between LNY (economic growth represented by GDP) and LNX (exports).

A 1% increase in exports will increase economic growth by 0.992378%. In other words, a unit increase in exports will increase economic growth by 0.992378. This shows that there is a positive relationship between exports and economic growth (GDP). In interpreting the coefficients of $\beta_1$ (beta), it explains the strengths of the coefficient of correlation and the slope. For β1, it has a positive relationship. Thus, when exports increase, economic growth also increases.

R Square ($R^2$) is usually called the 'goodness of fit coefficient' or the coefficient of determination. $R^2$ denotes the amount of variation in the dependent variable that can be attributed in the variation of the explanatory variable. A large $R^2$ coefficient provides an indication that the fitted model explains the data sufficiently. 71.87% of the variations in economic growth (LNY) can be explained by exports (LNX). Thus, it can be said that the fitted model explains the data sufficiently.

R (r) is the coefficient of correlation which shows how strong or weak the relationships between the variables are and whether it is positively or negatively related. To calculate the value of 'r', the researcher takes a square root of R Square ($R^2$) found in Table 2. In finding the correlation of economic growth (LNY) and exports (LNX) or when calculating 'r', it gives a value of 0.8478. 84.78% indicates a strong positive relationship between economic growth and exports. Since log (LN) was used to generate the OLS regression output, any heteroscedascity (unequal variance) has been removed. This shows a true picture of the results obtained in the statistical analysis. By using log (LN), any extreme values (outliers), have been removed to show consistency in the data points and show a true picture of the economy.

Heteroscedascity means unequal variance. OLS is based on the assumption of equal variance. Since there is equal variance, OLS is best and efficient. F- Statistics is very close to zero (0.000034 or 3.35978E-05) as shown in Table 2. This indicates that there is homogeneity of variance. One attractive feature of log is that the slope coefficients measure the elasticity of Y (economic growth) with respect to X (exports), that is, percentage changes in Y for a given percentage change in X.

D. SCATTER GRAPH SHOWING THE RELATIONSHIP BETWEEN EXPORTS AND ECONOMIC GROWTH

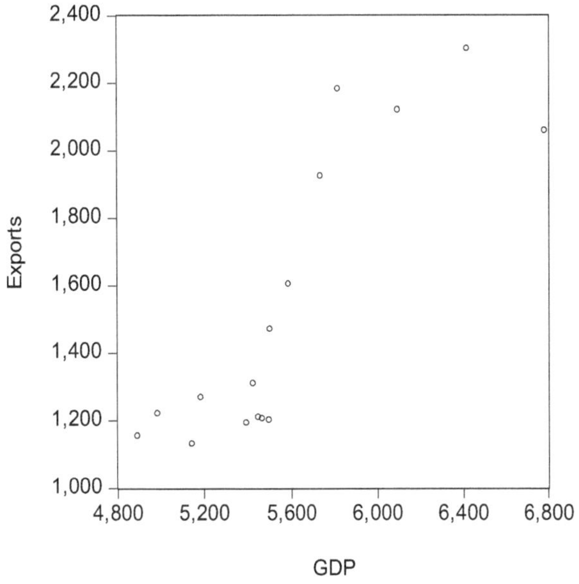

Source: Eviews Econometrics Software

The above scatter graph shows that there is a positive relationship between economic growth (LNY) and exports (LNX). The data points are upward sloping indicating a positive slope. An increase in exports would imply that economic growth would also increase.

E. RESIDUALS

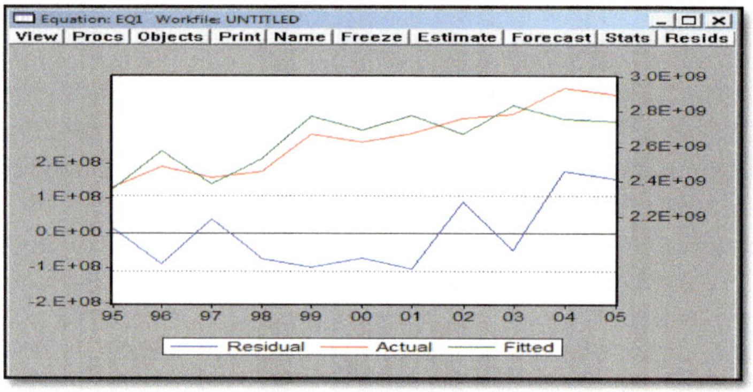


Source: Eviews Econometrics Software

The residuals lie between -1 and 1. This shows that there is consistency in the data points. There is a very close gap between the actual and the fitted line. The residual is closer to 0. The residual line does not fluctuate much, indicating that the residual plots show a good pattern (line of good fit).

Thus, exports are positively related to economic growth. From the statistical analysis, it can be concluded that exports has a strong positive relationship with economic growth. Therefore, increase in exports would lead to an increase in economic growth. The variations in economic growth can be explained by exports.

## 5.0 CONCLUSION, FINDINGS AND RECOMMENDATIONS

Thus, exports are positively related to economic growth. From the statistical analysis, it can be concluded that exports has a strong positive relationship with economic growth. Therefore, increase in exports would lead to an increase in economic growth. The variations in economic growth can be explained by exports.

Exports earnings are vital for Fiji's economy. It contributes significantly to Fiji's GDP and economic growth. Fiji's domestic exports, which largely comprises of agricultural and fisheries commodities include sugar, fish, coconuts, taro, copra, pawpaw and ginger. Other major exports include garments, mineral water and gold which earn a huge amount of foreign currency for Fiji. Fiji also has extensive mahogany timber reserves which are exported. In terms of value adding, the most important manufacturing activities are the processing of timber for furniture, canning and semi-process of fish, value adding and preserving of fruits and vegetables for the export markets. Another growing export is furniture made of palm (coconut) wood. Potential for the agriculture can be found in the production and export of high value niche agricultural produce. Products that give the best returns from labor and land resources include root crops, fresh fruits, vegetables and virgin coconut oil. Given the enormous export potential within the agriculture sector, the government plans to intensify its Export Promotion Programme through awareness programmes for farmers (World News, 2017).

Moreover, new programs will be funded to target the development of ginger, cocoa and rice. Fiji adopted an export oriented, outward looking approach with regards to trade relations. Fiji's main trading partners namely Australia, New Zealand, United States, England and Japan. The government of Fiji has decreased the export income tax to give incentives to producers to increase production for export purposes. Fiji exporters to use world priced inputs into their products to make them more competitive and to operate at their maximum potential. The government has introduced tax free region from Tavua to Korovou. This gives incentive for farmers who engage in agriculture, beef and dairy farming. The motive is to revitalize these industries to increase exports. Some of the methods the government has used to increase exports are import substitution and trade barriers. Import substitution is producing goods locally which were previously imported. One example of import substitution is potato farming. However, it is still in the initial production stage. The government uses trade barriers such as tariffs, embargoes, import quotas to restrict imports so that domestic production increases and more is exported. Subsidies are given to industries such as sugar and agriculture to increase production for export purposes.

The potential sectors that can be further developed to boost export earnings are garment, sugar, tourism industry and agricultural sector. Tax free zones should be given to garment industry so that garment production increases for export purposes. Garment industry is an export intensive industry that produces garment products mostly for export. Sugar industry can be further developed by giving subsidies to cane farmers to increase cane production so that more sugar is produced for export. Since Fiji's has abundance of land, more land should be used for sugarcane farming and to renew the land leases that had expired. The government should negotiate with European Union (EU) in further extending the trade agreement to provide preferential prices for Fiji's sugar. The government should also look for other potential markets apart from EU who are willing to buy Fiji's sugar at preferential prices that are above the world market price. Tourism is another major sector that can boost export earnings. More money should be allocated in the government budget for the tourism sector so that Fiji is continuously promoted in overseas. This will result in more visitor arrivals thus will foreign exchange earnings will increase. This can also lead to an increase in demand for Fiji made products overseas, thus, exports will increase. The second largest export commodity is water mainly comprising mineral water, therefore, government should provide subsidies to increase the production in the sector. Another policy recommendation is to expand the small and medium enterprises to expand the range of export commodities by Fiji and also expand the production of the existing commodities. The policy makers in Fiji should focus on further developing its export sectors to reap the gains of international trade and also focus on re-exports as its consists of a major component of total exports.

Lastly, the government should give subsidies to the agricultural sector, dairy, ginger farming, beef, fisheries and forestry so that the production increases for export purposes. Sweet biscuit are also in demand from foreigners, so subsidies needs to be given to domestic producers to increase production for export purposes. Trade theories such as Adam Smith's Absolute Advantage, David Ricardo's Comparative Advantage and Hecksha Ohlin's theory of trade apply to Fiji's exports. Thus, export is strongly and positively linked to economic growth.

## 5.1 LIMITATIONS OF THE RESEARCH STUDY AND DEFINED PARAMETERS

There are some limitations to this research project. Firstly, the study period for research and analysis purpose for the exports and economic growth of Fiji was only for 16 years. The research project was carried out in a developing country and may not resemble the views of developed nations. Time was also one of the limitations, since the research project was carried out within one semester (within three months) to be assessed. This area is a very interesting area and further in depth research could be done on this area.

## REFERENCES

Abu-Qarn, A. S. and Abu-Bader, S. (2004) "The validity of the ELG hypothesis in the MENA region: cointegration and error correction analysis", Applied Economics, 36, 1685 95.

Adjaye, A. 2010, "Contemporary Economic Policy Journal: The Implications of European Union Sugar Price Cuts, Economic Partnership Agreement, And Development Aid for Fiji, vol.28.no.1.pp.52-64.

Alkhuzaim, Waleed M. (2005). 'Export-Led growth hypothesis: Causality analysis for oil-based Gulf Cooperation Council countries', Doctoral dissertation, Colorado State University, Fort Collins.

Anon, (2015). [online] Available at: http://www.foreignaffairs.gov.fj/trade-policy/fiji-s-trade-policy/multilateral-trade/fiji-s-membership-to-the-world-trade-organization-wto [Accessed 27 Oct. 2015].

Atlas.media.mit.edu. (2017). OEC – 'Fiji (FJI) Exports, Imports, and Trade Partners'. [online] Available at: http://atlas.media.mit.edu/en/profile/country/fji/#Exports [Accessed 6 Apr. 2017].

Bahmani-Oskooee, M. and Alse, J. (1993), "Export Growth and Economic Growth: an Application of Cointegration and Error Correction Modeling", The Journal of Developing Areas, pp: 535–42.

Balassa, Bela (1978) 'Exports and Economic Growth—Further Evidence'. *Journal of Development Economics* 5:2, 181–9Bhagwati, J. (1988), *Protectionism*. MIT Press, Cambridge, MA.

Chemeda, F. (2001). 'The Role of Exports In Economic Growth with Reference to Ethiopian Country'. In: *Annual Meeting of the American Agricultural Economics Association in Chicago*.

Country Partnership Strategy (2014 – 2018): http://www.adb.org/sites/default/files/linked-documents/cps-fij-2014-2018-ea.pdf (accessed on 30th October, 2015).

Dodaro, S., 1993, "Exports and Growth: A Reconsideration of Causality", Journal of Developing Areas, pp: 227-244

Economic Analysis: Summary. (2014). 1st Ed. [Ebook] Country Partnership Strategy: Fiji, 2014–2018. Available At: Https://Www.Adb.Org/Sites/Default/Files/Linked-Documents/Cps-Fij-2014-2018-Ea.Pdf [Accessed 30 Oct. 2015].

Feder, G. (1982) 'On Exports And Economic Growth', Journal Of Development Economics, 12: 59-3.

Holman, J.A. and Graves, P.E. (1995), "Korean Exports Economic Growth: An Econometric Reassessment", Journal of Economic Development, pp: 45–56.

Frca.org.fj. (2015).' Fiji Revenue & Customs Authority'. [online] Available at: http://www.frca.org.fj/ [Accessed 27 Oct. 2015].

Foreignaffairs.gov.fj. (2017). Home. [online] Available at: http://www.foreignaffairs.gov.fj [Accessed 27 Oct. 2015].

Gujurati,D. (2003). Basic Econometrics. McGraw Hill Irwin: Gary Burke.

Henriques, I. and P. Sardosky (1996), 'Export-led Growth or Growth driven Exports? The Canadian Case', Canadian Journal of Economics, Vol. XXIX, pp. 540–55.

Heshmati, A. and Peng, S. (2012). International Trade and Its Effects On Economic

Jung, W. S. and Marshall, P. J. (1985). "Exports, growth and causality indeveloping countries", Journal of Development Economics, pp: 1-12.

Krueger, A. O., (1978), "Foreign Trade Regimes and Economic Development: Liberalization Attempts and Consequences", Cambridge, MA: Ballinger.

Lin, J. and Li, Y. (2001). Export and Economic Growth in China: A Demand-Oriented Analysis. [online] Available at: http://cerdi.org/uploads/sfCmsContent/html/197/JustinLi.pdf [Accessed 6 Apr. 2017].

Lucas, R.E. (1990), "Why does not capital flow from rich to poor countries", American Economic Review, 80, 92-6.

Merza, Ebrahim. (2007) 'Oil exports, non-oil exports and economic growth: Time series analysis for Kuwait (1970-2004)', Doctoral dissertation, Kansas State University, Manhatan.

Narayan, S. And Narayan, P. (2004). Determinants Of Demand For Fiji's Exports: An Empirical Investigation. The Developing Economies, 42(1), Pp.95-112.

Ndulu, B. and N. Ndungu (1998), 'Trade and Growth in Africa', in I. Zubair and M.S. Khan (eds), Trade Reform and Regional Integration in Africa, International Monetary Fund, Washington, DC.

Performance in China. China Economic Policy Review, 01(02), P.1250009.

Quddus, M. and Saeed, I. (2005). An Analysis of Exports and Growth in Pakistan. The Pakistan Development

Pugel, T. (2007). International Economics. McGraw Hill Irwin: Gary Burke.

Prasad, S (2000). Determinants of Exports in Fiji. Suva, Fiji.

Prasad, R. (2004). Fiji's Export Competitiveness: A Comparison with Selected Small Island Developing States. Reserve Bank of Fiji, [online] 2004(06), p.Working Paper. Available at: http://www.rbf.gov.fj/docs/2004~06%20WP.pdf [Accessed 27 Oct. 2015].

Rbf.gov.fj. (2015). Reserve Bank of Fiji - Home. [online] Available at: http://www.rbf.gov.fj/ [Accessed 27 Oct. 2015]

Rogers, A. (2000). An Analysis of the Determinants of Fiji's Imports. Suva, Fiji.

Ram, Rati. (1985) Export and Economic Growth: Some Additional Evidence, Economic Development and Cultural Change, 33, pp. 415-425.

Ram, R. (1986) Government size and economic growth: A new framework and some evidence from cross-section and time-series data. American Economic Review, 76(1), 191–203.

Ram, R. (1987) Exports and economic growth in developing countries: evidence from time series and gross-section Data, Journal of Economic Development and Cultural Change, 36: (1): 121-30.

Sprout, R.V.A., and J.H. Weaver (1993), "Exports and Economic Growth in a Simultaneous Equations Model," Journal of Developing Areas, pp: 289-306.

UNDP Pacific Office in Fiji. (2017). About Fiji. [online] Available at: http://www.pacific.undp.org/content/pacific/en/home/countryinfo/fiji.html [Accessed 4 Apr. 2017].

Vuki, L. (2014). 'World Forestry and Trees for Life. The Fiji Times, 29 March, 2014.

Shahbaz, M., Ahmad, K. and Asad, M. (n.d.). Exports-Led Growth Hypothesis in Pakistan: Further Evidence'.1sted.[ebook]Availableat:http://citeseerx.ist.psu.edu/viewdoc/download;jsessionid...?doi =10.1.1.704.4697.[Accessed 7 Apr. 2017].

Sharma, S. and Dhakal, D. (1994). 'Causal analyses between exports and economic growth in developing countries'. Applied Economics, 26(12), pp.1145-1157.

Statsfiji.gov.fj. (2017). International Trade Statistics - Fiji Bureau of Statistics. [online] Available at: http://www.statsfiji.gov.fj/statistics/economic-statistics/merchandise-trade-statistics [Accessed 7 Apr. 2017].

Velnampy, T. and Achchuthan, S. (2013).' Export, Import and Economic Growth: Evidence from Sri Lanka'. 4th ed. [eBook] Journal of Economics and Sustainable Development. Available at: http://pakacademicsearch.com/pdf.../147-155%20Vol%204,%20No%209%20(2013).pdf [Accessed 7 Apr. 2017].

Witte, W. and Bhagwati, J. (1979). 'Anatomy and Consequences of Exchange Control Regimes'. Southern Economic Journal, 46(2), p.681.

World News. (2017). Investment Fiji. [online] Available at: http://www.investmentfiji.com [Accessed 7 Apr. 2017]

# 17

# Economic Crisis and Small Business in Erbil-Iraq

**Cuma AkBAY[1], Rizgar Saed Hussein[2], Bahzad Taher Salim[3], Sirwan Latif[4]**

**ABSTRACT**

This research investigates the impact of economic crisis in Erbil-Iraq on small business (SBs) sector using factor analyses model. The sample constitute data collected from 110 SBs by using cross sectional data and simple random techniques. Results indicate that economic recession has a negative impact on the SBs sector in Erbil in the last two years. Employing the simplified static analysis framework based on simulations revealed that the economic recession has influenced negatively influence Erbil economy. Increasing general inflation rate, decreasing living standards and purchasing power have negative impacts the growth of SBs in Erbil and eventually the economy of Erbil.

Keywords: Economic crisis, economic growth, Erbil, financial crises, small business.

---

## 1.0 INTRODUCTION

In the globalization era, the occurrence of economic crises have become more often than before. Thus, it is necessary to conduct a formal study to examine the impact of the current economic crisis and recession on the small businesses in Kurdistan's regional government (KRG) of Iraq, particularly the impact of the ISIS war and the reduction of the oil price on small enterprises during the years 2014 and 2015, thus the purpose of this paper is to present the impact of the economic crisis on small businesses in Erbil.

The financial and Economic crisis has and will continue to have a major impact on our whole society. More and more people will be affected by it both directly and indirectly and we have not yet seen the full scale of the crisis either economically or socially. Whenever we start to mention the word crisis we are always using two additional words: recession and depression. If we want to explain the crisis we have to identify these concepts also. Recession means in very simple words: slowing economic activities. There should be a contraction compared with a position previously accessed, this slowing down may be shallow or deep. Sometimes the word recession is used as a synonym of crisis. On the other hand, if the level of

---

[1] Professor, Sutcu Imam University –Turkey.
[2] Assistant lecturer, Soran University- Iraq-Erbil.
[3] Assistant lecturer, Erbil Polytechnic University –Iraq-Erbil)- Email: behzad82h@hotmail.com
[4] Assistant lecturer, Erbil Polytechnic University- Iraq-Erbil

economic activity stays at a low level for quite a long time; this situation is defined as depression (Ratko & Ulgen, 2009).

Small business enterprise is a sector of the economy that needs Kurdistan Region government's attention and other developing nations due to the role it plays in job creation and economic growth in the nation's economy. "Small business play an important role in the development of economy, by creating jobs, by supporting innovation and competitiveness and, emphasizing dynamism and market atomicity" (Mirela et al., 2014).

A small business is a business that is privately owned and operated, with a small number of employees and relatively low volume of sales. Small businesses are normally privately owned corporations, partnerships, or sole proprietorships. The legal definition of "small" varies by country and by industry. In the United States the Small Business Administration establishes small business size standards on an industry-by-industry basis, but generally specifies a small business as having fewer than 500 employees for manufacturing businesses and less than $7 million in annual receipts for most nonmanufacturing businesses. In the European Union, a small business generally has fewer than 50 employees. However, in Australia, a small business is defined by the Fair Work Act 2009 as one with fewer than 15 employees (Bahzad, 2010).

A small business can be started at a very low cost and on a part-time basis. Small business is also well suited to internet marketing because it can easily serve specialized niches. Independence is another advantage of owning a small business. One survey of small business owners showed that 38% of those who left their jobs at other companies said their main reason for leaving was that they wanted to be their own bosses (Bahzad, 2010).

Small businesses are vital in today's economy because many of the revenue obtained by the government are from business taxes. In addition, the existence of small businesses can stimulate the economy and hopefully improve the economies all around the world. Finally small businesses are important because it can provide more job opportunities for people so that the unemployment rate is low (Bahzad, 2010).

There is no extensive literature that studies how the crisis has affected Small Business in (KRG) during the financial crisis that began in 2007 spread and gathered intensity in 2008. Many countries have their researches on impact of these crises on their small and medium enterprises (SMEs). In Erbil there is also the crisis of 2014-2015 that appeared because of ISIS war and the fall of oil prices to $30 per barrel. However, there are some empirical studies in the literature that shed some light on this issue.

A sampling of earlier studies includes (Winarno, 2013), (Zhang, Li, & Liu, 2014), (Memon, Halepoto, & Shaikh, 2012), (Kazuo, Takanori 2012) and (Stamatović & Zakić, 2010). According to results, the global financial crisis have negatively impacted on economy, particularly on the performance of small and medium enterprises (SMEs). (Busega, 2014) analyzed the impact of the financial crisis on SMEs, hence lowering the demand for goods and services provided by businesses, which induced a restructuring of the available jobs, reducing the number of active enterprises, decrease turnover and limiting investments. (Yalman, Demirkoparan, & Aras), analyzes the financial crisis impact on SMEs and SMEs strategies during financial crisis in the Sivas province, the results show that the ratios of small-sized firms have more changes than middle-sized firms, also middle-sized firms are less affected from crisis than small-sized firms. While small-sized firms are generally managed traditionally with family business status, they fall behind to make professional provisions against crisis.

The main purpose of this paper is to specify how the economic crisis affected small enterprises during 2014 and 2015 in Kurdistan Regional Government (KRG) and specifically choosing Erbil province as a sample niche, thus the objectives of this paper can be expressed as follows: (1) How is the economic crisis affecting Products and Services? (2) How is the economic crisis affecting Marketing and Sales? (3) How is the economic crisis affecting Human Resources? and finally (4) How is the economic crisis affecting Financial Activities?

## 2.0 FACTOR ANALYSIS MODEL

The importance of factor analysis as a mathematical model to analyze the relationships between a large number of variables and interpreted in a few of the factors that reflect the reality subject to analyze the data, and disclosure of some relationships unexpected that look distinct at first and then clear it is not her little significance, and vice versa, so it can be explained by the factor model for $(p)$ variables as a linear function of $(p)$ of the averages of variables for $(q)$ of the general factors (Factor Scores) or (Common) and the (Unique Factor) for each variable, as if $(q < p)$, the factor analysis model can be formulated as follows: Li and Zhang (2007).

$$\underline{x}_j = \underline{\mu} + \Lambda \cdot \underline{f}_j + \varepsilon_j \quad ; j = 1,2, \ldots ,n$$

When:

$\underline{x}_j$ is a vector with the capacity $(p \times 1)$ for $(p)$ from variables.

$\underline{\mu}$ is a vector with the capacity $(p \times 1)$ for $(p)$ from the averages of variables.

$\Lambda$ is a matrix with the capacity $(p \times q)$ for $(p \times q)$ from factors loading.

$\underline{f}_j$ is a vector with the capacity $(q \times 1)$ for $(q)$ from factor scores or common.

$\varepsilon_j$ is a vector with the capacity $(p \times 1)$for $(p)$ from unique factor also called a vector of random error.

Thus all response for variables consisting from two parts, the first caused by general factors which is a linear combination of factors, and the second section comes through the only factor that contains all other effects in other factors.

### 2.1 ASSUMPTIONS TO SOLVE BY USING FACTOR ANALYSIS

There are a set of assumptions in the model of factor analysis that are summarized by the following points:

#### 2.1.1 EXISTENCE OF A CORRELATION BETWEEN A SET OF VARIABLES

This kind of correlation sometimes called Inter correlation, which is produced from the presence of common factors affecting it, and how much they represent these correlations back to the reality of those factors. Factor analysis seeks to interpret the correlation between variables with factors number less than of original variables used, and relies this hypothesis on the standard value of the variables. So variables turned into new variants of standard normal distribution with a mean is zero and variance of one, and so the impact of units of measure different variables is canceled. Based on this hypothesis divides the total variance to the three variations are:

##### 2.1.1.1 COMMON VARIANCE

The variance Common - also called quantities common (Communalities) or variance of general factors part of the total variation, which represents the contrast ratio explained by common factors from the matrix analysis of variance $(\Sigma)$ and can be calculated by using the total squares factor loading that variable and has the symbol ( $h_j^2$ ) and defined according to the following equation:

$$h_j^2 = \lambda_{j1}^2 + \lambda_{j2}^2 + \cdots\cdots + \lambda_{jq}^2 = \sum_{j=1}^{n} \lambda_{ji}^2 \quad ; \text{ i=1,2, ... ,q}$$

If the value of ( $h_j^2$ ) of the variable ( $j$ ) large and approaching the one they will show that this variable interferes in whole with factors derived, this means that the factor $(i)$ where that $(i = 1,2, \cdots ,q)$ was important and a real impact in the phenomenon studied. But if the Communalities signed between zero and one, this refers to the partial interaction between the variables and factors. Finally, if the

Communalities equal to zero then we can say that the Extracted factors cannot explain any part of the variation of that variable.

#### 2.1.1.2 SPECIFIC VARIANCE

It is a part of the total variation, but it is not correlated with the rest of the variables, but it is correlated with same variable:

$$b_j^2 = \psi_j^2 + e_j^2$$

When

$b_j^2$ is the specific variance for variable $j$.

$e_j^2$ is the error variance.

$\psi_i^2$ is the variance of unique factor.

#### 2.1.1.3 ERROR VARIANCE

It is the part of the variance that does not explain by general factors, and can be considered as residual or error and it is the result of the occurrence of errors during the withdrawal of the sample and measured or any changes that cannot control it leads to a lack of consistency in the data and it has the symbol $(e_j^2)$ and can be calculated as the following:

$$e_j^2 = 1 - (h_j^2 + b_j^2)$$

Each of the common and specific variance share to consistence the Reliable Variance:

$$R_{jj} = h_j^2 + b_j^2$$

### 2.1.2 REPRESENTATION OF THE CORRELATION BETWEEN TWO VARIABLES FROM LOADING VARIABLES OF COMMON FACTORS

This hypothesis is based on the assumption of a correlation between the two variables is calculated based on the nature and existence of common factors, and can be represented this hypothesis for independent factors and orthogonal by the following equation:

$$r_{jj'} = \lambda_{j1}\lambda_{j'1} + \lambda_{j2}\lambda_{j'2} + \cdots + \lambda_{jq}\lambda_{j'q}$$

This means that the correlation coefficient between the two variables is a product of the total loading variables of common factors between them, as this correlation can be represented using matrixes, as follows:

$$\begin{bmatrix} 1 & r_{12} & \cdots & r_{1q} \\ r_{21} & 1 & \cdots & r_{2q} \\ \vdots & \vdots & \ddots & \vdots \\ r_{n1} & r_{n2} & \cdots & 1 \end{bmatrix} = \begin{bmatrix} \lambda_{11} & \lambda_{12} & \cdots & \lambda_{1q} \\ \lambda_{21} & \lambda_{22} & \cdots & \lambda_{2q} \\ \vdots & \vdots & \ddots & \vdots \\ \lambda_{n1} & \lambda_{n2} & \cdots & \lambda_{nq} \end{bmatrix} \times \begin{bmatrix} \lambda_{11} & \lambda_{12} & \cdots & \lambda_{n1} \\ \lambda_{21} & \lambda_{22} & \cdots & \lambda_{n2} \\ \vdots & \vdots & \cdots & \vdots \\ \lambda_{1q} & \lambda_{2q} & \cdots & \lambda_{nq} \end{bmatrix}$$

## 2.2 THE CRITERIA FOR SELECTING THE NUMBER OF FACTORS

The different nature of the measuring variables led to appear several analysis methods for factors, which in turn makes very easy an estimate of factors loading matrix to reach to the initial solution. The most important factor analysis methods is the Principal Component Method which we will use in this research. On the other hand, the criteria or methods for selecting the number of factors are necessary and makes it imperative for the researcher to determine the number of important factors that explain the phenomenon studied in the relationship, particularly when adopting Eigen values in determining the number of factors which is equal to the rank of the correlation matrix. That is why we need a criterion to select the best from among these models by selecting the appropriate number of factors that interpret a great ratio from the total standard variation. It depends on the basis of the ratio aggregate of the variance that are explained by the factors, it should be this ratio is greater than or equal to 75% and this is referred to by Alchukrgi (2005).

## 3.0 METHODOLOGY

Data was collected from 110 SBs by using cross sectional data selected by simple random techniques. We selected a number of variables to investigate impact of economic crises on SBs in Erbil. The questions form concentrated around some of the key points such amount of suppliers, investment in innovations, marketing expenditure, pressure on prizes, sales, customers, postponement of recruitment, salary, viability of the business, finance, pay and profits. In *Table 1* as illustrated average and standard deviation of each variable in this study.

**Table 1:** Definition of variables in factor analyses model

| Variables | Explanation | Average | Std. Deviation |
|---|---|---|---|
| X1 | The amount of Suppliers is getting lower | 4.3727 | 0.8552 |
| X2 | We will not invest in Innovations during The following year | 3.918 | 1.150 |
| X3 | Our marketing expenditure has been reduced | 4.0091 | 0.8830 |
| X4 | There is greater pressure on prises | 3.645 | 1.193 |
| X5 | The sales volume has decreased | 4.6273 | 0.6617 |
| X6 | The amount of Customers has decreased | 4.4545 | 0.8635 |
| X7 | We will cancel/postpone recruitment that was planned before | 4.3364 | 0.7203 |
| X8 | Salary increases will be lower than planned | 4.1273 | 0.6788 |
| X9 | Our team is concerned about the viability of the business | 4.7727 | 0.5360 |
| X10 | Finance is getting harder to obtain | 4.5545 | 0.6984 |
| X11 | Our customers are taking longer to pay | 3.555 | 1.860 |
| X12 | Our forecast: profits will fall | 4.4273 | 0.6596 |

As shown in *Table* 2 the first factor explained 29.8% of the total variation. This factor contains three variables ($X_7$, $X_8$, $X_9$). The second one explained 14.7% of the total variation, which included ($X_5$, $X_6$). The third factor has a ratio reached at 12.4% of the total contrast ratio containing ($X_{10}$, $X_{12}$). The fourth factor has 9.9% of the total variation ($X_3$, $X_4$). The fifth factor explained 7.7% of the total variation containing ($X_1$, $X_2$). As well as it can be observed that the variable ($X_{11}$) has appeared among the factor (sixth) respectively.

**Table 2:** Illustrate the importance of the variables (significant effect) within factors

| No. of Factors | Var % | Important Variables | name |
|---|---|---|---|
| 1 | 0.298 | $X_7$, $X_8$, $X_9$ | Human Resources |
| 2 | 0.147 | $X_5$, $X_6$ | Marketing & Sales |
| 3 | 0.124 | $X_{10}$, $X_{12}$ | Financial Activities |
| 4 | 0.099 | $X_3$, $X_4$ | Marketing & Sales |
| 5 | 0.077 | $X_1$, $X_2$ | Product & Services |
| 6 | 0.066 | $X_{11}$ | Financial Activities |
| **Total Variance** | 0.811 | | |

*Table* (3) shows the factor analysis to the Small Business (variables) and the quantities of communalities.

**Table 3:** Matrix of rotated factor loadings and communalities

| Variables | Factor1 | Factor2 | Factor3 | Factor4 | Factor5 | Factor6 | Communality |
|---|---|---|---|---|---|---|---|
| We will cancel/postpone recruitment that was planned before | 0.784 | 0.097- | 0.256 | 0.236- | 0.109- | 0.100 | 0.767 |

| | | | | | | | |
|---|---|---|---|---|---|---|---|
| Salary increases will be lower than planned | 0.798 | 0.023- | 0.195 | 0.204- | 0.002- | 0.211- | 0.761 |
| Our team is concerned about the viability of the business | 0.825 | 0.126- | 0.042- | 0.102 | 0.174- | 0.024- | 0.740 |
| The sales volume has decreased | 0.072 | 0.927- | 0.065 | 0.007 | 0.153- | 0.029- | 0.893 |
| The amount of Customers has decreased | 0.161 | 0.869- | 0.003- | 0.308- | 0.032- | 0.057 | 0.880 |
| Finance is getting harder to obtain | 0.034 | 0.038- | 0.896 | 0.052 | 0.027- | 0.168- | 0.837 |
| Our forecast: profits will fall | 0.229 | 0.023- | 0.847 | 0.201- | 0.077- | 0.054- | 0.819 |
| Our marketing expenditure has been reduced | 0.044 | 0.143- | 0.188 | 0.851- | 0.208- | 0.067- | 0.829 |
| There is greater pressure on prizes | 0.484 | 0.178- | 0.101- | 0.617- | 0.122 | 0.053 | 0.674 |
| The amount of Suppliers is getting lower | 0.080 | 0.196- | 0.029 | 0.119 | 0.709- | 0.466- | 0.780 |
| We will not invest Innovations during The following year | 0.143 | 0.060- | 0.078 | 0.209- | 0.871- | 0.078 | 0.839 |
| Our customers are taking longer to pay | 0.061 | 0.051 | 0.195 | 0.049- | 0.073- | 0.929- | 0.915 |

* Represents a variable with a significant effect and that has loading greater than or equal to 0.5 or less than or equal to -0.5.

## 4.0 EMPIRICAL RESULTS AND DISCUSSIONS

We can notice that the rotated factor loadings values (variances within factors) as shown in Table (1) and thinking in any value has a significant effect (greater than +50% or less than -50%) starting of the sixth factor (F6) we note the highest load has been interpreted by the variable X11 (Our customers are taking longer to pay), which amounted to -92.9% of the yield variance with a very big negative impact. That means there is a very significant negative effect on small business in Erbil. The variable X5 (The sales volume has decreased) within the second factor (F2), which amounted to -92.7% and came in the second place in terms of its impact on small business, and this is evidence that the sales volume has decreased negatively.

On the other hand, the variable X10 (Finance is getting harder to obtain) has interpreted +89.6% of the total yield variance, within the third factor (F3) and this value is positively reflected and improves the economic crises of small business in Erbil. The three variables above are considered the most important variables in terms of the positive or negative impact on small business in Erbil. But the variable X2 (We will not invest Innovations during the coming year) has appeared in the fifth factor (F5) and also has the loading of -87.1%, that means there is significant effect negative.

The second factor (F2) which is X3 (The amount of Customers has decreased) and the percentage loading factor have reached - 86.9% which indicates that there is a negative effect. But the fourth factor (4) is X3 (Our marketing expenditure has been reduced), it has ratio of saturation is -85.1% of the common variance, that indicates there is a negative effect. As well as the twelfth variable (Our forecast: profits will fall) comes in third factor is equal to +84.7% has impact positively on the small business.

While we find that the ninth variable within the first factor (F1) has a positive significant influence +82.5% on small business in Erbil. The variable X8 (Salary increases will be lower than planned) from the first factor (F1) has a +79.8%, which have a positive effect on small business. On the other hand, the variable X7 (We will cancel/postpone recruitment that was planned before) of the first factor (F1) has a +78.4% of the Common values of variance and which have a positive effect on small business.
Finally, we can say about the effects of the last two variables, X1 (The amount of Suppliers is getting lower) and X4 (There is greater pressure on prizes) within the factors (F5, F4) with the loadings factor (-70.9%, -61.7%) respectively, are not having significant affects on small business, because they have a small value of the ratio of variances.

## 5.0 CONCLUSION

Small enterprises play an important role in any country's economy and are considered vectors of growth in economic, creating jobs and strengthening the middle class in any society. The Kurdistan economic recession significantly reduced the purchasing power of the population, hence lowering the demand for goods and services provided by businesses, which induced a restructuring of the available jobs, reducing the number of active enterprises, decrease turnover and limiting investments.

The small business (SB) sector in Erbil is currently under a process of consolidation and improvement, which requires further support of public policies in promoting and supporting managerial and entrepreneurship education. Overall result suggests that for small business it is getting harder to obtain finance after crisis. Moreover, there is a great pressure on prices, while payment delays are increasing, sales volumes decreasing, Additionally, marketing activities and number of customers has decreased.

## REFERENCES

Alchukrgi, Thanon Younis Thanon (2005) "Using the Matrixes Q-mode and R-mode in factor analysis". unpublished Master Thesis, Faculty of Computing and Mathematical Sciences, University of Mosul.

Bahzad.T.Salim, (2010), The Finance Aspects of Building a Small Business In Kurdistan Region-Iraq: A Comparison with Sweden, master in business administration, Lebanese French University-BMU, internship with university of Picardie jules verne France, Erbil.

Busega, I. (2014). Impact Of The Financial Crisis On Small And Middle Enterprises In Romania. The Differences Between Urban And Rural Evolutions. *Global Economic Observer,* 2(2), 186.

Memon, M. A., Halepoto, A. H., & Shaikh, F. M. (2012). Global Financial Crisis in South Asia and its Impact on Pakistan's SMEs Sector by Using CGE Model. *Journal of Asian Business Strategy,* 2(4), 84.

Mirela Ionela & Daniela Livia & Andreea Claudia. (2014), The role of small and medium enterprises in improving employment and in the post-crisis resumption of economic growth in Romania, theoretical and applied economics, volume XXI (2014), no.1(590), Bucharest.

Ogawa Kazuo & Tanaka Takanori. (2012), The global financial crisis and small- and medium-sized enterprises in Japan: How did they cope with the crisis, RIETI discussion paper series 12-E-012, Japan.

Ratko, Z., & Ulgen, K. (2009). The Impact of Economic Crisis on Small and Medium Enterprises: in perspective of Swedish SMEs.

Stamatović, M., & Zakić, N. (2010). Effects of the global economic crisis on small and medium enterprises in Serbia. *Serbian Journal of Management,* 5(1), 151-162.

Winarno, T. (2013). Assessing the Impact of Recent Global Crisis on Small and Medium Enterprises (SMEs): Evidence from Indonesia. *Journal of Emerging Economics and Islamic Research,* 1(1), 1-13.

Xiangfeng Liu. (2009), Impacts of the global financial crisis on small and medium enterprises in the people's republic of China, ADBI working paper 180, Tokyo: Asian development bank institute.

YALMAN, İ. N., DEMİRKOPARAN, F., & ARAS, O. Financial crisis impact on SMEs and SMEs strategies during economic crises: a case of Sivas province. *Sivas, Turkey. Available at: http://www. opf. slu. cz/kfi/icfb/proc2011/pdf/67_Yalman. pdf (accessed 15 May 2013).*

Yoruk, N. (2001). Son Ekonomik Krizin KOBĠ'ler Üzerine Etkisi ve Tokat Ġli Örneği. G.Ü. İ.İ.B.F. Dergisi, vol. 2.

Zhang, J., Li, J., & Liu, C. (2014). Robust factor analysis using the multivariate t-distribution. *Statistica Sinica,* 24, 291-312.

# Permissions

All chapters in this book were first published in IJBSR, by LAR Center Press; hereby published with permission under the Creative Commons Attribution License or equivalent. Every chapter published in this book has been scrutinized by our experts. Their significance has been extensively debated. The topics covered herein carry significant findings which will fuel the growth of the discipline. They may even be implemented as practical applications or may be referred to as a beginning point for another development.

The contributors of this book come from diverse backgrounds, making this book a truly international effort. This book will bring forth new frontiers with its revolutionizing research information and detailed analysis of the nascent developments around the world.

We would like to thank all the contributing authors for lending their expertise to make the book truly unique. They have played a crucial role in the development of this book. Without their invaluable contributions this book wouldn't have been possible. They have made vital efforts to compile up to date information on the varied aspects of this subject to make this book a valuable addition to the collection of many professionals and students.

This book was conceptualized with the vision of imparting up-to-date information and advanced data in this field. To ensure the same, a matchless editorial board was set up. Every individual on the board went through rigorous rounds of assessment to prove their worth. After which they invested a large part of their time researching and compiling the most relevant data for our readers.

The editorial board has been involved in producing this book since its inception. They have spent rigorous hours researching and exploring the diverse topics which have resulted in the successful publishing of this book. They have passed on their knowledge of decades through this book. To expedite this challenging task, the publisher supported the team at every step. A small team of assistant editors was also appointed to further simplify the editing procedure and attain best results for the readers.

Apart from the editorial board, the designing team has also invested a significant amount of their time in understanding the subject and creating the most relevant covers. They scrutinized every image to scout for the most suitable representation of the subject and create an appropriate cover for the book.

The publishing team has been an ardent support to the editorial, designing and production team. Their endless efforts to recruit the best for this project, has resulted in the accomplishment of this book. They are a veteran in the field of academics and their pool of knowledge is as vast as their experience in printing. Their expertise and guidance has proved useful at every step. Their uncompromising quality standards have made this book an exceptional effort. Their encouragement from time to time has been an inspiration for everyone.

The publisher and the editorial board hope that this book will prove to be a valuable piece of knowledge for researchers, students, practitioners and scholars across the globe.

# List of Contributors

**Sumati Srinivas**
Radford University, USA

**Bertram C. I. Okpokwasili**
Associate Professor, School of Business Administration, Georgian Court University, Lakewood, NJ

**Hasret Balcioglu**
Department of Business Administration, Cyprus International University, North Cyprus, Mersin 10 Turkey

**Kket E Ewa**
Department of Accountancy, Cross River University of Technology, Ogoja, Cross River State, Nigeria

**Egu U. Inah**
Department of Accounting, University of Calabar, Calabar, Cross River State, Nigeria

**Mesut Sert**
Department of Public Finance, Akdeniz University, Turkey

**Cem Doğan**
Mustafa Kemal University Faculty of Economics and Administration Science

**Ünal Arslan**
Mustafa Kemal University Faculty of Economics and Administration Science

**Liang-Xin Li**
Business school, Hunan International Economics University, Hunan, Changsha 410205, China

**Safaa Tabit**
Department of Economics, Mohammed V Rabat - Agdal University, Faculty of Juridical, Economic and Social Sciences, Morocco

**Charaf-Eddine Moussir**
Department of Economics, Mohammed V Rabat - Agdal University, Faculty of Juridical, Economic and Social Sciences, Morocco

**Nagmi M. Moftah Aimer**
Social Sciences Institute, Department of Business Administration, Kastamonu University, Turkey

**Mohamed Elheddad**
University of Hull, Hull Business School (HUBS), United Kingdom

**Madan Lal Bhasin**
Professor, School of Accountancy, College of Business, Universiti Utara Malaysia, Sintok, Kedah Darul Aman, Malaysia

**Ömer Uğur Bulut**
Philosophy of Doctorate

**Sadık Rıdvan Karluk**
Professor (retired)

**Bertram C.I. Okpokwasili**
Georgian Court University, Lakewood, NJ

**Dr. Reem Shaher Al-Araj**
Assistant Professor, Faculty of Management & Finance, Middle East University

**Salma Slimani**
Researcher, Department of economics, Mohammed V Rabat -Agdal University, Faculty of Juridical, Economic and Social Sciences, Morocco

**Shivneil Kumar Raj**
Assistant Lecturer, School of Business and Economics, The University of Fiji, Lautoka, Fiji

**Priteshni Pratibha Chand**
Assistant Lecturer, School of Business and Economics, The University of Fiji, Lautoka, Fiji

**Cuma AkBAY**
Professor, Sutcu Imam University -Turkey

**Rizgar Saed Hussein**
Assistant lecturer, Soran University- Iraq-Erbil

**Bahzad Taher Salim**
Assistant lecturer, Erbil Polytechnic University -Iraq-Erbil

**Sirwan Latif**
Assistant lecturer, Erbil Polytechnic University- Iraq-Erbil

# Index